SHAW

Y0-BRC-836

The Dynamics of
Small Groups

The Dynamics of Small Groups

CECILIA L. RIDGEWAY

University of Wisconsin—Milwaukee

ST. MARTIN'S PRESS *New York*

Library of Congress Catalog Card Number: 82-60480
Copyright © 1983 by St. Martin's Press, Inc.
All Rights Reserved.
Manufactured in the United States of America.
76543
fedcba

For information, write St. Martin's Press, Inc.
175 Fifth Avenue, New York, N.Y. 10010

cover design: Myrna Sharp
book design: Judith Woracek

ISBN: 0-312-22369-2

Dedicated to Jaqueline Ridgeway

Contents

6 Status Differentiation, 160

7 Leadership, 205

Preface

A text that covers the subject of small groups should fulfill two basic goals. First, and foremost, it should offer a thorough and readable presentation of existing theory and research on group processes. Second, it should encourage reader interest by presenting an analysis of concrete groups in a way that allows students to see the relevance of abstract findings to their own experiences as participants in society. Too often the study of small groups has been presented entirely in the abstract, removed from a larger sociological context; a text should not only discuss internal group dynamics but should offer a clear analysis of groups as vital units in a larger social structure. Such an analysis also makes easier the integration of material taught in small group courses with that covered in other sociology, communications, business, and education courses.

The Dynamics of Small Groups accomplishes these goals through a series of interrelated steps. First, it offers a rigorous and thorough discussion of group theory and research. Although the emphasis of the book is sociological, and primary attention is paid to the development and operation of group structure, the psychological literature on group processes is considered in detail as well. Second, the subject is presented in as readable, clear, and lively a style as possible, making frequent use of concrete examples to illustrate the abstract concepts being discussed. A distinctive element of this text is a series of boxed features—extended examples and commentaries on major sociological topics essential to the study of small groups. Chapter summaries and illustrative tables and graphs will also help the student to assimilate the material.

The central focus of the book is on the internal workings of small groups, but within a concrete sociological context. Chapters 4 through 7 form the core of the book, addressing the fundamental processes of communication, conformity and deviance, status, and leadership in group structure. These chapters emphasize the emergence of group properties from the dynamic interaction of the members. In addition, I have complemented the usual detailed consideration of group structure with a chapter on group culture (Chapter 8)—a vital aspect of group behavior which is too often neglected in textbooks on small groups. I have tried to incorporate the most recent findings as well as classic studies into my analysis of these processes.

These core chapters are framed by Chapters 1, 9, and 10, which offer a thorough consideration of the external relations of small groups to the larger social structure. Chapter 1 discusses the prevalence, importance, and functions of small groups in society. The final two chapters (Chapters 9 and 10) are devoted to an analysis of actual primary and task groups in contemporary society and to their characteristic processes and problems. I should note that significant consideration is given to primary groups *throughout* the text; most small group texts, after giving brief lip service to primary groups, focus almost entirely on task groups. Yet the emotional importance of primary groups makes them a focus of student interest as well as sociological significance. The book concludes with an epilogue speculating on the way current changes in society are likely to affect our system of small groups.

Finally, because groups represent the convergence of individual and social processes, classic group studies have been conducted from a variety of sociological and psychological perspectives. To increase students' understanding of these divergent studies, I have included a chapter (Chapter 2) outlining the major theoretical orientations out of which most group research developed. In order to provide students with basic tools for understanding the research they will be reading about, I have added (in Chapter 3) a brief survey of research methods used in group studies.

In writing this book, I was aided immeasurably by the comments and suggestions of several reviewers: Richard J. Bord, Pennsylvania State University; Thomas L. Connor, Michigan State University; Timothy J. Curry, Ohio State University; Tove Helland Hammer, Cornell University; Malcolm W. Klein, University of Southern California; D. Randall Smith, Rutgers University; Henry A. Walker, Stanford University; and James Wiggins, University of North Carolina. I acknowledge their assistance with gratitude. In doing so, however, I should note that they are in no way responsible for the book's shortcomings, for which I alone bear responsibility.

Cecilia L. Ridgeway

I

The Study of
Small Groups

1

An Introduction to Small Groups

WHAT ARE SMALL GROUPS?

What are small groups? Are they somehow different from large groups? Why study them separately? Of what importance are they? These questions create a frame of reference from which the importance of studying small groups can be appreciated. Only with some understanding of the answers to these questions does the scientific study of small groups become meaningful.

Perhaps the easiest way to indicate what is meant by small groups is to list some examples. Friendship groups, committees, a corporate board, the president and his advisers, families, the lunch group at work, a dating couple, the city council, and a teenage gang are all examples of small groups. What do they have in common? First of all, they are all small enough that the members can deal with one another on a *face-to-face* basis. This key quality begins to suggest why small groups are different from large groups. If there are too many people, more than twenty or so, it becomes very difficult for everyone to deal with everyone else at once, and thus the large group breaks down into subgroups. People begin to deal with only a few members face-to-face and relate to the rest of the group indirectly. When this happens, the group as a whole has lost its personal character. We can see then that groups that maintain face-to-face interaction among all their members are of necessity small groups, usually having from two to twenty members.

But our examples have more in common. Each meets on a regular basis and shares an identity or sense of purpose. Thus, each small group has a character of its own and is a recognizable social entity to its members and to outsiders. This is what distinguishes a group from a simple collection of people. Six strangers in an elevator are not a small group.

If a group meets together with a common purpose, it tends to develop an additional quality as well. The members come to share some common ways of doing things and a set of often informal rules by which the group operates. Indeed, much of what we discuss in this book will deal with the way shared patterns of behavior develop in groups and the consequences these have for the members. If we combine the several attributes we have discussed, we have a more formal definition of small groups. According to Crosbie (1975), "a small group is a collection of people who meet more or less regularly in face-to-face interaction, who possess a common identity or exclusiveness of purpose, and who share a set of standards governing their activities."

Now that we have a better idea of what a small group is, let's go back to our list of examples again. Can it give us any hints as to the relative importance of small groups? Why should we study them? A cursory glance at this list makes it clear that we all spend a great deal of our lives in small groups. After all, they include friends, family, romantic relationships, the people at work. This fact suggests two ways in which small groups are of interest to us as individuals. First, when something absorbs a great deal of time and energy, native curiosity makes most people want to know more about it, how it operates, what makes it tick. Second, we might suspect that any activity that plays such a large part in daily living will substantially influence our individual behavior and feelings of self.

Yet another look at our list of small groups might suggest an additional point to the thoughtful reader. Several of the groups mentioned are important decision-making bodies. Boards of corporate directors, city councils, and the president and his advisers are groups whose decisions often have far-reaching impact on our lives. Even the less august but ubiquitous committee is responsible for many of the vital decisions affecting our lives and communities. For instance, hiring and firing decisions for many types of jobs are made by small committees, as are decisions on the type of building and development a city will allow. In fact, in a large, complex society like our own, the most important decision-making entities are usually not single individuals at all, but rather, small groups. Why this is so is something we will explore. But the fact of it suggests that small groups are a vital part of the larger social structure.

Our discussion so far has alerted us in a general way to some basic insights about small groups. First, we have seen that small groups are characterized by face-to-face interaction and seem to be different from larger groups in some ways. Second, small groups appear to be a vital aspect of an individual's life and possibly a major determinant of individual behavior. Third, such groups are an important element of the social structure of the larger society. The twin insights of the importance of groups to individuals on the one hand and to society on the other are the keys to understanding their social significance. A fuller understanding of these insights will give us a frame of reference, a perspective from which to approach the major topic of this book: the internal structure and operation of small groups themselves. Therefore let us consider each of our three points in greater detail.

WHAT MAKES SMALL GROUPS DISTINCTIVE?

The Effect of Size

When we consider changes in the size of a unit such as a group, we usually consider it to be a change in *quantity,* the number of members, not in *quality,* the basic nature of the group. But is this reasonable? Georg Simmel, an eminent social theorist from the turn of the century, was one of the first to realize that, with social groups, the situation may not be so simple. The effects of changes in size alone are not only quantitative: they will ultimately produce a qualitative change in the social organization of the group.

The single most important reason for this is that with the addition of each extra person the number of possible relationships in the group goes up dramatically (see Table 1.1). With two people, just one relationship is possible. But with three, there are three possible two-person relationships and one possible three-person relationship. Moreover, there are also the indirect relationships between two members through the third, and the relationship between each member and the group as a whole. And so it goes for even larger groups.

The proliferating possibilities that come with greater size change a number of things about the quality of interaction among the members and the nature of the internal problems faced by the group. Simmel (1950) sums them up like this: "The larger the group is, the more easily does it form an objective unit up and above its members, and the less intimate does it become . . . ." Size, then, changes two interrelated aspects of the group. First, the addition of new members dilutes the intimacy of the relationships among its members. Second, the more complex relationships that come with expansion of the group make the smooth coordination of group members' behavior harder to achieve. As a result, the group tends to develop a formal organization and explicit rules and regulations to control members' behavior. As Simmel points

Table 1.1. The Effect of Group Size on the Number of Possible Relationships

Group Size	Direct Relationships	Indirect Relationships
DYAD: John and Mary	John and Mary Total: 1	None
TRIAD: John, Mary, and Mike	John and Mary Mary and Mike John and Mike John, Mary, and Mike Total: 4	John and Mary through Mike John and Mike through Mary Mary and Mike through John Mary and the Group John and the Group Mike and the Group Total: 6
4-PERSON GROUP: John, Mary, Mike, and Sue	John and Mary Mary and Mike Mike and Sue John and Mike Mary and Sue John and Sue John and Mary and Mike Mary and Mike and Sue John and Mike and Sue John and Mary and Sue John, Mary, Mike and Sue Total: 11	John and Mary through Mike John and Mary through Sue John and Mike through Mary John and Mike through Sue Mary and Mike through John Mary and Mike through Sue John and Sue through Mary John and Sue through Mike Mary and Sue through John Mary and Sue through Mike Mike and Sue through John Mike and Sue through Mary John, Mary, and Mike through Sue Mary, Mike, and Sue through John John, Mike, and Sue through Mary John, Mary, and Sue through Mike John and the Group Mary and the Group Mike and the Group Sue and the Group Total: 20

out, the increasing formality of the group further interferes with intimacy.

The increasingly formal, objective quality of the group that comes with greater size has a number of specific consequences. As the group develops a more formal organization, a division of labor often evolves, and members begin to take on more specialized roles. It is no longer true that everybody does everything interchangeably. Rather, certain people end up in charge of specific aspects of group life. When role differentiation like this occurs, there is a general, although not inevitable, tendency for the group to develop a status hierarchy. The initial rough equality of members begins to change into clear inequalities of power and prestige.

As the group becomes more and more organized, it begins to seem to its members like an independent thing with a life of its own. The members feel less and less as though they, personally, are the group. The group begins to seem like some objective thing that they join but do not create. This has two consequences. First, it encourages members to take less personal responsibility for their actions within the group. As Simmel noted, people in groups larger than two or three often delegate personal duties and responsibilities to the group as a whole, giving the group new power to direct their behavior and opinions.

Second, the split between the individual and the group makes the individual feel less important, replaceable. In a dyad, a two-person group, the nature of the group is totally dependent on the unique personalities of the two members. If either of them is replaced by someone else, the group will be so completely transformed that it becomes a different group altogether. At the other extreme, the structure and nature of a large organization like a business or government bureaucracy are largely independent of the unique personalities of the people who work inside it. If one or two quit, new ones will be hired and the organization will go on very much as before. Between these two poles lie most small groups. Personalities *do* matter, and a change in membership will significantly change such a group. But the structure of the group does acquire some independent existence, and a potential remains for tension between the individual and the group.

A moment's reflection will show that each of the consequences of growing size, if allowed to continue, will eventually destroy the distinctive person-to-person quality that defines small groups. Beyond a break-off point of somewhere under thirty and usually around twenty people, the gradual changes introduced by group size so transform the basic nature of the group that it becomes a different sociological entity. The gradual quantitative change has become a qualitative change creating the difference between small groups and large ones.

Thinking about this, one might be tempted to go a step further. If it is increasing size that ultimately destroys the distinctive characteristics of small groups, wouldn't the truest, purest form of small groups also be the smallest: the dyad? As usual, things are not so simple. Let us look at Simmel's analysis of the dyad and triad (three-person group) to see why. This discussion will also illustrate how the addition of new members complicates social relations in a small group.

THE DYAD.   According to Simmel, in a dyad both members feel themselves confronted by another person in an immediate, reciprocal relationship. There is no buffer between them.[1] This creates possibilities for great intimacy, a degree of closeness that is difficult to achieve in any other type of relationship. It is this very exclusiveness, the "just you and me" quality of dyads, that gives them such potential for emotional sharing, for importance in personal life. As we have noted, dyads are completely dependent on the unique personalities of the two individuals. Consequently, they provide prime situations for members to express their individuality, and this makes dyads seem special to their members.

But the very same qualities make the dyad unstable as well. The mutual dependency of the members makes the relationship inherently insecure. If one person withdraws, the relationship is finished. Furthermore, there are always direct and immediate dangers in interaction. What if conflicts, disagreements, or hard feelings develop? There is no third person to help absorb the hostility or to mediate in an argument. There are no formal group rules or regulations to appeal to in resolving differences. Finally, the very potential for intimacy, for specialness, raises the level of expectations. What if the desired intimacy is not attained or cannot be maintained over extended interactions? The disappointment when this happens eats away at dyads. For their members, then, dyads are "endangered and irreplaceable" (Simmel).

The smallest small group, therefore, has the advantage of exceptional closeness, but the disadvantage of instability. The overlapping relationships and sense of groupness that come with more people can provide a permanence to balance against the shock of interpersonal conflict, even if some price is paid in intimacy. Simmel's analysis of the triad shows how the addition of even one person to the dyad begins to build these structures. The triad, however, is still not the most stable of small groups.

---

1. Simmel (1950:129) argued that this is not quite true for married couples. Marriage is such an established social institution that it often does create an abstract sense of a group with which the newly wedded couple must learn to deal.

THE TRIAD.   The most important consequence of a third member is that the two other members now have an indirect relationship with each other through the third member, as well as their own direct relationship. Simmel uses the example of the married couple who have their first child. The new baby binds them together in their shared concern for its welfare and increases their commitment to stay together as a unit. But, ironically, it also makes a little distance between them, breaks the dyadic circle of intimacy by focusing attention away from one another and toward the baby. To Simmel, the third member is like a bridge between two banks; it connects the banks but also measures the distance between them.

Simmel points out three possible roles that a third member can play: (1) the nonpartisan or mediator, (2) *tertius gaudens* ("the third who enjoys"), and (3) the divide-and-conquer role. All are distinctive to groups of three or more; they cannot occur in dyads. Any one of the three members can play these roles, not just a new third member. Also, members can change from one role to another.

The nonpartisan, or mediator, is essentially the role of the go-between who helps the other two handle their conflicts. A mediating third person can break the vicious cycle of mutual vehemence that tends to escalate emotional conflicts between two people. The intervention of the mediator forces the two parties to put the conflict on more objective, less emotional grounds, and this makes it easier to resolve. Recall that a dyad is unstable partly because it lacks such a person. The mediating role, then, serves to stabilize and perpetuate the group.

It is not an easy role to play, however. For minor conflicts, it may be manageable, but when the conflict is more serious, the third person will find it harder to maintain a disinterested, nonpartisan status. Both conflicting parties will demand that the third person show his or her loyalty and take sides. To them, nonpartisanship seems like repugnant fence-straddling (Simmel). If the third party is emotionally involved with both the others, it will be a very painful situation. Think of the dilemma of the children in many contested divorce cases (Nixon, 1979). Should they choose sides? How? If they do, don't they risk losing the affection of both the conflicting parties?

Simmel notes that the role of the mediator is occasionally made easier when the conflicting parties come to him or her for arbitration. In this situation, the arguing members have agreed to let the third member settle the dispute. This does give the third person more power to actually resolve things, making the situation a bit easier, if still not pleasant. But in real groups, experience suggests that arbitration is not very common as a method for resolving conflicts.

In the *tertuis gaudens* role, the third member reaps benefits from the competition between the other two members, who vie for his or her attention, support, or affection. (In some ways this is the opposite of the mediator who is victimized by the strife between the other members.) In the *tertuis gaudens* situation, the third person may be relatively innocent in this process in that he or she does not instigate or encourage the tension between the other two. This happens, for instance, when one member heaps attention and benefits on the third in order to annoy or upset the other member. Or the two members could be relatively jealous of each other and vie with each other because of their desire for a more exclusive relationship with the third person. This is the famous, troublesome romantic triangle. However, as the example of the love triangle reminds us, the third member may not always be so innocent. Indeed, he or she may actively seek the flattering, powerful position of the *tertuis gaudens* and try to maintain it by playing the two members against one another, encouraging their rivalry. But if the two members ever manage to get together and present a united front, the game is over for the *tertuis gaudens*. The mediator role gives the triad advantages of stability over the dyad. But the potential for the mediator to be transformed into a *tertuis gaudens* shows that the triad has its potential for disturbance as well.

The third member's ability to disturb the group, as well as bind it together, is particularly clear in the "divide-and-conquer" role. Here the third member, in order to enhance his or her own power, actively seeks to break up any two-person relationship that may exist between the other members. If the two members do not have any personal alliance established, the third person tries to ensure that none develops by pitting them against one another. Of course, the third member can't go too far in this. If the two members become too hostile to one another, they may quit the group, leaving the third person with no one to have power over. So the divide-and-conquer third, like the *tertuis gaudens*, must walk a delicate line between encouraging rivalry between the two other members and keeping the triad intact.

From Simmel's analysis, we see that the triad enables whole sets of complex relationships to develop that aren't possible in the dyad. These elaborate three-way relationships are the beginnings of group structure. As groups get even a little bit larger—four, five, six members—the shifting relationships of the triad begin to crystalize into a more clear-cut, stable (that is, more slowly changing) social structure made up of regular, recognizable patterns of relationships among the members.

As we have seen, one of the benefits of an increasingly organized and established group structure is greater permanence and stability: the group can better survive the whims of an individual member. This is already apparent in the triad. Even in the *tertuis gaudens* and the divide-and-conquer situations, the benefits received by the troublesome third party are entirely dependent on maintaining the existing structure of the triad. This usually inspires a mischievous third to keep his or her disturbances within bounds and helps the group survive.

THE IDEAL SIZE.   Now let's go back to the question of the ideal size for a small group. We've seen that the extreme of smallness, the dyad, has a wonderful potential for intimacy but pays a price in instability. At the other extreme, a group of twenty to thirty is likely to develop an elaborate, stabilizing group structure, but the chance for intimacy among all the members will be slight. Thus, common sense dictates that the ideal small group, the one which can both maintain some intimacy and achieve moderate stability, will be some size in between. And sure enough, studies of the effect of size on small groups have shown that groups of about five or so seem to be most satisfactory to their members (Hare, 1952; Bales, 1954; Slater, 1958; Hackman and Vidmar, 1970). Below that number, members often felt that the burden of keeping the group going was too great. Above it, people complained that their opportunities to participate became too limited.

The discussion of the effects of size on small groups should provide a clearer idea of why we study small groups as a special kind of organization. Small groups are qualitatively different from large ones. With luck, our discussion has also fleshed out for the reader our notion of what small groups are and given some sense of their dynamics and distinguishing characteristics.

THE IMPORTANCE OF SMALL GROUPS TO INDIVIDUALS

Dependence on Groups

George Homans (1950), a prominent sociologist, once argued that small groups are the *essential human group.* In human history, said Homans, nations, societies, cities, large organizations, all come and go, but families, friendship groups, and small bands of people persist. As long as people survive, they seem to band together in small groups. Why is this? What do groups mean to individuals that they should constantly create them?

In a way, it all goes back to the fact that people are born into a group, a family. Even if a child is not raised by the person who gives it birth, a child must be raised by *somebody*. Therefore, from the beginning, the child depends for its very survival on being a member of a group made up of at least the baby and its caretaker. Usually, of course, the group that raises the child is a bit larger. But in any case, it is the child's physical and emotional dependence on its caretaking group, its family, that sets the stage for people's lifelong involvement in small groups.

In the course of growing up, children learn to rely on groups for two basic needs: emotional sustenance, and assistance in managing tasks that they cannot accomplish alone. After fifteen or so years of such help from their caretaking group, children are skilled enough to go out into the world alone. But they carry with them those habits of using groups to help them deal with their lives. Groups are the most powerful tool the individual has for managing the physical and emotional uncertainties of adult life.

The fact that adults look to groups for emotional sustenance and aid in accomplishing tasks sets the foundation for two types of small groups that exist in our society: *primary groups* and *task groups.* Briefly, primary groups specialize in the emotional relationships among the members. Task groups are organized to accomplish specific instrumental goals, or tasks, giving minimal attention to the personal relationships among the members. We will describe these groups in their pure form, which sociologists call an "ideal type." But actually, the two types represent the polar extremes of a continuum, not a clear-cut dichotomy (Acock, Dowd, and Roberts, 1974). The truth is that all small groups have some primary- and some task-group qualities. What groups differ in is the relative emphasis they give to one over the other.

We will discuss the ideal types of primary and task groups in order to gain a feeling for the basic dimensions involved. We need to know something about their general characteristics and their impact on us as individuals. We also need to know which groups in our society function mostly as primary groups and which are more task oriented. However, in conducting such a discussion we do not want you to be misled into thinking of primary and task groups as a set of rigid pigeonholes. Remember that the distinction represents a continuum. There are many groups in our lives that cannot be neatly classified as more one than the other.

Primary Groups

The term *primary group* was first introduced into social science by Charles H. Cooley in 1909. His definition captures better than almost any other the feel of primary groups (Cooley, 1909):

> By primary groups, I mean those characterized by intimate face-to-face association and cooperation. They are primary in several senses, but chiefly in that they are fundamental in forming the social nature and ideas of the individual. The result of intimate association, psychologically, is a certain fusion of individualities in a common whole, so that one's very self, for many purposes at least, is the common life and purposes of the group. Perhaps the simplest way of describing this wholeness is by saying that it is a "we," it involves the sort of sympathy and mutual identification for which "we" is the natural expression.

Cooley used *primary* to describe these groups because he believed they were the place where basic primary human qualities were learned and expressed, and also because such groups hold a place of primary importance in the individual's life (Dunphy, 1972).

Primary groups have all the essential qualities of small groups: face-to-face association, small size, a sense of group identity, and group norms. But as Cooley's definition makes clear, they have additional qualities as well. These can be summarized as: (1) significant emotional attachment among the members and a relatively personal quality to interaction, (2) relative permanence or long duration, and (3) diffuse, nonspecific purpose.

Of these, the first—emotional attachment—is the critical distinguishing quality of primary groups. The second, relative permanence, is really a necessary condition for the development of emotional attachments. It takes time for people to form significant bonds with one another. When a group meets three or four times and then dissolves, the members simply don't have the opportunity to form the involvements that make a group primary in nature. We should note, however, that relative duration, while a necessary condition for primary groups, is not a sufficient one. Just because a group meets together frequently over a reasonable length of time does not, by itself, ensure that the members will form significant attachments to one another. Finally, we must caution that relative permanence does not mean that primary groups last forever, only that they are generally longer-lived than more impersonal groups.

The third characteristic of primary groups, nonspecific purpose, is a consequence of focusing on the emotional relationships among the members. When the main reason for getting together is to share one another's company, it really doesn't matter what the group does. When the group does decide to engage in a specific activity—go bowling, for instance—it does so mostly to create an occasion for being together. The real business of a primary group is not any outside activity at all. Rather, it is tending to one another's feelings, attitudes, opinions, and life problems.

PRIMARY GROUPS AND THE INDIVIDUAL.   As Cooley said, the purpose of primary groups is to deal with the selves of the members. This is the key to understanding why primary groups are so important to the individual; it also explains the source of the primary group's power over individual behavior and opinions. Primary groups are the one place a person can go to be responded to as a whole person. In most aspects of our lives—in our jobs, in civic roles, and so on—we perform a specific role. We present certain parts of ourselves that are relevant to that role, and keep back the rest. But primary groups are the place where you can let your hair down and freely express all the various aspects of yourself.

A place where you can be yourself is important for many reasons. Only there can you seek (and ideally receive) approval for the basic inner "you," rather than for your skill at performing some role. Such approval is the foundation of personal self-esteem. Access to groups where such approval is received contributes to each person's overall well-being and psychological stability. Also, a chance to be yourself is one of the best opportunities you have to discover for yourself who you really are. Consequently, primary groups become one of the major devices that most people use to develop and maintain their self-identity.

Individuals not only gain self-discovery and approval from primary groups, they also gain information about the world, particularly the social world. Most of what individuals learn about the norms of our society—its do's and don't's and how-to's—comes from the primary groups of family and friends. Of course, this begins in childhood, but it continues throughout adulthood. When you take a new job, one of the biggest problems is learning the ropes. You'll learn a certain amount from official rules and regulations and impersonal advice from others. But only when you have been there long enough to form personal friendships with other workers will you gradually be filled in on all the unofficial strategies people use to cope with the official rules and demands of the job.

College freshmen experience the same sort of problem when they first arrive on campus. Most have read the official publications the college sent them and looked around the campus. But they still don't know how college life really works. They don't know where to go on campus to meet people, they don't know if its all right to call a professor at home, they don't know which instructors are supposed to be good and which aren't. To answer such questions they need to strike up acquaintances with other students in their classes or dorms. Once they do that, their new friends will teach them the way the system really operates, adding dimension and meaning to their picture of campus life.

Finally, primary groups offer people support, encouragement, and potentially relief from the vicissitudes of life in a complex, impersonal world. In a large, industrialized society, much of our lives are spent negotiating jobs that combine high pressure with a work environment that is often impersonal to the point of being dehumanizing. Similarly, the bureaucratic nature of the government and business institutions we deal with often makes people feel as if they don't count for much. In this context, the warmth and self-affirmation provided by primary groups makes them seem like snug harbors in an indifferent sea. "Haven in a heartless world" was the phrase historian Christopher Lasch (1977) used to describe the family in industrialized society. The support people receive in primary groups strengthens them to cope with demands placed on them by the outside world. This in turn makes it possible for society to maintain its demanding social structure.

All these positive things offered to individuals by primary groups are, of course, only potential benefits. There is no guarantee that the primary groups to which any particular person belongs will succeed in providing all the types of support and aid described. Think of all the marriages that fail. These are primary groups that could not provide what their participants wanted or needed. It is also possible for individuals to be cut off altogether from primary-group membership at some time or another in their lives. Later, we will discuss some of the social conditions in which this may occur.

Imagining what it would be like to be cut off from all close, intimate groups brings home the fundamental importance of primary groups to the individual. People's dependence on primary groups for so many of the satisfactions of life gives these groups enormous power over their members. More than any other kind of group, primary groups have the power to form, maintain, and change people's attitudes, beliefs about the world, and their behavior as well. The fact that they have such power gives us a hint as to their importance to society as well. Whether people support the norms and structure of society at large depends a lot on whether their primary groups encourage them to do so.

TYPES OF PRIMARY GROUPS.   Now that we have some idea of the characteristics of primary groups and their importance to the individual, we are in a position to describe some of the types of groups in our society that function largely as primary groups. Dexter Dunphy (1972) has summarized these groups rather well.

1. Families
2. Free-association peer groups of childhood, adolescence, and adulthood; delinquent gangs and some small cohesive political elites (cabals); most close friendship groups
3. Informal groups existing in organizational settings such as classroom groups, factory work groups, small military units
4. Resocialization groups such as therapy groups, rehabilitation groups, and self-analytic groups

The first three categories of groups are quite familiar. But the last is an interesting insight of Dunphy's. We noted that primary groups are largely responsible for teaching people the rules and regulations of society and how to function in relation to them. Sociologists call this process *socialization*. But what happens if, as an adult, you feel you don't function very well in relation to society, and if your friends or family don't seem to be able to help you? One thing you might do is turn to specially constructed primary groups designed to retrain—that is, resocialize—people's everyday habits of dealing with others and society. These resocialization groups include therapy groups, parenting groups, consciousness-raising groups, and so on. We will have more to say about them, as well as the other categories of primary groups, in Chapter 10.

We can properly refer to families, peer groups, friendship groups at work, and resocialization groups as primary groups because they spend the greatest portion of their energies functioning as primary groups for their members. But that is not all they do. Recall that there are no pure primary groups. Families, friends, and informal work groups all engage in serious task activities as well. Families, for instance, worry about managing household finances. Work groups develop strategies for dealing with the boss's demands. Each of these groups is called primary because its concerns are much closer to the primary end of the group continuum, not because it is a pure type.

Task Groups

Task groups are groups created by their members to accomplish a specific goal. The goal can vary from making a policy decision, to solving a complex problem, to creating a group product like a television script, to carrying out such activities as sailing a large sailboat or moving a piano. The diversity of these goals illustrates the way task groups proliferate through all aspects of our society and into the personal experience of almost everybody.

To be of interest to us, task groups must show the defining qualities of a small group: small size, face-to-face interaction, and some sense of group identity and norms. This means that five members of a road crew who are assigned to work in the same place, but who pay no attention to one another and stick to their assigned individual jobs, cannot properly be called a task group. On the other hand, if the same workers decided to coordinate their activities together so that all of them could finish sooner, they would become a task group. The key difference is that, in the second case, the workers developed a sense of themselves as a group (a group identity) and developed some informal norms for coordinating their behavior so they could work together as a whole.

In addition to the basic qualities of small groups, task groups have their own distinguishing characteristics. First, they have a highly specific purpose, the accomplishment of their chosen task. Second, the relationships among the members tend to be primarily instrumental, rather than affective. Third, they are frequently characterized by relative impermanence.

The first of these is self-evident, but the second and third require some elaboration. Relationships among task group members are instrumental: each person relates to the others primarily in terms of the assistance they can provide in accomplishing the task. Interaction among the members is shaped by the requirements of the task and the relevant skills each has to offer. As a result, members tend to emphasize only those aspects of their selves that are pertinent to the job at hand and to play down other more personal concerns. This encourages an emotionally cool, work-oriented, "professional" atmosphere in the group. The dominance of this atmosphere does not mean that people have no emotional reactions to one another in task groups. Of course they do. But it is not legitimate for them to bring these up openly before the group. Officially, in a task group, members are not required to like one another, only to be able to work with one another.

The relative impermanence of task groups arises from their concentration on the accomplishment of a specific goal. When such a goal is fulfilled, the reason for that group's existence is removed. The group is then likely either to formally disband or to just drift apart. Occasionally, a group that has been successful and enjoyable for its members will search around for a new task in order to continue working, but this is the exception. The actual life of a task group can vary from a few hours to a few years, but, in general, their average lives are shorter than those of primary groups.

TASK GROUPS AND THE INDIVIDUAL.   Task groups are important to the individual for a number of reasons. On the most basic level, task groups are a vital tool for doing work that is too much for one person to accomplish alone. Obvious examples are physical tasks that require more than one person, for instance, playing basketball or forming a car pool. Much of what we do in our daily lives would be impossible if we didn't regularly rely on others to join with us in a group to accomplish such physical tasks.

Less obvious are the ways in which we rely on task groups for nonphysical assistance. For instance, when faced with a complex problem to solve or a decision to make, people turn immediately to others. Often they seek out a group of friends or knowledgeable others who will help work through the problem. If a public official or member of a large organization is faced with a complex problem, that person is likely to set up a group of advisers or form a committee. Why? Really, there are two reasons.

First, people usually reason rightly or wrongly that several heads are better than one. Other individuals are likely to have different skills, knowledge, and perceptions of the situation. If the problem is complicated, difficult, or the consequences very serious, it often seems wise to pool together as much information and as many different points of view as possible. The obvious way to do this is to put together a group of differing individuals who can exchange ideas and, ideally, come up with a better, more carefully considered solution than any one person alone. This is the rationale behind the United States Supreme Court, where nine judges are used rather than the single judge who presides over lower courts. Are groups really able to solve difficult questions better than individuals? Yes and no. This complex question will be examined in Chapter 9. But underlying the ubiquitous formation of committees is an assumption, accurate or not, that groups can help resolve complex problems.

The second reason we turn to others in the face of difficult problems is less rational and more personal. If a problem looks difficult, complicated, or confusing, it is easy to feel a little overwhelmed by it. We as individuals feel insecure about our ability to handle it. And, if the problem is a serious one or its consequences grave, the responsibility for solving it alone is dismaying. So we turn to others, not only for their ideas, but to share the burden of responsibility. When a group makes a decision, responsibility for that decision is diffused among all the members—no single individual is on the spot. This makes groups, committees, and panels of experts particularly attractive when the decision to be made is a politically sensitive one with serious consequences for the future.

Task groups are important to individuals in other ways too. Usually they lack the emotional rewards of primary groups. But most people, over the course of their lives, are involved in more task groups than primary groups. This is partly because task groups are relatively transient, so the turnover is high. But it is also due to the fact that most of us spend as much or more time working and organizing our lives as we do socializing in primary groups. Thus task groups, despite their work-oriented, more impersonal nature, mediate between us and the achievement of many things that we want in life. Examples are respect for our skills on the job, a sense of mastery over our environment, achieving specific goals like car pooling, and a sense of accomplishment. It is not that we can't or don't achieve such goals outside of task groups. It is that, due to the proliferation of task groups in our society, many of the arenas where we have a chance to work toward them turn out to be groups. Task groups, like primary groups, have substantial power to influence individual attitudes, beliefs, and behaviors. It is probably true that task groups lack the ability of primary groups to change basic beliefs and core values. But they have a substantial capacity to shape beliefs and behavior in a wide variety of more mundane circumstances.

TYPES OF TASK GROUPS.   Listing specific examples of groups in our society that function primarily as task groups is easy to do. It is less easy to put these groups into neat, inclusive categories. Task groups differ basically according to who establishes them and by the type of task that confronts each. There are small task groups organized by large organizations to solve problems, make decisions, and oversee operations. Examples are boards of directors, internal study groups, committees and subcommittees, and advisory councils. Large organizations sometimes use task groups to organize production too, although this is less common. For instance, hospitals sometimes organize doctors into diagnostic teams. In some experimental factories, workers are organized into small teams that build a product from start to finish. Scriptwriters also work together as teams in the production of television shows. Professional athletes sometimes work together in teams small enough to be true small groups. Another category of task groups includes those created by people in voluntary organizations, such as community action groups, grass-roots political groups, Little League teams, and so on. Finally, there are informal task groups that are developed by individuals outside any organizational environment. Examples are car pools and reading groups.

Again, we must caution that there are no pure task groups, just as there are no pure primary groups. The groups we have discussed are relatively more task oriented than socially oriented, but none is utterly without primary-group qualities. We can also think of groups that seem to fall very much in the middle between the primary and task extremes. An informal athletic team is an example—the kind of team where playing the game is important, but so are the friendships among the members. However, by describing the extremes of the primary group–task group continuum, some sense of the range of small groups as they actually appear in our society should be grasped.

THE IMPORTANCE OF SMALL GROUPS TO SOCIETY

The Link between Society and Individuals

In discussing the importance of small groups to individuals, we have repeatedly stumbled over the fact that they are a basic subunit in the larger organization of society. Families, for instance, are a fundamental building block out of which many aspects of society are created, including neighborhoods, cities, and socioeconomic strata. As a basic subunit, small groups perform a number of functions within the social structure of society as a whole that affect its operation and survival. To make our study of small groups meaningful, we need to understand these functions and their significance. The key to most of these arises from a single observation: small groups are the most important link between society as a whole and the individuals of which it is composed (Durkheim, [1893] 1933). The norms of the larger society, the behaviors in which individuals must engage in order to create the social structure, are taught to individuals by small groups as part of the socialization process. As we have seen, small groups have enormous power to shape people's basic beliefs and values, either in support of, or in opposition to the larger society. Once society's norms are learned, small groups continue to exert pressure on their members to conform with or to break them.

Both society and the larger organizations that make up its basic units are heavily dependent on small groups to teach and enforce societal norms. The power of large formal organizations to influence behavior is limited without the intervention of face-to-face processes. Our system for enforcing laws, for instance, assumes that the vast majority of citizens, thanks to small groups, know and willingly obey the law. As long as this occurs, society has the physical resources to track down the few miscreants and punish their disobedience. But if small groups stopped teaching the law and pressuring their members to obey it, all the police forces in the country would not be sufficient to handle the hordes of lawbreakers.

Society only continues as it is because people recreate it every day by acting in accordance with its demands. If a large proportion of citizens ceases to do that, the norms and the social structure itself are transformed. Small groups are a major determinant of individual citizens' behavior in this regard. We see then that small groups, as the intermediary between society and the individual, have enormous power to maintain or undermine the existing social structure (see Box 1.1).

The role of small groups as intermediaries has consequences for individuals as well. We have seen how people use their small groups to help them cope with the demands placed on them by the larger society. But the fact that society relies on small groups to deliver its values and norms to individuals affects those individuals as well as society. It means that people's sense of belonging to the larger society is quite dependent on their membership in the small groups that make human its values and rules. When you first take a job with a large organization—for example, a corporation or a university—you see the huge building and all those people working away in their identical little slots. It all seems so inhuman that it is difficult to imagine ever feeling like you belong there, let alone caring about the organization's goals and priorities. But as the days go by, you gradually become aware of a network of more personal relationships, of friendship cliques, political factions, and so on, that are like ivy covering the concrete walls of the institution. As you join these small groups, the organization acquires a human face, and you begin to feel you belong, that you are part of it. Whether its citizens feel they belong is in turn very important for society as a whole. The loyalty of its members is similarly crucial to a large organization. Only when the majority of citizens feel committed to a society can its social structure be maintained.

Box 1.1.   SMALL GROUPS AND PRODUCTIVITY IN JAPAN

Thirty years ago "made in Japan" was a sign to most Americans of cheap, poor quality goods. That is no longer true. Today, Japanese products set the standard for quality, efficiency, and value in industries from automobiles to electronics to cameras. The productivity of Japanese industry has become the envy of the Western world. How did they do it? What is their secret?

Part of the answer lies in the Japanese use of small groups to harness their employees' energies to the goals of the larger corporation. In *The Art of Japanese Management,* Pascale and Athos (1981) point out that the small work group is the basic building block of Japanese corporations. Japanese organizational charts show only groups, not individual positions or titles. In identifying themselves Japanese managers emphasize their group identification rather than their personal job titles. Management decisions are made through a repeated process of group discussion until a consensus is reached among all the affected people.

Workers on the production line are also encouraged to develop group relations with their immediate co-workers. For instance, the people who actually work on a particular aspect of production are brought together in "quality circles" of from two to ten people (Ouchi, 1981). In these circles workers talk about any problems they encounter with current production techniques and make suggestions about how they can be improved. Management takes these ideas seriously, and after thorough discussion many are implemented. When a group's suggestion improves productivity, it is not the individual who voiced the idea but the group as a whole that receives a bonus. The notion is that the individual could never have made such a suggestion without the stimulation and support of the entire work group. Many groups save their bonuses to pay for a big party at the end of the year. In this way the individual's self-interest is linked to the group's well-being, and through that to the corporate goals.

The small work groups Japanese corporations create exist mainly for task-oriented reasons, but management encourages the members of these groups to spend time socializing as well as working (Ouchi, 1981). There are two ways this is done. First, the corporation sponsors after-hours dinners, banquets, and cocktail parties where work-group members can get to know each other in an informal way (and perhaps blow off steam about personal frustrations within the group).

Second, during work hours, substantial attention is directed to socioemotional relations in the group as well as to task matters. Man-

Box ·1.1.   *(continued)*

agement and workers alike explicitly acknowledge that the work group must succeed at a human level first if it is to be an effective unit of production.

This is quite a change from the way task groups are viewed in American organizations (Pascale and Athos, 1981). In the "stick to the facts" atmosphere of U.S. business, getting the job done is usually the only legitimate matter of concern for an American work group. Spending too much time on personal relations among the members is seen as wasteful. In effect then, the work groups created by Japanese corporations have more primary-group qualities than do their American counterparts. So the Japanese not only use small groups more extensively in their corporations, they also make these groups more emotionally involving for their members.

What are the consequences of making work groups more emotionally involving? To begin with, it increases people's sense of commitment to the group and makes them more willing to work hard to benefit it. More of a worker's personal identity gets involved. Doing your best starts to matter more when you know it will earn you approval and recognition from people you care about. As we know, primary groups have a great deal of influence over the beliefs and values of their members. So work groups that are more primary-oriented are more effective at inducing individual workers to adopt the company's goals as their own, to really care how the corporation does. By using small work groups with primary as well as task qualities, Japanese corporations tap their employees' energies more fully and ally them more directly with the interest and values of the organization as a whole. An executive of Mitsushita, a major Japanese corporation, described the process like this:

> . . . when one of your organizations—like IBM, for example —*really* gets its members to "think" [IBM's motto] or to believe that "IBM means service," it is no longer an ad slogan. It becomes a belief system for thousands of people who work for that company—a human value beyond profit to which their productive lives are dedicated. No less is true for the business philosophy of Mitsushita. (Pascale and Athos, 1981)

To say that copying the Japanese will automatically improve American business productivity is to oversimplify. Japanese management is rooted in Japanese culture, and there are major differences between the beliefs and values of that culture and those of American society. However, fundamental lessons *can* be learned from the Japanese use of small groups, and particularly from their added emphasis on the human side of those groups. These basic lessons, when adjusted to the values of American society, may well point the way to increased productivity for U.S. business as well.

Alienation and Anomie

The topic of people's sense of belongingness to large-scale organizations naturally raises the issue of *alienation*. Let us look at the way this concept and a related one, *anomie*, are understood by sociologists. Both concepts provide an excellent illustration of the linking role small groups play between individuals and society. Alienation is a feeling of distance between yourself and a group. It is a sense of not belonging, of not being part of the group's "we." When an important small group in a person's life collapses, particularly a primary group, it is precisely this sense of "we-ness" that is destroyed. The individual feels the loss of the secure base the group offered. Not only does he or she feel cut off from what the small group provided, the person feels cut off from many aspects of larger society as well. Since groups link a person with the rest of society, the group's collapse leaves the individual stranded outside the mainstream of the norms, values, and rewards of society. He or she feels alienated, and the alienation has spread from the small group to the larger society.[2]

Of course, most people belong to several groups, and while the disintegration of an important one may leave them feeling somewhat alienated, they can usually cure this by reestablishing themselves in other groups. However, if people's focal primary groups collapse (their families, for example), or perhaps a whole network of their groups disintegrates simultaneously (in a disaster, for example), they will feel more than just alienation. They are likely to also suffer a crisis of anomie, of normlessness and meaninglessness. In this situation, they have lost not only a basis of emotional security, but also the central mechanisms by which we structure reality and maintain our sense of selves. Recall that people rely on groups for basic information about themselves and the nature of social reality. They are cut off from this as well when their groups collapse. Durkheim ([1894] 1951) argued that a disproportionate number of suicides occur where individuals are in situations of severe anomie.

No matter what causes a person's small groups to collapse, the consequent alienation and anomie are miserable for the individual. But they become a serious problem for society as well when whole sectors of the population experience them at the same time. This can happen

2. Some would argue that a person could be closely allied with personal small groups and still feel alienated if the groups themselves rejected society's norms and values. But this form of alienation does not carry the sense of personal loss, isolation, and powerlessness often associated with the term.

when people's primary groups are threatened, not by internal strife, but by pressure from outside. Conditions of rapid social change, social mobility, economic hardship, or sudden crisis can uproot the members, disorganize the group, and overwhelm its ability to adapt. Members may be set in competition with one another, or forced to desert the group for other organizations. The society itself may set up inconsistent demands that destroy the group's ability to connect its members to society. For instance, our society stresses achievement and success as the measure of a person's worth. And yet there are whole groups of people in our society who, because of their racial, ethnic, or economic background, find the pathways to achievement blocked. These people are in a double bind. Society tells them to achieve and doesn't let them do so. When a large sector of people and their primary groups are put under this kind of pressure, widespread alienation and anomie are inevitable. With this will come much greater violation of society's norms, and an increasing threat to the basic social structure. Society is dependent on people's membership in workable small groups, particularly primary groups, and on the basic support of these groups to maintain the morale and commitment of individual citizens and to ensure the essential well-being of the social structure (see Box 1.2).

Group Functions in Society

Now that we have some idea of the linkage small groups provide between individuals and society, we are in a position to consider more carefully the role small groups play in the operation of society and its larger organizations. The following list suggests some of the most important of these roles. Some will be clear from our discussion so far, while others will require more elaboration.

1. Small groups are largely responsible for socializing individuals into the norms and values of society and larger organizations. They are also responsible for resocializing adults to adapt to new or changing social conditions.
2. Small groups are society's major mechanism for routine social control over the behavior of individuals. The official means of norm enforcement available to large-scale organizations cannot successfully maintain control without the social pressure of small groups.
3. Small groups provide a mechanism by which the larger society can harness the personal motivation of the individual to organizational or societal goals. The classic example comes from stud-

Box 1.2.   PRESIDENTIAL ASSASSINS

When someone is cut off from small groups—from friends, family, and co-workers—two things happen simultaneously. As a social isolate, the individual loses the network of relationships we all use to maintain our personal identities, that which we rely on for the information and feedback necessary to keep firmly in touch with reality. At the same time, society loses its ability to control the person's daily behavior. It can no longer ensure that he or she will stick to fundamental rules of social conduct. This combined loss of social control and threat to personal stability is a formula for disaster.

Nowhere is this better illustrated than in the case of people who commit shockingly antisocial crimes, such as the assassination of a president. Such people are almost always disturbed individuals. However, their problems and distortions of reality have been exacerbated by their isolation from small groups. As their intentions turn murderous, they are not discovered and stopped by others because few people have any real contact with them. Because no one knows or cares what they do, they succeed in planning and executing their seemingly unthinkable crimes.

History has offered us a recent example in the case of John W. Hinckley, Jr., the man who, on March 30, 1981, tried to kill President Ronald Reagan. Hinckley clearly fit the pattern: a disturbed isolate whose crime went unstopped because he was cut off from all group relations. According to reports of testimony given at his trial (Press et al., 1982), Hinckley began to withdraw from group ties in adolescence. He had no friends as a teenager, spending his time alone in his room and becoming increasingly preoccupied with music. Although he still had his family, his relationship with his parents became more distant, less open. When he went away to college he invented a girlfriend in his letters home as a ploy to get more money from his parents. Because he had no true group ties at college, there was no one to challenge him on his imaginary girlfriend, and, according to psychiatrists, she became real to him. Because of Hinckley's growing distance from his parents, they did not realize the girlfriend was a ruse until after his arrest.

As Hinckley's mental problems grew worse, his ability to maintain group attachments deteriorated even further. This in turn meant that there were even fewer people around to help him distinguish between fantasy and reality, and no one close enough to realize the depth of his problems. Out of college, he couldn't hold a job. He became obsessed with the movie *Taxi Driver* and developed a crush on Jodie Foster, the actress who played its heroine. He collected guns

Box 1.2   *(continued)*

like the film's violent, disturbed protagonist. He fantasized a relationship with Foster, following her around and trying to call her on the phone. He wrote his psychiatrist that "I have remained so inactive and reclusive over the past 5 years I have managed to remove myself from the real world" (Press et al., 1982).

The final turn to violence came when his last group tie was severed. Hinckley's parents had continued to support him and take him in in times of crisis, despite his emotional estrangement from them. But now, following the unfortunate advice of a psychiatrist, they refused to take him back, cutting off their relationship with him altogether. This was three weeks before the assassination attempt. With no one to exercise any control over his behavior or provide any check on his fantasies, Hinckley began to concoct plans for violence. He considered a mass slaughter at Yale, where Foster was enrolled. He thought of hijacking a plane and demanding Foster as ransom. In Washington D.C., Hinckley happened by chance to see a newspaper report outlining President Reagan's official schedule. Deciding that killing the president would impress Ms. Foster, he got a gun and shot Ronald Reagan and three others as they left the Hilton hotel.

Fortunately, Hinckley did not succeed in killing the president. However, in the past assassins have killed four U.S. presidents. Three of the four assassins were very much like Hinckley: disturbed people with few group contacts to stop them from developing and carrying out murderous intentions. Considering their stories briefly will make clear how Hinckley's case was typical.

Most recent, of course, was the case of Lee Harvey Oswald, who shot President John F. Kennedy. Although much more rational than Hinckley, Oswald was also a troubled man cut off from others. He too lacked the group ties necessary to control his behavior or shine the light of reality on his imaginings (Ford and Stiles, 1965). By young adulthood his family was fragmented and he was alienated from its members. Having conceived a plan to emigrate to the USSR, he deliberately avoided forming a close attachment with anyone. Once in the Soviet Union, however, he found he could not form many contacts there either. Although he did marry a young Russian and bring her back to the United States, their relationship soon deteriorated to violent quarrels and estrangement. Isolated from others and alienated from both the United States and the Soviet Union, he carried out the assassination of President Kennedy.

In 1901 Leon Czolgosz shot and killed President William McKinley. His case too fits the basic pattern (Johns, 1970). At the time of the assassination he was withdrawn, emotionally troubled, and alienated from family and friends. He attempted to join the radical political

Box 1.2   *(continued)*

circles around Emma Goldman, the well-known anarchist. But Goldman (1931) reports that her friends rejected Czolgosz. He seemed strange and asked so many questions the anarchists thought he was a government spy. Without even other radicals to check his dangerous intentions, he carried out McKinley's murder.

In 1881, Charles J. Guiteau killed President James A. Garfield. Guiteau was another seriously disturbed man whose relationships with others had always been problematic, who was violently estranged from his wife and family, and who had no one to stop him when he began to live in his own dangerous delusions (Rosenberg, 1968). Finally, there was John Wilkes Booth, Abraham Lincoln's assassin. Booth is the one exception to our pattern. Although a political fanatic, Booth was not a loner cut off from small-group relations. The circumstances of his deed were atypical, however. The nation was embroiled in the Civil War, and Booth, an ardent Southern sympathizer, murdered Lincoln as the leader of the North.

That Hinckley and three of the four successful presidential assassins were loners, estranged from group relations, is no accident. With more group ties any one of these people could have been stopped. Of course, the problem is self-feeding. A disturbed person has difficulty maintaining group relations. However, the loss of those group ties makes emotional stability even harder to achieve. Finally, as the person becomes dangerous, there is no one near enough to stop him or her. All this underscores for us the vital importance of small groups, not only to us as individuals, but to society as a whole. The entire society relies on small groups to keep its citizens sane or, failing that, to see that they get help. It relies on small groups to maintain a basic control over our behavior for the sake of us all.

ies of soldiers. What makes people fight hard, risking death, for the abstract goals of their nation? Stouffer et al. (1949) studied American troops in World War II and found that the biggest determinant of combat effectiveness was the existence of satisfying primary relationships within the soldiers' peer groups. Shils and Janowitz (1948) discovered that the secret of the German army's effectiveness in the war was its organization into small platoons, which promoted the development of primary-group relations among the soldiers. Soldiers fight best for their buddies, and as long as the army can keep the loyalty of the buddy groups within it, soldiers will fight and die for their country's goals. Small groups allow society to tap the motivation of individuals for more peaceful means as well.

4. Small groups provide large organizations with a decision-making and problem-solving mechanism superior in some cases both to single individuals and to large groups in resolving difficult problems. We have already mentioned the skill- and information-pooling aspects of task groups as well as their ability to allow sharing of responsibility for the final decision. As we shall see in Chapter 9, these aspects give groups certain advantages as problem-solving mechanisms, although they can create problems as well. However, for now it is enough to note that the formal business, government, and educational institutions of our society increasingly rely on task groups as their major decision-making entities.

5. Small groups are society's basic source for new elements in its culture. Most new cultural beliefs, life-styles, and behavior patterns that are ultimately adopted by the society as a whole start first in small groups of individuals. We will have more to say about the culture-creating aspect of groups in Chapter 8.

6. As Crosbie (1975) notes, small groups mediate many individual events that ultimately become societal events. Examples are education, divorce, delinquency, migration, suicide, all of which begin as small-group events and end as social statistics. As a result, small groups can be instruments of social change as well as social control.

7. Finally, the informal small groups that spring up within large organizations sometimes form a sort of parallel structure to that of the formal organization. As Acock et al. (1974) point out, this informal network sometimes operates to pursue the organizational goals when the formal procedures fail. But this cuts both ways. Informal networks can be used to undermine the organization as well.

The many functions played by small groups make it quite clear that society is thoroughly dependent upon small groups for its survival. This has two implications. First, it is vitally important for society that the vast majority of its citizens have access to small groups to which they can belong and through which they can be linked to the larger social structure. If this does not occur—and there is never a guarantee that it will—high levels of social disorganization, crime, alienation, and anomie are inevitable. Second, to survive as it is, society must maintain the loyalty and support of the small groups within it. Small groups can wield their power against the larger social structure as well as in support of it. There is a middle course, also, in which pressure for social change is transmitted from individuals up through small groups to modify the social structure without fundamentally challenging it.

Small Groups and Society: Past and Present

What is the present state of the relationship between small groups and contemporary society? To answer this question, we need to acquire a historical perspective on the current situation. Nineteenth-century social thinkers were impressed by the impact of urbanization and industrialization on social life. Toennies (1887), in particular, realized that people's small-group relationships were being transformed by these forces. Toennies argued that the basis of social relationships were shifting dramatically from those of *gemeinschaft*—communal, face-to-face, primary relationships—to those of *gesellschaft*—the impersonal, contractual relationships of the marketplace. Traditional rural society had been organized around the classic, multipurpose primary groups of family, community, and church. But this society was being replaced by a new urban one where life revolved around impersonal economic or official relationships. In our terminology, then, Toennies thought that task-oriented associations and groups were displacing primary ones. Indeed, Toennies and other theorists of his time predicted that primary groups would ultimately disappear. Since most of these thinkers recognized the vital importance of primary groups to society, they viewed this trend with alarm.

From our position, a century later, we can confirm that the modernization process has continued apace. Has it destroyed the primary group? What has it done to the task group? It certainly is true that relatively impersonal, or secondary (as opposed to primary), dealings with others have become the basis of modern life. With this has come the creation and proliferation of task-oriented small groups throughout the organizational structure of our society. On the other hand, as sociologists began to realize in the 1930s, primary groups have not been destroyed in the process. They remain as important as ever, but they have been changed.

The keystone of traditional primary groups, the family, has indeed been badly buffeted by the development of modern society. Several of its many functions, such as education and adolescent socialization, have been stripped from it (Dunphy, 1972). It has been reduced in size to the nuclear family of parents and two to three children. But the family has not been destroyed by these changes. Indeed, its streamlined form has increased its flexibility and adaptability to the urban environment. It remains a fundamental social institution of our society.

In the meantime, many of the functions stripped from the old multifunctional primary groups of family and community have been dispersed among new, more specialized groups (Dunphy, 1972). The job of socializing teenagers, for instance, has passed to a variety of adolescent peer groups. For some, new groups such as communes and day-care cooperatives have taken over many basic family functions.

The primary and task groups that have arisen differ from their older, traditional equivalents in several ways. First of all, urban mobility has turned the new groups into more truly voluntary associations than were most in the past. In a traditional rural community, you must choose your groups from a very limited range and there is seldom an option of leaving later. But in a mobile urban environment, there are many groups that can be joined or withdrawn from pretty much at will.

Because of the number of small groups available in an urban environment, each can be much more specialized and limited in scope. Most flourishing new groups focus around specific age and interest groups and concentrate on performing only one or two functions for the individual. As a result, more and more (but not all) of the individual's small groups emphasize only emotional expression or task accomplishment or socialization, rather than combining all three as the traditional family or community groups did. Examples are friends that gather only for mutual enjoyment, or sports groups that get together primarily for task reasons. And then there are the recently proliferating number of groups designed specifically as resocialization groups. They teach new patterns of adjusting to society or make up for past socialization difficulties. It is clear that neither the primary nor the task group is going out of business, despite the predictions of nineteenth-century theorists.

A LOOK AHEAD

By now, we have some indication of the answers to our three original questions: why are small groups important to the individual, why are they important to the larger society, and what are the distinguishing characteristics that make them different from other forms of social organization? Our discussion of these issues will provide a frame of reference, a sociological and psychological context, for the main business of this book: an analysis of the internal dynamics of small groups. Our study will be more meaningful if this context is kept in mind. Small groups do not exist in the abstract; they operate in societies and affect individuals. With this in mind then, we will turn our attention from what Dunphy (1972) has called the *suprastructure* of small groups (composed of the individuals who are the members) and the *superstructure* (the institutions and society in which groups operate), to the level of small groups themselves. Our discussion of the distinguishing characteristics of small groups has given us some idea of what to expect. But other tasks lie ahead. We need to analyze, among other things, the emergence of group structure, and the importance of that structure in determining the character and behavior of the group. To do that we must first discuss the theoretical orientations and research methods that have been used to examine groups. These will be the topics of Chapters 2 and 3. Chapter 2 will conclude with a review of the basic theoretical notions that guide the rest of our analysis.

Chapters 4 through 8 take up the fundamental processes by which small groups operate and out of which group structure and culture emerges. We begin with a discussion of communication and the development of interaction patterns, cohesiveness, and interpersonal attraction in Chapter 4. Chapter 5 goes on to the development of norms and the problem of social control. This leads naturally to a discussion of conformity and deviance in small groups and their impact on group structure. In Chapter 6, we take up the issue of status differentiation among members and the emergence of hierarchies. The questions are why and how this occurs and what the consequences are for group functioning and relationships among the members. Once status differences develop, questions of leadership and power are raised, and this is the topic of Chapter 7. Finally, Chapter 8 addresses the emergence of small-group culture. We discuss the nature of small-group culture, how it develops, what aspects of group experience are likely to be enshrined within it, and how it affects the group's management of its internal and external problems.

Having surveyed fundamental group processes, we will turn our attention from groups in general to task and primary groups in particular. Chapters 9 and 10 each do two things: discuss processes unique to task or primary groups, and delve more deeply into the dominant examples of these groups in contemporary life. In Chapter 9, dealing with task groups, we will examine factors affecting group productivity, problem solving, and creativity. Decision-making groups within large organizations will be discussed more specifically. Primary groups are the focus of the last chapter, with special attention to factors affecting the emotional climate of a group and the relationship between group and individual development. Groups such as the family, friendship groups, and resocialization groups will be explored. The final two chapters will return us to the actual social and psychological contexts in which present-day small groups operate.

2

Theoretical Approaches to Small Groups

One of the most remarkable features of small groups is their diversity. Each particular group is composed of unique personalities operating in a distinctive setting. No two are exactly alike. Life in a small group seems to be made up of tiny specific events and details. How do you pull all these together to describe the overall pattern or structure of behavior in a particular small group? Even harder, how do you isolate basic processes that characterize not only this group but all small groups? To do this, you need a theory of, or at least a general theoretical orientation to, small groups.

A *theory*, as social scientists use the term, is a set of logically related concepts or propositions that describe relationships among aspects of the phenomena being studied (Olsen, 1968; Shaw and Costanzo, 1970). Theories are extremely useful because they suggest an outline for the forest as a whole rather than for just the trees. They provide a framework that the researcher can use to begin to see past the overwhelming detail of small-group life. The concepts defined in the theory focus attention on certain details considered most important in understanding the group, allowing others to be disregarded. A theory will further suggest that certain details are affecting other aspects of the group, and this will give the researcher a start in understanding how the group maintains itself, changes, and develops. Of course, the best theory will be the one that simply, neatly, and most accurately describes what goes on in groups. But a theory need not be proved entirely accurate to be useful. Often, a theory that ultimately seems seriously flawed will have focused people's attention on important new aspects of groups. A theory can start people asking the right questions, even if it fails to answer them itself.

Because theories do suggest a particular view of the way groups

work, they invite researchers to compare that view with careful observations of group processes themselves. This is the process of *theory testing.*
In the next chapter we will discuss some of the techniques used to test
small-group theories and to explore group behavior. Data acquired from
observing groups may match a theory very well, or they may be so
contrary as to suggest that the theory is entirely wrong. More commonly, however, data support some aspects of a theory but challenge
others. The researcher usually responds by modifying the theory to
account for the new evidence. You see, then, that the relationship between theory and data is dialectical. Researchers use theories to guide
their observations of groups. They then use the information acquired
from these observations to develop and improve their theories (see Box
2.1).

Although social scientists agree to the usefulness of theory, they
often differ on the types of concept systems that they believe should be
called theories. Some prefer to reserve the term *theory* for sets of concepts
that are tightly and rigorously organized in terms of formal logic. Others
will accept as theories groups of concepts that are organized in a looser,
more intuitive fashion. Another area of controversy is the extent to
which theories should be general and all inclusive. Some favor overall
theories that try to account for all aspects of group life. Others find
theories that focus on specific group processes such as power or leadership to be more useful. Specific theories are often called *minitheories.*

There is considerable overlap between these controversies. General
theories that deal with all aspects of groups also tend to be those that
are more loosely structured. We will call these *theoretical orientations.* They
provide conceptual frameworks that guide a researcher's overall approach to groups, rather than specify precise relationships among particular group properties. On the other hand, more rigorously organized
theories are usually also minitheories in that they limit themselves to
specific group processes. Often, however, these minitheories develop
within the general framework of some larger overall theoretical orientation.

Let's consider an example to clarify the difference between theoretical orientations and more specific minitheories. Exchange theory is one
of the theoretical orientations we will discuss later. It argues in favor of
an overall approach to group behavior, one which defines interaction as
an exchange of rewards and costs and assumes that each member seeks
to maximize rewards and minimize costs. Emerson's (1962, 1964) pow-
er-dependency theory is a minitheory that uses an exchange orientation. Instead of focusing on all aspects of group behavior, power-
dependency theory deals only with the development and maintenance

Box 2.1.   ON THE NATURE OF SMALL-GROUP THEORY

One of the chief contributors to our theories about small groups is Harvard sociologist George C. Homans. Later in the chapter we will have more to say about Homans's specific contributions. But for now, let's listen to what he says about the nature and usefulness of theories about group behavior.

The behavior of men, usually in small numbers, has inspired the largest part of human literature and eloquence. . . . But until recently this great mass of observation has led to nothing. Some leaders, perhaps those of the past more than those of the present, have shown great capacity for handling men in groups, but their know-how could not easily be communicated in words from one man to another. There have been a few maxims of practical wisdom, always at odds with one another because the limits of any single maxim were never stated. Whatever a man did, he could always find a rule to back him up. But until recently there has been little growth. Our knowledge is Babylonian. Our proverbs are carved on the pyramids. A new fact in physics or biology fits into an old theory, or by not fitting starts a new theory. Either way one can build on it. . . . But every adventurer in the science of human behavior from Aristotle to Freud has had to make a fresh start, or something like it.

If the outlook has changed since the opening of this century, the reason is that we have begun to sketch out systematic theories of human behavior and to use them. Einstein taught the world, what it ought to have known long ago, that no theory is permanent. If an old theory survives new conquests of science, it survives as a slave. But even the most fragile theory has its uses. In its lowest form, as a classification, it provides a set of pigeonholes, a filing cabinet, in which fact can accumulate. For nothing is more lost than a loose fact. The empty folders of the file demand filling. In time the accumulation makes necessary a more economical filing system, with more cross references, and a new theory is born. (Homans, 1950:4–5)

There are always more observations than can possibly be summed up in any one theory; or rather, if the theory is to be formulated at all, it must leave many observations out of account. Galileo took a fateful step for science when he left

Box 2.1   *(continued)*

friction out of the study of motion. He framed, for instance, his law describing the motion of a ball rolling down an inclined plane on the assumption that there was no friction between the ball and the plane. He was justified in doing so because he could set up his experiments in such a way that they approximated this ideal state more and more closely, although they never quite got there. And he could not have framed a simple, general law if he had not used this method. . . . Abstraction is the price paid for generalization.

The method of abstraction seems to create no such mental conflict in physics as it does in sociology. Electrons are members of a group—the atom—, and if we were electrons and knew man's theory of the atom, we might be amused by it, . . . The theory would seem so gross, so statistical, so simplified, even if it was adequate enough to show man how to split electrons out of the group. But we are not electrons; we study the atom from the outside; we have no way of comparing the theory with the reality, and therefore our shortcomings create no mental conflict in us. This is not true of our social theory. We have inside knowledge of our own society, and this immediate familiarity with group behavior is at once an asset and a liability. It is an asset because we always have our experience to check our theories against. They must be in some degree true to experience. It is a liability because people are too easily able to say of any social theory, "You have left such and such out." They are quite right: we always leave something out. We must if we are to make theories at all. But such people make no attempt to see what we have got in. . . . They do not understand that a theory may be true, and yet not the whole truth.

Source: Excerpted from *The Human Group* by George C. Homans, copyright 1950 by Harcourt Brace Jovanovich, Inc., renewed 1978 by George C. Homans. Reprinted by permission of the publisher.

of power differences. These are defined in exchange theory terms as the control of rewards and costs. The theory is formulated in rigorously logical terms that can be used to specify the precise consequences of particular power relations.

In this chapter we will discuss the major theoretical orientations that have developed in the study of small groups. Often there are several particular theories within each orientation. Rather than discuss the details of each, we will present the basic theoretical approach shared by members of that school of thought. Our purpose is to familiarize students with the basic perspectives that have created much of our current knowledge about groups and to extract concepts that will be used throughout the book. In focusing on general theoretical orientations in this chapter, we do not intend to neglect the many valuable minitheories in the field; rather these will be taken up in later chapters dealing with the specific processes that are the subject of those theories.

We will discuss four basic theoretical orientations: *field theory, exchange theory, systems theories,* and *group and individual approaches.* After describing these theories, we will draw concepts from each to provide an outline of the theoretical perspective that guides the presentation of material in this book. In pointing out that there is something to be learned from each perspective, we do not wish to create the impression that there is no conflict among these orientations. Many of the issues debated by these theories remain unresolved, a subject for disagreement among thoughtful people.

THEORETICAL ORIENTATIONS TO SMALL GROUPS

Field Theory

Probably the person most responsible for interesting American social scientists in the study of small groups was Kurt Lewin. An emigrant from Nazi Germany in the 1930s, Lewin brought with him an intense desire to understand the behavior of people in groups. His approach to the study of group processes, which Lewin called field theory, or group dynamics, profoundly influenced an entire generation of social scientists and is still important today.

As Shepard (1964) has noted, Lewin's impact was due to three things. First, he took a *phenomenological position* toward behavior. That is, he felt that to understand a person's behavior, it must be analyzed in terms of what that person subjectively perceives, rather than in terms of what an outside observer thinks is "objective reality." Second, he showed great *ingenuity in research design.* He pioneered in the use of laboratory settings and experimental designs to study group phenomena. He was particularly talented at combining experimental control with the creation of a realistic, meaningful context in which to study important group processes such as leadership climate and decision making. Third, Lewin was influential because of his *theoretical system.*

Lewin's theoretical system has its roots in the school of psychology called Gestalt that grew up in Germany between the two world wars (Deutsch and Krauss, 1965). A central notion of Gestalt psychology is that people do not experience the world in terms of bits and pieces, but rather organize their perceptions into holistic systems or fields of experience (Koffka, 1935). According to this view, the way you react to a particular event will vary depending on the context, or field, in which you perceive it to have occurred.

Lewin (1939, 1947a, 1947b, 1951) applied the concept of field to groups as a whole, rather than just to individuals. The *psychological field,* or life space, of a group consists of all the things and people in the immediate environment that have positive or negative emotional importance (called valence) to the group. Groups are oriented towards goals. These goals generally involve approaching positively valenced objects in the life space and moving away from negative ones. Goals have a dynamic quality then. They activate forces pulling the group members toward some things in the life space and away from others. In response to these forces and in pursuit of group goals, members are continually changing their position (locomoting) within the group field. It is this locomotion over time that constitutes the dynamic development of groups. The direction of a particular locomotion will be a grand result (vector) of all the conflicting forces in the group's field at that time.

The reader may notice that the actual concepts of Lewin's theory, locomotion, valence, vector, have an abstract mechanical quality that makes them difficult to apply to group behavior in any single, obvious, and clear-cut manner. Because this was always a problem, field theory researchers other than Lewin tended to use the theory as a guide to the general type of group processes that should be studied rather than as a detailed set of theoretical propositions to be tested. The central concept to emerge out of field theory research is group cohesiveness (Shepard, 1964). Cohesiveness refers to the extent to which a group is bound together or close-knit in feeling. In classic field theoretical terms, Festinger (1950) defined it as "the resultant of all forces acting on members to stay in the group." People working within the general field theory perspective have linked cohesiveness to the development of group norms (Festinger, Schacter, and Back, 1950), to leadership style (Lippitt and White, 1952), to group productivity (Schacter et al., 1951), to conformity and influence (Festinger, 1950), and to a variety of other areas. In a more recent use of field theory, Janis (1972) explained poor decision making ("group-think") by government policy-making groups in terms of the pressure of cohesiveness.

Although field theory produced many classic contributions to the study of small groups, it has not proved to be a complete success as a theoretical orientation. We have mentioned the difficulty in applying its abstract, mechanistic concepts. In addition there are major aspects of group life, such as role differentiation and status systems, for which it could not adequately account (Olmstead, 1959). As a result, the specific details of Lewin's theoretical system, such as his notions of valence, vectors, and locomotion, are rarely used today. Instead, it is the underlying assumptions of his theory that have proved of lasting importance. Since we will draw upon some of these assumptions ourselves, they are worth specifying.

Three basic assumptions of fundamental importance to small-group research can be extracted from the overall approach of field theory.

1. What creates a group is the process of members becoming *interdependent* with one another. Two people are interdependent when a change in the behavior of one affects the other. Because of interdependence among group members, different aspects of the group, such as its norms, leadership patterns, friendship networks, all affect one another—and are themselves interdependent.

2. Because of interdependence, a group must be analyzed as a *whole system* (or field). This means that one aspect of the group, say its communication patterns, cannot be understood except in relation to the other aspects of the group (for instance, the friendship network or status structure).

3. Groups are dynamic in that they contain many conflicting forces that cause group members to change and readjust relationships over time. Groups are almost never static.

Dunphy (1972) pointed out two additional contributions that field theory has made to our current understanding of small groups.

4. It is important to examine groups in relationship to their outside environment.

5. Goal orientation and group integration must be recognized as two central facts of all group life. It was Lewin who pointed out that groups focus much of their concern on accomplishing goals. Field research in general has also emphasized the importance of

group integration (or cohesiveness), which is the process by which members keep themselves united as a group.

Exchange Theory

Exchange theory is one of the more influential of contemporary approaches to interpersonal relations and, by extension, small groups. It comes at small-group behavior from a very different point of view than that of field theory. Instead of viewing the group as a holistic entity that shapes individual behavior, exchange theory focuses on the individual-to-individual dealings among the people who happen to make up the group. The holistic aspect of the group is less important. Exchange theory's primary concern is to analyze the way individuals control one another's behavior by exchanging rewards and costs. It tackles the problem by assuming from the start that people in relationships as well as in the economic market try to maximize the rewards they receive, and minimize the costs they incur, by seeking rewarding experiences and avoiding painful ones.

The alert reader will see a similarity between these assumptions and reinforcement theories of behaviorist psychology. Actually, one of the originators of exchange theory, George C. Homans, developed the basic notions of exchange theory in an explicit attempt to extend B. F. Skinner's basic reinforcement principles to an analysis of complex social behavior (Homans, 1961). Homans argued that the more rewarding a particular interaction is (in that it gives you something you value), the more likely you are to repeat the interaction (up to a satiation point where you tire of the reward). On the other hand, there are at least two people in any interaction. Other people are not going to join in a repeated interaction unless there is something in it for them, too. Consequently, to engage in repeated rewarding interaction, you must be prepared to give rewards as well as receive them.

Rewarding others usually requires that you give up something (time, effort, or whatever). Homans labels what you give up as the *costs* of interaction. He then assumes that people are *profit-seekers* in interaction, in that they will seek out and maintain high-profit interactions while letting low-profit ones lapse. However, as exchange theorists Thibaut and Kelley (1959) have pointed out, how high a profit rate must be in order to motivate you to maintain a relationship depends on the alternatives you have. You may continue a relationship with a very low profit rate if it is nevertheless better than any of your alternative possibilities.

Obviously, for a group to emerge, the members will have to have repeated interactions with one another, and that means they must develop and maintain mutually satisfactory patterns of reward/cost exchange. From the point of view of exchange theory, this is not easy, since each member is assumed to be maximizing his/her own gain. However, it is assumed that once the group emerges, the members, if they stay in it, find the group rewarding (or at least more rewarding than the available alternatives). Therefore, they are willing to develop some norms to regulate exchanges in the interest of preserving the common good.

Among the norms developed will be rules of *distributive justice* that define what is a fair exchange between members. An exchange is fair, says Homans, when the rewards are in proportion to each member's contributions. According to Homans, if you put more into an interaction than someone else, you feel you should get more out of it than they do. If you get less than "is fair," you are likely to feel angry and seek some redress. Exchange theorists who have pursued the notion of distributive justice norms (called equity theorists) argue that you may get some help in seeking redress since groups actively attempt to enforce distributive justice norms by rewarding members who abide by them and pressuring or punishing members who don't (Walster, Walster, and Berscheid, 1978). However, both Homans (1974) and the equity theorists recognize that difficulties may still arise because members may not be in complete agreement about the value of varying rewards and contributions.

Using these basic concepts, exchange theorists have attempted to account for a wide variety of group phenomena, including the emergence of status hierarchies, the problems of status inconsistancy, the exercise of leadership, and the problem of social control. However, exchange theory has attracted criticism as well. Some of it comes from people who are offended by exchange theory's assumption that people behave as perpetual profit-seekers. This is a matter of philosophical taste. However, Homans (1974) has answered his critics by noting that exchange theory in no way assumes that the only rewards people value are material ones. If people value honor, or altruism, or love, then those are rewards too, and people will take profits in them as well.

There is also the problem that exchange theory, particularly Homans's version of it, is explicitly *reductionist* in perspective. That is, it reduces the causes for social behavior in groups to the psychological causes of individual behavior, rather than seeking causes in the structure of the group itself. Many small-group researchers, but particularly the system theorists (to be discussed later), disagree, arguing that once groups develop, they take on a life of their own and evolve qualities that cannot be entirely explained by the individual qualities of the members.

Although thoughtful people disagree on this matter, we in this book will tend to favor the latter argument.

Another criticism raised is that Homans has not tested his basic assumptions themselves, but rather has used them to explain social findings after the fact (Nixon, 1979). Furthermore, his basic concepts—reward, cost, profit, value—are defined somewhat vaguely, so that they might be subtly reinterpreted to "fit the facts" of different situations (Turner, 1974). Of course, Homans's basic propositions could be tested, and indeed Crosbie (1972) has tested some of them and found qualified support. But, Nixon (1979) notes that the range of behavior to which exchange principles can be applied has not been determined. They may not apply quite as broadly as the theory's proponents have argued.

The final criticism leveled at Homans's exchange theory is that it is *tautological*, in that the basic concepts are defined in terms of one another so that the argument leads us in circles (Turner, 1974). For example, if someone argues that we like people we spend time with and we spend time with people we like, that is a tautology. If we ask what the first key concept "liking" means, we are referred to the second key concept "spending time with." If we then ask what that means, we are sent back to the first concept. The trouble with tautologies is that they cannot be disproved. Homans's theory is certainly not a simple tautology in the sense of our example. But it does come dangerously close to tautology at some points. For instance, it is troublesome when it is first argued that people only maintain "profitable relationships," and then it is assumed that, therefore, all current ongoing relationships in which people are engaged must be profitable to them.

Considering the problems with exchange theory, it is probably not wise to take it as the single best theory by which to analyze small groups. However, it should not be dismissed out of hand either; there are many situations in which its principles can be usefully applied. In addition, the overall perspective of exchange theory alerts us to some basic aspects of group life with which even the theory's critics are likely to agree:

1. People do pursue their own interests to a great extent (if not necessarily to the extremes suggested by exchange theory).
2. The interests of individual group members are not always compatible with each other or with the group as a whole.
3. Consequently, group members are continually negotiating and renegotiating compromises among their conflicting interests.
4. Groups tend to develop norms to regulate these negotiations (such as distributive justice norms) in order to minimize destructive consequences to the group.

Social Systems Theory

Systems theorists argue that the key to understanding groups is to focus on them as networks of people who function together as a holistic entity, a system. A *system,* as it is defined in these theories, has five basic characteristics. First, it is composed of members who are *interdependent* with one another. This is a point shared with field theory. Second, for a collection of people to form a system, there must be *interaction* among the members. It takes interaction for one person's behavior to affect another's. Thus, it is only through interaction that interdependence can have its effect. When people interact with one another under conditions of interdependence, they create the third characteristic of systems: *emergent properties.* Emergent properties characterize the group as a whole rather than the members as individuals. These new group qualities *emerge* from interaction among the members. For instance, they may create a distinctive group identity, or a sense of oneness, of unity with their fellow members. They also create norms, roles, patterns of behavior, all of which systems theorists view as emergent qualities of groups. Because of emergentism, systems theorists argue that the group as a whole is more than just the sum of its parts, its individual members.

The fourth major characteristic of a system follows from the first three. Because members forge themselves through interaction into a distinct, unified entity, systems develop a sense of *boundary* between themselves and the outside world. This boundary may be somewhat vague, and may change frequently. But it serves to distinguish members (and almost-members) of the group from those who are clearly not members. It makes the distinction between the "we" of the group and the "they" of outsiders. Finally, systems are *dynamic* in that they are constantly changing and evolving. Even when relatively stable patterns of behavior develop a leadership pattern in a group, for instance, these patterns are not static. They are maintained by a continued balancing and rebalancing of opposing forces in the group. From a systems point of view, groups are like waves in the ocean; the patterns only appear through the continual motion of the component parts.

You may have noticed that there is some overlap between a systems approach to groups and a field theory approach. They share a view of groups as dynamic holistic entities made up of interdependent members. Indeed, some systems theorists were strongly influenced by this aspect of field theory. But the two approaches differ in many ways also. Systems theorists view the group from the objective perspective of an outside observer. They use the properties of groups *as systems* (interdependence, emergentism, boundedness, interaction, and dynamism) and the problems to which the system responds to explain the way groups develop and change. The emphasis is on the emergence and operation of group *structure* (differentiated roles, a status system, and so on). Field theory also recognizes certain systemlike properties of groups, but it approaches these from the *subjective* perspective of the members. As a result it focuses on the changing *psychological climate* of the group and its effect on the members' behavior. The emphasis is on ongoing group processes rather than the evolution of group structure.

Within the general orientation of social systems theory, there have been many different specific theories of groups. We will focus on three different types of systems theories. The first type, called functionalist theories, developed around a group of Harvard sociologists, Parsons, Bales, and Hare, during the 1950s. The second came from another Harvard sociologist during the same period, the aforementioned Homans. Although he has since abandoned the approach for exchange theory, Homans in *The Human Group* (1950) proposed a distinctive systems approach that still has currency. Our final systems approach comes from the broad orientation of general systems. General systems theory developed out of biology, engineering, and cybernetics but has been applied to social behavior by people such as Miller (1955) and Buckley (1967).

PARSONS, BALES, AND HARE.   Talcott Parsons was a sociologist concerned primarily with theories of entire societies. However, with the aid of two younger colleagues, R. F. Bales and A. Paul Hare, several aspects of Parsons's theories were expanded to apply directly to small groups. Parsons's theories added new emphasis to the notion that societies and groups are actually holistic systems organized along lines of interdependence among the parts. To survive, said Parsons, all social systems must meet certain basic *functional prerequisites,* which define fundamental tasks or functions that must be accomplished to keep the system going. The social structure of a society or group (or any other social system) arises out of its efforts to meet these basic functional requirements on an ongoing basis. Parsons, Bales, and Shils (1953) defined the functional requirements of groups as the following:

1. *Pattern maintenance:* The cultural and behavioral patterns that give the group its distinctive character must be maintained. In small groups, this means that the individuals must share a commitment to maintaining the group's distinctive identity (Hare, 1976).
2. *Adaptation:* A group must successfully relate to its environment

(both social and physical), overcoming environmental threats and obtaining from the environment needed resources.

3. *Integration:* The group must develop rules for coordinating the activities of its various parts and achieving a certain sense of cohesiveness.

4. *Goal attainment:* Groups have to develop sufficient organization and control over their behavior to at least minimally accomplish the tasks or goals for which the members have joined together.

According to functionalist approaches, different groups will develop differing social structures and patterns of behavior to meet functional requirements. But once a group has evolved a set of behaviors that at least minimally satisfies all four functional needs, it is likely to stick to that pattern of behavior unless strongly pressured to change. This is what the functionalists mean when they say that groups (and all social systems) tend to settle into an *equilibrium state.* From Parsons's perspective, social systems that survive are those which develop mechanisms for reasserting their equilibrium when destabilizing events occur, so that the equilibrium becomes self-maintaining.

Parsons's view of social systems has been criticized as too conservative, placing too much emphasis on the way social systems preserve themselves without adequately considering the countervailing tendency for social systems to change. When Bales applied the functionalist approach to small groups, he avoided some of these problems by adopting a much more dynamic, tension-ridden view of the equilibrium concept. He did agree, however, that groups tend to evolve into an equilibrium state.

Bales argued that the attention of small groups, or at least task-oriented small groups, alternates between two basic problems: (1) issues associated with accomplishing the group's task, called *task demands;* and (2) issues associated with maintaining smooth working relationships among the members, called *socioemotional demands.* We can see that task demands involve the accomplishment of the adaptation and goal attainment functions, while socioemotional demands deal with the integration and pattern maintenance functions. However, Bales (1950) argued that there is a basic antagonism between what groups do to accomplish their task and what they need to do to meet socioemotional demands. Task accomplishment involves the direct exercise of control over members' behavior, often the development of a status hierarchy where some have more power than others. These actions may interfere with the warm congenial feeling of togetherness that serves the group's socioemotional needs so well. In turn, excessive preoccupation with smooth interpersonal relations will result in a very pleasant group atmosphere but may interfere with task efficiency.

Despite the rivalry between socioemotional and task demands, a group must minimally satisfy both to survive. A group that utterly fails to accomplish its goals will suffer problems of morale and disorganization of the sort experienced by an athletic team that never wins. Groups highly skilled at their task will still go nowhere if the group members can't get along with one another. Accordingly, says Bales, successful groups develop a kind of dynamic equilibrium state in which the attention of group members alternates rapidly between task and socioemotional problems. The notion that equilibrium in groups is characterized by rapid alternations in group attention has not been as widely accepted as have some other notions of Bales'. However, the concepts of task and socioemotional demands, interdependent and yet somewhat antagonistic, have proved to be a fundamental contribution to small-group theory and have been widely influential in group research.

To achieve a stabilizing equilibrium between task and socioemotional needs, without creating excessive confusion, group members begin to develop specialized roles that emphasize aspects of one or the other need. Members become task or socioemotional specialists. Out of this initial role differentiation the group begins to evolve a status hierarchy, and indeed an entire social structure. For Bales then, the competitive but interdependent relationship between task and socioemotional demands is the engine that drives the social structure of small groups. We will examine this aspect of Bales's theory more carefully (and critically) in Chapter 6.

Despite its contributions, functionalist theory has been heavily criticized on several counts. Its alleged conservative bias has already been mentioned. It has also been accused of being teleological in arguing that, because groups must meet basic functions to survive, whatever surviving groups do must be designed to meet those functions. Teleologies explain present events in terms of final, ultimate purposes. They have been a persistent problem for functionalists, although some have avoided the problem better than others. Bales, for instance, is better in this regard than Parsons. A third criticism cites functionalism as tending to reify social systems, treating them as autonomous creatures with a mind of their own. Although some functionalist thought has fallen into this trap, others have been more careful. In general, the small-group functionalists, such as Bales, Hare, and Olmstead, have been more reasonable in this regard.

Because of the dangers of teleology and reification, it is best not to take the functionalist argument too literally. But that doesn't mean that we need to dispose entirely of the notion of function. Surely it still makes sense to argue that there are certain basic problems with which groups must grapple to survive. The four functional prerequisites, and Bales's notion of task and socioemotional demands, do as good a job as any in specifying the general nature of these problems. Using categories as heuristic devices, as Nixon (1979) notes, can be useful in analyzing group structure. The danger to be avoided lies in assuming that all group behavior is directed toward these functions or toward the system's survival. It is also dangerous to use functions for after-the-fact explanations of what a group has done.

HOMANS'S SYSTEMS THEORY.   In *The Human Group* Homans put forth a systems theory that, while sharing some concepts with the functionalists, differs substantially in its approach. Homans agreed that groups should be analyzed as systems that are characterized by interdependence and can achieve an equilibrium state. However, Homans (1961) characterized this state as a "practical equilibrium" to distinguish it from what he thought was the overly mystical nature of the functionalist concept. Homans imagined equilibrium not as a state in which no change occurred, but as one in which the change that occurred was regular and recurrent, so that no new *kind* of change happened. As a result, Homans considered change to be as basic a tendency in groups as the tendency to stability. Indeed, Homans did not assume that groups automatically or inevitably reached an equilibrium at all. Unlike the functionalists, he did not consider equilibrium states to be an inherent aspect of social systems, only a characteristic which sometimes appears.

Homans also rejected the notion of functional imperatives as the explicit causes of group social structure. Nevertheless, we see a faint echo of functionalist notions in his concept of the *external* and *internal* system. Homans recognized that the sociophysical environment sets certain basic conditions for groups that develop within it—and puts certain pressures on them. Indeed, in Homans's view, it is often people's reactions to their environmental situation that leads them into interaction with others and, ultimately, into small groups. Consequently, he considered all those group behaviors and events that were in response to the outside environment to be the group's external system. For instance, if several typists in an office pool form a friendship group, all their behavior directed toward dealing with their jobs and the work organization constitutes their group's external system. However, to evolve into a true group, the members' joint behavior has to go beyond just dealing with the outside. It has to go on to develop some independent interests of its own (for example, having lunch together, developing friendships). All the behavior, feeling, and events devoted to these interests constitute the group's internal system. How complex and elaborate the internal system of a group can become depends on how much autonomy the group has from its surrounding environment. For instance, if our typists are not allowed to talk to one another while working and are closely supervised, they will have very little chance to develop shared behaviors and interests beyond the narrow concern of their jobs.

Homans analyzes group behavior in terms of three basic elements: *activities* (things group members do as part of the group other than interact with others), *sentiments* (members' feelings and beliefs), and *interaction* (reciprocal behavior between people). Both the external and internal systems are composed of a set of all three elements. Homans's theory consists largely of demonstrating the interdependence between each of these elements and between the group's external and internal systems, which Homans's elements comprise. To illustrate, he makes the following argument about the development of a group in a work situation. Sentiment, such as a desire for money, leads group members to engage in job activities that in turn require them to interact with one another about job matters. This is the external system. However, its last element, interaction, leads to feelings of liking, which form the sentiment element of the internal system. Once the workers begin to like one another, they begin to engage in nonrequired activities (for example, eating lunch together) and additional interaction. This internal system of sentiments, activities, and interaction in turn affects how they feel about their jobs (external sentiments, the way they perform job activities, and job-related interaction.) Out of this pattern of interdependence, group members begin to *standardize* their behavior in some ways (that is, develop shared norms) and *differentiate* it in other ways (develop status differences and specialized roles).

Homans's theory is valuable for its dynamic view of groups, which incorporates change as easily as stability. However, some of his concepts are used more today than others. The concepts of activities, sentiments, and interaction as basic behavioral elements have fared least well. But his concepts of the external and internal system and the interdependence between them have become fundamental notions in small-group studies.

GENERAL SYSTEMS THEORY.   The goal of general systems theory was to develop a basic set of abstract principles that would account for the operation of *systems* (groups of interdependent elements) of any type, be they biological, mechanical, social, or whatever. It was general systems theory that was responsible for finalizing the definition of systems—that is, bounded groups of interdependent elements (for us, members) that have emergent characteristics (Miller, 1955). However, they would add one more concept as well, that of *feedback*. Feedback is interaction between two entities in which the behavior of one brings forth a response from the other that in turn shapes the next response of the first one, and so on, in a circle of mutual influence. Buckley (1967) pointed out that interaction among group members is a feedback process. It is feedback that causes groups to develop emergent properties like shared norms, opinions, and patterns of behavior.

However, once these characteristics have emerged, feedback among the group members doesn't stop. Neither does the constant feedback relationship between the group and its environment. Some of the ongoing feedback in groups and with the environment will influence group members to support and maintain the group's norms and patterns of behavior. Buckley (1967) calls this the *structure-maintaining* aspect of social systems. It corresponds to the equilibrium notion suggested by other social systems theorists. But just as important is the other type of feedback, virtually always present in groups, which gradually pushes group members away from the established beliefs and behavior, pressuring the group to change its social structure. Buckley (1967) calls this the *structure-elaborating* aspect of groups. It causes groups as a whole to gradually change their rules and behavior over time.

The point is that both structure-maintaining and structure-elaborating types of feedback are going on at the same time, all the time, in small groups. The result is a kind of *moving equilibrium* in which the members of groups, at any one point, all more or less agree on the group structure, but where, over time, the structure that they agree upon gradually changes. Imagine, for instance, a dating relationship where you are less emotionally involved than your partner. At this point it will be clear to you both that you are the powerful one in the relationship, the one who can afford to call the shots. But what if you gradually become more dependent in the relationship yourself? The power balance will change, and before long it may be apparent to you both that it is now your partner who has the greater power. The power structure of the group, and the equilibrium it represents, has shifted.

Moving equilibrium describes the reality of small groups and structures better than the equilibrium concepts offered by other social systems theorists. Indeed, the concept of structure-elaborating and structure-maintaining feedback is general systems theory's major contribution. But in other ways, general systems theory has proved disappointing to social scientists. Its very "generalness," its attempts to account for all types of systems, have made its concepts so abstract as to be of limited use in explaining the reality of everyday groups. As a result, rather few concrete studies of small groups have employed a pure general systems theory approach.

The Group and the Individual

There is no single unifying theory explaining the influence of small groups on individuals. Instead, the ideas to be presented here derive from a diverse collection of theories. Most of the researchers in this area never actually considered themselves small-group theorists per se, although they contributed concepts that have proved of lasting value to group studies. What they had in common was a view of groups as powerful determinants of individual behavior. Because these theories emphasize the relationship between the group and the individual, rather than the structure of the group itself, they take a more psychological approach to groups—in contrast to the primarily sociological perspectives discussed so far. They seek to understand both the social and psychological bases for the group's power over the individual.

In the first chapter we pointed out that, among the human species, the young do not grow up alone: they are raised as members of a group, a family. In the first few years of existence, the child's physical survival depends on being accepted into a group relationship with some person or persons who will at least minimally assist the child in meeting its basic needs for food, shelter, and—as some have suggested—human contact. According to Jones and Gerard (1967), the child's dependence on a caretaking group has two components. First, the child is *effect dependent* on the group for assistance in achieving desired outcomes (or effects), for instance, getting food. Second, the child is *information dependent* on the group as well. This means that the child relies on the group for basic information about the world in which it lives. For example, the primary caretakers give the child its first examples of language and social expectations for behavior. As the child grows into independence, his or her effect and information dependence on groups moderates but does not disappear. Even adults continue to need the assistance of friends, relatives, and associates to achieve some outcomes in the world that they could not accomplish alone. Also, through all those years of childhood, people learn to manage their dealings with the world and meet their basic needs largely through membership in groups and relationships with other people.

Adults, then, generally carry with them certain habits of effect or information dependence on groups. Both types of dependence naturally affect the way people in groups deal with one another and the patterns of behavior that develop. Each gives a group a particular power over its individual members. Understanding the consequences of these two types of power will help us understand how groups influence individual behavior. In addition to information and effect dependence, groups have a third source of power over individuals. As anyone who has passed through adolescence knows, groups have the ability to influence our sense of who we are and what we think of ourselves. We need as well, then, to look at theories describing the relationship between groups and the individual's sense of self and identity. Let us begin with theories that deal with information and effect dependence and the types of group processes each sets in motion. We will then go on to theories of groups and the self.

INFORMATION DEPENDENCE.   Festinger (1954) proposed his theory of social comparison to account for some of the major group processes resulting from members' information dependence. Social comparison is a *cognitive* theory in that it emphasizes the importance of people's perceptions and knowledge in determining their behavior. Festinger assumes that people need to establish the correctness of their beliefs, values, attitudes, and working definitions of social reality in order to act reasonably on the basis of them. Working definitions of social reality consist of the person's interpretation of what is going on (or went on) in a social situation.

The first and most satisfying way of convincing yourself of the validity of a belief is by directly testing it against your own physical experience. For instance, if you want to be sure that your belief about the depth of the local lake is correct, you could row out and measure it. Or you could refer to an expert source, like a geography book with data on the depth of local lakes. But then you would be assuming that the experts themselves had directly measured the lake. So, either way you would be relying on evidence of a direct physical test of reality. We can get such information to check the validity of most of our beliefs about the physical environment. But can we physically test our beliefs about the social environment? Can we go back to the party last night and directly test whether what we thought happened really did? Obviously not. Many of our most important beliefs are about social reality. Examples are beliefs about our relationships with others, about whether we are good or attractive people, about what constitutes success, about what the rules of social situations are.

How do we assure ourselves that the beliefs we hold about social reality are essentially valid if they generally cannot be directly tested?

According to Festinger, we turn to others and compare our version of social reality with theirs. The more people who agree with us, the more secure we feel that our version of social reality is valid and "true." Of course the people who are most available to turn to are the members of the small groups to which we belong: families, friends, work associates. This is particularly true since, as Festinger points out, it will be the opinions of "co-oriented peers," those we see as similar to us, whose opinions will be most important in confirming our beliefs.

The need to find others with whom you can compare your beliefs is one of the major reasons why people band together in small groups, especially in situations of uncertainty. But in any group, members will rely on one another, through the process of social comparison, to develop agreed-upon, shared definitions, not just about the group itself, but about the outside environment and about the individuals in the group. To develop such shared beliefs and maintain the members' security in them, new members who enter the group with discrepant beliefs will have to be influenced by the others to change their opinions.

The position of these new members raises an important point. What happens when people seek to confirm their beliefs by comparing them with those of their fellow group members and find that the others disagree? They can try to cling to their opinions despite the opposition. But how easy is it to remain convinced that you are right when everyone tells you that you are wrong? In the face of such opposition (which is a type of conformity pressure), most people change their beliefs. So we can see that the social comparison processes, which arise out of people's information dependence, become a foundation for conformity pressure in groups and for the processes by which group members influence each other's beliefs.

EFFECT DEPENDENCE.   People's dependence on groups to achieve desired outcomes has many consequences. However, we will focus on theories dealing with the emotional results of effect dependence, and how this shapes the emotional lives of groups. The theories we are about to discuss, in contrast to cognitive approaches like social comparison, emphasize the primacy of emotional reactions in determining behavior. They generally derive from Freud's *psychoanalytic* approach to behavior. Although there are many areas of conflict between the cognitive and psychoanalytic views of individual behavior, that is not our concern here. Rather we are interested in the unique insights psychoanalytic approaches can give us into the emotional dimensions of group life. We can combine these insights with complementary ones offered by social comparison theory to increase our understanding of the power groups wield over their members.

In *Group Psychology and the Analysis of the Ego*, Freud argued that people originally band together in groups because of a shared problem with a powerful authority figure. Through dealing with the shared authority problem, group members begin to develop positive ties with one another as well.

This argument tells us that under conditions of effect dependence, for example, a shared problem with an authority figure, people's attention and the emotional life of the group will focus first on problems of power, control, and authority. Since the group has a shared goal, it is immediately faced with the problem of deciding how to accomplish that goal. And from this arises the question of power: who will be most influential in deciding the group's behavior, and whose interests will be most satisfied by the behavior the group decides on? Struggling with these issues, group members get to know one another more intimately, making shifting alliances. Out of this arises the question of affection: who likes whom?

These days it is recognized that people form groups for many reasons, of which a shared problem with an authority figure is only one. In this respect, Freud's analysis was too narrow. But his argument remains of interest because it highlights the emotional consequences of the shared experience of effect dependence. People share effect dependence whenever they join together in a group to achieve some goal that they feel they could not accomplish on their own. That goal might be to find affection, to get something done, or to just have fun. In fact, people are likely to become effect dependent upon any group that they are willing to put some time into.

Taking their cue from Freud, a number of group theorists have suggested that *power* (or control) and *affection* are the two fundamental dimensions in the emotional lives of all small groups (Bennis and Shepard, 1956; Mills, 1967; Leary, 1957). Power and affection are called *dimensions* because an individual's power over others in the group can range from very high to very low, and the affectionate feelings between members can vary from very warm and positive to indifferent to very negative and hostile. Freud showed us that these basic emotional dimensions in group life arise out of the members' effect dependence on one another.

From infancy, people begin to deal with the problems of power and affection in relationships. By adulthood, they have a whole history of experiences that will have shaped their present orientation. When they, as adults, enter into new small-group situations, they bring their past history with them. As a result, no group of adults starts from scratch on the problems of power and affection. Each of the members has his or her own preferred way of dealing with these issues. Out of the mix of the members' different, possibly conflicting orientations to power and affection, the emotional life of the group takes shape.

SELF AND IDENTITY.   The third source of power groups have over individuals derives from their ability to influence a person's sense of self and personal identity. To understand this influence we need to consider theories that explore the relationship between an individual's self and his or her experience with groups. These theories take what is called an *interactionist* approach to behavior. Unlike purely sociological theories on group structure, or psychological theories on the responses of the individual, these theories concentrate on the actual process of interaction itself.

At the turn of the century, C. H. Cooley ([1902] 1964) argued that the relationship between groups and our sense of self is a fundamental one, suggesting that our relationships with others are the mirror into which we look to discover who we are. According to Cooley, our social self is a "looking glass self" learned from the reactions of others to our behavior. Those relationships with the biggest impact on our sense of self are those we have with the primary groups to which we belong. Recall that it was Cooley who argued that primary groups are the shaping grounds for selves.

Cooley's notion of our sense of self as something somehow learned through our relationships with others was made explicit by G. H. Mead (1934). Mead argued that children first gain self-awareness by observing other people's reactions to their behavior. By doing this, they begin to realize what kind of impression that behavior must have created to have brought about such a response. This in turn gives them their first sense of what the social meaning of that behavior must be. Over time, children piece together bits of information gained in this way to form both an image of themselves and an idea of what others think of that image. Both become fundamental components of the self. As a result, selves are a kind of imagined relationship between us and our general notions of others who view us in certain ways that we take to be true. Selves are social in nature, and important for us. They are acquired through the child's membership from infancy in the primary groups of family and friends.

Mead's insights into the self point out a number of things about the relationship between groups and an individual's sense of self. First, since selves are learned through interaction with others, others have the ability to influence our sense of self. By confirming through their reactions our present sense of self, they can help us maintain our current self-identity. By disconfirming that self, they help us or force us to change it. Because of this, our current sense of self is dependent on the group relationships in which we are involved. If these should change substantially, our sense of self is likely to be somewhat altered in the process. As an expression of this point, sociologists speak of self-identity as being *situated* within a specific set of group contexts. We can see, then, that one basis for the power groups have over individuals is their ability to influence the individual's sense of self. Knowing this, individuals will often prefer membership in one group over another on the basis of its impact on their self-image.

Let us summarize what we have gathered from our discussion. First, according to Jones and Gerard, people learn from infancy to be, in varying degrees, both effect dependent and information dependent upon groups. The fact of group members' information dependence on one another sets in motion what Festinger called the social comparison process, where people test the validity of their social beliefs against the opinions of others. The process of social comparison in turn establishes a foundation for conformity pressures and influence processes. Out of members' effect dependence on one another arise the basic emotional dimensions of group life. According to Freud and others, these dimensions center around problems of power or authority and problems of affection. A member's relationship to the group's emotional life is a major source of its influence over him or her. Finally, we saw that an individual's self and sense of identity is largely acquired through membership in groups and remains situated in a network of group relations. As a result, groups acquire another significant source of power over the individual in their ability to influence self-image.

A PERSPECTIVE ON GROUPS

Now that we have reviewed the major theoretical orientations on small groups, we can present an overview of the perspective that guides the presentation of material in this book. Most closely allied with that of the social systems theorists, but also employing concepts from each of the three other views presented, this general perspective will not limit the substantive material on small groups in the following chapters. We intend to consider a wide variety of specific information on small groups, some of which fits neatly into our perspective, some of which does not. But the perspective will function as a heuristic device, a framework from which we will interpret the results of small-group research.

This text adopts the point of view that people come together in groups primarily to deal with shared problems and to benefit from one another's company. To satisfy these needs, the members of a prospective group must learn to coordinate their actions, at least minimally, with one another. The first problem faced by all small groups is socioemotional. The second is the task itself: to maintain the commitment of its members, groups must minimally accomplish shared goals. The task problems of groups generally revolve around dealings with the outside environment and the mobilization of the members' skills and resources for task accomplishment. The socioemotional problems of groups usually focus on the distribution of rewards and costs in the group, on affection, on attitudes toward power and control, and on questions of individual self-definition.

Although all groups deal with both task and socioemotional issues, the nature of each and their relative importance will vary from group to group. Work groups, committees, and athletic teams are all examples of groups with explicit task-oriented goals. The task aspects of an informal friendship group are much vaguer. Similarly, the socioemotional goals of the group may vary from the simple need to maintain civil working relations among the members to a strong concern with real intimacy, as with a dating couple.

As Bales pointed out, task and socioemotional problems in groups are interdependent in that one cannot be successfully managed unless the other is also at least minimally dealt with. And yet there are times (although this may not be inevitable) when efforts that further task goals interfere with socioemotional ones, and vice versa. For instance, telling jokes in a hard-pressed work group may relieve some potentially disruptive tension among the members, but it will also take time away from work.

In an effort to manage these competing problems, groups gradually develop two mechanisms: a social structure and a group culture. Each represents a technique or tool for distributing the efforts of group members among task and socioemotional issues. Of the two, the more familiar is social structure, which consists of a set of specific relationships among the group members. The concept of social structure includes leadership patterns, status hierarchy, role differentiation, and communication and friendship networks.

Although Roberts (1951) and Olmstead (1959) noted its importance some time ago, small-group culture, on the other hand, remains an understudied area. A group's culture consists of its collective representations of itself, shared past experiences, and habits of collective behavior (like wearing a gang jacket or going to the movies on Wednesday night.) The line between social structure and culture is not a neat one. However, culture generally consists of shared values, symbols, beliefs, and group behaviors, while social structure is the pattern of relationships among the group members (who talks to whom, who has power, and so on). We will examine small-group cultures in more detail in Chapter 8.

Groups develop neither social structure nor culture by magic, however. Rather, group members create culture and social structure through interaction with one another and through the process of mutual influence. It is important to remember that people come to groups with their own personal needs, ideas, and ways of doing things. Even if group members share from the beginning a general agreement on some group goals (which is not always the case), there will be considerable disagreement over how goals should be accomplished and who should benefit the most from the plan adopted. There will always be conflicting interests and a need for substantial negotiation before any clear, stable pattern of relationships (social structure) and sense of collective identity (culture) are established.

If people bring such disparate interests to groups, how is it that they manage to compromise on a particular social structure and culture? Here we draw upon the notions of people's effect and information dependence upon groups. People usually want the group to exist because they need something from it and need the others to help them get it. This creates the basis for interdependence among group members, a defining quality of group life. It also gives group members the power to influence one another's opinions and behavior, and a means by which members can be induced to compromise. Through a process by which everybody in the group influences everybody else, a shared, agreed-upon way of doing things gradually evolves. This becomes the group structure and culture.

The social structure and culture of small groups are never static. But after the initial period of rapid change and development, group structure and culture usually (but not inevitably) become more stable as change occurs more gradually. In other words, structural and cultural patterns in groups are best thought of as the kind of moving equilibrium described by systems theorists. Groups show this interesting mixture of stability and change because they have within them mechanisms that both maintain and elaborate structure and culture, as Buckley (1967) pointed out.

The maintaining aspects of group structure and culture again flow from people's dependence on groups, and the powers it gives groups over their members. Since group members are interdependent, communication and interaction among them leads to mutual influence and ultimately to conformity pressures. These tend to keep things the way they are in the group, preserving the status quo. These processes are just an extension of those by which structure and culture are agreed upon in the first place.

The elaborating mechanisms in group structure and culture come primarily from two persistent sources of change: the outside environment and the desires of group members. Changes in the outside environment put new pressures on the group and create opportunities for new types of behavior. For instance, if some members of a friendship group at work are transferred to a different building, for the first time the group may have to start meeting after work in order to be together. The activities the group engages in after work are likely to be different from those during work hours. As a result, the group's cultural patterns will change and, possibly, so will the structure of relationships among members.

Individual group members remain a source of group change because they periodically seek to renegotiate the rewards and costs they receive under the present social structure and culture. For instance, a group member may try to achieve more power or less responsibility in group decisions. Or a member, dissatisfied with the way the group is pursuing its goals, may try to talk members into engaging in new activities. In a dating couple, one member may feel that the emotional communication in the relationship isn't open and warm enough; another may feel that the relationship has become too intimate and want to pull back emotionally. All these examples represent attempts on the part of individual members to pressure the group into changing its patterns of behavior (culture) or relationships (structure) to make their participation in the group more personally satisfying. No group structure or culture is likely to satisfy all the needs of all group members all the time. So pressures to change from individual members are endemic in groups. When combined with the fact that the outside environment is often changing as well, we begin to see why group structure and culture are never static. Even the smoothest-operating group has its strains and conflicts.

The structure and culture a group develops can be more or less effective in accomplishing group goals and satisfying individual members. The overall success of the group in these matters is reflected in the group's *cohesiveness* and *integration*. If individual commitment to the group disappears, the group perishes. There is absolutely no guarantee that group members will hit upon a social structure and culture that will mobilize their energies and keep them committed to the group (that is, achieve high cohesiveness). Groups frequently fail. Even more frequently, they evolve a structure and culture that does only a minimal job of managing problems. The result is a group that never quite goes out of existence, but which is tense or listless, its members dissatisfied but not quite unhappy enough to leave the group. So, while many groups survive happily for a time, they are all vulnerable, and none have magic qualities that guarantee their persistence.

It is clear that we view group structure, culture, and cohesiveness as factors that emerge from the interaction of group members with one another and with the outside environment. In other words, we accept the notion that groups are *dynamic systems* in the sense defined by social systems theorists. Furthermore, we accept the idea that since culture and structure develop out of members' interdependence, the various aspects of structure and culture are themselves interdependent. For instance, changes in the cultural identity of a group may well affect the leadership structure. It is necessary, then, to examine aspects of small groups from a holistic perspective. This does not mean that we must focus on all aspects of the group at once. But it does mean that we must examine a part of the group, say, the communication network, in relationship to the other aspects of group structure and culture.

SUMMARY

In order to see through the diversity and detail of small-group life to the basic underlying processes, we need the guidance of a theoretical perspective. A theory is a set of logically related concepts that describes relationships among the phenomena being studied. When a theory provides a general conceptual framework for analyzing groups rather than specifying precise relationships among specific group properties, it is best called a theoretical orientation. In this chapter we reviewed the four theoretical orientations that have guided most of the research done on groups. After describing each we extracted basic concepts which inform our discussion of groups throughout the book.

The first theoretical orientation discussed was Kurt Lewin's *field theory*. Drawing upon Gestalt psychology, Lewin argued that groups must be understood in terms of the shared psychological field, or life space, they create for their members. This field arises out of the members' interdependence and gives the group the quality of a holistic system. Using the terms valence, locomotion, and vector, field theory describes group development in terms of the goal-seeking behavior of the members, which causes them to continually change their position in the group's life space. Field theory produced a whole tradition of research focused around the causes and consequences of group cohesiveness. However, today the major influence of field theory derives from its underlying assumptions rather than its specific theoretical concepts. Most important are its assertions that groups are holistic entities arising from the interdependence of the members; that, as a result, a particular aspect of the group, such as leadership, can only be understood in relation to other aspects of the group; and that groups are dynamic and continually-changing entities.

Exchange theory focuses on the individual-to-individual dealings among group members rather than on the holistic aspect of groups. Borrowing from reinforcement principles in psychology, exchange theorists such as Homans seek to explain how group members control each other's behavior and create group structure through the exchange of rewards and costs. They assume that people's behavior in such exchanges is guided by a desire to maximize rewards and minimize costs. In an effort to maintain mutually rewarding patterns of interaction, group members develop norms to regulate exchanges in the interest of the common good. Among these are distributive justice norms, the special concern of a branch of exchange theory called equity theory. Despite criticisms of reductionism and tautology, exchange theory has been very influential in the study of status, leadership, and social control. From our point of view, it offers valuable insights into the conflicting interests group members bring to the group and into the negotiations and norm building that arise from these conflicts.

Like field theory, *social systems theory* views groups as networks of people who function together as holistic entities—systems. Systems are characterized by interdependence and interaction among their elements (the group members), by emergent properties that characterize the group as whole, and by boundedness and dynamism. Parsons's, Hare's, and Bales's functionalist branch of systems theory further argues that social systems must accomplish the basic functions of pattern maintenance, adaptation, integration, and goal attainment to continue their existence. Group structure evolves to meet these functions and gradually settles into an equilibrium state. Bales provided an influential view of this process in arguing that it represented the group's effort to balance between the competing problems of task accomplishment and the maintenance of smooth socioemotional relations. In contrast to the functionalists, Homans's systems theory viewed equilibrium, not as a state where change ceased, but as one where no new kind of change occurred. His view of the external and internal systems in group behavior and structure has been very influential. The General Systems Theory apof Miller and Buckley further emphasized the importance of change as well as stability in groups. Through the feedback process of interaction, groups develop structure-elaborating as well on structure-maintaining mechanisms, with the result that groups evolve a continually moving equilibrium.

A diverse set of theories focusing on the *group's impact on the individual* formed our fourth theoretical orientation. Groups influence their members through the processes of information dependence, effect dependence, and the development of self-identity. Festinger's theory of social comparison describes how people rely on their fellow group members to interpret and define social reality. Drawing from Freud, a number of psychoanalytically oriented theorists have argued that effect dependence gives rise to the two fundamentional dimensions of a group's emotional life: power and affection. Interaction-oriented theorists such as Cooley and Mead have described how individuals' sense of self develops from, and is rooted in, their network of group relations.

This chapter concluded with a description of the general perspective this book holds on small groups. This perspective borrows concepts from all four theoretical orientations but is most closely allied with that of systems theory. We argued that people form groups to manage shared problems and to benefit from each other's company. This interdependence gives rise to the basic task and socioemotional problems faced by all groups. Through the members' efforts to manage these sometimes competing problems, groups develop two interdependent emergent properties: a social structure and a culture. Consisting of the pattern of relationships among the members, group social structure includes the status and leadership system, role differentiation, and communication and friendship networks. Group culture consists of shared values, symbols, beliefs, and norms. Social structure and culture are created through the process of mutual influence among the members. However, given the conflicting needs and interests of the members and the changing challenges of the group's environment, there is no guarantee that a workable structure and culture will evolve. If it does, it will represent a moving equilibrium that changes over time. Groups are never static. The structure and culture of the group will be more or less adequate to the task of accomplishing group goals and satisfying individual members. The overall success of the group in these matters is reflected in the group's cohesiveness and integration.

3

Methods of Small-Group Research

Once you have a theory about small groups, how do you go about checking its validity? Or, what if you don't yet have a specific theory but do have some general theoretical notions which you want to use to guide an exploration of some aspect of groups—perhaps in the hope of developing a more specific theory. In either case, you need to observe small groups and note what goes on in them in some systematic way. You need, in other words, to organize your observations into a systematic research *method*. Only with systematically acquired evidence will you have a logical basis for saying whether the predictions of your theory have been supported. Since theories describe processes that are general to whole categories of small groups, testing those theories usually requires you to compare what goes on in one group with what goes on in another. This can't be done unless you have a systematic way of observing both groups. Even if the goal of your research is simply to describe a particular group, you will need a systematic research method if you want to gain an accurate picture of the group's dynamics.

Adopting a systematic research method requires a series of careful decisions. First, you must carefully *specify your research problem* so that you know precisely what it is you want to learn about groups. Next, you need to decide which basic method of investigation is most appropriate to the goals of your research. In small-group studies, this usually means a choice among *experimental, observational,* or *survey research designs.* Then you must consider whether it would be better to gather your group information in a *laboratory setting* or in a natural *field* setting. Finally, you need to settle upon the specific *techniques* you will use to measure group processes. As we will see, there are a wide variety of both objective and subjective techniques that researchers use to record group behavior.

To fully appreciate the data collected on small groups through research studies, you need to know something about the basic issues. involved in identifying research problems and choosing research methods and techniques. This chapter is designed to give you a brief introduction to those issues. Since they are often quite complex, what we will present here will be greatly simplified. However, our goal will be to provide you with enough basic information to understand the research studies discussed in the remainder of the book.

SPECIFYING THE RESEARCH PROBLEM

The first step in any research method is to be very clear and explicit about what you are looking for. What aspects of the group are of interest to you and what exactly do you expect to learn about them? It is only after you have clarified what you want to know that you can specify the types of information you need to gather about groups.

This step is easier if you are conducting research to test a specific theory. In that case, the theory itself predicts a particular relationship between two or more aspects of the group. This prediction to be tested becomes a *hypothesis*. The aspects of the group addressed by the hypothesis become *variables* to be measured by the researcher. The hypothesis generally specifies that a change in one variable goes with a change in another. The variable presumed to cause the change is called the *independent variable;* the variable affected by the change is the *dependent variable.* For instance, a researcher might propose that a change in a group's communication method (independent variable) will change the pattern of friendship (dependent variable) in the group.

By developing a hypothesis, you make the goals of your research explicit. This process is clearest when you formulate your hypothesis from a theory you wish to test. However, not all research into groups tests theories. Sometimes investigators develop and test hypotheses from personal hunches about the way groups work (although such hunches are usually guided by the assumptions of some general theoretical orientation). Still other research does not attempt to test a specific hypothesis at all but seeks rather to explore or describe some aspect of groups.

Even in exploratory research, however, it is important to clearly formulate your research problem. Sometimes this means identifying an independent and dependent variable and asking what the relationship is between them. A researcher, for instance, who feels that the control of money has great impact on the power relationships in a marriage may do exploratory research to find out what the nature of that impact is. Or an investigator interested in a particular dependent variable, say, the effectiveness of group leaders, might want to know what independent variables affect it. Researchers also do the reverse, focusing on a particular independent variable and asking what effects it has on the group. Specifying a research problem, then, means identifying the independent and/or dependent variables of interest to you, and formulating, if possible, hypotheses about the relationships among them.

TYPES OF RESEARCH DESIGNS

Once you have a clear idea what you want to know about groups, you are then in a position to decide which method would be best for gathering the information you need. Over the years researchers have developed a wide variety of specific designs for studying groups, but most of these can be classified into one of three basic types: *experimental, observational,* or *survey designs.* Each has its advantages and disadvantages. Which is best depends on the goals of the study and on the practical limitations it faces. When an investigator chooses a research design, he or she usually makes another decision: whether the study would best be conducted in a *laboratory* or in a *field* setting.

Experiments

Most people are familiar with examples of experimental research in the physical sciences; but some find them hard to visualize in the social sciences. Yet experiments are probably the single most commonly used design for studying group processes. Experiments are designed to test theories of cause-and-effect relationships in group processes. This is done by actually manipulating the independent variable under controlled conditions and observing whether it produces the expected effect in the dependent variable. Suppose you hypothesized that a member's competence at the group task affects his or her influence in the group. To test this notion experimentally, you must change the competence level of group members and measure whether that in turn changes their influence level.

If the dependent variable (influence) does change as expected, you can be reasonably sure that it was caused by the independent variable *if* you have controlled for other possible causes. Experiments involve not only manipulation of the independent variable then, but also controlling for *extraneous variables.* Extraneous variables are aspects of the group or its situation that are not relevant to the hypothesis but might also cause a change in the dependent variable. For instance, people's influence in the group might be affected by the extent to which they are liked by the others, or by their prestige in the larger society, as well as by their competence at the task. You must take steps to ensure that the change you observe in influence could not have been due to these other factors, rather than to your manipulation of competence.

There are many ways to control for extraneous variables. However, one of the most common involves the use of a *control* group. The logic is straightforward. The investigator selects or creates two groups that are similar with respect to all the extraneous variables likely to affect the dependent variable. Both groups are put through an identical set of experimental procedures, with one important exception: in the experimental group the level of the independent variable is manipulated, while in the control group it is not. The researcher then compares what happens to the dependent variable in the control group with the way it behaves in the experimental group. Any difference between the two should have been caused by the change in the independent variable. Using a control group, then, is one way to ensure that the effects you observe in an experiment are in fact due to the cause you are interested in, and not to some entirely different factor.

LABORATORY EXPERIMENTS.   Experiments can be conducted in either a laboratory or field setting. Most take place in laboratories specifically designed for the purpose of the experiment. This makes it much easier for the experimenter to manipulate the independent variable and control for extraneous variables. Hollander (1960), for instance, wanted to test a hypothesis about the way nonconformity affects a group member's ability to gain high status in the group. He could have observed real groups, waited for instances of nonconformity to occur, and watched what happened to status. But that would have meant observing a great many groups, just hoping for examples of nonconformity, and Hollander could never have been sure whether the changes he saw in status were due to nonconformity or to some other aspect of the member's behavior. So Hollander instead designed a laboratory experiment, and he employed a confederate to play the role of the nonconforming group member. A *confederate* is a person who poses as a regular member of the group but actually works for the experimenter and behaves according to a plan. By using a confederate Hollander was able to stage different degrees of nonconformity and observe its effects under conditions where extraneous variables—such as the nonconformer's expertise or attractiveness—could be controlled. Using a confederate, however, does mean deceiving the other group members, which, as we shall see, can raise ethical issues.

Laboratory experiments can use real groups, such as families or groups of college friends who come to the laboratory to participate in a study. Generally, however, such experiments rely on groups that are created in the laboratory by the experimenter. The goal is to put people in specially designed situations that elicit particular types of behavior. For instance, the experimenters might give a group of people a problem to solve together as a group. The problem itself might be relatively artificial—that is, not one which people would encounter in real groups. But the way people in the experiment go about negotiating with one another to solve the experimental problem will be very real. And it is this behavior that the experimenter wants to study. Thus the experimenter has used a relatively artificial setting to create a realistic representation of some aspect of actual group behavior, in this case, group problem solving and decision making.

Usually, in an experiment, the researcher does not try to recreate all aspects of groups at once. Instead, the experiment usually focuses on one or two specific group processes—the effect of cohesiveness on group productivity, for instance. The experimenter tries to insure that all aspects of the processes he or she wants to study are brought into play and that other group processes are held constant. In this way, the researcher can pinpoint the operation of these specific processes alone.

One of the biggest advantages of laboratory experiments is this ability to identify the individual effects of different group processes that, in actual groups, operate together in a confusing manner. Another obvious advantage is the ability to test cause-and-effect relationships in a clear way. This is vital for actually testing theories and judging their usefulness.

Because of these advantages, a great deal of small-group research employs the laboratory experiment method. We will draw extensively on these studies, but note their limitations as well. For laboratory experiments do have a major disadvantage, and that is the problem of realism. How well does the behavior created in the laboratory actually correspond to what happens in groups? Often, as we shall see, behavior in the laboratory does reasonably represent what goes on in certain situations in certain types of groups (see Box 3.1, "Can Laboratory Studies Be Realistic?")—but it does not represent all groups or all situations. We need to be very careful not to overgeneralize on the basis of laboratory experiments.

There is an ethical issue to be considered as well. By definition, experiments manipulate the group members' experience in the group. The researcher is responsible for any intentional or unintentional effects

Box 3.1.   CAN LABORATORY STUDIES BE REALISTIC?

Some students are suspicious about laboratory studies from the beginning. They are unconvinced that the intentionally contrived circumstances of the laboratory create social processes real enough to tell us anything about actual groups. While laboratory studies do vary in their relevance to particular groups, there is nothing inherently unrealistic about what goes on in them. In most cases, an investigator only wishes to study one or two group processes at a time, and so does not try to recreate the full richness of an actual group. However, it is perfectly possible to do so—or at least come close to such lifelike reality.

A dramatic example is Zimbardo's (1973) laboratory study on the effects of prison life. Zimbardo wanted not to look at one or two specific processes but to examine the total effect of a prison system on the people involved, the prisoners, guards, and wardens. So he recreated the key elements of that system in a laboratory—just a set of rooms in the basement of a Stanford University building. The results were frighteningly realistic.

Zimbardo began by creating the physical environment of a prison. Bars for doors made some rooms into cells; others were furnished as guard's and warden's quarters; a blocked-off corridor became the prison yard. Then participants were recruited from college-aged males living in the university area. All were similar in race and class background. They were given a battery of psychological tests to ensure that all were emotionally stable, well-adjusted people. Finally, a flip of a coin decided whether a participant would be a guard or a prisoner. Note that these procedures allowed Zimbardo to control for extraneous variables like personality differences between the guards and prisoners, or the possibility that the participants behaved the way they did because of psychological problems. With these variables controlled, we can be reasonably sure that the behavior Zimbardo observed was created by the prison situation itself.

With the mock prison and participants ready, the experiment began. Police in screaming squad cars dragged the "prisoners" out of their homes on the morning of the first day. Upon arrival at the laboratory, they were stripped naked, searched, and deloused by the "guards," now sporting kaki uniforms, mirror sunglasses, and billy clubs. The prisoners' clothes were taken from them and replaced by a short, humiliating smock with a number on it. The "warden" (Zimbardo's research assistant) read them the prison rules: no talking except in specific places, all prisoners to be referred to by number only, permission required to smoke or use the toilet, and so on.

Box 3.1 *(continued)*

In these and other ways, Zimbardo recreated key elements of the prison situation. It was his intention to run the experiment for two weeks, each day carefully recording the behavior of the participants and looking for changes induced by the prison situation. What happened was much more dramatic than he anticipated. In just a few days the contrived laboratory prison transformed average middle-class young men into cruel, contemptuous guards and apathetic, subservient prisoners. Before the study one "guard" said this about himself: "As I am a pacifist and non-aggressive individual I cannot see a time when I might guard and/or maltreat other living things" (Zimbardo et al., 1973). Three days after the study began, the same guard recorded in his diary: "I made sure I was one of the guards in the yard because this was my first chance for the type of manipulative power that I really like—being a very noticed figure with almost complete control over what is said or not . . . I sat on the end of the table dangling my feet and contradicting anything I felt like . . ." (Zimbardo et al., 1973)

So real were the social processes created in the laboratory that Zimbardo himself reports being swept away by them. On the second day one of the prisoners became victim to extreme depression, uncontrollable crying, and fits of rage. However, Zimbardo reports being reluctant to let the man go. He was convinced in his role as prison superintendent that the prisoner was trying to "con" him and his prison staff. On another occasion the guards picked up a rumor that a mass escape was planned. Instead of studying the rumor process, Zimbardo reports making an impassioned plea to the local city police department to transfer his prisoners to the actual city jail to foil the plot.

Events were clearly becoming much too real. On the sixth day Zimbardo stopped the study for ethical reasons. Had he realized in advance how powerful his study would be, he probably would not have started it. However, having done so, he now took steps to ensure that the participants suffered no permanent psychological harm. Encounter debriefing sessions gave people a chance to vent their feelings and talk through the moral and ethical issues involved. Follow-ups during the following year made sure there were no lasting effects.

Zimbardo's study makes it quite clear that social behavior created in the laboratory can be very real indeed. Of course, laboratory studies, like all types of research, vary in quality. Some do a better job of recreating the processes they wish to study than others. However, simply because a study is conducted in a laboratory does not make it inherently unrealistic. Zimbardo's study also raises another point. In studies with human participants, there is often a trade-off between complete realism and the ethical problems of manipulating people in serious or harmful ways. In such situations, ethical considerations must come first.

this manipulation might have on the people participating in the experiment. Manipulations that cause people significant discomfort—embarrassment, anxiety, self-doubt, or even physical pain—raise serious ethical issues.

The use of deception in experiments also poses ethical questions. Whenever the experimenter misleads participants about what will occur, deception is involved. For instance, the use of a confederate involves deception, since the naive participants do not realize that he or she is working for the researcher. Deception is also involved when an experimenter presents the object of a study as one thing when it is really another. For instance, a study of the relative influence of males and females in mixed-sex groups might be portrayed as a simple study of group decision making. Such deceptions are used to prevent participants from becoming self-conscious about the behavior under study and changing it accordingly. Clearly, it is best if experiments employ no deception at all. However, the use of small degrees of deception that do not place the participants in an embarrassing or uncomfortable situation is probably not too serious a problem as long as it is explained to the participants in the end. Ethical issues must be considered in all group research, but it is particularly important to meet high ethical standards in experiments because they manipulate human behavior.

FIELD EXPERIMENTS.   An alternative to the artificiality of the laboratory study is offered by the field experiment. This research design combines the experimental method with the study of actual, fully developed groups in natural settings. In many ways, it represents the best of both worlds—the control and explanatory clarity of an experiment with the realism of actual groups. Consequently, some of the most interesting studies we have on small groups are field experiments. Lewin, Lippit, and White used this method in a classic study of the effects of different leadership styles on group behavior (Lippitt and White, 1952). Working with recreational groups for ten-year-old boys, they trained the adult leaders of these clubs to act in an authoritarian, democratic, or laissez-faire manner and then observed the effects on group behavior (see Chapter 7 for a fuller discussion of this study). The result was a significant contribution to our understanding of the relations between leaders and groups.

The trouble with field experiments is that they are very difficult to do well. Because of the "real-life" setting one cannot always control all the unforeseen changes that may come from the outside environment —severely disrupting the study and making the results difficult to interpret. Also, the very realism of field experiments increases the potential for ethical problems. It is people's real life, not just their isolated experiences in the laboratory, that is manipulated, and the impact is likely to be much stronger. As a result, we have relatively few good field experiments to point to in the literature of small-group research, despite the many advantages of the method.

WHEN ARE EXPERIMENTS USEFUL?   The logic of an experiment requires the investigation to specify independent and dependent variables and to know enough about their relationship to be able to delineate relevant extraneous variables that might interfere with it. As a result an experimental design is most appropriate to the type of research where the investigator has a specific hypothesis to test. The experimental design is particularly useful for testing the validity of theories, since it alone tests directly for the existence of proposed relationships between group aspects. However, it is much less appropriate in exploratory research where either the independent or dependent variables are uncertain. In that situation a less controlled research design is more informative.

There are practical and ethical constraints on the use of experiments as well. From a practical standpoint, experiments are limited to the study of independent variables that the researcher is capable of manipulating. For instance, the hypothesis that "Jewish people tend to form close-knit families" cannot be tested experimentally. There is no practical way to manipulate the religious background of a given person. It would be better to study a hypothesis like that with a survey design. There are also hypotheses that would be unethical to test experimentally. "Extreme fear causes a decline in group coordination" is an example. It would not be ethical to place people in situations of extreme fear just for the sake of study. However, this hypothesis might be examined by studying real-life situations, such as war or natural disasters, where people have been placed in this situation. Experimental designs can be extremely useful for understanding group processes, but only if they are used appropriately and their results are not generalized beyond their legitimate scope.

Observation

Observational designs are built around direct observation of small groups. The researcher is actually present to see how the group behaves. They differ from experiments in that the investigator makes no effort to manipulate an independent variable. Rather, group processes are allowed to unfold without interference while the researcher records what happens. They also differ from surveys where the investigator relies on indirect methods of observation such as interviews with the members or questionnaires.

Observational designs differ depending on how the investigator has structured the conditions under which the group is observed. In a completely *unstructured design,* you simply pick a group and record in detail what goes on in it. Several years ago a group of media people used unstructured observation to examine the nature and concerns of the contemporary American family. They picked a few families whose external characteristics seemed to make them typical, and, with the families' agreement, planted video cameras in all the main rooms of their homes. The cameras were left rolling all day long for weeks recording almost all of the families' interactions. The results were fascinating. However, they were also overwhelming in their detail and a bit confusing in terms of what they had to say about the group dynamics of families. There was no logical way to sort out what was characteristic of American families in general from what was idiosyncratic about a few particular cases. The results did, however, present stimulating new ideas about what might be going on in contemporary families. Unstructured observation, then, is most appropriate to exploratory research—that is, where you are not seeking conclusions about groups, but rather want to know what are the most important questions to ask. As a result, it is usually used at the preliminary stage in a research project, when the investigator is in the initial process of choosing independent and dependent variables and formulating a hypothesis.

When researchers already know what specific group processes they want to study, *structured observation* is usually more appropriate. Here the researcher tries to reduce the overwhelming detail of group processes by focusing the group's behavior in some way. The researcher might assign the group a particular task or ask the group to follow a certain set of procedures in their discussion. A researcher interested in the relationship between money and power in families, for instance, might give several families a financial task to work on and observe the way the members act toward one another. Bales (1950; Bales and Slater, 1955) used structured observation to gather evidence on his theory of the task and socioemotional dimension of group behavior. He created five-person groups from a population of peers (male Harvard sophomores), gave them a specific human relations problem to discuss, and set certain procedural ground rules (the members had to begin by introducing themselves and were instructed to come to a group decision). Within these structures the groups were allowed to develop without interference, and the task and socioemotional behavior of their members was recorded.

Bales's studies took place in a laboratory setting where observers could sit behind one-way mirrors and record group behavior. Because it is easier for an investigator to control conditions in a laboratory, structured observation studies often take place in that setting. However, they can also be carried out in a field setting. One might use structured observation to study children's groups at camp, for instance.

The greatest advantage of observational studies is their realism. There is rarely any doubt that the researcher is recording real social processes rather than artificial ones created by his or her own intervention in the group. Observational studies also expose researchers to the rich complexity and diversity of actual small groups. This is particularly true if the researcher studies existing, fully developed groups in a field setting. Since this complexity is often in disturbing contrast to the rather simple notions of our theories, observational studies can provide an important corrective. They are also rich breeding grounds for new theoretical ideas garnered from watching the fascinating twists and turns of unfettered group interaction.

However, there are some disadvantages to the observational approach as well. It is easy to get lost in the swift-moving details of unstructured group interaction and to lose sight of the forest for the trees. This can be partially corrected by using a structured interaction design, but not without some loss of the realism that makes observational studies so valuable. Also, our theories and hypotheses generally deal with only one or two specific aspects of group processes, not all aspects at once. It can be very difficult, through observation alone, to clearly distinguish the effects of one set of group processes from the effects of all others. This can make it difficult to effectively test a theory with an observational design. Observational studies are probably best for generating hypotheses and for providing a final, crucial test of realism for hypotheses whose predictions have been confirmed in more controlled designs.

Surveys

Survey designs study group processes indirectly by asking the members questions about their experiences. Of our three research designs it is probably the one least frequently used to study group processes. The reasons are that it yields a relatively small amount of information about any one group and that information is always from the point of view of the individual members, not the group as a whole. Group processes that an observer might see, but which would go unnoticed by the members, will be difficult to detect with a survey design.

It is hard to get a detailed picture of a group behavior from a survey study.

However, it is usually faster and simpler to survey members about their group than it is to directly observe group interaction or conduct an experiment. As a result, survey designs compensate for the limited information they gather on any one group by collecting data on a great many groups, usually far more than can be practically studied by any other method. This makes survey designs particularly appropriate when you want to understand something about a whole population of actual small groups, for instance, corporate boards of directors or high school friendship cliques. Survey studies, by the way, are almost always field studies of existing groups in their natural setting.

It is possible to gather information on a whole population of groups by surveying every group in it. But that is often impractical and unnecessary, too. There are methods for selecting a smaller *sample* of groups that will be representative of the whole population. Most common is a *random* sampling, in which groups are chosen to be in the study by a technique which gives every group in the population an equal chance to be included. Most survey designs study a representative sample of groups in order to say something about the population as a whole. Coleman (1960), for instance, collected data on the cultural values of high school groups by asking the students in a sample of American schools to name the members of the "leading crowd" in their school and describe the activities they would most like to be associated with. In a study of primary groups, Litwak and Szelenyi (1969) used a sample of families to discover the types of favors people prefer to ask of relatives, rather than of friends and neighbors (see their study in Chapter 10).

Thus, when you want to characterize a whole population of groups (or contrast two populations), a survey design is usually best. Surveys are also useful for studying variables not subject to manipulation or control by the researchers, either for practical or ethical reasons. To use a survey design, however, the investigator must have the research problem worked out in enough detail to know what questions to ask. Unlike observational studies, surveys never discover things that the researcher did not know to ask about in the first place. Within these confines, survey designs can be used both for descriptive exploratory studies and for testing hypotheses. When they test hypotheses survey designs are limited to showing an *association* between two variables. Because the independent variable is not manipulated in survey designs, you cannot say with confidence that the association is causal in nature.

It should be clear, then, that each of our three designs has its advantages and disadvantages. Experiments offer precision and confidence in testing hypotheses, but they also may suffer from a lack of realism that limits the generality of the findings. Also, for both practical and ethical reasons, not all group variables are subject to experimental manipulation. Observational studies have the advantage of realism and expose the researcher to the rich complexity of real interaction that can be an important corrective to overly simple theories. However, this very complexity makes it difficult to pinpoint the specific processes necessary to test theories. Survey designs provide only limited data, but they gather that data on a larger number of groups, which makes them useful for studying whole populations of existing groups.

Which design is best depends to some extent on the nature of your research problem. Are you testing an exact hypothesis or is the study more exploratory in its goals? It also depends on your personal belief in the value of realism versus control, and the need for large samples. There are trade-offs in each of these designs. When you have a research problem that could be studied in more than one way, you must choose on the basis of the type of information you believe to be most valuable. These are issues over which thoughtful people disagree, and, as we shall see throughout this book, different researchers have made different decisions in their own work.

TECHNIQUES OF DATA COLLECTION

The research design investigators choose organizes the logic by which they argue whether a particular notion about small groups is true. But they still need a systematic way of recording the evidence by which they will measure their independent and dependent variables and make their logical argument. There are two general types of data collection techniques commonly used: *objective* measures and *subjective* measures. Objective measures record information about the group from the point of view of an outside observer, a person who can see the group as a whole, free of the particular biases of individual members. Subjective measures give information about the group as it is perceived by the members themselves; thus, only subjective measures can record what a behavior actually meant to the group members themselves.

We can see that the two techniques give different types of information about groups. Both are quite valid. As we shall see, which is the most appropriate to use depends to some extent on the type of research design employed by the investigator. However, it also depends on the sort of questions asked by the researchers. For instance, "Who is the most influential member of the group?" is a question asked from an objective point of view. It requires an objective measure, such as one that identifies the person whose suggestions were most often adopted by the group as a whole. But to ask, "Who is the group leader?," is to ask a question about whom group members *perceive* to be the most powerful and influential person. Leaders are only truly leaders if they are acknowledged by their followers. So a subjective measure is needed. Sometimes a researcher will try to compare objective information on a particular aspect of a group with a subjective view of the same aspect. This matching can say a great deal about what is going on in the group.

Under the general groupings of objective and subjective techniques, there are a wide variety of specific devices for observing and measuring small-group behavior. We will discuss some of the most commonly used ones. These will serve as illustrations of objective and subjective measuring techniques and give insight into the studies we will discuss later that use these techniques.

Objective Techniques

One of the best known objective techniques is Bales's Interaction Process Analysis. A trained observer records each communication that occurs between group members in terms of (1) who said it, (2) who received it (to whom was it directed), and (3) what types of content it contained. Bales (1950) created 12 categories by which the content of the communication can be classified. As Figure 3.1 shows, these categories were developed explicitly to test Bales's theory of the task and socioemotional dimensions of group behavior (discussed in Chapter 2). Six of the categories record members' efforts to deal with the group's task environment; the rest record members' expressions of antagonism or support for one another. Since the basic notions of task and socioemotional dimensions have become so widely accepted by small-group researchers, people have found these categories useful in studying a wide variety of group problems. Consequently, interaction process analysis, or some simplified version of it, is now used by some researchers as an all-purpose tool for recording group behavior and for testing very different theoretical ideas.

One main reason for its popularity is the breadth of behavior recorded by this technique. It registers the emotional tone of group interaction, as well as its task directedness. Exercising and accepting influence is also recorded, meaning measures of group structure can easily be developed by looking at who *talks* the most, who is talked *to* the most, and whose ideas are most accepted by the group. This technique is also very flexible in application. It has been used to record group

Figure 3.1. Bales's Twelve Categories of Interaction

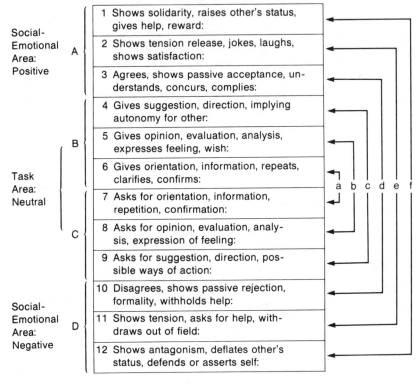

KEY:
a Problems of Communication
b Problems of Evaluation
c Problems of Control
d Problems of Decision
e Problems of Tension Reduction
f Problems of Reintegration

A Positive Reactions
B Attempted Answers
C Questions
D Negative Reactions

Source: Reprinted from *Interaction Process Analysis* by Robert F. Bales, copyright 1950, 1976. Reprinted by permission of the University of Chicago Press and the author.

behavior in observational studies, such as Bales's (1950), and in experimental designs, as, for instance, by Eskilson and Wiley (1976), who used it to measure some of the dependent variables in their experiment on sex composition and legitimacy in groups (this study is discussed further in Chapter 7).

The major disadvantage of interaction process analysis, however, also develops out of its wide scope of observation. It takes several carefully trained recorders to accurately observe and code even a brief interaction between a few people because so much information must be taken down about each communication. As a result, the technique is cumbersome and expensive. If the researcher only needs observations on an isolated aspect of group behavior, say influence, use of a simpler technique is probably more appropriate. There are many such straightforward measuring techniques available.

There is also the problem of having all those observers sitting there watching the group. This is a drawback that other objective methods for recording group interaction share. The presence of many observers runs the risk of making the group self-conscious, of distorting its behavior. In field settings with natural groups, observation by trained observers also raises practical problems. These are often surmounted by videotaping the group interaction, and having observers code it later. In laboratory studies, another way of handling the problem is to put observers behind a one-way mirror where they can view the group without being visible themselves.

Subjective Techniques

THE INTERVIEW-QUESTIONNAIRE APPROACH.   The two most common techniques for gathering information from the point of view of group members themselves are *interviews* (or questionnaires) and *participant observation*. Discussing these should illustrate the types of subjective information that can be gathered. Let's take the interview-questionnaire approach first. If you want to know group members' perceptions of each other and the group itself, you can, of course, simply ask them—which is what this technique does. There are, however, many ways to do this.

First of all, you can administer your questions in a face-to-face interview with each group member or through written questionnaires. Interviews give the investigator a chance to clarify, on the spot, any questions respondents do not understand and to follow up on the basis of their answers. However, they are very time-consuming and expensive for the researcher. A good practical alternative is the questionnaire, which, although it often yields data less rich than that gained through an interview, is quick and easy to administer.

A second choice to be considered is the degree to which questions should structure and focus the answers they elicit. *Open-ended* questions simply ask group members to describe one another; the researcher can then analyze these descriptions to see who was perceived as likable or influential or whatever. More common are *structured* questions, which ask group members to rate one another on various characteristics of interest to the researcher. For instance, the researcher might ask: Who has the best ideas? Who is the friendliest? How would you rate each group member in terms of influence over group decisions?—and so on.

A well known, and more sophisticated, questionnaire technique for measuring group members' perceptions of one another is called *sociometry* (Moreno, 1960). Really a device for measuring the network of relationships among group members, sociometry provides information from which the researcher pieces together a picture of the group's social structure as seen by the members themselves. In the original form of the technique, each group member is asked to name the people with whom he or she would most like to spend time. The researcher usually asks the question in terms of some specific activity that is relevant to the group, for instance, "Name the person you most like going to the movies with." Members also name the people they least like to spend time with.

The researcher then compares the group members' choices to discover who named whom. Usually it happens that one or two people are named by almost everybody in the group. These are the sociometric "stars," the most popular, the high-status members, the leaders. There may be a sociometric "reject" too, someone who is named by most others as the least preferred member. If two or three people all name one another over others in the group, we have evidence of an informal clique, or coalition.

Cliques, leaders, and isolates become most obvious when the group's sociometric choices are graphically displayed in a sociogram. Each member is represented by a circle, and sociometric choices are represented by lines between the circles. The number of lines, or preferences, connecting all the group members indicate the group's overall cohesiveness.

Because sociometry is simple to administer and flexible, it can be adapted to measure a wide variety of group traits. For instance, group members are often asked to rank each other in terms of specific characteristics ("best ideas," "most helpful," and so on) as well as emotional preference. Because of its adaptability, this ranking procedure, which developed from sociometry, has become one of the most widely used measurement techniques in small-group research.

The interview-questionnaire technique can be used in survey, observational, and experimental designs in both field and laboratory settings. Indeed, it is the only technique appropriate to survey designs, which are, after all, a method for polling people on their opinions. Sophisticated sociometric measures are primarily used to study natural groups in field situations. However, simple rankings of group members by one another are used in laboratory studies as well to tap perceived group structure. Even experiments whose emphasis is on objective data collection techniques often conclude by having the group members fill out a postexperimental questionnaire in which group members' perceptions are assessed.

PARTICIPANT OBSERVATION.   This subjective technique is used in observational studies of natural groups in field settings. The researcher actually joins the group as an observer, getting to know all the members, spending a great deal of time with them, and accompanying them through the group's activities. Through this process, the researcher learns what it is like to be a group member and what the world looks like from inside the group. Also, as the group members develop rapport with the researcher, they begin to let him or her in on the "inside scoop," what the group members really think about themselves and the group.

You can see that the name "participant observation" has an accurate connotation: the researcher actually participates in the group. However, the word "observation" also alerts us to the fact that, throughout this participation, the researcher continually analyzes the experience of the group from a social scientific point of view. As an aid in doing this, the researcher keeps extensive notes on what happens in the group. A researcher can then check to see if a particular small-group theory can account for what is described in the notes. If it can't, the researcher must ask why, and thinking about the experience of the group may suggest some possible answers. In this way, the researcher may be able to revise and improve the theory, or even come up with a new one.

Participant observation sounds deceptively easy, since it is only a more formalized version of what we all do when we analyze what goes on in groups we are members of. But actually, it is very difficult to do well. The difficult part comes in learning both to be close enough to the group to gain full information and yet still to be able, mentally, to stand back from what is happening and analyze it scientifically. Because it is difficult, many efforts at participant observation have disappointing results. However, an example of a study where participant observation was done well is William F. Whyte's *Street Corner Society*. Whyte (1943) spent two years "hanging out" with an Italian street gang in Boston during the Depression. From his observations he was able to discern some basic relationships among the status structure of a group, the group's environment, and the behavior of individual members. Many of these findings will be discussed in later chapters.

SUMMARY

To gain reliable knowledge about small groups, you need a systematic method for studying them. Adopting a systematic method requires you to carefully specify in advance the nature of your research problem, to choose a research design and setting appropriate to that problem, and to settle on a technique for collecting the data you need. Specifying a research problem means being very clear and explicit about what precisely you expect to learn about groups. You need to pinpoint the independent and dependent variables of interest and be as precise as possible about the relationships you expect among them. When you can state in advance that you expect a particular relationship between two group aspects, then you are ready to engage in hypothesis-testing research. However, if you do not know what the relationship might be, or are uncertain about the relevant dependent or independent variables, you need to do exploratory research.

Once the problem is specified, there is the question of choosing a research design and setting. Experiments test causal relationships directly by manipulating the independent variable, under conditions controlling for the effect of extraneous variables, and examining its effect on the dependent variable. As a result experiments are most appropriate for hypothesis-testing research. The difficulties of manipulating some aspects of group behavior and controlling for others encourage researchers to conduct most experiments in a laboratory setting. However, this may result in a loss of realism, which can limit one's ability to generalize on the results. Conducting the experiment in a field setting can sometimes overcome this problem, but this is often difficult to manage. Experiments are limited to the study of group variables that are subject to manipulation by the experimenter. There are special ethical considerations in the use of experiments as well, since they actually manipulate human behavior.

Observational designs differ from experiments in that the researcher makes no attempt to manipulate the independent variable.

Rather, the investigator simply observes the group directly, under more or less structured conditions, and records as carefully as possible what unfolds. Observational studies can be conducted in either a field or laboratory setting. The major advantage of this approach is its realism. Observing groups in open interaction can stimulate new ideas and provide an important corrective for overly simple theoretical notions. However, the inability to control for external variables makes it difficult to pinpoint the effects of specific processes. As a result, observational designs, although they can be used for hypothesis testing, are most useful for generating new hypotheses.

Of the three, survey designs are the least frequently used to study small groups. They provide indirect observations of groups by asking their members to relate their own judgment of the group. Although they gather only a small amount of data on any one group, they generally study a large number of groups. Usually a representative sample of groups is surveyed so that conclusions can be drawn about a whole population of groups in the society (all urban families, for instance). Surveys study real groups in a field setting, and they can be used for both exploratory and hypothesis-testing research.

After a design is chosen the researcher must settle on one or more techniques for gathering data on groups and measuring the independent and dependent variables. Objective techniques gather information on the group from the point of view of an outside observer. One commonly used objective technique, which we discussed in detail, is Bales's interaction process analysis. Subjective techniques gather information from the point of view of the group members themselves. One approach is to question the members directly through interviews or questionnaires. Sociometry is a commonly used questionnaire technique. Another subjective technique is participant observation, in which the researcher joins the group and combines the analytic approach of a researcher with the knowledge of an insider. Objective and subjective techniques provide two different types of information about a group, both of which are valid. Which specific techniques are best depends on the nature of the research problem and the design that has been chosen.

II

Fundamental Processes in Small Groups

4

Communication, Cohesiveness, and Group Development

Communication is the vital process out of which small groups emerge. It is the immediate mechanism by which a group evolves a social structure and culture. And it is through communication that groups maintain their habitual patterns of behavior. In fact, communication is one of the most critical aspects of interaction among group members, the way they influence each other's behaviors and the way the group is brought to life. This makes the communication process a natural place to start our consideration of small-group organization and development.

In Chapter 2 we argued that people join or create small groups in order (1) to accomplish some goal that requires the assistance of others and (2) to satisfy personal needs through interaction with others. These two requirements create, in the backs of group members' minds, pressure to communicate about two classes of need (Golembiewski, 1962). First, the desire to keep the group going forces communication aimed at resolving the group's task and socioemotional problems. Second, each member will engage in communication to achieve some satisfaction of their own personal needs for social comparison, affection, dominance, and so on.

Communication arising from either of these pressures will gradually cause group members' relationships with one another to become in some ways more unified and their opinions and behavior to become more standardized (Golembiewski, 1962; Homans, 1950). But at the same time, communication alerts group members to their differences in needs, abilities, behaviors, opinions. In the process of communication, members may begin to emphasize certain of their differences, particularly those that point out their distinctive skills and characteristics. These, in turn, become the foundation for a division of labor, for a status hierarchy, and for varying degrees of friendship. So, communication leads to differentiation among the group members as well as to unity and standardization. The dual process of standardization and differentiation are the means by which groups become unified wholes with, on the one hand, shared behaviors and opinions and yet, on the other, individual members who can play distinct roles and have different relationships with one another.

Because communication is the vehicle for both standardization and differentiation (Golembiewski, 1962), the nature of the communication patterns in a group affects the type of social structure a group develops and how it evolves and changes over time. There are two aspects of a group's communication patterns that we will consider. First is the question of who talks to whom. Are there some people who talk to everybody on a regular basis, and others who talk only to one or two members most of the time? This is the question of the group's *communication network*. We can think of a communication network as the lines between group members along which communication most frequently flows. The second aspect of communication patterns concerns the content of communication and how this is related to the way the group changes and develops over time. This is the problem of *group development*.

A group's communication network in turn affects the degree of *cohesiveness* that it achieves. We will examine this relationship, and then look a little more thoroughly into cohesiveness in its own right. What makes a group "stick together," achieve that sense of unity and oneness? And this question will lead us to a number of other aspects of group life that flow out of communication, including the patterns of friendship among the members and the development of role specialization and a status and leadership structure.

After exploring communication networks and cohesiveness in groups, we will turn our attention from the *organization* of communication in groups to its *content*. Instead of asking who talks to whom, we will look at what types of things are said. We will see that the content of communication is one of the motors that drives change and evolution in groups. In our consideration of group development, we will examine the phases groups go through in terms of the issues or problems that dominate the group's attention and communication.

COMMUNICATION NETWORKS

When people first come together in a group, what do they do? They greet each other—they begin communicating. In a polite way they begin to investigate each other: they ask questions; they reveal information about themselves; they try to form a general outline of each other that will help them decide how each member fits in with their goals and needs. In short, they try to decide how they wish to relate to each other. At this early stage in the group, it often happens that almost everybody talks to everybody else. But before long, in the process of trying to deal with one another and the group task, a distinct pattern of communication develops, with people talking more to some members than to others (Crosbie, 1975; Golembiewski, 1962). Clear channels of communication will develop between some members but not others. Over time, this network of channels will become a stable, habitual aspect of group life.

Theoretically, of course, the communication network that evolves in a group could include clear, open channels between each and every member. Why shouldn't every member talk equally with every other member? But, in practice, this seems to happen only rarely. Why? When two people are members of the same small group, what kinds of factors facilitate or block the development of clear channels of communication between them?

To answer this question, we need to consider two types of situations in which small groups develop. In the first, the group is formed by the members themselves without much interference from the outside environment or larger social organizations. As a result, there are few external constraints on the communication patterns that can develop. In the second type, the group develops in a highly structured environment, for instance, in an apartment house. We will examine these two group settings separately.

Freely Formed Networks

When groups are free to form their own networks, one of the important factors affecting communication between members is the status of the communicators. There are two types of status that are important here. First, there are *external status characteristics* (Berger et al., 1977), which are valued characteristics or signs of social standing in the outside world that individuals bring with them to small groups. Examples are a wealthy background, a prestigious occupation, or, in our society, being white or male in a racially or sexually mixed group. These external status characteristics may have no relevance to the activities or concerns of the newly forming small group. But, as we will see in Chapter 6, they still carry a certain aura of prestige.

The second type of status is *internal status.* This is the standing, the position, that an individual achieves within the status structure of the small group itself. In the long run, this is the important type of status in a small group. However, when members of a newly forming group first come together, no group status structure has yet emerged. So, at this point of initial communication among the group members, nobody has any clearly defined degree of internal status. But they do have high or low external status characteristics.

Many aspects of external status characteristics are visible through physical clues, dress, manners, and so on. Even after the briefest glance around a room, most people have a pretty good idea of the external status characteristics of their companions. They also know how their own status characteristics compare with those of the others. They know if they are relatively high or low compared to their fellows. How does this affect whom they initially talk to and what communication channels develop?

There is reason to believe that, even in the first few moments of interaction, more communication is directed to members with high external status characteristics. Imagine a group of people who meet together in the interest of organizing a tax protest. The opening rounds of introductions soon make it clear that two or three members are very prominent people in town. Whom will everybody rush up to and address? The local dignitaries, of course. In a newly forming group, then, people who judge themselves to be relatively low in external status characteristics generally try to communicate more with higher external status members than with others like themselves. We say "generally" because, of course, there are exceptions, as when two low external status members turn toward each other to avoid communicating with the apparent "big shots." But if normally the "lows" are talking to the high external status members, who are the "highs" talking to?

Based on Larsen and Hill's 1958 study of communication patterns among boys at summer camp, Crosbie (1975) offers a possible answer to this question. He suggests that in the initial forming phase of a group, potential high-status members actually may talk down to likely low-status members in an effort to gain recognition and support. If we apply Crosbie's analysis to our situation with high external status members, we might expect that those high external status members who want to translate their status characteristic advantage into a high-status position within the group will initially communicate downward in an effort to build a constituency. For instance, one of the local dignitaries at our taxpayers meeting might want to become the group's leader and spokesman. To that end, he might try to chat in a friendly, interested way with the lesser citizens who come up to talk to him. This downward communication could seem flattering to the low external status members who receive it and increase their liking and respect for the high external status communicator. Such admiration and affection can become the basis for high internal status as the status structure of the group develops. On the other hand, high external status members who are not ambitious for status within the group are likely to turn to one another in their initial communication.

In the initial stages of interaction, we can see that visible external status characteristics will be an important determinant of who talks to whom. In the absence of any restriction on communication from the group's physical environment or task, it seems generally then, that the early communication network is an up-down one in terms of external status differences, with a positive bias toward those with high characteristics, but with a reasonable degree of communication between upper- and lower-status members.

In the course of this communication, group members gain more information about each other's task abilities and personal characteristics in addition to external status characteristics. Out of this exchange of personal claims and task contributions, a stable internal status structure begins to emerge. As we shall see in Chapter 6, this occurs rather quickly, usually after only a few hours—or even minutes—of interaction. But what interests us here is that the group's communication network changes along with the evolving status structure.

What tends to happen is this. As certain people begin to emerge more clearly as the high (internal) status members of the group, they begin to restrict their communication with low-status members. Instead, they focus their communication efforts on other high-status members, their peers in the group. Low-status members, on the other hand, continue to direct most of their communication to higher-status members. The result is a communication network organized vertically along the status structure, but biased upward in that the people on the top receive and give a lot more communication than the ones on the bottom. Note that this means that low-status members not only are talked to less than high-status members, they also talk to others less than high-status members, since fewer people are interested in what they have to say. As a result, the communication network is biased upward not only in direction, but in quantity of communication. An upward-biased network like this is one of the most consistent findings of small-group communication studies (Riley et al., 1954; Bales et al., 1951; Sherif, 1956; Kelley, 1951; Crosbie, 1975). We see, then, that the communication network evolves from an up-down pattern in terms of external status characteristics to an upward-biased pattern in terms of internal status as a stable status structure emerges in the group.

So far, discussion has focused on groups made up of members with differing levels of external status characteristics. (This is most often the case in small groups. Since gender is an external status characteristic, dating couples follow this pattern. So do most committees.) However, what of peer groups, which by definition don't fit this description? How do communication networks evolve when the members of a newly formed group are external status equals—in that the members are all of about the same age, race, sex, and socioeconomic background? (Many friendship cliques and some work groups are like this.)

Assuming that nothing in the outside environment structures the communication patterns, the communication network in peer groups evolves together with the internal status structure. At the very beginning, there is rather open and free communication among all the members. But, before long—some say as little as ten minutes (Fisek and Ofshe, 1970)—some members usually begin to acquire more influence and prestige than others and a status structure begins to emerge. The growing internal status differences between some members begin to limit the once-open channels of communication. High-status people begin to protect their new position by reducing the number of direct dealings they have with low-status members. They direct their own communications mostly to other high-status members. Low-status members may continue to try to talk with high-status members as before, but they don't get much in the way of direct answers. The channel has been blocked. So eventually they redirect most of their efforts toward people who are only slightly higher status than they. As a result, a chain of communication emerges that matches the status hierarchy. Once again, the chain is upwardly biased in that the higher-status members both talk more and are talked to more than the lower-status members.

When groups are free to form their own communication networks without interference from the outside environment, it is clear that status is the critical variable in determining who talks to whom. If the group begins with people who differ in external status characteristics, then even the initial moments of communication will be structured by this variable. But in these groups as well as peer groups, the shape of the relatively stable network that finally emerges will depend on the nature of the internal status system that develops.

Networks Structured by the Environment

When a group develops within a specific physical location, like a place of work or an apartment house, its communication network is often prestructured by that environment. Consider what happens when three friends sit at a lunch counter. The person in the middle can easily talk to both of the other people, but the persons on the ends can only talk comfortably to one other person. The end people, to talk to one another, must lean forward or backward in an awkward position. In this situation, they will probably give up trying to talk directly to one another, instead focusing on the middle person. This of course leaves the middle person in a privileged place in the communication network.

In our lunch-counter example, the physical environment set certain constraints on the flow of communication, making it easier to maintain some communication channels over others. Faced with such constraints, people usually find it easier to change their own behavior than to try to alter the rather inflexible environment. As a result, the communication network, which is a social creation of the members themselves, ends up reflecting the physical arrangement of the members in space.

When a group develops among people who are spending a great deal of time in a particular physical place, you are likely to see this same effect. For instance, the flow of communication in a friendship or work group in a large office will be affected by whose desk is next to whose, the presence of things like dividers or walls, and job regulations that restrict people's movement. Similarly, if your office or dorm room is at the end of a corridor and far from the nearest staircase or exit, fewer people are going to walk by and talk to you than if you are in the middle of the hall or near a main entrance.

The basic principle is clearly one of *proximity.* The more people directly near to you in space, the greater number of communication channels there will be available for you to develop. Of course, after the group becomes more established, you may not choose, for reasons perhaps of social status, to maintain open channels with all the people near you. But, for group members who are not located near you in space, you don't even have this opportunity. As we shall see, when the environment prestructures the flow of communication in this way, the communication network itself can become a major determinant of the friendship patterns and status structure that emerge in the group.

WESTGATE AND WESTGATE WEST.   To get a better idea of how the physical environment structures communication in a real-life setting, and how this in turn affects the type of relations that develop among group members, let's look at a classic study of the development of friendship groups in a married students housing complex at MIT (Festinger, Schacter, and Back, 1950). Festinger and his colleagues studied two projects. The oldest, called Westgate, consisted of a series of small, single-story houses arranged in U-shaped courts. The newer project,

Westgate West, was made up of more modern two-story apartment buildings. We can see, then, that the physical arrangement of Westgate and Westgate West prestructured the communication pattern among the residents in slightly different ways (see Figure 4.1). What effect would this have on the friendship groups that developed?

Festinger predicted the following: the smaller the physical distance between people, the greater the likelihood that they would have contact (communication) with one another; the more contact between people, the greater probability of a friendship forming, and, ultimately, the greater the chance of the individual friendships knitting together into a genuine group (Festinger, Schacter, and Back, 1950). We should note, however, that Festinger made these predictions knowing that the people in the housing complex were all going to be rather similar in age, background, and interests just by virtue of being married students at MIT. As we shall see when we discuss cohesiveness, proximity has its strongest effect on friendship when the people involved are basically similar in major ways.

Festinger and his colleagues tested these predictions by collecting a variety of data. To get at the relation between proximity (physical distance) and friendship, they asked each resident to name the three

Figure 4.1. Westgate Court and Westgate West

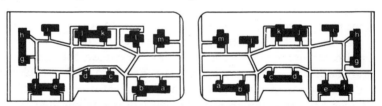

Schematic Diagram of the Arrangement of the Westgate Court

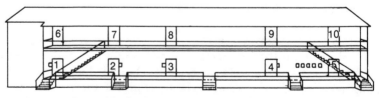

Schematic Diagram of a Westgate West Building

Source: Reprinted from *Social Pressures in Informal Groups* by Leon Festinger, Stanley Schachter, and Kurt Back with the permission of the publishers, Stanford University Press. Copyright 1950 by the authors.

persons in Westgate or Westgate West they saw the most of socially. Note that this is a sociometric technique for measuring group structure, one of the devices for studying groups mentioned in Chapter 3.

The results clearly confirmed the investigators' predictions. Most of the residents named people from their own courts (Westgate) or building (Westgate West) as the ones they saw the most, socially. However, they were next-most likely to name people from adjacent courts or buildings. Looking at the choices made within each court of Westgate, tenants were most likely to choose their closest neighbors as friends, next-most likely to choose those two doors away, and third-most likely to choose those three doors away.

There were some interesting exceptions to this general pattern that illustrate particularly well the effects of the communication networks established by the environment. In Westgate, the end houses on each court faced out away from the court rather than in toward the center, as did the rest of the houses. This in effect put the people living in the end houses on the periphery of the communication network of the court. Interestingly, the end-house residents were much less likely to be named as close social contacts by the other members of their court than were people whose houses were more centrally located. In Westgate West, there were also some interesting exceptions to next-door-neighbor friendship patterns. There, people who lived by the stairs were much more likely to have friends on the next floor, presumably because the stairway provided an easy pathway for communication with their upstairs neighbors.

Having shown that proximity is indeed associated with the friendship patterns that develop, the researchers decided to gather clear evidence that these patterns did represent active communication channels among the residents. They fabricated a rumor that a national news story was going to be written about the housing projects and planted it with individuals in two Westgate courts. A week later they went back and traced back the spread of the story. They found that the stories had clearly traveled along the lines of friendship established among residents of the courts.

Recall that Festinger predicted not only that proximity would affect communication and friendship, but that ultimately it would increase the chance of individual friendships growing together into a cohesive group. They were able to show clear evidence that cohesive groups had developed among the residents of several courts and buildings. But the courts and buildings prestructured the communication patterns among the residents somewhat differently. The separation of floors in the two-story buildings of Westgate West created an obvious barrier to communication. Did this adversely affect group formation? Because of problems with the data, the investigators were unable to answer the question definitively. But they cite some suggestive evidence that indicates the following: where the tenants allowed the physical barriers to inhibit the development of friendships between floors (24 percent of the buildings), cohesive groups did not form in the building as a whole; in the remaining buildings, however, people did manage to make between-floor contacts, and there cohesive groups were much more common. Thus, when the environment prestructures the communication network, it sets constraints on but does not wholly determine the group development that follows.

There is one additional effect of communication networks that Festinger and his colleagues uncovered. The end houses of the Westgate courts, you will remember, faced outward and thus were on the periphery of the court's communication network. At one point in their study, the researchers examined the extent to which residents of a court developed similar opinions on issues relevant to the housing project. They found, among other things, that people in the end houses were much less likely to share the opinion of others in the court. Seventy percent of the end-house people disagreed with the majority opinion, compared to 34 percent of those whose houses faced in towards the court. Clearly, members of the courts influenced one another's opinions through communication. Those on the periphery of the network received fewer communications and, so, were less likely to be talked into agreeing with the others. Here, we see an example of the way the flow of communication can increase the degree of standardization among group members.

The study of the Westgate and Westgate West housing projects makes it clear that the structure of the communication network in turn affects a number of aspects of the group as it develops. First of all, the flow of communication is likely to affect the development of friendships, what is often called the sociometric structure of the group. The communication pattern also affects group cohesiveness, the extent to which the individual friendships knit together into a distinct unified group. Once a group has emerged, the communication pattern will also affect the group's ability to influence all its members to adopt shared opinions and beliefs.

In the study, group communication patterns were prestructured by the physical layout of the housing projects. But the interdependent relationships discovered between the communication network and a group's friendship patterns, cohesiveness, and influence processes are likely to hold for freely formed groups as well. The only difference would be that, in freely formed groups, the communication network is more flexible and changes more easily in response to other aspects of the group. Therefore, the communication network of a freely formed group is likely itself to adapt to the emerging friendship patterns and status structure, as these aspects of the group in turn adapt to it.

What about the relationship between communication and status in groups where the communication pattern has been structured by the outside environment? Festinger and his associates did not investigate the question of status in the MIT housing projects. However, there is another tradition of research on communication networks that can help us answer this question. It will also give us greater insight into the way networks affect group cohesiveness, and show how differing types of networks affect the group's ability to deal with different sorts of problems.

BAVELAS'S COMMUNICATION NETWORKS.   In contrast to Festinger's field research method, Bavelas (1950) and Leavitt (1951) used a laboratory to experimentally vary communication networks and examine the effects on group processes. Bavelas and Leavitt used five-person groups and arranged their communication networks into several patterns, including those shown in Figure 4.2. Notice that each of the four networks differs in the *distance* between positions (*A* and *E* can talk to each other directly in the circle but are separated in the chain by three other people) and the *centrality* of any particular position. The position of greatest centrality in any network is the one closest to all other positions. We can see from Figure 4.2 that, of the four networks, the wheel is the most centralized, followed by the *Y*, the chain, and, finally, the most decentralized, the circle.

How does the centralization of a group's communication patterns affect the emergence of its status structure? This was one of the first questions to interest Bavelas and Leavitt. In an experiment with groups organized into wheels, *Y*'s, chains, and circles, Leavitt (1951) gave groups a task to work on, and at its completion, asked each group member, "Did your group have a leader? If so, who?" In the wheel, the person in position *C* was named the leader 92 percent of the time. In the *Y* and the chain, *C* was named 68 and 48 percent of the time, respectively, but in the circle no one position was named any more often than any other. These findings have been confirmed in several subsequent studies (Shaw, 1954; Shaw and Rothschild, 1956).

Clearly, the more centrally located you are in the group's communication network, the more likely you are to emerge as a high-status member. This makes sense if you think about it. Someone in a centralized position has greater control over the flow of information in the

Figure 4.2. Four Communication Networks for a Five-Person Group (studied by Bavelas and Leavitt)

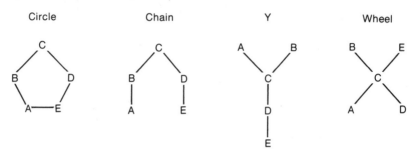

Source: Reprinted from "Some Effects of Certain Communication Patterns on Group Performance" by H. J. Leavitt, in *Journal of Abnormal and Social Psychology*, 46 (1951). Reprinted by permission of the author.

group. Information is a source of power. The more you have of it, the more influence you are likely to have over the other members and the decisions they make. Imagine a group of reporters assigned by their newspaper to cover the White House. Because one has personal friends in the White House staff she always hears about leaks and newsbreaks before the rest of them. As a result, the others start going to her for information, placing her in the center of their communication network. This in turn gives her a great deal of control over what they know and when, and with that control comes power over their behavior and decisions. Not surprisingly, people who wield such obvious informational power in the group are soon accorded status and prestige as well. When the communication network is preset by the outside physical or social environment, it becomes the skeleton around which the group's status system develops.

The centrality of your position in the communication network affects your attitude toward the group as well. Which would you enjoy more, occupying position *C* in the wheel or position *A*? Or think about sitting together talking with your friends. Is it better to have a chair in the center of the group or off on the periphery? In a more centralized position, you can talk to whomever you want, you have more personal independence (Shaw, 1964, 1978). Since independence is related to satisfaction, the more centrally located you are in the group's communication network, the more enjoyable you are likely to find the group. Several studies have confirmed this point (Shaw, 1964, 1981). In Leavitt's (1951) study, for instance, the person in the most centrally located position had an average personal satisfaction rating of 7.8, compared to 4.6 for those in peripheral positions.

The total morale of the group, however, depends upon the satisfaction of all the group members, not just the few in centralized positions. Overall, group satisfaction is highest where all positions are equal in centralization, and therefore independence. These are the decentralized, democratic networks. Among the networks in Figure 4.2, for instance, group satisfaction is highest in the circle, followed by the Y, the chain, and the wheel (Shaw, 1981).

It appears that centralized networks cause more negative feelings among group members than do decentralized, more egalitarian patterns. The overall satisfaction of members with the group and the negative or positive feelings among the group members are related to the group's cohesiveness. It seems, then, that it is easier to create a cohesive, high-morale group if the communication pattern is kept open and decentralized. This does *not* mean that a group with a centralized communication network cannot be cohesive. It can, but it will have the added difficulty of overcoming the dissatisfactions felt by the members stuck on the periphery of the network.

There is a popular assumption that centralized communication networks are more efficient at getting things done even if they are less pleasant for the members. Trying to discover whether this is true has been a major thrust of research on communication networks. The results offer us further insights into the way the structure of communication can fundamentally alter the operation of a small group.

The relative efficiency of centralized networks depends on the type of task the group is trying to accomplish. Centralized networks are more efficient in handling relatively simple tasks that primarily require the pooling of information. But when the task is more complex (technical or human relations problems, for instance) decentralized networks are faster and make fewer errors. According to Shaw (1964, 1978) tne reason for this is something called *position saturation*. The idea is that there are only so many communications at a time that one person can deal with effectively without being "saturated" or overwhelmed. Complex problems require the group members to exchange much more information. In a centralized network, all these communications go through the person in the central position, who is inundated. McFeat (1974) uses the example of a taxi dispatcher. All calls both from the taxi drivers and from people wanting taxis have to go through him. Think how harrassed he will get at rush hour, and of the mistakes he may make as a result. A decentralized network remains efficient in this situation because communications are spread out equally and no one person is overburdened.

This may sound very abstract, but it has lots of applications. Because a group having more open, decentralized communications can deal with more information, it is likely to come up with more creative responses to situations it finds itself in. It is not surprising, then, that writers who work for advertising companies or the media often organize themselves into small democratic work groups even within the hierarchic, bureaucratic organizations that employ them. Most informal friendship groups in our society maintain relatively open, decentralized communication networks that help their members cope with the sometimes overwhelming demands of modern society. In general, whenever groups are free to form their own communication network, they may adjust it to better deal with the types of problems they typically face. Also, large organizations may self-consciously structure the communication networks of the small decision-making groups created within them in order to take advantage of the differing efficiencies of these patterns.

Our examination of both freely forming and environmentally structured groups has demonstrated an intricate interdependence between the pattern of communication and almost every other aspect of the group's structure and operation. There is a close association between the flow of communication and the group's status structure on the one hand, and its sociometric (friendship) structure on the other hand. In addition, communication networks affect certain aspects of the group, such as its degree of cohesiveness and its ability to accomplish differing types of goals. When a small group develops within a large formal organization—a business or government bureaucracy, for instance—or in a single physical location, its communication network is often prestructured by this environment. In that case, the group's patterns of status, friendship, cohesiveness, and task success usually develop around the skeleton provided by the rather inflexible communication pattern. In freely formed groups, those same qualities—including communication networks—emerge together and adapt to one another. We will take up issues concerning the development of a status structure and the group's task efficiency in later chapters. But now, let us turn our attention to the development of group cohesiveness, its sources and consequences, and to the related problem of the group's sociometric structure.

COHESIVENESS

Of all the aspects of groups that arise out of the process of communication, cohesiveness is one of the most fundamental. The strength or solidarity with which a group is bound together is a basic dimension that defines the degree of "group-ness" or unity that a set of people achieve. At the extreme low end of the cohesiveness scale are collections of people so tenuously linked together in their behavior that they can hardly be considered a group. At the other end are close-knit, unified sets of people that seem to embody what we mean by "group."

Defining Cohesiveness

Out of this intuitive notion of what cohesiveness is, Festinger constructed a more formal definition. Cohesiveness, he said, was the "total field of forces which acts on the members to remain in the group" (Festinger, 1950). This has been the most influential, if controversial, definition of the concept ever offered. At the level of abstract understanding, most small-group researchers would agree with it. After all, if cohesiveness refers to the strength with which a group is glued together, then to refer to that "glue" as a field of social forces holding members together makes sense. The controversy develops in deciding exactly what is meant by a field of forces. What concrete aspects of the group are being referred to? Festinger's definition does not say. You may have realized by now that this definition is one derived from Lewin's field theory (see Chapter 2). We see here an example of the problems of operationalization which were a major weakness of that approach.

COHESIVENESS AS INTERPERSONAL ATTRACTION.   In practice, Festinger (1950) measured cohesiveness as the number and strength of friendship ties group members have with one another compared to those they have with outsiders. In other words, he measured cohesiveness sociometrically, in terms of interpersonal attraction among the members. He did this because he was studying informal friendship groups in a housing project (the Westgate study just discussed). In such groups, which are a type of primary group, it seems reasonable to assume that the links between members will be based on interpersonal attraction. In most primary groups, the interdependence among the members seems to be largely *social* rather than *instrumental,* meaning that they rely on one another for company rather than for accomplishing specific tasks.

The problem is that later researchers went on to make sociometric measures *the* indicator of cohesiveness for all types of groups (see for instance, Cartwright and Zander, 1968). Some even defined the concept solely in terms of interpersonal attraction (Lott and Lott, 1965). Surely there is more that holds a group together, even a primary group, than friendship alone. And what about task groups such as committees and so on? It seems particularly inappropriate to define the cohesion of a smoothly working, efficient committee solely in terms of friendship among the members.

A BROADER VIEW.   A more complex conception of cohesiveness is needed. Let's begin by defining cohesiveness as the extent to which features of the group bind the members to it. This definition is similar to Festinger's, but a bit more specific. Feldman (1968) has pointed out that there are at least three different ways in which small groups bind their members to them. First, members can of course be bound to the group through links of friendship and mutual liking. Feldman calls this aspect of cohesiveness *interpersonal integration*.

However, members can also be bound to the group through the nature and effectiveness of its organizational structure. This is what we shall call a group's *structural-functional integration* (Nixon, 1979), a second aspect of cohesiveness. It refers to the success with which a group's social structure coordinates the members' behavior in a way that both allows an effective pursuit of group goals and the maintenance of good working relations among the members. Think of an efficiently organized committee that uses its members' time and talents effectively and smoothly. Compare that to one of those ineffective committees to which we have all belonged. In those your efforts seem to be wasted because they are not properly coordinated with those of others, the meetings go in circles, nothing gets done, and, as a result, frustration builds and tempers flare. How cohesive can the inefficient committee ever be? Although structural-functional integration arises from the way the group is organized—how well its parts fit together—rather than from the affection of the members, it is as fundamental to cohesiveness as is friendship.

The third way a group can bind its members to it is through a set of shared beliefs, rules, or practices. Feldman (1968) calls this third aspect of cohesiveness *normative integration*. It refers to the degree of consensus group members achieve about what the group is, how it should operate, and what its rules are. It reflects the extent to which the members have developed shared, agreed-upon norms for governing group life.

When faced with these three rather different aspects of cohesiveness, some writers have chosen to deal with each as a separate concept (Nixon, 1979; Wilson, 1978). Often, the term *cohesiveness* is used to refer to interpersonal integration alone (Cartwright and Zander, 1968) and the more structural aspects of normative and structural-functional integration are called group integration. We, however, will use the word *cohesiveness* to refer to the combined result of all three types of integration acting simultaneously in a particular group. Cohesiveness captures best that sense of a group that fits happily together, works smoothly, and creates a sense of satisfaction for its members.

Although all three types of integration contribute to the group's overall cohesiveness, they are each somewhat independent of the others. Feldman (1968) used friendship groups among campers to study the relationship among the three types of integration. Interpersonal integration, he found, was related to both structural-functional and normative integration, but the latter two were unrelated to each other. So the nature and effectiveness of the group's organization is linked to development of shared norms by the pattern of personal relationships among the members. It is out of the members' reactions and dealings with one another that structural-functional and normative integration are created.

A group's purpose or type will determine the relative importance of each type of integration in determining it's overall cohesiveness. In more primary-oriented groups, like Feldman's campers or Festinger's Westgate residents, interpersonal attraction will clearly be the most important. Specialized roles, the development of a status system, and the mutual influence out of which norms are created, all grow out of the initial friendship bonds established among the members. If the members stop liking one another, groups like this usually dissolve. Without friendship, the cohesiveness of socioemotionally oriented groups is almost impossible to maintain.

It is interesting to think of the family in this light. The family is an atypical primary group in that its task functions (raising children, managing finances, running a household) are as important as its socioemotional ones. But what happens to a family when husband and wife lose all affection for one another or when there is a serious break between parent and child? Often the family dissolves under the pressure. Occasionally, a couple who no longer like each other stay together for task reasons (to care for the children, share finances, and handle the outside environment together). But this kind of compromise is usually strained and difficult to maintain. Such families, in other words, are usually low in cohesiveness even if they manage to survive.

The story is quite different for task groups, however. When a group's main purpose is simply the accomplishment of a task, it is structural-functional integration that will be most important for overall cohesiveness. What matters to such groups is efficiency and success at the task. Think of the president's advisers. When problems develop among them it is not because they don't like each other. That is often irrelevant. Usually, dissension is over who reports to whom, who is in charge of what, and who gets to see the president and when. The source of bickering and disunity is the group's organizational structure. It is the viability of its structure that is most important to a task group's cohesiveness.

Interpersonal integration is much less important in task groups than structural-functional integration—and probably less important than normative integration as well. Members need only maintain cordial working relationships; actual friendship is unrequired. Indeed, it is possible for a group of people who actually dislike one another to hold together as a group in order to accomplish some goal that is very important to them. However, such active hostility certainly does weaken the group, lowering its overall cohesiveness.

Normative integration is most important in groups whose members have come together to express a shared interest or ideology. Religious groups or political action groups are examples. In groups like this, shared commitment to a specific set of beliefs and norms is what holds the group together. If conflict develops over core beliefs, the group usually cannot maintain sufficient cohesiveness to survive.

Having taken the time to understand the complex nature of group cohesiveness, you might ask, what good is it? What difference does it make if a group is high or low in cohesiveness, as long as it has the minimum cohesiveness to stay together? This is the next question we will turn to: the consequences of group cohesiveness. After we have some understanding of the effect of cohesiveness on group life, we will turn to the factors that allow a group to achieve high cohesiveness.

The Consequences of Cohesiveness

Since a highly cohesive group is one that binds the members tightly together, it naturally is one which the members actually care about, one to which they feel committed. Because they value the group, members put more energy into group activities in a cohesive group. With more effort coming in from each member, cohesive groups have more collective resources to apply toward group goals and activities. Out of these simple observations come the major consequences of cohesiveness for group life. We will see differences between high and low cohesiveness in (1) the amount and quality of communication in the group, (2) the group's ability to maintain the loyalty and satisfaction of its members, (3) the power of the group over the opinions and behavior of its members, (4) the group's ability to achieve its goals, and (5) the extent to which group culture is elaborated. Let's examine these consequences more carefully.

AMOUNT AND QUALITY OF COMMUNICATION.   It makes sense that members of a close-knit group will talk to each other more. Because they value the group, they try to take part in its activities, and that means interacting with other members. There is clear evidence from field experiments conducted on friendship groups and others that the greater the cohesiveness, the more communication activity in the group (Lott and Lott, 1961; Shaw, 1981). In addition to greater communication in any given session, it also seems likely that cohesive groups meet more frequently, further increasing the amount of communication among members.

It appears that the structure and quality of communication is different in cohesive groups as well. The investigations of Back (1951) found that regardless of whether the cohesiveness of the group derived primarily from either interpersonal attraction among the members, task orientation, or group prestige, certain effects on communication were observed. Members of cohesive groups not only participated more, but participation was spread more equally among them. In other words, it is less likely in a cohesive group that a few people will do all the talking. Instead, everybody takes part at least to some extent. In an atmosphere of cohesiveness, the quality of communication is likely to be more friendly and cooperative as well, and more oriented toward keeping the group together (Back, 1951; Shaw and Shaw, 1962). In low-cohesive groups, members direct fewer of their communications to matters concerning the whole group rather than themselves and are generally more agressive and less cooperative (Shaw, 1981). We see, then, that there is a reciprocal relationship between a group's communication processes and its cohesiveness. The pattern of communication affects the development of cohesiveness, which in turn encourages communication.

MEMBER LOYALTY AND SATISFACTION.   If everybody talks more and what they say is friendlier, it is not surprising that members seem to enjoy high-cohesive groups more than low-cohesive ones. Studies of a wide variety of groups, including friendship groups among construction workers (Van Zelst, 1952), decision-making groups at business and government conferences (Marquis, Guetzkow, and Heyns, 1951), Air Force groups (Gross, 1954), and experimental laboratory groups (Exline, 1957) all report that members of highly cohesive groups are more satisfied with their group experience. Think how much more satisfying it is to be a member of a primary group of family or friends when the group really feels unified, together. Indeed, much of the real pleasure of group participation comes from those moments of high cohesiveness when everybody in the group seems to pull together as one. Cartwright and Zander (1968) suggest that high cohesiveness leads to greater acceptance, trust, and confidence among the members, which in turn helps each member feel a sense of security and personal worth. Naturally, a group that offers such satisfactions to its members is going to inspire their loyalty. As a result, highly cohesive groups have an easier time maintaining their membership. Fewer people lose interest and drop out.

POWER OF THE GROUP OVER ITS MEMBERS.   If people are enthusiastic about a group, they are more willing to make some personal adjustments, even sacrifices, to remain a member. This gives the group a certain power over their behavior and opinions. We see this power most clearly in the group's ability to enforce its norms. A highly cohesive group can bring much greater pressure to bear on an individual member to conform to the group's accepted opinions and ways of doing things.

Festinger, Schacter, and Back (1950) looked closely at the effects of cohesiveness on the opinions of residents in housing project groups. First they measured the opinions of each resident in Westgate and Westgate West toward a controversial tenants' organization. They found clear evidence that the individual courts in Westgate had formed definite norms defining the group's opinion toward the tenants' organization. Some courts favored it, some opposed it; but the point is that most groups had achieved a collective stand on the issue, a normative view. In Westgate West, the situation was somewhat different. The groups there were much newer and had been exposed to the issue of the tenants' organization for only a short time. Not surprisingly then, the investigators found little evidence that the friendship groups of Westgate West had developed any norm defining a group opinion on the issue.

Next, Festinger and his colleagues measured the cohesiveness of the different buildings and courts. As we have seen, their measure was based solely on interpersonal attraction, which is less than ideal. However, since these were friendship groups, this was not too serious a problem. Degree of cohesiveness was then compared to the homogeneity of opinion on the tenants' organization among the members. This was done by finding the dominant opinion in each court and building, and then looking at the number of residents who deviated from it. In Westgate, they found that the more cohesive the court, the fewer deviates it had. In other words, the highly cohesive courts had been more successful in influencing or pressuring their members into conforming with the group's normative view.

It was a different story in the buildings of Westgate West. There, group cohesiveness was unrelated to homogeneity of opinion. Why?

Since the Westgate West groups had not developed clear norms on the issue, the greater power of cohesive groups to enforce norms was useless in this situation. The groups had no norm to pressure their members to conform to. We see, then, that the power cohesive groups have to influence their members is not all-encompassing. Rather, it is limited to issues the group has taken up as matters of concern, and about which it develops some sense of normative agreement. On those issues, however, highly cohesive groups have much greater ability to bring about conformity than do low-cohesive groups. Shaw (1981) reviews a number of studies that support these general conclusions.

There is an interesting paradox about the point that highly cohesive groups put more pressure to conform on their members. This paradox derives from the fact that cohesive groups also increase their members' ability to resist the conformity pressures put on them (Back, 1951; Jones and Gerard, 1967). When a group is very cohesive, it can tolerate much more resistance and rebellion from its members without risking disintegration. As Golembiewski (1962) says, it is an "elemental law of small group physics" that the greater a group's cohesiveness, the greater the force necessary to pull it apart. Think of things you can shout in anger at your family that you wouldn't dare say to friends. That is largely because families usually are more cohesive than friendship groups. You are fairly sure your family won't break off relations with you because of your unkind words—but your friends just might. The cohesiveness of a group, then, is a variable that increases the conformity pressures put on the members, and yet, at the same time, it can potentially increase their freedom to rebel against those pressures. Both effects derive from the fact that people value their membership in highly cohesive groups. They are willing to both change themselves more and put up with more from others in order to remain a member.

GOAL ATTAINMENT.   If the members of a group agree on a goal they want to attain, they have, in a way, adopted a norm about that goal. We already know that cohesive groups are better at inducing their members to follow group norms. We might expect, then, that highly cohesive groups will be more successful at mobilizing their members' energies and directing them toward a goal. As a result, high-cohesive groups should be better at achieving their goals than low-cohesive ones. Indeed, a number of studies show exactly that effect (Berkowitz, 1954; Goodacre, 1951; Shaw and Shaw, 1962; Van Zelst, 1952).

The association between cohesiveness and goal attainment is precisely why athletic coaches are always so preoccupied with the spirit and togetherness of their teams. They know from personal experience that a team's cohesiveness can make the difference between winning and losing. However, there is an interesting twist to this association. The only goals that cohesive groups are better at obtaining are those they genuinely set for themselves. Often these are not the same goals expected of them by outsiders, such as employers, a large organization, or even small-group researchers. Seashore (1954) for instance, found that high cohesiveness in industrial work groups was related to either high or low productivity, depending on the standards of production established by the group members themselves.

Homans (1950) gives a classic illustration of this in his description of a work group in an electrical plant during the Depression. The work group adopted a production goal not so high that they would work themselves out of a job in hard times, but not so low as to cause trouble from the management. When someone produced more than the group goal, he was called a "rate buster" and systematically harassed into slowing down. On the other hand, underproducers were called "chiselers" and similarly pressured to speed up.

The point is that, just because highly cohesive groups are more effective at goal attainment, it does not follow that they will always be more productive in the eyes of outsiders. If a cohesive group sets high productivity as its goal it will be more productive than a less cohesive group. But it may not want to be very productive. It may even set social activity as its primary goal. Consider a group of students who go to the library together one night a week. An outsider might expect their group cohesiveness to be related to the degree to which they pressure each other to work hard at the library. But what if the group actually goes to the library as an excuse to socialize? They will use their group resources to achieve the goal of having a good time.

We should consider primary groups in this light also. The major goals of primary groups are usually social: keeping each other company, engaging in mutually enjoyable activities, or dealing with one another's personal feelings and problems. A highly cohesive primary group will be more able to have a good time together. If the group values such activity, they are also likely to provide a more supportive atmosphere in which the members can air their feelings and troubles. All these are examples of a cohesive group's better ability to draw upon the energy of their members and achieve their chosen goals.

ELABORATION OF GROUP CULTURE.   Highly cohesive groups generally develop a more complicated group culture (Dunphy, 1972). When a group achieves that sense of solidarity that comes with cohesiveness, it tends to develop little behavioral routines that members enact together to express their sense of togetherness. Examples might be an informal initiation, or a particular set of inside jokes or ways of kidding one another that the members repeat just to affirm their sense of groupness. Often these rituals center around symbols like gang jackets, a particular handshake, or a group emblem that the members adopt to represent themselves. These little rituals are routinized behavior but differ significantly from everyday behavior in that they carry a special meaning for the group members, an assertion of what the group feels itself to be. As Dunphy (1972) points out, these behaviors become routinized and repeated in groups because they give the group members a means for focusing their collective attention on the central meanings of the group's life. They also help the members establish a psychological "we-they" boundary between themselves and the rest of the world. Because group rituals and symbols allow an expression of togetherness and group definition, they in turn reinforce the group's cohesiveness. There is a circular relationship here: as a group becomes more cohesive, it is likely to develop little rituals and other aspects of a more elaborate group culture; enactment of these rituals in turn feeds cohesiveness.

We can see that the consequences of high cohesiveness are mostly good, effects one might want in many small groups. There is a hint of a dark side to cohesiveness in the increased conformity pressures, and indeed, as we will see in Chapter 9, this can cause some problems for decision-making groups. Nevertheless, it is clear that cohesive groups are more satisfying to their members, more able to agree on things, and better at achieving their goals. Given these advantages, it follows that we should ask: how does a group manage to become cohesive?

Sources of Cohesiveness

Many of the sources of cohesiveness we will consider flow logically out of our discussion of the nature of group cohesiveness. We will look at the following factors, all of which can affect cohesiveness:

1. Special norms and practices designed to build members' commitment to the group
2. Interpersonal attraction among the members
3. Social structure and leadership style of the group
4. Type of interdependence among the group members
5. Group's relationship to its outside environment
6. Attractiveness of the group's goals and activities

COMMITMENT-BUILDING NORMS AND PRACTICES.   There are some specific norms and practices that groups adopt to increase their members' commitment and, as a consequence, improve cohesiveness. The sociologist Rosabeth Kanter uncovered a number of them in her efforts to understand how groups like communes and religious cults manage to maintain their membership and stay together (Kanter, 1968, 1972a, 1972b). Examining these will give us a feel for what links a member's own desires, beliefs, and feelings to group goals in a way that binds the member to the group.

Kanter (1968, 1972b) argues that there are three ways in which a person can feel committed to a group. They can be committed for *instrumental* reasons, which is to say, they are loyal to the group because it is a means by which they can achieve things they want. They can also be committed for *affective* reasons, meaning that they have meaningful, emotion-laden relations with others in the group. Finally, they can be committed because of a *moral* or *evaluative* connection they feel with the beliefs the group embodies. These three types of commitment correspond neatly with our notions of the structural-functional, interpersonal, and normative aspects of group cohesiveness. Indeed, they are simply a restatement of those aspects from the point of view of the individual member rather than the group as a whole.

Kanter found six techniques groups use to increase each type of commitment. Few groups use all these techniques, but most use some at one time or another. All six techniques are based on a fundamental observation: increasing your commitment to a group involves not only getting something from the group itself, but also giving up something outside the group. Both the getting and the giving up increase the strength of your connection to the group.

A member's instrumental commitment to the group can be increased by norms and practices requiring either *investment* or *sacrifice* or both (Kanter, 1972b). Norms that require you to invest a great deal of your time, energy, money, or property in the group increase your commitment in a straightforward way. The more you put into a group, the greater your stake in its survival and success. This is one reason why some religious cults require their members to give all their worldly possessions to the group.

More complicated are norms requiring that you sacrifice something to become a member of the group. The basic idea behind sacrifice norms is this: the more it costs you to get something, the more you value it when you have it. Fraternities and military academies like West Point sometimes use "hazing" and other harsh initiation practices for just this reason. So do teenage gangs. Athletic teams make their members give up smoking and staying out late. Other groups might require their members to go to great effort or inconvenience to attend meetings.

Do these sacrifice norms really increase commitment? Yes. Aronson and Mills (1959), for instance, showed that women who were forced to go through an unpleasant, embarrassing initiation process ended up more attracted to the group than women who were allowed to join in a more straightforward manner. Numerous other studies have shown that, when people are forced to endure substantial costs for something, they end up justifying their efforts by deciding the goal was worth it (Festinger, Riecken, and Schacter, 1956; Festinger, 1957; Bem, 1967, 1972). That norms and practices requiring sacrifice really do build commitment points out that the techniques groups use to enhance their cohesiveness are not always positive for the individual member. They can require suffering and conflict as well as offer rewards.

A member's effective commitment to the group can be enhanced by practices that increase the member's sense of fellowship and *communion* with one another and by norms that require *renunciation* (Kanter, 1972b). As groups develop their own culture, they often evolve practices and rituals designed to give the members a sense of togetherness. A family might make a point of spending at least one Sunday a month together on an outing—going to an amusement park or on a picnic. Religious groups get together and sing. Teenagers gather to listen to their favorite music and trade confidences. These are communion practices that increase a member's emotional bond with the group.

Renunciation norms ask members to give up some of their friendships with outsiders in order to concentrate their loyalties, emotional life, and need satisfactions within the group. In the extreme case, groups like religious cults or fanatical political groups may try to cut off all personal relations outside the group, either by withdrawing physically to an isolated place (as Peoples' Temple members moved to Jonestown, Guyana, see Box 4.1) or by adopting strict codes of nonconfidence in outsiders. However, even everyday groups like high school friendship cliques or romantic relationships usually ask their members to withdraw from competing relationships as a sign of loyalty and commitment.

The techniques of *transcendence* and *mortification* can be used to increase people's moral or normative commitment to a group (Kanter, 1972b). Groups offer their members transcendence by expressing their view of the world in terms of an ideology that links the members to forces or traditions greater than themselves. A political action group might express its views in terms of the "struggle for freedom by oppressed people everywhere." A hispanic gang might call itself the "Aztecs" to link its cult of toughness to the warrior cultures of ancient

Mexico. A taxpayer group might adopt the American Revolutionary slogan "Don't tread on me" to connect its concerns with the founding ideals of the country. The effect is to make the group seem more important and attractive to the members, to make them feel that, by belonging, they are linked with great forces in history.

Mortification is perhaps an overly dramatic name for the practice of criticizing those aspects of a member's behavior or beliefs that reflect standards other than those of the group. Mortification is one aspect of the process of maintaining group norms through the punishment of deviance. In a teenage group, for example, any member who violates the group standards of "coolness" is usually ridiculed. However, this process points out how groups increase their members' normative commitment to the group by inducing them to define their own self-value in terms of group norms. In groups like communes or fanatical political and religious cults requiring intense commitment from their members, the mortification process is often increased by formal sessions for self-criticism or the criticism of others. In Jonestown, for instance, members who were reported to have doubts about the cult were forced to make long confessions of their "sins" to the Reverend Jones. In the end, of course, Jonestown members were so committed to the group that they were induced to commit suicide at the request of their leader (Box 4.1).

Commitment-building techniques all serve to increase members' psychological involvement in the group, and this contributes substantially to its overall degree of cohesiveness. These techniques are important, not only for themselves, but also because they illustrate the subtlety of the process by which people's personal beliefs, needs, and sense of self become bound up with those of a group. However, specific norms and practices for building commitment are not the only way that members become more involved in a group. There are also a number of more general processes, which go on all the time in all groups, that are very important for cohesiveness. There are, for instance, the processes by which members come to like and enjoy each other's company, and factors such as the group's organization, leadership, and its relationship to the environment. It is to these more general sources of cohesiveness that we now turn.

INTERPERSONAL ATTRACTION.   Anything that increases group members' attraction to one another will increase the group's interpersonal integration, which of course is an aspect of cohesiveness. What makes group members like one another? A full consideration of all the factors affecting people's attraction to one another is naturally beyond the scope of this book. However, we can suggest some basic factors that

Box 4.1.   COMMITTED ENOUGH TO DIE: THE JONESTOWN
TRAGEDY

In 1978 a commune of 900 people committed suicide in the jungles of Guyana. At the command of their leader, the Rev. Jim Jones, they gathered around and drank a potion of Kool-Aid laced with cyanide. How could it happen? How could people be so committed to a group that they would kill themselves at their leader's request?

The answer is complicated. But one important factor was the set of commitment-building norms and practices Jim Jones instituted in the commune. At one time or another, the Jonestown commune used all six of Kanter's (1972b) techniques (investment, sacrifice, communion, renunciation, transcendence, and mortification) to make the members feel that their very selves were synonymous with the group and its leader. At the end, when the increasingly psychotic Jones told them they were about to be destroyed by their enemies and must all die together, most did so willingly.

The Jonestown communards were members of the People's Temple, a Marxist religious group originally dedicated to social justice, racial integration, and the ideals of love and equality among all people. The group was founded by Jones in San Francisco during the 1960s. However, increasing criticism from the U.S. press and his own growing paranoia led Jones to Guyana with a group of his followers to build Jonestown, a utopian commune in the jungle. Let's see how commitment-building techniques helped bring the Jonestown members to the point of dying at their leader's request.

In the People's Temple, members were encouraged to sell all their personal property and give the proceeds to the church. This, of course, is an investment technique for increasing commitment. One follower who later defected recalled how he gave the Temple his house, turned over to it his salary as district attorney, sold his sports car, and started buying his clothes at the Salvation Army (Winfrey, 1979). Having given everything to the Temple and gone off to the jungle, many Jonestown victims had nowhere to run and nothing to go back to when the suicide call went out.

During the actual suicide event, Jones cunningly forced a final investment to ensure that people would go through with their own deaths. He ordered the commune's "nurses" to begin squirting poison into the mouths of the group's babies. "After you watched your child die," said Paula Adams, who survived by being absent from the commune that Saturday, "you'd think, 'What's there to live for. I may as well die'" (Winfrey). When you have invested everything, even the lives of your children, you are too committed to turn back.

Box 4.1   *(continued)*

Moving to Guyana also meant renunciation of personal relationships outside the commune. Many followers left husbands and wives, children and parents, to go to Jonestown. Once there, they found themselves in the middle of the jungle, isolated from all other contacts. Jones dismissed all complaints about family separations. In a classic example of a renunciation norm, Jones insisted that personal alliances only diminished a person's concern for the group's true cause, the victims of social injustice (Winfrey). The only fellowship a dedicated member should need is that of his or her fellow believers.

The Jonestown group also used communion practices to increase commitment. Particularly in the early days, there was an enormous emphasis on warmth and love among the members. One survivor recalled that when she first visited the People's Temple, "a force of love just slapped you in the face" (Winfrey). Another remembers, "When you walked into the church, everybody greeted you with hugs. I had never experienced this kind of love before" (Winfrey). Although harsh circumstances and Jones's growing psychosis made the last months oppressive rather than loving, the group still engaged in ritual demonstrations of togetherness. In a horrible way, the final drinking together of poison was just such an act of communion.

Probably the most important commitment technique in the Jonestown commune was transcendence. "I went into this group to serve mankind by building a tightly knit utopian society which would be a model," said one man who later became disillusioned (Winfrey). Above all, Jim Jones promised his followers dedication to great ideals, to justice and equality for all, to an end to racial hatred. Even the idea of mass suicide was presented as a "revolutionary" act that would go down in history as the greatest testament against racism and oppression ever known (Winfrey).

To demonstrate their commitment to the cause, Jones asked his followers to abide by a number of sacrifice norms as well. They were not allowed to smoke or drink. They were forced to survive on a limited diet. On several occasions they were also asked to demonstrate their willingness to make the ultimate sacrifice. Jones held mock suicide calls where people were fed what they thought was poison. When they didn't die, Jones would tell them it had been a good lesson. After one, a survivor remembered that "We all felt strongly dedicated, proud of ourselves" (Winfrey).

Finally, to break through the members' last defenses and link their innermost feelings with the group, Jones used mortification techniques. One follower recalled that he told his people a perfect world would come about "only when people destroy their own egos from within and replace them with a collective ego" (Winfrey). To do this, Jones said he would have to play tricks on his followers, embarrassing

4.1   *(continued)*

and criticizing them. For instance, people's spouses might be asked to attack them in front of everyone. One man was asked to sign a document saying that Jones, and not he, was the real father of his child. All the members were asked to write long incriminating letters of "self-analysis." In doing so, they turned the keys to their self-worth over to the group and its leader.

Each of these techniques sucked the Jonestown members deeper into the group and pulled them further and further away from the outside world. In the end, everything they had was rooted in the group; they had almost nothing outside it. When forced by Jones to choose between dying with the group or being left without it, most chose to die. With the bulk of the members stepping up to die willingly, the hundred or so who were less enthusiastic were overwhelmed and forced to die as well.

influence a person's sense of compatability with his or her fellow group members. One of the most important of these is *similarity* among the members. There is substantial evidence that the more similar you think a person is to you, the more you will like them. Most of the research has focused on similarity of attitudes and opinions (e.g., Newcomb, 1961; Byrne, 1961); but there is also evidence that similarity of personality characteristics (e.g., Griffitt, 1966) and social economic background (Byrne, Clore, and Worchel, 1966) increases attraction between people (Huston and Levinger, 1978). If, for instance, you join a group and discover that most of the members come from a similar background to yours (they too grew up in the suburbs or had working-class parents, for example), you immediately feel more comfortable and find it easier to talk. If you also discover that they agree with you about many things and share your interests, you'll probably begin to feel that you might really become friends. Your attraction will only be increased if you find that they also share some of your personality characteristics, like being fun-loving, or introspective, or competitive.

However, when it comes to personality needs—for love, power, recognition, and so on—it is compatibility, not similarity, that counts (Shaw, 1981). For instance, two people who both have a need for dominance have incompatible needs. But when one has a need to nurture and the other has a need to be nurtured, their needs are compatible. What matters for attraction is that the needs of one person satisfy the needs of the other.

It is often argued that simple quantity of interaction is related to attraction as well (Homans, 1950). The basic idea is that the more time you happen to spend with another person, for whatever reason, the more you will like them (Festinger, Schacter, and Back, 1950). Results showing friendship to be related to *proximity* are often interpreted in this way. Certainly you are likely to choose your friends from those whom your environment places you in contact with on a regular basis. Proximity and interaction provide the opportunity to get to know another person, which may lead to attraction. On the other hand, it may give you the evidence you need to actively dislike the other person. So it seems that proximity and interaction only provide the opportunity to be attracted to someone, without determining that in the end you will like them.

GROUP STRUCTURE AND LEADERSHIP STYLE.   Our discussion of the structural-functional aspect of cohesiveness points out that the fit between the group's organizational structure and the task and socioemotional demands it faces will greatly affect the cohesiveness it achieves. If the organizational style of the group makes it inefficient in achieving its goals, the members will become frustrated and angry, tension will build and cohesiveness will decline. The organizational aspects we have in mind here are the group's status structure, communication network, and friendship patterns. From Shaw's (1964) work we might expect, for instance, that a committee with a highly centralized communication network would find complex decision making a frustrating, inefficient experience and suffer low cohesiveness as a result. Similarly, if a group's social structure makes it ineffective in handling interpersonal conflict or providing minimal satisfaction of its members' needs, such socioemotional difficulties are likely to eat away at the group. When we consider task and primary groups in more detail in Chapters 9 and 10, we will discuss which types of organization are better suited to particular goals.

It is also important for cohesiveness that members reach some consensus about what the group structure is. The first aspect of this consensus is a simple shared recognition of who has status, who doesn't, who is friends with whom, and so on. Most groups do not have to interact long before differences in status, friendship, and communication begin to emerge. It is usually only a little bit longer before the fact of those differences is recognized by almost all the members. Achieving a shared acceptance of the distribution of status is often more troublesome. Yet this is vital if a consensus is to develop about the group structure. Often members feel their position in the status hierarchy is unfairly low or that of someone else is too high. As Homans (1961) pointed out, members must feel the status system of the group is equitable if their commitment to the group is to be maintained. Status struggles are a recurring kind of conflict in small groups.

The extent to which a group's organization requires active participation from all members also affects cohesiveness (Couch and French, 1948; Cartwright and Zander, 1968). For instance, when a group divides up a task so that each member has to do a part, everybody gets involved in the group effort and, as a result, feels more a part of the group. The consequence is a greater sense of unity and cohesiveness. We can contrast this to a situation where, because of the group structure, a few people do all the work while the others are on the sidelines.

Lewin extends this argument to suggest that groups with democratic leaders who encourage member participation will be more cohesive than groups with authoritarian leaders (Lippitt and White, 1952). However, while this may be true of some situations, it is certainly not true of all. While authoritarian leaders do not encourage participation in decision making, they do, if they are a bit charismatic, encourage the members' *emotional* participation in the group. Since a sense of emotional involvement is every bit as important as decisional involvement, groups with charismatic authoritarian leaders can be very cohesive. An example might be a fanatical group of terrorists who accept the absolute dictates of their leader and function as a highly coherent unit.

One way to divide a task so that everybody must participate is to evolve a specialized division of labor (Durkheim, [1893] 1933). According to this system, members specialize in different aspects of the group's task, so that the group as a whole is dependent on each member to contribute his or her part to the task solution. Because specialization makes everybody dependent on everybody else, it can increase cohesiveness by increasing structural-functional integration. However, there are limits to this in small groups because specialization also increases members' social isolation from one another (Baker, 1981). If group members become so specialized that they never do the same things, they begin to lose touch with one another and an emotional distance grows up between them. Think of what happens when a husband and wife play such different roles in their relationship that, in the end, they hardly know each other. Although a specialized division of labor provides gains in cohesiveness through improved structural-functional integration, if it is taken too far, these are outweighed by losses due to declining interpersonal integration. We can say, then, that the extent to which a group's structure is adapted to its goals, the acceptance of that structure by the members, and the extent to which the structure successfully encourages member participation all affect the cohesiveness the group achieves.

TYPES OF INTERDEPENDENCE.   Competitors are as interdependent as cooperators, but there is a fundamental difference in the kind of relationship they achieve. When group members are united together to achieve some collective goal, they are cooperatively interdependent. The experience of relying on one another and working together as a team builds a sense of unity, increasing the group's cohesiveness (Deutsch, 1949). But if the group goes after a goal that only one or a few members will win, the members become competitors, stop trying to help each other along, and the coherence of the group declines. Imagine being a member of a basketball team and facing two very different situations. In one, you are working together to win a spot in the playoffs for the team. In the other, the team is playing before a judge who will pick one member for a best-player prize. Think how differently you would act toward your teammates in each. In actual groups, members often are aware of the divisive potential of competitive interdependence, and they may try to avoid adopting competitive group goals. But sometimes the outside environment forces such goals upon them. When three friends are unemployed, what happens when they all hear about a single job opening?

Actually, the pressure of the outside environment can work in the opposite way, forcing a cooperative goal on a group as well. One of the more interesting ways this occurs is when the group is attacked or threatened by the outside environment. The members rally together to defend the group (Janis, 1963). This is why competition between two groups can increase the group spirit and cohesiveness of each. Sherif and Sherif (1953) conducted an ingenious field experiment that demonstrates this effect. Two groups of twelve-year-olds at summer camp were allowed to develop without knowledge of each other. In each group, friendships formed and a status system evolved. Then the two groups were brought into competition with one another by means of a camp contest. During this competition, strong hostility developed between the groups, but, internally, solidarity increased. Participants tended to overestimate the performance of fellow group members in comparison with the competitors, and, in one group, a new leader was installed to make the group more effective. So the threat of outside competition not only increased feelings of unity, it encouraged changes in group structure to make them more successful in pursuit of their goals. Both factors improved the groups' overall cohesiveness.

There was an interesting final twist to this study. Not wanting to leave the two groups of campers in a state of hostility, Sherif and his colleagues staged a camp emergency, hoping it would unite the two warring factions under a single cooperative goal. They deliberately

damaged the camp's water supply, and the common problem of fixing a truck and getting it into town to get water forced the campers to work together in a cooperative fashion. In doing so, the campers overcame their hostilities and welded themselves into a single cohesive group.

RELATIONSHIP TO THE OUTSIDE ENVIRONMENT. We have just discussed one aspect of a group's relationship with its environment in terms of the competitive or cooperative goals the environment encourages. Now we turn to another aspect of this relationship that also has important effects on group cohesion. Outside environments allow small groups varying degrees of autonomy. When a group's social or physical environment puts a great many constraints on the behavior of group members, limiting their alternatives, the group has very little freedom of operation (Homans, 1950; Wilson, 1978). We have seen how the physical environment can prestructure a group's communication patterns, which affects in turn its status and friendship patterns. Even more important are constraints from the social environment. Work groups, like committees and decision-making groups, are likely to have certain rules laid down for them by the larger organization in which they operate. Neighbors, community, the economy, and larger society all put a number of constraints on the family, dictating many of the terms according to which a family must live.

If you think about it you will see that types of groups vary greatly in the extent to which group life is constrained and regulated by the outside environment. Total institutions such as prisons and mental hospitals control almost all aspects of their inmates' lives. On the other hand, informal friendship groups operate with few outside constraints. How will this affect the cohesiveness these groups achieve? Let's consider what happens when a group tries to form under conditions of minimal autonomy. If, for instance, patients in a mental hospital tried to form a group, they would find their opportunities to get together, and their activities while they were together, almost totally constrained by the environment. With so little freedom to maneuver, how likely is it that the members will be able to learn enough about and adjust sufficiently to each other to develop a workable group structure, and to establish and maintain norms for their behavior, even to evolve a real friendship network? Clearly, the less autonomy a group has, the harder it is to achieve real cohesiveness (Wilson, 1978). On the other hand, when a group has a great deal of autonomy, that alone does not guarantee cohesiveness. It is just that the more autonomy a group has, the greater the opportunity it has to achieve cohesiveness.

GROUP GOALS AND ACTIVITIES.   The last source of cohesiveness is very straightforward. Quite simply, the more attractive members find the group's goals and activities, the more they will commit themselves to the group, and the more cohesive it will be (Cartwright and Zander, 1968). You are obviously going to feel more involved in a group that pursues a goal you think is worthwhile, in that it satisfies your personal needs or matches your values. The group's basic activities also can have some intrinsic value to you in that you find them pleasurable or interesting, and this increases commitment.

A group's goals or activities can also seem attractive because of their prestige value or social importance. For instance, struggling with national problems may not seem inherently pleasurable, but the members of a president's cabinet are likely to feel very good about it because of the enormous prestige and social impact of what they do. The prestige of a group, then, is a factor that increases its possibilities for cohesiveness.

Clearly, the cohesiveness of a group is affected by a wide variety of factors. Since cohesiveness really reflects the extent to which group members come together and act as a unit, it is something that emerges from the way all aspects of the group fit together at a given time. In our less than comprehensive survey, we have seen that it is affected by commitment-building norms and practices, interpersonal attraction among the members, the fit between group structure and both group goals and the personal needs of members, the type of interdependence among the members, the group's relationship to its environment, and the attractiveness of its goals and activities. Because so many factors are involved, high cohesiveness is better thought of as a delicate changeable state than as an enduring stable characteristic of a group. While groups that remain together very long do not usually drop below a certain minimal level of cohesiveness, their overall cohesiveness will still vary considerably over time.

GROUP DEVELOPMENT

Group cohesiveness is a product that develops out of communication among the members. The fluctuating cohesiveness of the group, over time, in turn affects the process by which it pursues its goals. As the group members struggle to organize themselves in pursuit of their group goals, their attention and, therefore, the content of their communication progress from one aspect of the problem to another. When one aspect is resolved, the topic of group communication shifts to the next.

This is the process of *group development.* It represents the stages in the life-cycle of a group. The more cohesive a group is at any point in time, the greater its ability to resolve the problem of its current stage and go on to the next. Indeed, this is one of the major ways in which high cohesiveness aids goal attainment. So we see that, in the issue of group development, our concerns with both communication, now viewed in terms of content, and cohesiveness come together.

Although researchers have long had the sense that groups progress through a natural series of stages over their life-cycle, describing these stages has not been easy. The earliest attempt came from Bales (1950), working with decision-making groups in the laboratory, and people such as Bion (1961) and Bennis and Shepard (1956) who were working with therapy groups. Focusing on such different types of groups, they naturally developed rather different theories. We will come back to Bennis and Shepard's approach when we look more closely at primary groups in Chapter 10. Bales's model was so general that some attempts have been made to apply it to primary as well as task groups (Shaw, 1981). Bales delineated three stages:

1. *Orientation,* where group members collect information about the task and each other

2. *Evaluation,* the critical assessment of that information

3. *Control,* where members begin to regulate each other's behavior in order to take group action toward the goal

These stages contain some insights about group development, but they are so general as to be less informative than one would like.

The dramatically different types of goals adopted by task and primary groups posed serious problems for the creation of a group development theory appropriate to all small groups. The trick was to find a system by which the very different focal concerns of task and primary groups could be viewed as varieties of the same basic process. Then it might be discovered whether the order in which these types of concerns are dealt with follows any regular and usual sequence in both task and primary groups.

One of the first efforts of the sort came from Tuckman (1965). Based on a review of previous work drawn mostly from therapy groups, he proposed four stages of group development. He attempted to generalize his stages beyond the therapy context and argued that they could be applied to work groups as well. Stage 1 is *dependence and testing,* in which group members attempt to define the nature and boundaries of the "task" they face. (As Tuckman uses the word "task," it simply

means the goal the group sets for itself. Thus, the task can be a socioe-motional issue like self-development or having a good time, or a more classically work-oriented task like problem solving or decision making.) "Dependence" refers to the fact that, at this stage, each member tends to look to others to define the situation for him or her. In stage 2, the topic of communication switches from a definition of group goals to struggles between the members for the types of relationships they will have. Tuckman calls this stage *intragroup conflict*. Out of the resolution of this conflict comes the *development of group cohesion*, stage 3. Members accept the now-formed group structure. Communication focuses on the main-tenance of the newly achieved harmony and the avoidance of conflict between members. Finally, having developed a group structure and resolved emotional relations of the members, the group settles down to efficient work toward its goal. Members carry out their functional roles in the group structure with a minimum of conflict, allowing the group to devote its energies to the task. This last stage is called *functional role-relatedness.*

In addition to suggesting these stages, Tuckman (1965) argued that groups would vary in the speed with which they progressed through them. Groups such as committees that know they will meet for a short time only try to proceed rapidly to the fourth stage, spending minimum attention on the early stages. They may use aids to make this easier, such as external definitions of the problem they are working on. The more concrete the group's task, the more likely the group is to be successful at such a rapid progression. But if the problem is complex, the group may bog down and have difficulty achieving its goal because it did a poor job of defining and agreeing on its task in the first place, or perhaps because it never resolved the relationships among the group members. Longer-lived groups, and this includes most primary groups, can take more time and deal with these problems over weeks or months.

Tuckman's (1965) stage theory has been quite influential. However, Hare (1976) notes that since it was proposed a number of additional group development studies have been completed. Hare argues that when these are considered along with Tuckman's work and that which preceded him, a pattern of stages can be seen that is more truly general, in that it applies equally well to both task and primary groups. You will recall from the last chapter that Hare is one of the proponents of a functionalist approach to small groups. Not surprisingly, then, he sees group development in terms of the order in which the group takes up its functional problems.

Hare takes Parsons's four functional problems (discussed in Chap-ter 2)—pattern maintenance, adaptation, integration, and goal attain-

ment—and essentially argues that groups deal with them in just that order. First comes the initial *pattern maintenance* stage in which the group tries to decide what kind of group it is and what its goals are. The beginning of the development of a group identity, this stage has an obvious correspondence to Tuckman's stage 1. Once the group has some idea of its purpose, members make beginning efforts to deal with it. In the process, they develop and display to each other their varying skills in regard to the group goal. This is Hare's *adaptation* stage. In the next phase, the members restructure their relationships to one another to make better use of the varying skills they possess. In other words, they evolve a social structure by which they mean to pursue the group's goal. Hare calls this phase *integration*. Next comes *goal attainment*, where the members carry out their roles to achieve their task. This is obviously equivalent to Tuckman's last stage. Hare, however, adds a fifth stage, a return to pattern maintenance, when the group members redefine the group and their relationship to it as the group prepares to disband.

The advantage to Hare's approach is that his functional stages really are general enough to apply to both primary and task groups. And yet they retain enough specificity to be meaningful and informative. Their disadvantage is one which is often encountered in functionalist analyses. The approach appears to overemphasize the rationality of the process by which the social structure evolves, implying that this process will be freer from conflict and more likely to result in an efficient task structure than is often the case. The advantage of Tuckman's approach is that this conflict is made explicit. Overall, though, Tuckman's theory does seem better suited to primary groups than to work groups.

A more recent model of group development avoids this disadvantage of Tuckman's approach but preserves many of its insights. It essentially follows Tuckman's stages but labels them in a manner applicable to a wider range of groups. Caple (1978) suggests that groups begin with an *orientation* stage in which members try to find out who they all are and what they are trying to do together. At this stage the members do not coordinate their behavior with one another very well, and there is much tentativeness and mutual testing. The second stage is *intragroup conflict*, just as it is in Tuckman's model. The following stage of reconciliation and the development of consensus is called the *integration* stage. Next comes the *achievement* stage where the group finally gets down to productive work on its goals. Unlike Tuckman, Caple adds a fifth stage as well, called *order*, in which the members, now basically satisfied with the group, become interested in preserving it as it is rather than changing it.

Caple's approach represents something of a synthesis of the distinctive insights of both Tuckman and Hare. Overall, while there are differences in the approaches of all three, there is also a great deal of overlap. They all agree that groups begin with a stage of orientation and goal definition and do not begin to work efficiently and productively until much later, usually about stage 4. There is general agreement about what goes on in the middle period of a group as well. It is a time of testing among the members, out of which the social structure emerges. The major disagreement among these theories is in how this middle period should be divided into stages and what aspect of the process should be emphasized. For our purposes, we can set this disagreement aside and accept the basic outline of group development that they all share.

That shifts in the content of communication can be used to outline the stages in the life-cycle of a group brings home for us the centrality of the communication process in group life. Communication is the vehicle by which the group comes to life. Out of communication, the group's structure, culture, and cohesiveness are created. The network of communication among members forms the skeleton of the developing group structure, affecting and being affected by the status and friendship patterns that emerge. How well these products of communication function together in the group in turn determines the group's cohesiveness. As we have seen, cohesiveness has many consequences. One of these is the success the group will have in surmounting the challenge posed by each stage in its life-cycle. Since communication phenomena lie at the heart of group structure and processes, considering them has forced us to touch upon almost all aspects of group life.

SUMMARY

Through the process of communication, groups form, develop, and change. Through communication, group members simultaneously develop shared norms and behaviors and are alerted to one another's differences. Thus communication becomes the vehicle for the dual processes of standardization and differentiation in groups. As a result, the nature of the communication patterns in a group affect the type of social structure a group develops, its friendship patterns and cohesiveness, and the way the group changes over time.

Although theoretically every group member can talk equally to every other member, in practice this rarely happens. Instead a distinct communication network develops with more frequent and open communication between some members than others. When groups are free to form their own communication networks without interference from the outside environment, status is the critical determinant of who talks to whom. Differences in external status characteristics will structure even the initial moments of interaction. However, in these as well as peer groups, the shape of the network will depend on the internal status system that develops. In general, status differences produce an upwardly based network in which higher-status members both talk more and are talked to more than lower-status members.

When a group develops within a large formal organization or in a single physical location, its communication network is often prestructured by the environment. In that case, the group's status and friendship patterns usually develop around the skeleton provided by the rather inflexible communication pattern. To understand the way a communication pattern structured by the physical environment can affect the development of friendship and cohesiveness in a group, we examined in detail the Festinger et al. (1950) study of the Westgate and Westgate West housing complexes for married students at MIT. To see the effects of prestructured communication networks on status, we looked at the work of Bavelas (1950) and his colleagues. We found that the more centrally located a member is in a network, the more likely he or she is to emerge with high status. In addition the overall centralization of a group's network affects its efficiency at different types of tasks and the morale of the group members.

Of all the aspects of groups that arise from communication, cohesiveness is one of the most fundamental. Cohesiveness can be defined as the extent to which features of the group bind the members to it. We distinguished three components of cohesiveness. First, there is the bond among the members due to their personal attraction for one another, called interpersonal integration. In the past cohesiveness has often been measured solely in terms of this component, but we argued that it alone cannot explain the nature of small-group solidarity. Second, members can be united by the interlocking roles they play in the group's organizational structure. We called this structural-functional integration. Finally, members can be bound together by the shared norms and beliefs of the group, or normative integration.

Since a highly cohesive group is one that binds the members tightly together, it naturally is one that the members care about. Because they value the group, members put more energy into group activities. With greater effort coming in from each member, cohesive groups have more collective resources to apply toward group goals. Out of these observations come the major consequences of high or low cohesiveness. More cohesive groups have more positive communication among the members, are better able to maintain the loyalty and satisfaction of their members, have more power to influence their members' behavior and opinions, are better able to achieve their goals, and develop more elaborate group culture.

What makes groups cohesive in the first place? First of all, groups may knowingly or unknowingly adopt specific norms and practices designed to increase the members' commitment. These generally work by either focusing positive experiences for the members within the group or by requiring members to endure some hardship for the group. Cohesiveness is also increased by factors such as similarity and need compatibility, which encourage interpersonal attraction among the members. A social structure and leadership style that is adapted to group goals, is accepted by the members, and encourages member participation is another source of cohesiveness. Cooperative interdependence, whether brought on by a group goal or by a threat from the outside environment, increases cohesiveness as well. The outside environment can also affect a group's opportunity to become cohesive by influencing the degree of autonomy and freedom of action the members have. Finally, the prestige and attractiveness of a group's goals and activities affect its cohesiveness.

As group members struggle to organize themselves in pursuit of their group goals, their attention, and therefore the content of their communication, progress from one aspect of the group situation to another. This process of group development represents the stages in the life-cycle of a group. The more cohesive a group at any point in time, the greater its ability to resolve the problems of one stage and go to the next. Describing a sequence of stages that characterizes all kinds of groups is difficult. Several different models have been proposed, and there is no general agreement about which is the best. After reviewing some of the major models, we concluded that, despite differences, most agree on the following general sequence. Groups begin with an initial phase of goal definition and orientation, go into a period of conflict and structure building, followed by reconciliation and acceptance of the new structure, and only then move into a period of productive work toward group goals.

5

Conformity, Deviance, and Social Control

One of the most striking aspects of small groups is the apparent control they wield over their members' behavior. A brief look at an adolescent friendship group, whose members dress each morning in virtually identical ways, who use the same slang and have the same tastes, is enough to convince most people that small groups not only establish standards of behavior for their members, but actively induce conformity to them. And, for most of us, the personal experience of having belonged to a group is proof that the question of conforming to group standards or deviating from them is a central problem of group life. In this chapter, we will attempt to understand how and why conformity and deviance occur in groups.

American culture so prizes individualism that it is often difficult to use the word conformity without evoking images of mindless, sheeplike behavior. But the fact is, conformity to social norms makes social organization possible for small groups as well as society as a whole. If people did not agree to some basic rules of behavior, they could not coordinate their actions with others because no one would have any idea what anyone was going to do next. As a result, no collective goals could be achieved: no dams and highways built, no governments run, no personal relations established. Imagine what it would be like just to drive a car if most people refused to conform to basic highway norms such as driving on the right side of the road. Conformity, a necessary part of social life, is sometimes even an aspect of enlightened self-interest. In fact, most of us willingly conform to the rules of our social groups throughout most of our daily behavior.

Conforming most of the time does not mean conforming all the time, however. Because we all occasionally break the rules of our social groups, deviance is a persistent aspect of social organizations of all kinds, including small groups. Interestingly, "deviance" is not an entirely nice word in our culture either. It conjures up an image of aberrant, antisocial behavior, the behavior of an outcast. The fact that both conformity and deviance have negative connotations perhaps reflects a basic conflict in American culture. But it also highlights an even more basic conflict between the interest of the group and the interest of the individual. Actually, since groups are made up of individuals, this is better viewed as a conflict between that part of ourselves whose needs are met by the group and that part which wants to be independent. We will see this conflict underlying most of the processes of deviance and reaction to deviance in small groups.

In some ways, deviance is also a necessary part of social life. When a group member breaks a rule, he or she offers the group an alternative to the way things have always been done. This makes deviance a driving force for change in small groups. Since the ability to adapt to changing circumstances is a prerequisite for group survival, deviance can actually help the group in some situations. But group members are seldom aware of this aspect of deviance. In the eyes of most, deviance appears as an attack on the group and its beliefs. Of course, high levels of deviance can truly destroy a group. As a result, the most common reaction will be an effort to pressure the deviate to bring his or her behavior back in line with the group's norms. Efforts on the part of the group majority to reduce or eliminate deviance are what is called the *social control* process in small groups (Crosbie, 1975).

Our task in this chapter is to understand the processes of conformity, deviance, and social control in small groups. Conformity we take to be a member's willing or unwilling adherence to group norms. Deviance is behavior that violates or contradicts group norms. Social control, on the other hand, is the group's attempt to reduce or eliminate deviance once it occurs. The central concern of all these processes are the actual norms of the group. Therefore, we will begin by examining the nature of group norms, looking at how they are established and the role they play in group life. This will provide a standpoint from which to analyze differing types of conformity and deviance in small groups and their relationship to group development and change. Next, we will consider sources of conformity and deviance as well as their consequences for the attainment of status and influence in the group. We will then turn to group reactions to deviance in an effort to understand the social control process. Thus equipped with a working knowledge of conformity, deviance, and social control, we will analyze those aspects of group structure that increase or decrease pressures for conformity and deviance. Finally, we will address the implications of conformity processes in small groups, both for larger organizations and for the individual's adherence to the rules of society as a whole.

GROUP NORMS

One of the most fascinating aspects of people, when they come together in groups, is that after only a few minutes of interaction they settle on rules to coordinate and govern their behavior. The shared, agreed-upon rules of behavior that group members establish among themselves are what we call *norms*. Some are societal norms that members apply to their group. An example might be the use of the majority vote to decide issues. Others are idiosyncratic norms evolved by the group itself. Norms define the kind of behavior that is expected from a group member (Hare, 1976). They do this by specifying not only what members should do, but also what they should *not* do. For instance, in a group of friends, norms may require a willingness to listen to each other's problems but may also prohibit excessive demands for help and attention. So norms not only prescribe—they proscribe.

It is difficult to discuss norms without using words like "should" that carry a sense of moral judgment and obligation. Norms are for the most part derived from the goals the group values and wishes to attain. They define the kinds of behavior the group members think is necessary for or consistent with the realization of those goals (Hare, 1976). This gives norms an evaluative quality. Since the behavior specified by the norm has consequences for the achievement of the group's goals, that behavior takes on a sense of being either acceptable or unacceptable to the group. As a result, there is a moral sense of "should" attached to norms. This in turn gives rise to *sanctions*—that is, rewards and punishments—which are associated with conformity to, or deviance from, norms.

The evaluative quality of norms distinguishes them from mere behavioral regularities among group members. An outside observer might notice that the members of a committee all dress in more or less the same way. But, unless the committee members have a shared evaluative sense of the correctness of that dress style, or the inappropriateness of different styles, this would not be a social norm of the committee. Instead, the standardized dress style might be the result of chance factors, or of norms of a larger organization within which the committee operates. Norms, then, are not just observed, average behavior; they are specifications of preferred, expected behavior.

For norms to carry this evaluative quality, they must be recognized and acknowledged as legitimate by the majority, or at least a powerful minority, of group members. This is the sense in which norms are shared and agreed upon. Because of the informal quality to much of small-group life, many of a group's norms are not articulated in an explicit fashion. Indeed, group members might never devote any conscious thought to the informal norms of their small group. But they will demonstrate their implicit recognition and acceptance of these norms by using them as shared standards by which to judge each other's behavior.

Group norms generally address themselves to classes of behavior rather than specific actions. As Sherif and Sherif (1969) note, norms are "generalizations that epitomize events, behavior, objects, or persons in short-cut form." This gives norms a sort of ideal-typical quality. Interestingly enough, people usually build into norms a recognition of their quality as generalizations. Norms typically do not define a single ideal behavior as the only permissible one. Rather, they define a range or *latitude of behavior* that is considered acceptable or unacceptable (Sherif and Sherif, 1969). Providing for a latitude of behavior in response to norms allows the practical variation of people and circumstances to be taken into account.

The Formation of Norms

One of the best illustrations of the easy, almost unconscious way people in groups form norms comes from a classic experiment by Sherif (1936). Sherif took advantage of a well-known visual illusion called the *autokinetic effect*. When people view a stationary pinpoint of light in a completely darkened room, the light appears to move. Since the movement of the light is an illusion, any estimate a viewer might give of the distance it moved will be entirely a product of their personal or social standards of reference (within certain physical limits).

Sherif asked people to estimate how far the light moved under two different conditions. In one, subjects sat in a room with two or three others. They gave their estimates to the experimenter out loud, so that they could hear one another's responses. Although in the first round, individual estimates were rather different, they rapidly converged on a single group estimate. In other words, even in this minimal group situation, people were influenced by each other's choices and quickly evolved a shared, agreed-upon estimate of how far the light moved. In the course of a few minutes they had established a norm defining the group's beliefs about the light. Different groups agreed on different norms. For instance, one group adopted a 2-inch estimate; another said 4.5 inches. But in all groups the members' individual estimates merged together into a distinct consensus. After three sessions together as a group (members were exposed to the light 100 times in each session) the group members were split up and tested alone. Interestingly, they continued to use the norm that their group had established to guide their estimates even when alone.

Of course, the immediacy with which individuals merged their opinion with others in this experiment is partly due to the strangeness of the situation. The individual group members had no frame of reference to judge the illusory light, so, naturally, they turned to one another to establish one. In an example of the social comparison process, members checked the validity of their opinions by comparing them with those of their companions. When there was a discrepancy, they felt insecure about the accuracy of their own estimates, and so, compromised with those of their groupmates. This is the way groups form agreed-upon opinions, tastes, and judgments about themselves and their surrounding environment. Out of this process of norm formation through social comparison, groups develop a shared perspective on the world, a definition of their own reality.

However, you might ask how often people are in such an unfamiliar, ambiguous situation as the one in the Sherif experiment. Don't people usually bring with them well-formed personal opinions on most topics when they join a group? How easily are group norms formed when the members already have personal views on the matter?

That is the situation Sherif (1936) investigated in the second half of his experiment. This time, Sherif first tested his subjects alone. Over the course of several exposures to the light, he found that individuals developed a personal standard for themselves, a consistent estimate of the distance they thought the light moved. Sherif then put together people with widely divergent personal standards (for instance, less than 1 inch versus more than 7 inches) and tested them in a group setting. In the first group session estimates converged substantially toward one another. For instance, the person estimating more than 7 inches dropped to 4, while the person estimating 1 inch increased to 2. But it was only in the second or third group session that the individual estimates merged entirely into a clear group norm. The process of norm formation proceeded in the same way when people joined the group with their own personal norms as it had in the first phase of Sherif's experiment. Once again people changed their opinions when they found they were very discrepant with those of others. However, the process was slower since people had their own personal standards to overcome.

As we shall see, social comparison is not the only process by which groups form norms. But it is one of the most subtle and pervasive. It nicely illustrates how people need little more than to be in one another's presence before beginning to negotiate rules for dealing with one another and coordinating views on matters of mutual concern. That, of course, is why people form norms in the first place, to enable them to coordinate their behavior together. There are really two sides to this process. The first is achieving agreement on matters of joint concern and establishing norms to maintain that agreement. The uniformity achieved among the group members in this way makes it easier for them to deal with one another, to know what to expect from each other. This is what the social comparison process does.

The second side to the process is developing norms to regulate areas of actual or potential disagreement and conflict among the members (Thibaut and Kelley, 1959; Bonacich, 1972). When members have strongly held beliefs on matters of real concern to them, they may resist pressures to uniformity, despite the cost. Even more frequently, conflicts develop over the rewards and costs individual members expect to gain from the group's activities. For example, what if a couple disagrees on what they like to do on Saturday night. She likes to go to movies; he likes to meet friends at a bar or party. How do they resolve the conflict? They could spend every Saturday evening arguing over what to do. Occasionally, one might win, sometimes the other. But, say Thibaut and Kelley (1959), the costs of constantly bickering are likely to outweigh the pleasures of occasionally getting to do what you want. So group members in this situation usually develop a norm to regulate the conflict. For instance, our couple might decide to alternate between doing what she wants one Saturday and what he wants the next. The norm provides a rule by which the conflict can be resolved without continual argument among the members. In this sense the norm substitutes for the process of continually trying to influence the conflicting member (Thibaut and Kelley, 1959).

Group members generally recognize that serious conflicts of interest can destroy the group. When such conflicts break out, there is usually an effort by the group to formulate some rules to regulate the conflict. It is often pointed out that formal procedures in small groups, such as voting on group decisions, are usually a result of efforts to regulate conflict through norms. Of course, there is no guarantee that a group will be successful in this process, or that the conflicting members will stick to the compromise norms. But we can see that when the process of norm formation through mutual influence and voluntary agreement hits a stumbling block, the group will react by trying to establish compromise norms to substitute for the stalled influence process. Because of this, groups usually develop more detailed and elaborate norms in those areas of group life where there is real or potential conflict than in those areas where the members easily agree. Roommates, for instance, often disagree over matters of housekeeping and standards of cleanliness. To avoid recurring conflict, they frequently develop very specific systems for dividing up household tasks and rotating each member's responsibility for them. A maze of intricate norms can serve as a clue to an outsider trying to locate the tension spots in a group's existence.

Classes of Small-Group Norms

The process of norm formation leads us naturally to the question of the differing classes of norms small groups develop. As we have so often said, people generally come together in groups to pursue some goal or purpose. The early periods of interaction are usually spent developing some consensus on what these goals or purposes should be. Here, norm formation begins. Because the types of behavior consistent with achieving one set of goals can be different from those of another, the process of agreeing on the group's purposes is also the process of agreeing on certain ground rules, basic norms for behavior in the group. Norms are the means by which group goals are attained (Hare, 1976).

To successfully pursue a goal, groups must develop norms that adequately address two fundamental problems. As we pointed out in Chapter 1, first comes the task problem, the issue of dealing with the group's environment and organizing group resources toward the goal. In response to task issues, a group will form norms defining the group's perceived relationship with its environment, a method for dividing up work toward the goal, and usually a status or leadership system. Second, the group must develop norms for dealing with the socioemotional issues of the satisfaction of individual needs and the maintenance of smooth working relationships. The particular norms a given group develops to deal with its task and socioemotional problems will vary enormously. But since the type of goal the group chooses will affect the nature of its task and socioemotional problems, as a result this choice establishes a certain range into which the group's norms are likely to fall. It is through this process that primary groups, for instance, end up having considerable similarity in the general nature of their norms despite the fact that they are made up of very different people. The norms members evolve together create the group's structure and style of life. They form what is called the *normative order* of the group.

In the process of creating the group's normative order three different types of norms are formed: procedural, role, and cultural norms.

Procedural norms establish the basic ground rules for interaction among the members. Is the tone of interaction to be serious and work-oriented? Playful? Emotionally open? Cool and emotionally neutral? Will members speak freely, interrupting each other? Or will each person wait his or her turn? Will decisions be made by an informal consensus? By formal majority vote? By a group leader? Under what circumstances will the group get together, and how often will the group meet? These are all examples of the kinds of decisions groups make as they evolve their basic operating procedures. The type of choice a particular group makes will depend on its goals, the personalities of its members, and the task and socioemotional problems these give rise to.

Since procedural norms establish the basic framework for interaction in the group, they apply equally to all members. But groups adopt some norms that apply only to specific members. These *role* norms define the distinctive behavior the group expects from a particular member. For instance, one member might be expected to be the "idea person," another, to relieve tension by telling jokes and making wisecracks. One of the major sources of the role norms ascribed to a member is his or her niche in the status hierarchy. From the leader to the lowest-status member, each position in the status system carries a set of normatively expected behaviors. When an individual moves into a particular status niche, he or she is expected to take on the behaviors appropriate to it. Other determinants of members' role norms are their duties in the group's division of labor (this is usually closely linked to status position) and their position in the sociometric structure of the group.

Last, groups create *cultural* norms. These define the group's collective beliefs, attitudes, values, myths, rituals, and self-image. Together a group's cultural norms define its own unique perspective on reality. They specify the group's understanding of what it is, what its surrounding reality is like, and how it is located in that reality. Some of these norms are simply informational in character, representing the group's assessment of the facts describing itself or its environment. Others are emotionally laden group stands on issues of great concern to members. For instance, a family may prize its norms of self-reliance. "Nobody in our family needs to ask help from strangers, we take care of each other," is an example of a cultural norm.

Such beliefs and values qualify as group norms because individuals are expected to adhere to them if they wish to be fully accepted members of the group. Not all attitudes or beliefs group members happen to share will meet this criterion. We can imagine a group of friends who happen to agree on most political issues. But when the friends get together, they do not worry about politics. As a result, political beliefs do not become a defining aspect of membership in their group, and if someone with different beliefs joined it would not be a problem.

Cultural norms evolve more slowly than other classes of norms. The framework for procedural and role norms is usually in place after only a few brief periods of interaction. But a group's culture builds up bit by bit over a longer period of time. As a result, short-lived groups like some committees or work groups (and most laboratory study groups) manage to establish only a few cultural norms, ones which usually outline a few basic beliefs or assumptions about the group's situation. But a long-lived group, a family, for instance, will develop an intricate structure of cultural norms defining its beliefs and traditions. We will have more to say about cultural norms in Chapter 8.

Conformity, Deviance, and the Normative Order

The norms of a group together make up its normative order. As the framework of this normative order begins to emerge, emphasis in the group usually shifts from the formation of new norms to the maintenance of the existing ones. This shift signals the development of an equilibrium state in the group. Recall that our conception of equilibrium does not imply a cessation of change in the group's normative order, only a slowing of the pace of change. Also, it is good to remember that while most groups agree on the fundamentals of their normative order and, therefore, achieve an equilibrium, there is no guarantee that this will happen. Most of us have experienced groups bogged down from the beginning in a battle over the basics, groups in which no normative order ever clearly emerged.

With these caveats clearly in mind, let us turn our attention to the majority of groups that do develop a stable normative order. These are the groups that, after some initial ups and downs, shake down to a reasonably regular manner of operation. In such groups the processes of mutual influence by which norms were formed in the first place are redirected toward achieving conformity to those norms and controlling deviance from them. By pressuring one another to uphold the norms, members create and maintain the group's equilibrium. Without conformity and social control efforts, a relatively stable social structure and easy effective interaction would be unattainable in groups. An appropriate level of conformity and social control is necessary if group members are going to be able to relate successfully to one another and together take significant steps toward achieving the group goals. Conformity and social control, then, are the fundamental processes by which the group's social structure and culture are maintained—and its goals pursued.

Moderate levels of conformity, and therefore a stable social structure, are achieved in the face of persistent pressures for deviance, innovation, and change. In Chapter 2 we noted that all groups contend with two ever-present pressures for change: the group's changing outside environment, and the needs and interests of the individual group members. In addition, internal pressures to change may exist in the form of contradictory group norms or a clumsy, ineffective group structure. Such pressures encourage members to break with the norms, to do things differently, to deviate. If the deviation falls outside the latitude of acceptable behavior associated with the norm, efforts to bring a member back in line are likely. So a stable normative order is only maintained by a continual dynamic process of deviation and control.

The constant small—and occasionally large—deviations from the group's norms do not leave those norms unaffected. Because efforts toward social control are often only partially successful, and because deviance sometimes suggests preferable ways of doing things, the norms themselves are gradually altered. As a result, the normative order evolves and changes over time. The result is what we called in Chapter 2 a moving equilibrium. The stability achieved by conformity, then, is never complete. And indeed, the rate at which a group's norms and structure change can be seen as a result of the particular balance between effectiveness of conformity pressures in the group, and the strength of pressures for deviance.

It may have occurred to you that sometimes a group would be better off changing in response to deviance, rather than pressing for social control. This can be true, especially if a group's environment is changing rapidly, meaning it had better adapt or be destroyed. If a new boss joins an office with a whole new way of doing things, friends in the typing pool had better develop a strategy for dealing with him or her, even if it means changing some of their customary routines. Or if some members of a group are seriously unhappy with the way things are done, the group might be wise to try to make some changes. Forcing deviates back into the "mold" may cause enough tension to tear a group apart.

In theory, then, we can imagine an optimal level of pressures toward conformity and social control in a group. Pressures to conform would be strong enough to maintain a reasonably stable normative order that would allow the group to effectively pursue its goals. On the other hand, these social control efforts would not be so strong as to strangle all attempts at innovation in the group's norms. Without such innovation the group cannot change and adapt in response to significant new problems (Moscovici, 1976). As a theoretical concept, the notion of an optimal level of social control provides valuable insight into the dynamic relationship between the normative structure of a group on the one hand, and the processes of conformity and deviance on the other. But how likely is it that a real-life group will achieve this optimal level of social control? Perhaps not very.

The fact is that groups generally proceed on a trial-and-error basis in these matters. Some groups, through good fortune and the social skills of their members, do find, at least for a period of time, some middle level of social control that allows the group to carry on reasonably well. But other groups can and do overcontrol themselves. Imagine a political group that demands such rigid adherence to its ideological norms that virtually no dissent is tolerated. Feeling stifled, unable to respond to changing outside conditions, the members drop out one by one until the group is reduced to a tiny cell too small to have much political impact.

Groups can also err on the side of too little social control. It is common for groups to have so much trouble reaching consensus that group action becomes a tedious, frustrating, not very successful business. In effect, the lack of social control interferes with structural-functional integration, and thus cohesiveness. The members gradually get fed up with the delay, the disorganization, the ineffectualness of group activities, and begin to lose interest in the group. If something isn't done, the group will simply lose its membership and go out of existence.

The processes by which a group achieves conformity and reacts to deviance are the means by which the group's normative order is created, maintained, and changed. Through these processes the structure and culture of a group are both continually recreated and gradually changed in an ongoing dynamic. Thus the problems of conformity, deviance, and social control are at the very heart of group life. It is important, then, that we understand the causes and consequences of each. Let us begin by looking at sources of conformity in groups.

SOURCES OF CONFORMITY

Why do people conform? The answer lies in the fundamental processes that describe people's reliance on groups: information and effect dependence (Chapter 1). People rely on one another for basic knowledge about the reality with which they must contend. In addition, as social comparison theory points out, people rely on the agreement of others to establish the validity of beliefs not subject to direct objective tests. Views about most aspects of social reality are of this nature. We saw how social comparison leads people to establish group norms in the first place. Once the norms are formed, the same process induces members to conform to them. The fact that group members all agree on the standards and beliefs of the group seems like evidence for the validity of those beliefs. In the face of such evidence, the group member accepts the group standards as his or her own. As long as group members continue to conform to these shared standards they have the security of knowing that their view of reality is supported by the group. If they deviate from them, on the other hand, they are likely to feel out on a limb, prey to feelings of uncertainty and doubt about the validity of their unusual beliefs. If you doubt the power of this process, think about the rather startling beliefs maintained by flying-saucer cults, or messianic groups predicting the imminent end of the world. The members of these groups keep their beliefs despite the outside world because of the support and influence of their fellows.

When members conform on the basis of social comparison, they actually change their own beliefs and standards to those of the group. As a result, their conformity is not an unwilling, superficial compliance with the demands of others. Rather, the group norms are adopted as a matter of private belief as well as public behavior. Recall Sherif's experiment in which those who judged the light alone, after being taken out of the group, continued to abide by the group standard.

This kind of private as well as public change does not always characterize conformity based on effect, as opposed to information, dependence. People rely on others to obtain valued outcomes and, as a result, those others have some power to reward or punish them. People may go along with the group norms, then, to gain rewards from other members, or to avoid unpleasant costs. For instance, if the norm among your friends is to trade notes on your love lives, you may find yourself telling all despite your doubts because you want their approval and respect and don't want to be thought prudish.

Initially, rewards and costs are likely to produce only public compliance with the norms. But if the member continues to comply, he or she usually comes to accept the norm privately as well. Indeed, this is how new members learn most group norms. In the beginning, they do what is encouraged and avoid what is discouraged in the group. Over time, they come to understand and accept the norms that explain those rewards and costs.

Of course there are many kinds of rewards that group members can mete out to one another. But, for the inducement of conformity, perhaps the most important rewards are acceptance and social approval. In order to be accepted and approved of, the group member tries to be like other group members, to do what they do or they expect to be done. Nowhere is this clearer than with teenagers. As insecure adolescents, they copy each other assiduously in the way they dress, talk, and act, all in an effort to win approval and avoid ridicule. In exchange theory terms, they trade conformity for social approval from their groupmates.

The power of such inducements is dramatically demonstrated in a classic series of experiments by Solomon Asch (1955). Asch presented groups of people with a clear-cut judgment task. The subjects were shown two cards. One had a single black line on it, the standard line. The other had three lines on it. One was the same length as the standard line, the other two were of differing lengths. The task was to pick which of the three was the same as the standard line. When tested on their own, people gave fewer than 1-percent incorrect answers to this task. Asch was interested in whether a group could induce people to give an incorrect answer even in such an obvious and clear-cut situation.

To explore this question, Asch had his subjects, who were all male college students, give their judgments in the presence of seven to nine of their peers. But unbeknownst to the single naive subject in each group, all the other group members were in collusion with the experimenter. As the confederates were asked one by one to give their judgment, they systematically gave the wrong answer. It was arranged that the naive subject would always give his answer last or next to last. Imagine his confusion as he confronts an apparently black-and-white task and then hears his peers say one by one that black *is* white. He is in a situation of absolute conflict: should he abide by what he himself knows to be true, or go along with the group? What happened? Most of the time the naive subjects did stand by what they knew was true. But a full 37 percent violated the evidence of their own senses to agree with the group.

These results are particularly impressive when we realize the minimal nature of Asch's groups. They simply sat near one another and publicly announced their choices. Because the group members did not talk to one another, the majority could not engage in any direct efforts at persuasion or explicitly suggest to the subject that his behavior carried rewards or costs. Yet the subjects still felt the pressure of the majority's presence. They did not wish to stand alone, to appear different—and perhaps wrong and inferior—in the eyes of the majority. Implicitly, the majority could punish, or so it seemed to the subject, simply by judging him in their own minds. If the pressures to conform are substantial in such a minimal situation, imagine what they are in a well-established group.

In most real situations, the conformity pressures on a group member are not limited to either social comparison or rewards and costs. Usually both are present and are tightly intertwined. Actually, we can see some of both pressures acting in the Asch experiment. While the subjects felt an implicit ostracism to be associated with dissent from the majority, they also felt insecurity about the accuracy of their own judgment, despite the clarity of the task. The two forces together were often pursuasive.

Social comparison and reward/cost factors are sources of conformity that arise from direct group influence on a member. But another, less situational source of conformity exists that is often just as important in actual small groups, particularly those which persist over a reasonable length of time. Sometimes group members abide by a norm because they have internalized it as a personal standard of behavior (Crosbie, 1975). A college student, for instance, might defend her crowd's political beliefs, not just because they are the group standard, but because she has come to really believe in them herself—that is, she has absorbed them and now uses them to govern her own behavior. In this situation, members conform to group norms even when there are no apparent social comparison or reward/cost pressures on them. It is clearly an advantage for a group when its members have internalized its most important norms. In that situation, the members join with the rest of the group in policing their own behavior.

Members internalize those norms they have learned thoroughly and by which they have abided for some time. However, there is another reason why a member might internalize a norm: because it agrees with his or her own personal values and standards (Kelman, 1958). Again, this can be an important factor in actual small groups since people tend to join groups that do express their own personal values.

Clearly, groups wield powerful tools to induce their members' conformity to group norms. People conform to group expectations in order to be assured of the validity of their views, to gain social acceptance and approval, to avoid rejection, and to abide by personal standards when group norms have been internalized. Given these powerful sources, what are the countervailing pressures to deviate from the group norms? That is the question we turn to now.

SOURCES OF DEVIANCE

Deviance usually arises from two general sources: the members' knowledge of the norms, and their assessment of how the norm or its consequences affects them personally. Let us begin our discussion with the first, and less complex, source of deviance.

It goes without saying that conformity to a norm is impossible if you do not know what the norm is. Most norms in small groups are informal rules that are never explicitly stated or explained. To make things worse, these norms evolve and change over time. So a misunderstanding of what is expected of you is a real possibility in most small groups. As a result, you may inadvertently violate a group norm and only be aware of it when you see the group's reaction.

Well-established members are unlikely to make errors in regard to the group's more important norms, although they may occasionally slip up on a peripheral one. New members, on the other hand, must be *socialized* into the group before substantial conformity can be expected of them. They have to be taught the norms. A few of these, particularly if they deal with the core values of the group, may be explicitly related to the member. But most will have to be learned simply by observing the behavior of other group members. Some will only become clear through trial and error, by bumping into the reward structure of the group.

One's assessment of the personal consequences of a norm, the second source of deviance, can lead to deviance in several circumstances. One of the most important occurs when a group norm conflicts with the norms of a member's other reference groups. (Reference groups are groups whose norms and values people use as standards by which to judge their own behavior.) Most people belong to extensive networks of small groups, and more than one becomes an important determinant of their behavior. When a group norm conflicts with a central norm of an important reference group, a member may find that he or she simply cannot abide by it (Goode, 1960). For instance, a member of a teenage gang may back out of some particularly violent gang action because of competing pressure from his or her family. This point emphasizes again that groups exist in a larger social environment, with which they must deal. Groups must take into account the other competing memberships their members have. The norms that groups evolve cannot fly in the face of these other memberships if they are to be supported and maintained by the members.

In assessing the consequences of a norm, a member may also conclude that there will be more rewards and fewer costs associated with deviance than conformity (Homans, 1974). For instance, if a group member has taken a public stand on an issue and it now conflicts with the group norm, he or she may feel that, in backing down, the loss of face will be too great. There are personal costs to conformity. It is uncomfortable to feel you are acting inconsistently just for the sake of the group. And publicly yielding to pressure may make you feel weak and humiliated. In some situations, these costs might seem greater than those associated with deviance (Gerard, 1964; Crosbie, 1975).

A member may also see more long-range gains to be had from deviance, over conformity, in some situations. For instance, at times (which we will discuss later) nonconformity can be an aid to influence in the group. Also, deviance attracts attention, and sometimes the added attention from the other members may make the costs of the deviance worthwhile. Finally, because of inconsistent or conflicting norms, the group's reward structure may inadvertently encourage deviance in some cases.

A final and very important source of deviance is a member's desire to actually change a group norm (Moscovici, 1976). There are several reasons why this might occur. A member may feel that a norm does not allow sufficient satisfaction of his or her own needs and desires. Similarly, members may feel a norm unfairly rewards some members over others and thus is inequitable (Homans, 1974). Or a member may simply think a norm is ineffective for the group. It may seem to reflect an incorrect assessment of social reality. Or the member may think the norm impedes the group's attempts to achieve its goals. In each of these situations, a member violates the offending norm in an effort to convince the group to change it. Moscovici (1976) points out that this is a common occurrence in groups, and a major source of innovation in group life.

Clearly, the greatest cause of deviance is in the conflict between the interests of the group as a whole and the interests and desires of the individual member. But it is important to remember that some of the sources of this conflict lie in the structure of the group itself. For instance, the extent to which group norms are perceived to be just, and the status structure, to match the desires and skills of the members, will affect the overall levels of deviance. Although it is individual members who ultimately choose to deviate from the norms, the structure of the group may create some of the inducements to do so.

CONFORMITY, DEVIANCE, AND STATUS

Having considered why members conform or deviate, it seems reasonable to ask what the consequences of this behavior will be for their position in the group. Researchers have approached this issue by examining the impact of a member's conformity and deviance on his or her influence and status within the group. Questions have also been asked about the impact of one's status position in the group on the amount of conformity expected of him or her. Are high-status members expected to conform more or less than low-status members? These two sets of questions really address different points in the status process. The first looks at the effect of deviance on the initial attainment of status. The second asks whether status, once attained, influences the degree of conformity expected. We will explore both questions in turn.

Deviance and Status Attainment

A number of theorists have argued that to achieve high status, members must first spend time conforming to the group norms (Hollander, 1958; Homans, 1961; Kimberly, 1967). Thus, by conforming, a group member convinces the others that he or she is trustworthy and concerned about the group. Only when the group members have been assured that a member is group oriented rather than simply self-interested will they allow him or her high status and substantial influence in the group.

Certainly, it does seem reasonable to assume that group members will be more willing to allow someone influence over them if the individual in question can be trusted to be group oriented. Yet efforts to test the suggested relationship between conformity and status attainment have produced equivocal results (Hollander, 1960; Wahrman and Pugh, 1972, 1974; Ridgeway and Jacobson, 1977). Two of these studies even found a *negative* relationship between conforming to group norms and attaining status. How can we explain this?

The problem does not lie with the basic assumption that groups prefer to give high status to group-oriented members (Ridgeway, 1982). Rather, the difficulty appears to be that conformity to group norms in and of itself does not clearly communicate a member's group-oriented intentions (Ridgeway, 1978, 1981a). When people conform to group norms they are doing what they have been informally required to do by the rest of the group. When people do something they are required to do, the motivation behind their actions is inherently unclear (Kelley and Michela, 1980; Jones, Davis, and Gergen, 1961). Is their conformity motivated by a genuine desire to be cooperative and help out the group? Or are they perhaps being very self-interested, just doing what is easiest, what is expected of them, to avoid a hassle? You can't tell from the conforming behavior alone. So conformity by itself is not likely to convince the rest of the group of your group-oriented intentions, and, as a result, it does not seem to be an aid in achieving high status.

People do make judgments about how group-oriented a fellow member is, but they do so on the basis of evidence other than simple conformity. They rely on such characteristics as the attitude portrayed by the person's nonverbal behavior, the explicit remarks by the person, and so on. Since behavior like this does seem to communicate group orientation, it can increase a member's chances of attaining high status.

We know that deviance itself can sometimes serve important ends for a group. But can breaking with group norms help a person actually achieve high group status? The answer is complicated because it appears that nonconformity does several things at once. Unlike conformity, deviance usually is seen as a reliable indication of a member's true intentions. When you violate a group norm, you are going against what is expected of you. Therefore, you must be doing so because you really want to (Jones and Davis, 1965; Kelley, 1973). One can imagine circumstances when a person's nonconformity might indicate to one's groupmates the person's desire to help the group. But most of the time, group members would prefer that all members conform to the norms. Under most circumstances, then, deviance will seem to the group to be a self-oriented, uncooperative act. On this basis, deviance would seem to reduce a person's chances of achieving high status.

But there are other ways in which deviance can actually help in gaining status, at least under some circumstances. The fact is, nonconformity attracts attention, and the added attention can affect the way the group assesses a member's contribution to the group activities (Ridgeway, 1981a). As we shall see in the next chapter, one of the major determinants of status is the group's assessment of the quality of an individual's actual or potential contributions to the group's focal activities. So if members feel that they have high-quality contributions to make, salting their behavior with a little nonconformity may increase the rest of the group's awareness of those contributions. If the group does decide those contributions are good, the member's status in the group will increase.

Of course, the added attention brought by deviance could simply highlight the incompetence of a member's efforts in the group's activities. But deviance has another effect that reduces this likelihood. Moscovici (1976) has pointed out that nonconformity, especially in opinions and judgments, gives the appearance of bold self-assurance. When a person's efforts at the group activities are presented with such confidence, the group often assumes those efforts must be of high quality. So a moderate amount of deviance can make a member seem competent, at least as long as there isn't objective evidence to the contrary. This apparent competence is likely to increase the person's status.

Is there some way we can put these complex effects of conformity and deviance together and summarize their overall impact on status? First of all, it appears that conformity by itself does not help a person gain high status in a group. Nonconformity, on the other hand, can be an asset in achieving status both because it attracts attention and because it is self-assertive, which can enhance apparent competence when it accompanies a person's contribution to group activities. However, nonconformity has liabilities as well, since it appears self-interested. Putting these together, it would seem that a moderate level of nonconformity would be most effective for achieving status if the person has something significant to contribute to the group's activities. However, if a person clearly hasn't much to offer the group, nonconformity is likely to detract from status.

The effects of conformity and deviance are so complex because they affect the status process indirectly. Nonconformity offers the rest of the group clues as to a person's group-oriented or self-interested motivation in the group. Also, by attracting attention and appearing self-assured, a person influences the group's judgment about his or her contributions to group activities. The group's assessments of a member's motivation and contributions in turn directly affect the status he or she is allowed. The reason for conformity's limited impact is that it does not give clear cues to these status factors.

Conformity and Established Status

What happens once the group's status structure emerges? Do established high-status members conform more or less than medium-or low-status members? To answer this question, we need to consider the role norms which specify what is expected from a high-status member. The high-status people in a group are expected to uphold the group's basic values. They are also supposed to help the group solve its problems. These observations suggest two points about a high-status member's conformity. First, they are likely to conform closely to the group's most *important* norms, those that enact the group's primary values (Homans,

1974). These norms will be mostly cultural and occasionally procedural norms, but will also include the role norms defining the position of high-status members. Most groups consider it very important that their high-status members do what is expected of them.

That leads us to our second point. Under some circumstances, notably when the group has a problem to solve, high-status members are *expected* to *innovate* (Hollander, 1964; Homans, 1974). That is, they are expected in this specialized way to break the norms, to suggest to the group new beliefs or ways of doing things. Festinger's (1956) account of a religious cult that predicted the imminent end of the world offers a dramatic example of this. In anticipation of the end, the faithful sold their houses and quit their jobs. At the appointed date they gathered together to await the stroke of midnight. The hour came, but the world did not end. The group was in crisis. What did it do? It looked to its leader and prophet, a woman, to save it. At four A.M. she announced she had had a vision from God. She declared that, because of the group's great faith, God had decided to spare the whole world. In one stroke, she replaced the group's old beliefs with new ones and restored the group's faith in itself. For high-status members, then, conformity to their role norms requires occasional deviance from procedural and cultural norms. In fact, if a high-status member fails to come up with this innovative deviance when the group needs it, he or she will appear incompetent in the eyes of the group and be likely to lose status.

But what about non-innovative deviance, for instance, arriving at group meetings late? What is the group's reaction to such behavior from a high-status member? Hollander (1958) suggested that the essence of status in a small group is a particular degree of trust, esteem, and indebtedness on the part of the group toward a specific member. In reflection of its indebtedness, the group grants the member a certain amount of *idiosyncracy credits.* These credits reflect the group's willingness to tolerate a certain degree of idiosyncratic norm-breaking from the member. Since high-status members have acquired the largest supply of idiosyncracy credits, they are able to deviate more often from unimportant norms without censure than are medium- or low-status members. In other words, the group will tolerate behavior, such as being late to meetings, from high-status members that it would punish in other members. However, even high-status members have only so many idiosyncracy credits. If they push the group too far, breaking norms right and left, the group's patience will wear out and they may lose their high-status position as a result.

In contrast to high-status members, medium-status people conform fairly closely to all group norms (Harvey and Consalvi, 1960; Dittes and

Kelley, 1956; Kelley and Shapiro, 1954; Blau, 1960). They have fewer idiosyncracy credits, so deviance is less tolerated from them. Moreover, the norms describing their role in the group do not require or expect innovative deviance. Finally, they have enough standing in the group to care about it, to be motivated to preserve it by upholding its norms. These factors together make medium-status people perhaps the greatest conformers in the group. They are the ones whose behavior is largely responsible for the maintenance of all the group's norms rather than just its most important ones.

Low-status members have even fewer idiosyncracy credits than medium-status members, but they also have fewer reasons to be committed to the group. Because the group gives them fewer rewards than other members, they may become motivationally withdrawn from the group. As a result, they may not try to stick closely to the norms. Their low status may also be due to their relatively low ability at the group's focal activities. This lack of ability may in turn make it difficult for the member to do a very good job at norms related to these focal activities. For instance, in a group where fast talk and wisecracks are prized, a relatively inarticulate member will have genuine difficulty keeping up some of the norms. The result of these factors is that low-status members generally have fairly high levels of deviance (Crosbie, 1975).

We see, then, that the relationship between established status and conformity is curvilinear. For very different reasons, both high-status and low-status members show lower rates of conformity, while conformity among medium-status members is usually high. High-status members conform closely to the group's most important norms, but on those less important they have considerable latitude for deviance. In addition, certain amounts of innovative deviance are actually required of them.

SOCIAL CONTROL

Now that we have looked fairly carefully at the processes of conformity and deviance, let us turn our attention to the problem of social control. How does a group attempt to control deviance when it occurs? Since the social control processes are basically the conformity and deviance processes viewed from the perspective of the group rather than the individual, we should expect to see the same factors operating, namely social comparison and rewards and punishments. But, from the vantage point of social control, some interesting group processes set in motion by these factors become visible.

Persuasion, Rewards, and Norm Change

Let's start by looking at the social control process in action. In a classic experiment, Schacter (1951) measured how a discussion group reacted to a member who agreed with the majority from the beginning (the mode), to someone who disagreed in the beginning but changed to agreement with the majority (the slider), and to someone who persistently disagreed with the majority (the deviate). One of Schacter's most important findings was that the group initially directed most of its communication toward the deviate and the slider in an effort to persuade them to change their minds. As the slider began to "see the light," the pressure eased off him but kept up against the deviate. But when it eventually appeared that the group could not sway the deviate, they began to stop talking to him. At the end he was rated as the least-liked person, the sociometric reject. The slider, on the other hand, who had allowed himself to be persuaded, was rather well-liked, although the favorite was the mode.

What we see here are two different types of social control efforts: first persuasion, and second, when that does not work, the punishment of rejection. Persuasion (influence-oriented communication) as a means of social control arises out of the social comparison process (Festinger and Thibaut, 1951). Considering why this occurs offers an interesting insight into the peculiar power of the deviate in a group. For instance, why didn't the group in the Schacter experiment just threaten the deviate—"conform or we will reject you"—and if he refused, ignore him right from the beginning? The fact is that the group members needed the deviate to agree with them in order to feel confident of their own opinions. As long as he insisted on another point of view, it undermined the majority's confidence in the validity of their own opinions.

Disliking and refusing to talk to the deviate did not solve this basic problem. So naturally the group turned to this punishment as a last resort. This illustrates the potential limits on the effectiveness of rewards and punishments as a social control mechanism. If the deviate refuses the enticements and threats, the process escalates to the point where the group has no choice but to play its trump card and reject the member. But once the group ceases to deal with the deviate, it loses all power over him or her. Then the deviate can go on to violate the norms, if not in the center of the group (in a way, the rejected deviate is no longer a full member of the group), at least in its vicinity. Thus the deviate remains a thorn in the side of the group.

Of course most of us do not, most of the time, find it very easy to resist rewards and punishments directed toward us. Indeed, in the Schacter experiment, it is likely that in addition to receiving efforts at persuasion, the deviate received low-level punishments as well, for example, frowns, disapproving looks, sarcastic remarks. Most of us want to be accepted and approved by other people. It is hard to knowingly let yourself be disliked. Much of the time we react to disapproval by changing our behavior, allowing ourselves to be persuaded.

Rewards, punishments, and persuasion, then, often are effective means of social control (see Box 5.1). But as our consideration of the Schacter experiment shows us, they have their limits. What happens when the deviate remains adamant? Emerson (1954) replicated Schacter's experiment and got much the same results, except that he noted that the majority had actually moved its position somewhat toward that of the deviate. In other words, the deviate actually influenced the majority. This points out to us a third social control reaction possible from the group. The group can in fact *change the norm* to match the deviate's behavior or opinions, thereby resolving the conflict between the two (Moscovici, 1976). In effect, the group is "normalizing" the deviate's behavior.

When does the group react to deviance by changing the norm? Moscovici (1976) has done a number of experiments that suggest the key lies in the deviate's *behavioral style*. When a deviate adopts a particular stance, retains it consistently, and presents and defends that stance with confidence, logic, and coherence, the majority will be influenced (Moscovici and Faucheux, 1972; Moscovici and Nemeth, 1974; Nemeth and Wachtler, 1974; Levine, 1980). With such confidence and consistency, the deviate appears surer of the validity of his or her stance than the majority feels about its own. Beginning to doubt itself, the majority slowly changes its own view to something closer to that of the deviate.

Of course, the deviate must maintain this confident, consistent behavioral style in the face of what may be a barrage of persuasive efforts and disapproval from other group members. That isn't easy. Moscovici (1976) points out that such determined deviates are almost always disliked by the group to some degree, even when they are influential. However, they often also enjoy some admiration for their independence. As Moscovici notes, this reflects the ambivalence of groups toward their persuasive deviates. They are difficult; they cause trouble; and yet, they are a needed source of new ideas that may ultimately benefit the group.

On the other hand, the group is not at all ambivalent about a deviate whose behavior is inconsistent and unassured. They simply dislike such a person (Moscovici, 1976). Furthermore, the group feels

Box 5.1.   NORMS AND SOCIAL CONTROL IN AN AEROBIC DANCE CLASS

In gyms and recreation halls around the country a new sort of group is springing up—the aerobic dance class. A sociologist might find such a class a rewarding setting for some informal "participant observation" (wherein the observer joins and participates in a group but does not influence activities).

From the first day of such a class, many familiar dynamics of small-group behavior will be in evidence. On arriving the observer is likely to find a cheery, enthusiastic instructor who tells the class that not only will they become fit and beautiful, but that they are also going to have a *wonderful* time doing the dances. A certain theme to the teacher's efforts to inculcate norms and get the group to maintain them emerges. Group members pay a fee (the group "cost") for the aerobic dance class. To ensure that members continue attending, the teacher has to make sure each works hard enough to see results (slimming down, new agility, improved overall vigor—the "rewards"), but simultaneously the instructor has to induce each member into thinking he or she likes the experience (the "motivation"). Thus the stage is set for social control, based mostly on persuasion (charts and figures showing heart rates and statistics), with big doses of promised rewards ("Tired? Think how skinny you're getting!"), occasional resorts to jocular ridicule and punishment ("Give Mary a hand everyone, she made more mistakes than anyone"), and constant reminders of how pleasurable the group task is ("Isn't it *fun* to *boogie!*").

Besides these direct messages from the instructor—communicating the social norms of the class—the group has norm expectations of its own, some of which are more quickly discernible than others. As a beginner the participant-observer might not want to appear foolish by asking obvious questions, so, like any newcomer to a group, he or she is likely to resort to some informal social comparison. If the new member is late and the class is already busily performing routines, this will underscore one group rule: classes start strictly on time. Second, one's outfit should probably reflect the norm: if all the veterans wear leotards and tights, shorts and a tee shirt would be out of place. There will also be negative clues on what apparel is even less acceptable, especially if several newcomers should wear jeans or neglect to bring sneakers. Although no verbal messages are necessarily given, the newcomers are likely to quickly conform to the group's dress norms.

Over time other signals may emerge on the group's expectations of its participants. Beyond merely being on time, there will be still more procedural norms to be learned. Getting a drink will be allowed between dance routines but not during them. There should be no talking during routines either, other than to ask the instruc-

Box 5.1   *(continued)*

tor a question. And sit-ups are *always* done with knees bent.

Also to be grasped is an extensive set of cultural norms. The class includes "calls" that signal the different dance calisthenics. Students are expected to learn how and when to take their own pulse. (Soon even the greenest newcomer is likely to be chatting jargon like a veteran on technical subjects such as "target" and "maximum" heart rates.)

At the end of the class our participant might observe how he or she and other newcomers have been completely brought into the group. Each has acquired a niche in the status system, and the group as a whole has developed specific role norms outlining expected behavior in general. A woman marathon runner, for example, with a large wardrobe of chic exercise outfits, would probably move to the top of the status hierarchy. She might stand in the first row and trade jokes with the instructor. Everyone would expect her to perform better than the rest, and she probably would! However, if she ever failed to look like a Rockette at Radio City Music Hall, the instructor would probably scold or tease her relentlessly. There are costs as well as rewards associated with high status in the group.

The middle-status group members might be old-timers who have mastered the routines but who, for one reason or another, do not shine. Nevertheless, they would probably be expected to keep up a certain standard. For example, if a dancer from the middle ranks were to fall back in pace with a beginner so they could talk, the instructor might shout, "Margaret, that's too slow for you—speed up." Margaret has, in fact, broken two norms. One, talking during routines—a universal procedural norm—applies to everyone in the group. The other, slowing below her expected pace, applies only to people in her status level.

The participant whose enthusiasm is less than perfect and whose agility is not the best, can expect to end up in the bottom category of group status. As in all small groups, however, low status has its advantages. Poor performers benefit from the group's good humor, for one. Although low-status members might tend to group in the back where their botched steps would not be so obvious, other dancers would notice. However, better dancers are not likely to snicker. In fact, the group's expectations of the bottom level would probably be low enough that they might often win approving looks for achieving mediocrity, rewards the high-status participants would never gain so easily.

In any group, the dynamics of social control, the pressures toward conformity and against deviance, the powers of status and reward, are all likely to be visible—even in an aerobic dance class. And, in the end, the dynamics will have worked. Although the participant may never perform beyond the group's expectations, he or she might slim down and sufficiently internalize the group's norms to think the aerobics class was actually fun.

little pressure to normalize such a deviant's behavior because it does not threaten the majority's security in its own stand. Therefore, if persuasion and lower levels of rewards and punishments fail to have their effect, the group can comfortably reject the inconsistent deviate by excluding him or her from the group.

Variations in Group Reactions to Deviance

The strength of a group's reaction to deviance depends on several factors: what norm is violated, the extremity of the deviance, and the status of the deviate. It makes sense that group members will get more upset when the violated norm is central to the group's basic values or activities. We all know from personal experience that in every group there are some things you simply do not do without causing a severe reaction from the others, while there are other infractions that are considered more minor. Friends, for instance, will tolerate a lot from one another, but not attempts to seduce away their lovers. That violates the core norms of mutual support and loyalty in friendship.

There is experimental evidence to support everyday experience in this area. In Schacter's (1951) study, he varied the relevance of group discussions to the organizational purposes of the group (these groups were clubs formed around interest areas). When the topic was highly relevant to the group's central interest, the deviate's refusal to conform to the majority opinion constituted a violation of an important group norm. Therefore, we would expect that the deviate would be more strongly rejected in those groups than in groups where the discussion topic was of little relevance to group interests. That is exactly what Schacter found. Since then, additional studies have also found that the severity of the group's reaction is greater when the norm that is violated is important to the group's central values and activities (Mudd, 1968).

There is also evidence that the group's reaction depends on the extremity of the deviance. Recall that a norm defines a range of acceptable behavior. The further outside that range a behavior falls, the more deviant it will seem to the group, and the stronger will be their reaction to control it (Gerard, 1953; Mudd, 1968). For instance, you are likely to be less annoyed with a date who is fifteen minutes late than with one who keeps you waiting for three quarters of an hour. Finally, as we mentioned earlier, deviance on the part of a high-status member is often treated more gently by the group than the same behavior would be from a low-status member.

The structure of a particular group can affect the severity of its social control reactions as well. But most of these structural factors also affect the initial pressure on group members for conformity and deviance. This is not surprising in that the conformity, deviance, and social control processes are intertwined and continuous with one another in group life. Indeed, in many ways they represent different parts, or aspects, of a single group process. Now that we have a basic understanding of the dynamics of all three, let us examine how aspects of group structure can increase the intensity of conformity pressures and social control reactions on the one hand, and deviance on the other.

THE IMPACT OF GROUP STRUCTURE ON CONFORMITY, DEVIANCE, AND SOCIAL CONTROL

Pressures to conform have been found to vary with many aspects of a group's makeup. We will consider three of the most important. The broadest, and perhaps most powerful in its impact on conformity and social control, is *group cohesiveness*. Also important, however, are the *centralization of the communication network* and the *nature of the group majority*.

Group Cohesiveness

In the last chapter, we saw that highly cohesive groups have more power to influence their members' behavior and opinions. Naturally then, high-cohesive groups will be able to produce more powerful social control efforts than low-cohesive groups. The Schacter (1951) study, discussed in the previous section, provided clear evidence of this. In addition to varying the relevance of the discussion topic, Schacter also varied the cohesiveness of the groups. Some subjects were formed into groups ("clubs") whose focal interest matched the personal interests they had expressed before the experiment (high-cohesive groups). Others found themselves in groups organized around interests quite divergent from their own (low-cohesive groups). In the high-cohesive groups, there were more efforts to persuade deviates to conform and stronger rejections of them when they failed to do so.

There are several reasons why the group's reaction to deviance will be more controlling when it is more cohesive. If we think about it, these same reasons are likely to induce members to conform more in the first place.[1] First of all, in a cohesive group, the members are more commit-

---

1. Crosbie (1975) argues that cohesiveness may increase only social control, not voluntary conformity. But evidence such as Janis's (1972) showing self-censorship among the members of highly cohesive policy groups argues to the contrary.

ted; they care more about the group and its activities. Second, in a highly cohesive group there is an enjoyable sense of coordination among the members, a sense of working smoothly together as a unit. In this atmosphere, deviance appears like an interference, a betrayal of the group, a wrench in the works. Knowing this, and presumably feeling personally involved in the group, a member is likely to resist deviating in the first place. But when deviance does occur, the group will not react lightly.

A third factor that increases both prior conformity and social pressure is the greater level of communication and participation among the members of a cohesive group. Simply by interacting more, the members will subtly and persistently influence one another to behave and think in similar ways in regard to group concerns. This will produce more uniformity among the members, greater agreement about the group norms, and, therefore, more voluntary conformity. Moreover, if deviance does occur, this same increased communication will give the group greater opportunity to persuade and sanction the deviate.

Crosbie (1975; Crosbie, Stitt, and Petroni, 1973) argues that several of the antecedents of cohesiveness have an independent impact on conformity. That is, they do not affect conformity by increasing cohesiveness, but rather have a direct affect on their own. Whether their impact is independent or not, there certainly is evidence for an association between these antecedents and conformity. For instance, there is evidence that *friendship* among members increases conformity to the group's norms (Hare, 1976; Roethlisberger and Dickson, 1939). It makes sense that friends will influence each other's behavior and opinions more than nonfriends.

In Chapter 4 we noted that similarity among the members is one factor that increases group cohesiveness. It seems likely that *homogeneity among the group members* also increases conformity pressures. When Festinger (1954) proposed his theory of social comparison he argued that people would be most influenced by their comparisons with others who they felt were similar to them. If that is the case, then group members who are relatively similar in attitudes and background should exert more influence (and thus more conformity pressure) over one another than members of a more heterogeneous group.

Group goals that make the members *cooperatively interdependent* also increase conformity pressures (Deutsch and Gerard, 1955; Crosbie, Petroni, and Stitt, 1972; Berkowitz, 1957; Thomas, 1957; Camilleri and Berger, 1967). Obviously, if members are dependent on one another to achieve a desired goal, they will pressure each other to stick to the norms agreed upon for reaching that goal. Finally, anything that increases the *attractiveness of a group* for a member increases his or her willingness to conform to its norms (Festinger, Schacter, and Back, 1950; Back, 1951). However, since attractiveness of the group is often the measurement used to indicate cohesiveness itself (as was the case in Schacter's experiment), this amounts in practice to a restatement of the association between cohesiveness and conformity.

Decentralized Communication Networks

We have already noted that the increase in communication that comes with cohesiveness also increases pressures for conformity. We should suspect, then, that conformity pressures would also be greater in groups whose communication networks are decentralized. In a decentralized network, each member can exert direct pressure on most other group members, while, in centralized networks, the contact between some members is only indirect. Since direct contact is more influential than indirect contact, more effective mutual influence occurs in groups with decentralized networks (Shaw, 1981). Several studies confirm this fact (Goldberg, 1955; Shaw, Rothschild, and Strickland, 1957).

Groups with a decentralized communication pattern are generally democratic in their status and leadership systems. Centralized networks are found in more hierarchical and authoritarian groups (Chapter 4). Does that mean that informal conformity pressures are often actually higher in democratic groups? Yes and no. Conformity pressures from the communication process alone probably *are* greater in democratic groups. There, everybody exposes his or her opinions to everybody else and, as a result, opens him- or herself up to influence from all sides. In the restricted communication system of an authoritarian group, one's opinions are exposed only to a few others. However, communications are not the only source of conformity pressures. The enhanced power and status of leaders in an authoritarian group also gives them a greater capacity to influence—and coerce if necessary—the other members. Perhaps we should conclude that conformity pressures are not necessarily less intense in democratic groups than in authoritarian ones, even if they are not greater. However, the source of conformity is different in the two. In democratic groups, it comes from open communication. In authoritarian ones, it comes from differences in power and status.

The fact that decentralizing communication increases conformity pressure tells only half the story, however. One aspect of decentralization, you will recall, is that each member has greater autonomy in his or her communications and decisions. The very fact that all members can express themselves freely and actively participate in group decisions increases the *opportunity* for deviance. So decentralized, democratic groups actually do two things at the same time. They maximize for their members the potential for autonomous action (Feldman, 1973), as well as their exposure to conformity pressures. If a member should take this opportunity for independence and challenge the group norm, he or she is much more likely to actually convince the group to change if it is decentralized and democratic. This means that the norm-change reaction to deviance is probably much more likely in decentralized groups than in centralized, hierarchical ones.

Nature of the Group Majority

Are people more likely to conform to the group norm when the majority behind it is quite large? What would happen if there was another deviate besides you, would it be easier to resist the pressure to conform? Asch (1951, 1955) explored these questions in a series of experiments with line judgments like the one described earlier. Once again subjects were asked to judge which of three lines was the same length as a comparison line, but this time the size of the "majority" giving the obviously false answer was systematically varied from one to fifteen persons. The naive subject's conformity increased dramatically as the size of the majority grew from one to three or four people, but at that point it leveled off. It seems that once there are three or four people standing against you alone, there might as well be ten or fifteen: the pressure is about the same. More recently there have been debates about the precise number at which the impact of the majority reaches its maximum and then levels off (Gerard, Wilhelmy, and Conolley, 1968), but the basic idea has held.

The fact that it is harder to resist a larger majority is probably best explained in social comparison terms. When you are faced with one person who disagrees with you, there is no reason to assume that his view is any more correct than your own. But when two, and then three or four, of your groupmates unanimously agree that the group norm is the best response to the situation, your confidence in the correctness of your own belief is shaken. Of course, this is most likely to happen when the majority is composed of groupmates of equal or higher status than you (Hare, 1976). If you are a high-status member opposed by a majority of lower-status members, you may try to hold out and change the majority.

In all these experiments, the naive subject stood alone against a unanimous majority. Asch (1955) tried another variation in which one of the group members was secretly instructed to disagree with the majority and choose the obviously correct answer. In that situation naive subjects were willing to oppose the majority themselves and also name the correct answer 94 percent of the time. So if you have even one supporter, you're much more able to resist the group's pressure to conform. Actually, further work has shown that this "supporter" doesn't even have to agree with you; he or she simply has to join you in opposing the majority (Shaw, Rothschild, and Strickland, 1957). Anyone who is willing to break the unanimity of the majority makes it easier for you to deviate too.

As an interesting aside we might point out that in a group with relatively open, decentralized communication, you are much more likely to find out if someone in the group really does support you. At the very least, you are more likely to find someone who also disagrees with the majority. Maier and Solem (1952) argued that if the group has a democratic leader, he or she may stand by you just to ensure that your opinion gets a hearing. So increasing the likelihood that the majority will not be unanimous is another way in which decentralized groups increase the opportunities for deviance as well as pressure for conformity.

We can conclude, then, that conformity pressure will be higher, and social control reaction stronger, when a group is cohesive, or has some of the antecedents of cohesiveness, such as friendship or homogeneity among the members and cooperative interdependence in pursuit of a goal. Conformity pressures will be similarly high when the majority behind the norm is large and unanimous, and when the group's communication patterns are open and decentralized. However, it is important to note that decentralized communication also increases the potential for deviance in a group, as well as the likelihood that the group's social control reaction will be one of norm change rather than simply persuasion or punishment.

CONFORMITY TO WHOSE NORMS? THE SMALL GROUP VERSUS LARGER ORGANIZATIONS

Small groups enforce conformity to those norms that they have adopted as their own. But, as we noted in Chapter 1, these group norms may or may not be in accord with the larger organization or society in which the group functions. For a high school administration, the only appropriate norms for classroom behavior are discipline and learning. However, these may not be at all like the norms adopted by a group of teenagers attending the class. Similarly, a group of workers may not entirely accept and enforce the norms of management. When a conflict exists between the norms of a person's primary group and those of a larger secondary organization to which she belongs, there is substantial evidence that most people will put their allegiance with their primary group (Iwao, 1963; Bates and Babchuck, 1961; Baur, 1960). Consequently it is vitally important for larger organizations that the primary groups within them accept, at least in the main, the basic norms of the organization. Indeed, as we pointed out in Chapter 1, secondary organizations, and particularly society as a whole, are heavily dependent on small groups to support and enforce their norms.

It is probably rather rare for a small group to adopt as its own all the norms of a larger organization without question. Indeed, one thing small groups often do for their members is provide a context in which some resistance or frustration with the larger organization can be expressed. In this situation, small groups provide their members with the same kind of support for opposition to the organizational majority that the naive subject got from the fellow deviate in Asch's study.

On the other hand, it is difficult for a group to survive when it completely and utterly rejects the basic norms of its surrounding organizations. There are several reasons for this. As we mentioned earlier, people belong to several groups simultaneously. If the norms of one of them reject the norms of the others, the group will have difficulty enforcing the conflicting norms. (Of course, it is possible for a person to belong to a whole network of small groups that agree in rejecting the norms of the larger society. Indeed, that is how deviant subcultures are created and maintained. An example might be the world of gay people.)

A second reason why it is difficult for a group to utterly reject the norms of its surrounding social environment is that that environment is likely to react punitively toward the group. Larger organizations may put so much pressure on a small group that many of its members feel forced to quit rather than face the costs of remaining a member. This is what happened to the individual branches of the American Communist party during the McCarthy period of the 1950s. So groups whose norms deviate greatly from the prevailing norms of surrounding organizations have a harder time maintaining their members. As a result most small groups array themselves somewhere in the wide middle area between complete acceptance and utter rejection of outside norms.

The extent to which a person's small groups adhere to or resist the norms of the larger society has a great deal to do with that person's own overall level of conformity or deviance in society. People who maintain unusual, eccentric, or even illegal life-styles usually do so through membership in groups whose norms support these nonconforming behaviors. In other words, most people manage to be nonconformists in the larger society by being conformists within their small groups. We are not suggesting that people are never independent in their actions. Indeed, most nonconformists choose to belong to small groups with deviant norms when they could take the easier course of being more conventional. The point is that people use groups and the support of group norms to embolden their resistance to the norms and authority of larger organizations.

An experiment by Milgram (1965) shows how resistance to authority can be increased by small-group support. An experimenter ordered subjects to give increasingly strong electric shocks to another person, despite that person's protest and cries. Disturbingly, most subjects felt unable to resist the authority of the scientist-experimenter and complied with his demands (although the experiment was arranged so that no one was really shocked). But when Milgram had two confederates go in with the subject and refuse to give very strong shocks, 90 percent of the subjects then felt able to refuse the experimenter's demands themselves as well. The support of their fellows helped them to resist the coercive authority figure and stand up for their own standards of humane conduct. In the same way, the support of his co-workers might embolden a worker to protest against an exploitive boss. Of course, emboldening support from your fellows can have negative consequences as well. A teenager might think of stealing something, or taking a swing at a police officer; but only when his friends are egging him on does he actually do it—and get in trouble as a result.

Because of the power they have either to pressure their members to conform or encourage them to resist societal norms, small groups are double-edged swords for the individual as well as for larger organizations. Consequently, it is probably important for personal happiness that one choose one's group memberships carefully, allowing for a balance between one's need to belong and the costs of deviance on the one hand, and opportunities and support for self-expression on the other. Similarly, it is critical that if larger organizational structures are to function effectively, they maintain effective links with the small groups operating within them.

SUMMARY

Conformity is a member's willing or unwilling adherence to group norms. Deviance is behavior that violates these norms. Social control is the group's attempt to reduce or eliminate deviance once it occurs. Since all these processes revolve around group norms, understanding them requires us to first examine the nature and formation of norms.

Norms are the shared, agreed-upon rules of behavior members establish to govern their behavior together. Since they generally define ranges of behavior thought to be consistent with the group's goals, norms carry a moral connotation that gives rise to sanctions for conformity to and deviance from, them. From the moment people come together in a group, they begin to negotiate rules for dealing with one another and coordinating views on matters of mutual concern. There are two sides to this process. First is achieving agreement in matters of joint concern through social comparison, and then establishing norms to maintain that agreement. (Sherif's autokinetic experiment illustrates this process.) Second is developing norms to regulate areas of actual or potential conflict.

Groups generally develop three classes of norms that together make up their normative orders. Procedural norms establish basic ground rules for interaction and apply equally to all members. Role norms define the distinctive behavior that the group expects from each particular member. Finally, the group's shared beliefs, values, attitudes, myths, and self-image are embodied in cultural norms, to which individuals are expected to adhere if they wish to be fully accepted members.

As the framework of the normative order begins to emerge, the processes of mutual influence among the members are redirected from the formation of new norms to the maintenance of the existing ones. By pressuring one another to uphold the norms, members create a relatively stable social structure that makes effective interaction possible. However, this stability is achieved in the face of persistent pressures for deviance and change. Despite social control efforts, the constant small, and occasionally large, deviations from the group norms gradually alters them. As a result, the normative order evolves and changes over time. We can imagine an optimal level of social control that is sufficient to maintain reasonable stability but is not so strong as to strangle needed innovation. However, many groups fail to achieve this, exercising either too much or too little social control.

As Asch's experiments make clear, groups wield powerful tools to induce their members' conformity to group norms. People conform to group expectations to be assured of the validity of their views (social comparison), to gain social acceptance and approval and avoid rejection (rewards and punishments), and to abide by personal standards when group norms have been internalized. Deviance, on the other hand, usually arises from either of two sources: insufficient knowledge of the norms in the first place, or a negative assessment of a norm's consequences. The latter can lead to deviance when a norm conflicts with those of other reference groups, when it appears inequitable or ineffective, or when there are fewer rewards or more costs associated with conformity than with deviance.

The effects of conformity and deviance on the status people attain in groups are complex. Conformity by itself does not help a member gain high status. Nonconformity can be a help, however, since it attracts attention and is assertive, giving the appearance of confidence and competence. But nonconformity has liabilities as well, since it appears self-interested. The effects of established status on conformity are more straightforward. Both high- and low-status members deviate more, while medium-status members conform the most. Despite a wider latitude for deviance, high-status members must conform to core norms. They are also expected to engage in innovative deviance in some situations.

Groups exercise social control over deviance by means of three processes: persuasion, use of rewards and punishments, and norm change. In the last the group alters its norm to come closer to the position of the deviate. This reaction is most likely when the deviate shows a confident and consistent behavioral style and is able to resist the group's dislike.

The severity of a group's reaction to deviance depends on the importance of the violated norm, the intensity of the deviance, and the status of the deviate. Aspects of the group's makeup also affect the intensity of its conformity pressures and the strength of its social control reactions. Both are higher when a group is cohesive or has some of the antecedents of cohesiveness, when the majority behind the norm is large and unanimous, and when the group's communication patterns are open and decentralized. However, decentralized communication also increases the potential for deviance and the likelihood of a norm-change reaction on the part of the group.

Small groups enforce conformity to those norms that they have adopted as their own. These may or may not be in accord with the larger organization or society in which the group functions. Since groups often provide their members with a context in which some resistance or frustration with the larger organization can be expressed, it is unusual for them to enforce without question all that organization's norms. On the other hand, it is difficult for a group to survive when it completely rejects the basic norms of its surrounding organizations. The extent to which a person's small groups adhere to or resist the norm of the larger society has a great deal to do with that person's own overall level of conformity or deviance in society.

6

Status Differentiation

The most important aspect of small group structure is the status hierarchy. Because of its central role in controlling the activities and goals of the group, we have already said a good deal about status, particularly in regard to the communication patterns and conformity processes of groups. But we have yet to define status relations more formally. A member's *status* in a group refers to the degree of deference, esteem, and power to influence others that he or she acquires. Status is something that emerges from the relationship between a member and the rest of the group.

If we map out the patterns of power and deference among all the members, we have a picture of the group's *status structure.* Although we can imagine a situation where all members defer to one another equally, observations of actual groups suggest that this is exceedingly rare (Bales, Strodtbeck, Mills, and Roseborough, 1951; Parsons, Bales, and Shils, 1953; Fisek and Ofshe, 1970). Instead the status structures of groups are almost always characterized by differences in power and prestige among the members, even though there may be a few members of approximately equal standing in the group. The status structures of groups, then, usually describe a hierarchy in which members are arranged from highest to lowest in power and prestige.

The location of a member in this hierarchy is his or her status *rank.* Each rank in the hierarchy carries with it a set of normatively defined obligations to the group, as well as privileges. The highest-status members have, of course, the greatest power and prestige, but also the greatest obligations. In his study of a streetcorner gang in Boston, Whyte (1943), for instance, noted that "Doc," the gang's leader, spent more money on his followers than they did on him. The hierarchy determined how much he spent on any particular follower. The further down the ladder a member was, the less Doc was obligated to spend on him (see Box 6.1 "Status in the Norton Street Gang").

The difference between the highest and lowest status rank reflects

160

the degree of *status differentiation* in the group. Some groups—many adult friendship groups, for instance—have what is called a *flat* status hierarchy in that the highest- and lowest-status members differ only slightly in power and prestige. But dramatic status differences (*tall* hierarchies) are common also. Think of the advantage in power and prestige that a gang leader, or the most popular member of a high school clique, has over the other members.

If you consider the informal groups of which you personally are a member, you may not find it all that easy to clearly rank the members in terms of status. Your efforts may be assisted, however, by noting certain observable signs of power and prestige (Berger et al., 1974; Berger et al., 1977; Bales, 1950). Members' status ranks can generally be deciphered from three behavioral clues:

1. Their rate of participation in group discussion
2. The type of evaluation their comments and behavior draw from the group
3. The degree of influence they have over the group's decisions and actions

High-status members talk more, receive more positive evaluations from others, and are influential. We might note that high-status members talk more, not only because they are personally inclined to do so, but also because they are more frequently asked for their opinions by others (Berger et al., 1974). This point illustrates the mix between the individual's assertion of power and the group's choice to grant deference and influence that underlies status processes in groups.

Status Systems as Organization and Reward Allocations

Groups evolve their status systems out of two rather different types of pressure: (1) the need to organize in pursuit of the group's goals, and (2) the need to avoid destructive competition over the rewards to be gained from group activities. As Wilson (1978) points out, the first arises out of the fundamental agreement of group members to pursue certain goals as efficiently as they can, while the second stems from fundamental conflicts of interests among the members. Status structure, then, is similar to group norms in that it develops both as an expression of group unity and as a mechanism to regulate potential disagreements.

There are several reasons why the need to organize the group to accomplish its goals gives rise to a status structure. Since the members

Box 6.1   **Status in the Norton Street Gang**

In nearly every chapter we have made some reference to the fascinating study by Whyte (1943,1955) of the Nortons, a street gang in a poor Italian neighborhood of Boston. Now it's time to get to know Doc and his boys on Norton Street a bit better. Who were the members, and what were the status relations among them?

There were thirteen of them in all, Doc, Mike, Danny, Long John, Nutsy, Frank, Joe, Alec, Angelo, Fred, Lou, Carl, and Tom. Interestingly, they were not just kids but were all actually in their twenties. Living in the midst of the Depression, they had been laid off their jobs and were able to work only on an occasional basis. So they spent their time hanging out on the corner in the old neighborhood. Although most had known each other since childhood, they only coalesced as a real functioning group when Doc lost his job and began to show up on the corner again.

The men on the corner gradually became accustomed to acting together. They started doing favors for one another, which was particularly important since everybody went through periods of being broke and needing help. Before long they were tied together in a web of mutual obligations.

From the beginning Doc was their leader. He moved immediately into that position because of the reputation he brought with him from their teenage days. Doc was bright, and as a kid he had acquired a reputation for toughness, perhaps to compensate for his polio-impaired left arm. During their childhood years it had been Nutsy who was the leader of the neighborhood gang; Doc had been his lieutenant. Then one day Doc and Nutsy got into a fight and Doc won. Doc recalled that "After I walloped . . . [Nutsy], I told the boys what to do. They listened to me. If they didn't, I walloped them. I walloped every kid in my gang at some time" (Whyte, 1955). But toughness hadn't been Doc's only claim to status as a kid. As he also recalled, "They had faith in me. . . . It wasn't just the punch. I was the one who always thought of the things to do. I was the one with half a brain" (Whyte, 1955).

The kid gangs broke up as the boys got older and went on to jobs, but Doc retained his reputation in the neighborhood. That reputation gave him a set of specific status characteristics (toughness, intelligence, fairness) that he carried with him to the Norton Street Gang. He was also one of the oldest of the Norton Street group, which gave him a diffuse status characteristic advantage as well. The combination of Doc's specific and diffuse status characteristics moved him immediately to the top of the gang's emerging power and prestige order.

As Doc became the top man, his closest friend, Danny, moved

Box 6.1   *(continued)*

up to high status as well. Mike, another friend of Doc's who had been the leader of his own gang as a kid, also acquired high status. Like Doc, Danny and Mike were older than most of the other members. They became Doc's lieutenants, enforcing his orders with the lower-status men and relaying the men's concerns back to Doc. Together they formed what in the next chapter we will call a *conservative coalition* that supported Doc's leadership.

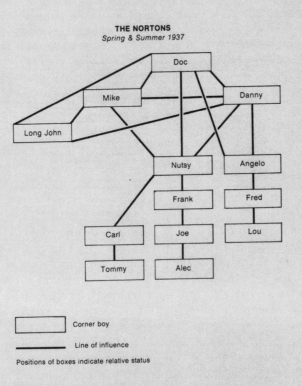

THE NORTONS
Spring & Summer 1937

☐ Corner boy

▬▬ Line of influence

Positions of boxes indicate relative status

Long John, one of the gang members, had an unusual position in the group. He was young and in the habit of gambling away his week's pay in the crap games. While the Nortons had nothing against running crap games, they considered the players in those games to be suckers. As a result Long John had little real influence over the other Norton men. However, he still held a fairly high position in the status hierarchy because he was an old friend of Mike's and, thus, had been taken up by the ruling triumvirate. When Doc, Danny, and Mike did something, they asked Long John along.

Finally, there were the other men whose status in the group was a result of their age, their former reputations, and the nature of their connections with higher-status members. Nutsy was as old as Doc but

Box 6.1 *(continued)*

had, of course, been defeated by him in the past. Angelo was in the middle of the group's age range and was a friend of Doc's. Fred and Lou were also in the middle age group and had been helped by Doc in the past. Frank and Joe were a year or so younger and were friends of Nutsy. Carl and Tommy were also friends of Nutsy's, but were among the youngest members. Alec was quite young and was only a friend of Joe's.

Those were the men of the Norton gang. What did they do together? They would sit around and talk, comment on passersby, go bowling on Saturday night, and sometimes hang out with the young women of the Aphrodite Club at the Norton Street Settlement House. Bowling and associating with the ladies were the major areas in which the Norton men gained or lost prestige. Interestingly, the men supported, heckled, and challenged one another in such a way that their bowling scores and success with the women were almost invariably a direct reflection of their status and influence in the gang.

have differing interests and skills, the group ideally would like to evolve an organizational structure that would best use all the members' talents. This usually means a division of labor, with members specializing in different aspects of the problem at hand. But a division of tasks implies the need for a system to coordinate the various specialized activities. When some begin to coordinate others' activities, power differences may easily develop. Group members may also feel it is simply more efficient to grant greater power and influence to those members who appear to be most skilled at the group's focal activities, again creating status differences. We should expect, then, that a member's assumed or perceived competence at performing the group's focal activities will be one determinant of his or her standing in the status hierarchy.

The need to regulate destructive conflicts of interest among the members creates status differences in a rather different way. We have often pointed out the personal rewards and need satisfactions people seek from group life—such as approval, esteem, and power. But problems arise because what it takes to completely satisfy the desires of one member may interfere with the need satisfaction of others. You, for instance, might want to be the best-liked, most-admired member of our group. But what if I also want to be the most popular? If you get all that you want, then I can't get what I want. Another difficulty stems from the fact that the group only meets for so much time and has only a limited amount of energy to spend on the individual concerns of its members. Consequently the attention and concern of the group is an inherently scarce resource for which the members compete.

However, perpetual conflict and competition among group members, each trying to maximize his or her personal need satisfaction, is potentially self-defeating. As exchange theorists point out, members must agree to offer some level of rewards to others if they expect to receive rewards themselves. Group members have a common need, then, to develop an agreed-upon system for exchanging rewards among themselves, one which will contain the conflicts of interest within normative bonds and prevent mutually destructive competition. Groups accomplish this by means of their status systems.

This status equilibrium is not achieved instantly, however. There is likely to be an initial status struggle in small groups. During this period, members attempt to cut the best deal for themselves that they can. When the dust settles—and this usually happens quickly (Fisek and Ofshe, 1970)—it generally becomes clear that some people have achieved more advantageous positions than others in terms of power and access to rewards. We will examine how and why this happens. But for now it is important to realize that despite their power, the "winners" of this struggle remain dependent upon the "losers" for the maintenance of their privileged positions (Emerson, 1962). Prestige and approval must be granted by others; in exchange for them, lower-status members demand certain task performances and duties from the high-status members. They also demand that the high-status members' exercise of power be limited by norms to certain agreed-upon "legitimate" channels. When a high-status member tries to wield power outside these channels, it will be considered illegitimate and will likely be resisted by the group. In this way, the norms that define the group's status structure transform the simple privilege of high power into the privileges and obligations of status ranks. Let us turn now to the question of those behaviors and attributes that determine the status a member achieves in a small group.

Sources of Status in Groups

FOUR CATEGORIES OF BEHAVIOR.   According to present research, there are four general classes of attributes and behaviors that enhance status in face-to-face groups. The first and most important are *external status characteristics* (Berger et al., 1974; Berger et al., 1976; Berger et al., 1980), which were first mentioned in Chapter 4. Characteristics of an individual that have high or low status value in the larger society and that are brought with the individual into the small group fall into this category. Some of these, such as age, sex, race, and physical attractiveness, are *ascribed* characteristics. People possess these through no fault or merit of their own, and yet they carry high or low status value for them. Others are *achieved* characteristics; they represent high- or low-status states that people attain through their own efforts. Examples are occupations, educational attainment, and acquired skills. We will discuss in some detail the impact of external status characteristics on a group's status system. But for now it is enough to note that high external status characteristics—for instance, being white, male, or well educated when other group members are not—gives you an advantage in achieving power and prestige in a small group. Having low external status characteristics compared to your groupmates—being female in a group of males, for example—is a disadvantage.

The second category of status-enhancing factors are signs of *objective competence* at the group's focal activities (Kimberly, 1972). If you are, in fact, very good at the group task and can demonstrate that clearly to your groupmates, your status will be improved. There are generally two ways you can do this. The first is to bring some direct sign of actual task ability with you when you enter the group. When Magic Johnson joins a new basketball team, he brings his whole history of success with him as a direct indication of his basketball ability.

The second way is to prove your competence on the spot. You do this by excelling at the group's focal activities—scoring winning points on an athletic team or winning a fight with a rival leader in a gang. This outlet is often not open to status seekers, however, for objective competence can only be demonstrated clearly when the group's task is unambiguous and the members share well-defined standards for evaluating each others' performance. And that just isn't the case for many of the types of activities that small groups engage in—tasks such as planning for the future, dealing with human relations, or making complex decisions. So objectively superior performances are not as common a source of status in small groups as one might think.

A third determinant of high status are what have been called *dominance behaviors*.[1] Recent evidence suggests that there are certain nonverbal behaviors, gestures, and ways of talking—for example, taking a seat at

---

1. Since *dominance* is the word used for these behaviors in most studies, we will use it here. However most of these behaviors, such as eye contact and verbal latency, are better thought of as simple self-assertions rather than as hostile, domineering behaviors or raw demands for submission. Indeed, it is possible that truly domineering behavior produces a different type of reaction—an emotional backlash of sorts—which affects status differently than do more everyday assertive behaviors.

the head of the table, direct eye contact, interrupting or seizing the conversational floor—that people use to signal their intention to assert themselves in a situation (Rosa and Mazur, 1979; Mazur et al., 1980; Nemeth, Wachtler, and Endicott, 1977; Willard and Strodtbeck, 1972). After a brief nonverbal struggle, those who, for whatever reason, are less comfortable with such behaviors will usually back down, leaving the dominator in a position of enhanced power that is likely to be translated eventually into high status. We shall see that there are a number of reasons why a person might engage in dominance behavior, or why he or she might back down in the face of such behavior from someone else. But the point for now is that such contests do go on, and do affect the status hierarchy that ultimately develops.

The fourth and final set of factors relating to individual status in a group are *socioemotional behaviors*. Like power, affection is a fundamental emotional dimension in small groups that affects the esteem members can command. As we shall see, this factor is more important in the status processes of primary groups than task-oriented ones, although even there it continues to have an impact.

There are two socioemotional variables that appear to affect status. The first is simply sociometric popularity, or likeableness (Feldman, 1973). As French and Raven (1959) pointed out, liking someone gives them *referent power* over you. You care about their opinion of you and, therefore, try to act in accord with their wishes in order to please them. When a member is well-liked by the rest of the group, his or her power in the group is enhanced. This referent, or sociometric, power becomes a basis for high status in the group. We should caution, however, that the most popular person is not always the highest-status member, since friendship is only one factor in the evolution of the status hierarchy.

The second sociometric variable is the member's perceived motivation toward the group (Hollander, 1964; Kelley and Thibaut, 1969; Kimberly, 1972; Meeker and Weitzel-O'Neill, 1977; Ridgeway, 1978, 1982). The distinction here is between members whose actions seem to be motivated by interest in the group and a desire to help it further its aims (group-oriented motivation) and those who seem to be motivated by simple self-interest or indifference to the group (self-oriented motivation). Cooperative, group-oriented members are more valuable to the group and, therefore, more likely to be rewarded with higher status than self-oriented ones. The cooperative, interested, helpful manner that goes with being group oriented seems likely to make the member more attractive and likeable as well. So in practice the two socioemotional variables that affect status are likely to work hand-in-hand.

PERFORMANCE EXPECTATIONS AND SOCIOEMOTIONAL JUDGMENTS. Simply listing the four major behavior categories that can affect status achievement in small groups is not enough if we are to really understand how these variables work. We must also take into account the phenomena of *performance expectations*. These are the expectations members form for their own and each other's performance at the group's focal activities (Berger et al., 1974). In effect they are rough estimates of a member's *perceived* (as distinct from objective) task competence. The performance expectations group members hold for one another are not necessarily conscious or rational. They are just working impressions formed about each other's abilities in performing the group's central activities.

Performance expectations have a dramatic affect on status because they act as self-fulfilling prophecies (Rosenthal and Jacobson, 1968). If people expect you to perform well they give you more opportunities to participate in the group's central business. And, because they assume you are able, they tend to evaluate what you do positively and actually encourage you to perform well. Having evaluated your behavior positively, they also are more likely to accept your influence. On the other hand, if others expect you to do badly, it is difficult to perform well, and even more difficult to be seen as having done well. Because they doubt your abilities, the others resist giving you much influence. In this way, then, high and low performance expectations are translated into differences in observable power and prestige (Berger et al., 1974, 1977). Remember that these observable signs (rate of participation, type of evaluation, and degree of influence) are in fact indications of status differences. So differences in performance expectations lead to differences in status.

There is reason to believe that three of our four sources of status —external status characteristics, objective competence, and dominance cues—affect status primarily by affecting the performance expectations members develop for themselves and each other. It is clear that this is how objective competence has its effects. If a football player can point to his "best player" award or to the number of points that he personally contributed to the team score, that is obviously going to create in his own mind and in the minds of his teammates certain expectations for his future performance, which in turn will affect his status on the team.

Less obvious and more interesting is the fact that external status differences also determine performance expectations. We will go into some detail on the effects of external status characteristics a bit later in the chapter. But for now it is sufficient to note that the reason why external status characteristics are an advantage or disadvantage in a group is that they carry with them high and low performance expectations (Berger et al., 1974; Berger et al., 1977). For instance, if you are a doctor in a group of office workers, people's first, almost unconscious expectation, rightly or wrongly, will be that you are more able than the others.

It seems likely that dominance cues also work their effects primarily through performance expectations, although this has not yet been clearly established. When you seat yourself at the head of the table, meet other people's gaze head on, speak up assertively, and argue fluently and articulately, what impression is created? Most people would say one of confidence and self-assurance. Such apparent self-confidence is usually read, moreover, as a sign of *competence,* unless what you are saying is in clear conflict with the facts (Moscovici, 1976; Moscivici and Faucheux, 1972; Moscovici and Nemeth, 1974; Nemeth, Wachtler, and Endicott, 1977). So assertive behavior not only creates power differences, it also creates the impression that you know what you are doing. This in turn leads your groupmates to evaluate your contributions more positively and generally to form high performance expectations for you, which result in high status.

If external status characteristics, signs of objective competence, and dominance behaviors affect status through performance expectations, what about socioemotional behaviors? Here the story is a bit different. Socioemotional behaviors seem to affect status through a rather different track, one which is as yet poorly understood. Maybe we can approach the problem this way. Performance expectations serve as the members estimate of the rewards to be had from task success if high or low status is entrusted to particular people. But as we have so often noted, people want socioemotional as well as task rewards from groups. Perhaps socioemotional behaviors affect status by giving some indication of the socioemotional climate that would be created in a group if a particular person were given high or low status.

It seems likely that in most groups both performance expectations and socioemotional factors will affect a member's status. However the relative importance of each set of factors will depend on the nature of the group and its goals. In task-oriented groups—committees and problem-solving groups—performance expectations will heavily outweigh the impact of socioemotional judgments. But in primary groups, such as friendship cliques, socioemotional factors will be an important determinant of status.

Now that we have a general understanding of the kinds of behaviors out of which status hierarchies are created, we are ready to look at the status process in action. To do this we must examine the processes by which status hierarchies evolve in groups. Because of the over-whelming impact of external status characteristics on the power and prestige rankings in groups, we will separate our examination into two parts. In the first, we will look at the evolution of status for groups in which the members begin as equals in external status. This is the famil-iar situation of the peer group. In the second, we will be interested in groups formed by people who differ in one or more external status characteristics.

THE EVOLUTION OF INTERNAL STATUS ORDERS

Groups of External Status Equals

Bales was one of the first to study the process of status evolution in groups of external status equals (Bales, 1950; Bales et al., 1951; Hei-necke and Bales, 1953). His groups were task oriented in that they were brought together under the guise of examining a problem in human relations. However, his results have been applied quite broadly to groups of all sorts. One of Bales's most striking findings was that, in as little time as a 45-minute discussion period, clear status differences emerged among the members (Bales et al., 1951).

Bales interpreted his results to mean that in such groups there is an initial state of equality between the members that changes through the process of interaction into a status-ordered set of relations (Fisek and Ofshe, 1970). Bales and others assumed that this occurred through a rational sorting process by which members gathered information about one another, identified those who were objectively more able to guide the group toward its goals, and granted them higher status in exchange for their competent services (Bales, 1950, 1953; Homans, 1961; Blau, 1964).

In an attempt to examine this view of status evolution in peer groups, Fisek and Ofshe (1970) formed fifty-nine discussion groups like those studied by Bales. They then made minute-by-minute observa-tions of the members' participation in the group discussion. Participa-tion, if you recall, is one of the key signs of power and prestige. At the end of the session, group members ranked one another's contributions in terms of guidance, best ideas, and ability at the task. These measures tapped the members' perceptions of one another's competence and in-fluence in the group.

Fisek and Ofshe's results were somewhat surprising. For about half the groups, things seemed to work as expected. Members began by participating about equally, then inequalities gradually developed, and by the end of the 45-minute session a stable hierarchy of participation rates had emerged. But, surprisingly, members perceptions of each other's competence and influence did not clearly match the differences in participation. Fisek and Ofshe interpreted this to mean that, while a clear dominance hierarchy had developed in the group, members had not yet become fully conscious of it. This evidence challenged Blau's (1964) and Homans's (1961) notion that members first perceive differences in one another's abilities and efforts and then grant status and dominance on that basis.

An even more striking challenge to this idea came from the other half of the groups Fisek and Ofshe studied. In these groups an unequal pattern of participation emerged within the first minute of interaction. Furthermore, the hierarchy that developed in the first minute remained stable throughout the entire 45-minute session. This means that members who became first, second, or third in the hierarchy during the initial minute or two of discussion, stayed in that place for the entire discussion. The question raised by this finding is, how can people rationally assess one another's abilities and efforts in just one minute? Something other than such judgments must account for the dominance hierarchy that emerged in these groups.

Members of these groups also ranked one another on perceived competence and influence at the end of the session. Interestingly, their final perceptions of one another corresponded closely to their differences in participation. High participators were seen as doing more to guide the group and having better ideas and greater ability at the task. Clearly, a definite status system had emerged in these groups that was recognized by all. Fisek and Ofshe suggest that this happened for these groups, but not the others, simply because a stable dominance hierarchy emerged so early. The members then had a longer time to become aware of this hierarchy, and to develop perceptions of one another based on it.

Based on their evidence, Fisek and Ofshe reject the exchange theory notion that members first develop perceptions of one another's abilities, then grant status on the basis of those perceptions, which in turn results in differential participation. Rather, they argue that the sequence works the other way. Members first establish stable differences in participation, which Fisek and Ofshe call a dominance hierarchy. On the basis of this members develop differential perceptions of each other. This in turn transforms the simple dominance hierarchy into a true, agreed-upon, status hierarchy.

SIGNALING DOMINANCE.   The question that remains is how groups of initial equals establish stable differences in participation rates. Whatever the process is, it must be something that can operate quite quickly, even though it need not always do so. For clues to the answer, researchers have turned to studies of the formation of dominance hierarchies in animal societies (Mazur, 1973; Chase, 1980). Recent evidence suggests that people may use nonverbal gestures to signal dominance in ways that, while more subtle, are nevertheless comparable to that of other animals, particularly other high-order primates.

Mazur and his colleagues have argued that people use facial gestures for establishing and maintaining dominant positions (Keating, Mazur, and Segall, 1977). Particularly important is looking directly at someone as a signal of dominance. In its extreme form this "eye-glance" signaling can lead to a "stare down" between two people contesting for dominance, but what happens in everyday interaction is more subtle and generally not hostile (Mazur et al., 1980). For instance, Rosa and Mazur (1979) found that in a group of peers, duration of initial glance was a good predictor of the status the member would attain by the end of the discussion session. People who "outglanced" their fellows, in that the other person looked away before they did, ended up high in the status hierarchy, as measured by their participation rate. Interestingly, there was little indication that the group members were even aware that this glancing contest had occurred.

Another nonverbal gesture that seems to signal dominance is verbal latency. Willard and Strodtbeck (1972) found that people who are quick to begin speaking tend to rank high in the status hierarchy of Bales-type discussion groups. Rosa and Mazur (1979) found similar effects for verbal latency in their groups, although it was not as powerful a predictor of status as eye glance.

In another study Mazur and his colleagues attempted to document how a simple, largely unconscious gesture like eye glancing could have an effect on status (Mazur et al., 1980). Apparently looking eye to eye at someone "stresses" them; that is, it increases their physical arousal level. This effect can be increased by using added signals like lowered, glowering eyebrows or an aggressive tilt of the head. Staring directly at someone allows you to manipulate their physiology. Some people who find this arousal more uncomfortable than others tend to back down sooner in a glancing contest. In the study, the less uncomfortable people were with direct eye-to-eye contact, the more likely they were to end up in a high-status position in the group.

We might speculate on why some people are more uncomfortable than others in dominance contests. One factor is probably a matter of personality. As we mentioned in Chapter 1, power is one of the basic emotional dimensions of group life, and individuals develop as part of their personalities definite dispositions for dealing with it. Some people are highly motivated to achieve dominant power positions in their relationships with others. There are others who are uncomfortable in such a position.

However, more important than personality factors are probably other factors that may vary from situation to situation. For instance, how competent you feel at the group's task is likely to affect the assertiveness of your behavior, and your willingness to stand your ground or back down. (We will discuss this more carefully in a moment, and also, when we discuss groups with external status differences, we will see that an external status advantage usually makes you more confident and assertive and inclines others to give way to you.)

Nonverbal gestures such as mutual glancing and verbal latency are events that can occur in just a few seconds of interaction. The fact that people can, and often do, establish stable patterns of deference based on these signals allows us to explain why Fisek and Ofshe (1970) found that dominance hierarchies emerged so quickly in some groups (although —it is important to remember—not all). However, exactly how dominance behaviors like out-glancing or being quick to start speaking translate into the higher participation rates Fisek and Ofshe found, is the next question we need to consider. Afterwards, we can go on to consider the larger problem of the way initial dominance and participation differences become true status differences.

DOMINANCE AND PARTICIPATION.   Studies of group communication have shown that people regulate the flow of conversation by rules of "turn taking" (Duncan, 1972). In a study of Bales-type discussion groups composed of external status equals, Burke (1974) found that about half the time the conversational floor was passed by one member to another in a regularized way with no interference from other group members. Furthermore, the people who achieved high status in the groups maintained their high participation rates, not by continually grabbing the conversational floor, but by having the floor given to them by others in an orderly turn-taking process.

Aware of the association between dominance signals and status, Burke gave the following account of his results. Speaking turns in conversation, he maintained, tend to be organized into larger units, which he called "interchanges." Interchanges consist of a group of successive speaking turns that all focus on the same topic or goal. Burke then suggested that highly active group members do not use their dominance signals to indiscriminately steal turns. Rather they use them at the conclusion of one interchange to grab the floor so that they may initiate an interchange of their own. When they do this, the active group members are likely to grammatically phrase their interchange in such a way that the people they address are obliged to return the floor to them after they have responded. For example, one active member might say, "I think this is a good idea. Tell me what you think." Then, after expounding on that idea, the member gives the floor to others for comments. However, by asking for reactions the member has effectively focused the conversation on his or her own ideas. As a result, when the commentators finish, the floor goes back to the originating member for further reaction and rebuttal. In this way active group members are able to control the discussion and maintain high participation rates without having to constantly interrupt others and steal turns. Burke's data generally support this interchange-structuring analysis of dominance in peer groups.

Burke's analysis suggests that people capitalize on their initial success at nonverbal dominance by going on to a more complex form of linguistic control over group interaction. In this way they translate the results of a simple dominance contest into more general differences in participation rates. As we have noted, it is the high participators who are ultimately seen as the most influential and, generally, the most competent members in a group. Once they are perceived by the rest of the group in this way, we can say that they have achieved fully recognized positions of high status in the group. But exactly how this happens, how dominance and participation differences due to dominance are translated into status, is something we need to look at in more detail. Doing this requires that we understand the role of performance expectations in the status processes of peer groups. It is also helpful to know something about the impact of objective competence. It is to an analysis of these that we turn now.

PERFORMANCE EXPECTATIONS, COMPETENCE, AND STATUS.   The evidence tells us that status hierarchies often evolve much too fast for them to be based on members' rational assessments of one another's abilities in regard to the group's activities. Does that mean performance expectations and competence play no role in who attains status in peer groups? Absolutely not. Dominance behaviors, performance expectations, and objective competence are interrelated in a complex series of ways. Furthermore, as we shall see, differences in dominance must be legitimized by performance expectations before they can be translated into true status.

Remember that the winners of nonverbal dominance contests tend to be those who feel the least uncomfortable in a dominance struggle

(Mazur et al., 1980). What factor is likely to make you more comfortable with the arousal caused by these struggles? Self-confidence, among other things. There are many sources of self-confidence in a situation, but surely a very important one is your own conviction of being competent at the task. That is, it is the high performance expectation you hold for yourself that creates your confidence. Of course, you can have a high performance expectation for yourself even when, objectively speaking, you are not particularly good at the task. However, in general, it is easier to feel convinced of your abilities if past experience has shown that you usually *are* better at this particular task than are most people. Consequently, people who are objectively more competent at a particular type of group activity usually approach it with greater confidence and enthusiasm. As a result they are probably more likely to initiate and win dominance contests with other members and, ultimately, to attain higher status in the group.

If your own initial expectations for your performance affect your dominance behavior, that behavior in turn affects the expectations others develop about you. Success at an initial dominance contest is likely to encourage your groupmates to perceive you as more able and begin to form a high performance expectation for you. Recall Moscovici's (1976) point that, unless there is clear objective evidence to the contrary, evaluations of competence are based on a confident, logical, consistent —we might say, dominant—behavioral style. Berger, Conner, and McKeown (1969) have shown that, in groups of equals, initial differences in members' evaluations of each other's behavior as competent or incompetent, which might be due to dominance, soon lead to differential expectations for performance. Once your groupmates expect you to perform well, they treat you accordingly, responding positively to your participation efforts and encouraging you to participate even more.

We can see some of this happening in the process of controlling conversational interchanges which we just discussed. To succeed in gaining the floor and controlling interchanges two things must happen. First, the member must be self-confident enough to initiate the control effort in an assertive way. But second, the rest of the group must allow him or her to get away with it: they must accede to the control attempt. At first, they may do this because they are not as confident about their own opinions as the would-be dominator seems to be about his or hers. Once they have acceded to an initial control attempt, they are more likely to perceive the dominator's ideas as competent and begin to form a high performance expectation for him or her. However, gaining the floor initially does not guarantee that high performance expectations will be formed. For instance, if the ideas the dominator expresses while he or she has the floor contradict the facts and are clearly incompetent, they will not evoke high performance expectations from the group. As a result, when the dominator attempts to control the next conversational interchange, he or she will be resisted. Group members may say, "We've heard enough from you, let's hear from someone else." The dominator's participation rate will begin to fall, and he or she will not end up with high status after all.

This analysis tells us that dominance behaviors are important in establishing initial participation inequalities in peer groups—what we have called a dominance hierarchy. However, for this dominance hierarchy to be translated into a full-fledged stable status structure, members must develop performance expectations for one another that correspond to their position in the dominance hierarchy. Because ideas stated assertively and confidently "sound better" than those stammered hesitantly (regardless of objective competence), this usually does happen. But it is not inevitable. So for dominance to lead to status, it must first be translated into performance expectations that give it legitimacy. Dominance behaviors, performance expectations, and objective competence are thoroughly intertwined in the emergence of status differences among peers.

SOCIOEMOTIONAL BEHAVIOR AND STATUS.   Before we leave our consideration of peer groups we should make some mention of the remaining source of status, socioemotional behavior. Simple observation makes it clear that this behavior does have an impact on status. In primary groups they probably do this in two ways. First, because the group's focal activities are socioemotional in nature, the relevant skills by which competence is judged and performance expectations are formed are social abilities. As a result, socioemotional behavior will affect status through performance expectations as well as by creating the impression of likeableness and group orientation.

Unfortunately, the precise role of variables such as liking in the status evolution process has never been clearly delineated. Early on, Bales and Slater (1955; Slater, 1955) proposed that there was some opposition between those behaviors necessary to guide the group forward on its task and the socioemotional behaviors required to be well-liked. Contributing to the task often means engaging in directive, controlling behavior. Since such task-oriented behaviors are essential to status, the assumption was that the highest-status person would not be the best liked. This suggests that there might be some role specialization between task and socioemotional behaviors, with each providing a different and opposing route toward higher status.

More recent work has challenged this view, however. It now appears that role specialization between task and socioemotional behavior, while it may occur, is in no way inevitable (Lewis, 1972; Bonacich and Lewis, 1973; Burke, 1967, 1968, 1971). More common than not, apparently, high-status, task-oriented members are also the best-liked members (Lewis, 1972; Burke, 1968). Additional evidence suggests that being task oriented in a group is positively related to being liked, although the relationship is not extremely strong (Morgan, 1974).

Clearly, we need to know much more before we can explain the role of liking in the development of status hierarchies. For now we can only say that it does seem to have a positive effect on status. It appears to have some association with the dominance and competence behaviors that are so clearly a part of the status evolution process. However it seems to have, as yet, poorly understood effects that are independent of those factors as well.

We can say a bit more about our second socioemotional variable, group-oriented motivation. Several writers have suggested that, all other things being equal, groups will be more willing to accord power and prestige to members who seem to be motivated by a desire to help the group rather than those who care only for their self-interest (Hollander, 1958; Kelley and Thibaut, 1969; Kimberly, 1972; Meeker and Weitzel-O'Neill, 1977). There is some experimental evidence to support this idea (Kelley and Thibaut, 1969; Ridgeway, 1982).

A person's motivation is important to the group because it provides some indication of what the person might do with power and prestige if he or she had it. Group-oriented people are more likely to use power and prestige to benefit the group as a whole and not just themselves. It makes as much sense, then, for a group to give high status to a group-oriented member of only average competence, as to give it to a highly competent but self-oriented member. Because of this, it has been argued that appearing group-oriented provides an additional path to status in groups of external status equals.

Ridgeway (1978) suggested that in such groups, members who attempt to attain high status through dominance and task-related behaviors will be successful if they can convince the group that they are *either* competent *or* group-oriented in motivation. There is no incompatibility between competence and group-oriented motivation, so it is quite possible that a member could appear to be both. But the point is that, in a group of equals, the members are likely to accept either qualification as sufficient for attaining enhanced status.

Kimberly and Zucker (1973) have gone a bit further suggesting that, when a group is in a state of uncertainty about achieving its goal, it will actively prefer having group-oriented members in its high-status positions, regardless of their competence. The idea is that, during difficult times it takes a group-oriented person to hold the group together, to smooth over the interpersonal tensions and redirect the group toward its goal. So the socioemotional track to high status should be most important when the group is in some kind of turmoil and needs someone to help it consolidate its resources.

Although these arguments about the impact of socioemotional variables seem reasonable, there is as yet little direct evidence to document them. The impact of these variables on the status processes of groups remains one of the areas of group studies most in need of further research.

Groups with External Status Differences

Now let us turn to the situation in which group members differ in their external status characteristics. This is actually more often than not the case in small groups. For instance, all mixed-sex groups are like this. So are any groups in which members differ significantly in age, education, income, or occupational status. Almost all committees, councils, boards, and other decision-making groups fall into this category. Also included are groups whose members differ in some type of externally acknowledged expertise, or are substantially different in physical attractiveness. In many friendship groups, for instance, some members are known to engage in more prestigious activities outside the group than others.

External status characteristics are important because group members use their differences in these things as a basis for assigning status within the group. As a result, a member who has higher status in the outside society, compared to the others, ends up with higher status in the group as well. When differences in external status characteristics are present, then, members tend to order their group's internal status system according to them. This process is called *status generalization*.

The importance of external status characteristics has been recognized for some time (Webster and Driskell, 1978). Torrance (1954), for instance, found such effects among three-man bomber crews in the Air Force. The pilot is officially in charge in such groups. But when he was outranked by another member in age, military rank, or other status characteristics, he was not in fact the most influential in the group. In a famous study of simulated jury deliberations, Strodtbeck, James, and Hawkins (1957) found that sex and occupational prestige affected who was chosen foreman, how much people talked, how competent they were judged to be, and, ultimately, who had the biggest impact on the jury's decision. In studies of biracial work groups Katz and his associates found that whites talk more, talk more to other whites than to blacks, and that even blacks talk more to whites (Katz, Goldston, and Benjamin, 1958; Katz and Cohen, 1962). We could cite many other examples of the way external status generalizes to status within a small group.

STATUS CHARACTERISTICS THEORY.   Berger and his colleagues have constructed a theory to explain how and why external status character- istics have such an impact on the status system of small groups (Berger, Cohen, and Zelditch, 1966, 1972; Berger, Conner, and Fisek, 1974; Berger et al., 1977). They have also suggested how the process of status generalization might be overcome. Since these variables are so impor- tant, we will look fairly carefully at Berger's theory. Doing this will allow us to see how the effects of status characteristics are related to some of the other sources of status we have already discussed, particu- larly, objective competence and group-oriented motivation. We will also speculate on their relationship to dominance behavior. It is good to keep in mind that all these factors continue to operate much as they did in groups of equals. But when differences in status characteristics are introduced, the effects of other variables become intertwined with the pervasive impact of the status characteristics themselves.

Before getting into the details of Berger's theory we should note that it is designed to deal with task-oriented groups only. Berger consid- ers a group to be task oriented if it has a goal, if the members have some idea of the difference between success and failure in achieving the goal, and if they feel that the contributions of group members affect the group's success in achieving it (Berger, Rosenholtz, and Zelditch, 1980). This definition of task orientation is broad enough to include most small groups, including many primary groups whose members do have dis- tinct goals in mind. However, more purely expressive, or socioemotion- ally oriented, groups may not fall into this category. There is every reason to think that external status characteristics affect internal status in these groups too. But the way these effects occur in such groups may not be precisely as described by Berger's theory. These caveats should be kept in mind as we take up the theory's main points.

Now let us turn to the theory of status characteristics itself (Berger et al., 1980; Berger et al., 1977). According to Berger and his associates, status characteristics affect group status because they carry with them evaluated—that is, positive or negative—performance expectations about the way the possessor of the status characteristics will behave compared to others who are higher or lower on the same characteristic.

Generally the expectation is that people with higher external status characteristics will perform better at a task than those with lower external status characteristics.

People form expectations for their own performance, based on their own status characteristics, in the same way that they form expectations for others. When people enter a group, a quick inspection of the others usually gives them a sense of where they stand in terms of status characteristics. This is particularly true for observable status variables like age, sex, or race, but other factors such as occupation or education can often also be discerned by outward signs like clothing and manner. If members conclude from this inspection that their status characteristics are higher than those of their groupmates, they are likely to expect themselves to perform better in the group and to be more competent than the others. With this in mind they are more likely to speak up in the group and participate actively in the group deliberations. They are likely to present themselves assertively and engage in more dominance behaviors. Furthermore, they will be less likely to yield to the influence of others. Those with lower status characteristics, on the other hand, are likely to feel themselves less competent. As a result they yield more in dominance contests and participate less (see Box 6.2). They tend to evaluate the contributions of higher external status members more positively than their own and, so, to yield more to their influence. In this way, members translate their differential expectations for one another's behavior into differential power and prestige in the small group.

This is the essential scenario described by status characteristics theory. We might note that it is quite compatible with the effects we saw in groups of external status equals. The major difference is that the impetus behind an individual's dominance behaviors and high participation rate is not personal disposition. Rather it is a shared set of performance expectations for the individual and the other group members that is based on their relative status characteristics. So, when group members differ in external status characteristics, it seems likely that it is these differences that create, through performance expectations, differences in dominance behaviors. These dominance differences in turn reinforce the performance expectations. Recall that when members are peers, the initial sequence is reversed: differences in dominance create differences in performance expectations. Both in peer groups and groups with external status differences, the status structure that emerges is ultimately based on performance expectations (with some admixture of socioemotional judgments).

Berger and his associates' theory of status characteristics goes on to differentiate between different types of external status and to explain

Box 6.2   Status and Dominance in Conversation

In our society, men have an external status advantage over women. Since people with status advantages behave in a more dominant way, we should see some hidden power plays in conversations between men and women. In recent years researchers have gone out and recorded everyday talk between men and women in all sorts of settings. They have discovered a number of interesting differences in the way men and women converse with one another.

One of the first things they noticed is that men interrupt women more than they do other men, and more than women interrupt other women (West and Zimmerman, 1977). Interrupting not only signals a sense of dominance in a relationship, it also actually controls the conversation by taking the floor and changing the topic to subjects the high-status person is more interested in. Here is an example of a conversation between two university students that West and Zimmerman recorded. The brackets indicate times when the man and woman are speaking at the same time. Notice the effect of the interruptions.

FEMALE: How's your paper coming?
MALE: All right, I guess. (pause) I haven't done much in the past two weeks. (pause)
FEMALE: Yeah, know how that
          can . . .
MALE: Hey, ya got an extra cigarette? (pause)
FEMALE: Oh uh sure. (hands him the pack) Like *my*
          pa . . .
MALE: How 'bout a match?
FEMALE: 'Ere you go. Uh like *my*
          pa . . .
MALE: Thanks. (pause)
FEMALE: Sure. (pause) I was gonna tell you
          my . . .
MALE: Hey, I'd really like to talk but I gotta run. See you. (long pause)
FEMALE: Yeah.   (West and Zimmerman, 1977)

Interestingly, West and Zimmerman found similar patterns of interruption in conversations between adults and children. We would expect that, since age is a diffuse status characteristic just like sex.

Besides interrupting more, men also control the topic of conver-

Box 6.2   *(continued)*

sation by failing to respond to many topics introduced by the women talking to them. Women, on the other hand, in their lower-status position, almost always respond to topics introduced by men. The result is that women work harder to keep the conversation going, but men have more control over what is talked about. Sociologist Pamela Fishman (1978) discovered these differences by recording many hours of ordinary conversation between three couples, all of whom thought of themselves as liberated from traditional sex roles. She found that the topics men brought up "succeeded," in that the other person responded to them, 96 percent of the time. However, the topics introduced by women only succeeded 36 percent of the time even though women were responsible for 62 percent of the total topics brought up (reported in Parlee, 1979).

One of the major ways men killed the topics women raised was by giving only a minimal response, like "um," which made the conversation hard to keep going. In response women would often use special strategies to try to increase their chance of getting a response. For instance, they might introduce their remarks by saying, "This is really interesting," or "D'ya know what?" (Fishman, 1978). The following excerpts from conversations recorded by Fishman illustrate how this works. In the first the man introduces a conversational topic and the woman responds.

> MALE: I saw in the paper where Olga Korbut . . .
> FEMALE: Yeah.
> MALE: . . . went to see Dickie . . .
> FEMALE: You're kidding! What for?
> MALE: I don't know.
> FEMALE: I can just imagine what she would go see Dick Nixon for. I don't get it.
> MALE: I think she's on a tour of the United States.
> FEMALE: Has he sat down and talked to her?
> MALE: (shows a picture in the paper)
> (conversation continues).   (Quoted in Parlee, 1979)

Now compare that with this excerpt where the woman tries to get a conversation going on a magazine article she is reading.

> FEMALE: I am really offended! That a magazine could publish this book. (pause, during which male does not respond) That someone could put together this kind of a book on muckraking sociology. This article I'm reading just (pause) just to aggravate myself, I guess, called "(title of article)" by Bill London. (pause, no response from male) It is the most sexist thing, overtly sexist-racist thing I have read in years.

Box 6.2   *(continued)*
MALE: Why?   (quoted in Parlee, 1979)

Interrupting and using minimal responses to control the topic of
conversation are only two of the many subtle dominance behaviors
people with status advantages use when dealing with those with lower
status. However, they are a good example of the way dominance
behaviors work. By a series of small, often unconscious, gestures,
people translate their external status advantage into power and influence in a face-to-face relationship. As long as these dominance gestures are legitimized by high performance expectations (as they almost
always are when there is an external status advantage), the person
with low status characteristics will accept them and, knowingly or not,
bolster the other's high status.

---

when and how they affect the performance expectations members hold
for one another, and consequently the status they achieve. In Berger et
al. (1974), it is noted that certain types of external status characteristics,
called *diffuse status characteristics,* carry performance expectations that are
quite *general* in that they are not limited to specific situations only.
Examples are status characteristics like sex, race, or age. These are
diffuse characteristics because, while they carry some specific behavioral expectations, they are not limited to those. Rather, they are assumed by our society to be more or less relevant to all situations,
whether this is reasonable from a logical point of view or not. In contrast
to diffuse characteristics are *specific status characteristics* that carry performance expectations limited to specific situations only. Specialized skills
or abilities are specific status characteristics. Mathematical expertise, for
instance, might function as a specific status characteristic among a group
of students.

The next question is this: how and when do members' differences
in diffuse and specific status characteristics affect their expectations for
one another's performance at the group's central activities (and therefore, their status in the group)? These are the problems of salience and
relevance. It appears that any diffuse or specific status characteristic on
which the members clearly differ will be used by them to form performance expectations for one another, provided only that there is no
evidence that clearly disassociates the status characteristic from the
group task (Moore, 1968; Berger, Cohen, and Zelditch, 1972; Webster
and Driskell, 1978; Freese, 1976). This means, for instance, that a group
of students becoming friends in the dorm will be influenced by differences among them that may be quite irrelevant to their goals of friend-

ship and mutual support. Perhaps some come from a wealthier background or have a better academic record. Relevant or not, these differences will affect the performance expectations the students form for each other and, ultimately, the power and prestige they have in each other's eyes.

Status characteristics that differentiate the members can be used to create performance expectations in one of two ways. First, the status characteristic might be directly relevant to the group task, the way mathematical ability is relevant to solving some puzzles. In this situation, status characteristics give rise to performance expectations in a direct and logical way. But second, and importantly, status characteristics that distinguish among the members also create performance expectations even when the status characteristic is *not* directly relevant to the group's activities. By what is called a "burden-of-proof process" a status characteristic that discriminates among the members is assumed to be relevant to any task activity unless proved otherwise (Berger, Cohen, and Zelditch, 1972). The burden of proof is on those who would argue that it is *not* relevant to the group activities. This is how status characteristics like race or sex end up determining who has power and influence even when they are utterly irrelevant to the group's activities. This, for instance, is what happened in the mixed-sex juries that Strodtbeck, James, and Hawkins (1957) studied.

In addition to those that discriminate among the members, any status characteristic that the members believe is relevant to success or failure at the task will have an impact on the expectations members form for one another. If, for instance, group members share a status characteristic that is relevant to their group goal, it will serve as an *equating characteristic,* establishing a peer relationship among them in that regard (Webster, 1977). Being a woman in a women's consciousness-raising group, for instance, becomes an important status characteristic that establishes a certain fundamental equality among the members. As we shall see, equating characteristics can reduce the impact of status characteristics in which the members differ.

By now it may have occurred to you that, either through actual relevance or through a burden-of-proof process, more than one status characteristic may influence the members' expectations for each other's performance in the group. How do members combine all this information to actually form expectations for themselves and for their groupmates? Berger and his colleagues argue that the information from different status characteristics is simply added together in the members' minds to form aggregate expectations for one another (Berger et al., 1976; Webster and Driskell, 1978). The more clearly and directly relevant a status characteristic is for the group's task, the more heavily it counts in forming these aggregated impressions. This means that directly relevant characteristics probably have a bigger impact on expectations than do those connected by a burden-of-proof process (Berger et al., 1980).

Sometimes a person's status characteristics give rise to inconsistent assumptions about their performance capabilities. In our society, for example, it is generally considered a higher status to be male than female. So, in a mixed-sex group, the members should generally have higher performance expectations for the males than the females. But what if one of the women is also a doctor, a very high-status occupation in our society? The performance expectation for a doctor should be higher than that for the non-doctors in the group. How, then, do the group members form an expectation for the woman doctor's abilities?

For years, it was thought that the woman doctor would be treated as either a woman or a doctor but not both. The basic idea was that the inconsistency between the woman's two status characteristics caused tension or discomfort for both her and the rest of the group (for example, Lenski, 1954; Kimberly, 1966; Zelditch and Anderson, 1966). To avoid this tension, the inconsistency in her status would be resolved by ignoring one or the other of the inconsistent characteristics. Theories differed on which status characteristic would be acted upon and which would be ignored. However, the usual idea was that the status characteristic least relevant to the group's activities would be the one ignored. So in a team of doctors working on a patient, the woman doctor would be just another doctor. In a women's group, however, she would be just another woman.

There is an alternative to this scenario, however. It is possible that, rather than ignoring either of the inconsistent characteristics, people simply combine them just as they do all other status characteristics (Berger et al., 1977). According to this view, a woman doctor should seem more able than other women, but less impressive than a male doctor.

Which approach is best supported by the evidence? The results are a bit mixed (for example, Freese and Cohen, 1973), but today the greatest weight of evidence supports the simple combining idea (Berger et al., 1977; Webster and Driskell, 1978). It appears that people simply add up the positive expectations associated with an individual's high status characteristics (for example, being a doctor) and subtract the negative expectations associated with low status characteristics (for example, being female) to create a kind of averaged expectation. So a woman doctor equals "more" than other women but still "less" than a male doctor.

In forming expectations, people seem to use all the information on status characteristics that they have. Even when a status characteristic is not directly relevant to the group's activities, it is not ignored just because it is inconsistent (Zelditch et al., 1980). So it seems that people simply combine inconsistent status characteristics when forming expectations for one another.

These are the basic tenents of status characteristics theory. What is particularly powerful about the theory is the way it describes how external status characteristics structure the status hierarchy of face-to-face groups even when they are irrelevant to the group's concerns. This, of course, is how status differences between blacks and whites, between men and women, and between other groups are maintained in face-to-face situations, even when the participants are free from overt racism or sexism. Anyone who has felt him- or herself to be at an external status disadvantage in a group knows how frustrating the status generalization process can be. It is not surprising, then, that a significant thrust of research on status characteristics has been to develop intervention techniques that can overcome the effects of status generalization. This is one of the topics we will consider next. Doing so will also allow us to gain more insight into the roles that objective competence and group-oriented motivation play in the status process of these groups.

THE ROLE OF OBJECTIVE COMPETENCE.   Before we go on, however, we should comment briefly on the effects of objective competence on group status processes when members differ in external status. We have seen that status characteristics have their effect by creating differential expectations for competence, which, through a process of self-fulfilling prophecy, tend to create real differences in participation and performance. But we have not discussed actual objective competence at the task.

What if a person with low status characteristics really is very good at the task and manages to demonstrate that fact in the group? Clear evidence of a superior performance should modify expectations held for that person and raise his or her status in the group (Berger, Conner, and Fisek, 1974). But, as we will see when we examine the status equilibration process, this doesn't happen very often. First of all, the pressure of low expectations makes it hard for anyone to perform well no matter how able he or she is. Athletes face this problem all the time. Suppose you are a talented tennis player, but you are also Ms. Nobody and you have been matched against Ms. Famous Champion. Experts who have seen you play think you have the talent to beat her, but the press and fans in the audience clearly expect you to lose. Comes the big game, you find yourself nervous, perspiring. Ms. Champion, on the other hand, is easy and relaxed. Every point she scores draws a roar of approval from the crowd. You find it hard to concentrate and make mistakes that make you even more nervous. Before long you are down in the game, and then in the set, and finally loose the match.

The pressure of low expectations are not the only thing that makes competence hard to prove when you have low external status. Just as important is the fact that most of the tasks dealt with by actual small groups are relatively ambiguous, often dealing with a problem of planning, decision making, or of human relations. As we pointed out earlier, there are no simple, clear-cut, objective criteria for evaluating competence at such tasks. This makes it doubly hard for the person to prove his or her abilities to the rest of the members, who are skeptical to begin with.

We can conclude, then, that demonstration of objectively superior competence should raise the status of a member with low external status characteristics. Similarly, demonstration of objectively inferior competence should lower the status of a person with high external status characteristics. However, due to the self-fulfilling nature of the expectations associated with high and low external status, such demonstrations are difficult to accomplish.

OVERCOMING STATUS GENERALIZATION.   There has been a move in our society of late to include more members of status-disadvantaged groups—for instance, minorities, women, and poor people—in various governmental planning and decision-making groups. The idea has been to insure that the opinions and interests of these people are represented in the decisions that are produced. However, the results of these efforts have often been disappointing. Despite their presence on various boards and councils, such people have often found that they have had little influence on the decisions made. They have been victims of the status generalization process.

Is there any way this process can be overcome, that people who differ in external status can relate to one another as true equals in power and influence? Fortunately, the answer is yes. We will examine two techniques that have been developed to accomplish this. The first uses additional information to modify the performance expectations people hold for themselves and others. The second uses the communication of a cooperative, group-oriented attitude to diffuse the resentment others feel when a low external status person tries to achieve higher status.

The first technique, the modification of performance expectations, was originally demonstrated in an interesting study by Cohen and Roper (1972). These researchers wanted to achieve equal status interaction between black and white junior high school boys working together on a task. In our society it is unfortunately considered higher status to be white than black. As a result, the white students, who were higher on the diffuse status characteristic of race, could be expected to dominate in such groups (Cohen, 1972). But Cohen and Roper felt this inequality could be overcome if it could be demonstrated to the students that the black kids were higher than the white kids on other specific status characteristics. The researchers trained the black students to build a transistor radio, making them high on a specific status characteristic (radio-building skill) on which the white students were low. Then they had the black students teach the white students how to build a radio. This created a second specific status characteristic, teachers versus learners, on which black students were again high and white students were low. Just as important, the teaching session provided a situation in which the specific status superiority of the black students could be dramatically demonstrated to all. Cohen and Roper assumed that this clear demonstration would alter the performance expectations black and white students held for each other.

At this point, then, the effects of the diffuse status characteristic of race were counteracted for both black and white students by two opposite-valued specific status characteristics. Consequently, the black and white students should now have been able to approach each other as equals. To test whether this was true, the students participated in a cooperative game after the teaching session. During the game, Cohen and Roper measured the influence and prestige accorded black and white students. It was generally equal. Cohen and Roper had succeeded in overcoming the generalization of the status characteristic of race.

Making equating characteristics relevant to the group's task can also reduce the effects of status generalization (Webster, 1977). For instance, if a group of parents of varying economic backgrounds gather to discuss their children's problems at school, emphasizing their shared status as parents will reduce the impact of their economic differences. However, to completely overcome status generalization, as Cohen and Roper did, it is necessary to outweigh the offending status characteristic with new, opposite-valued specific characteristics. If these new status characteristics are made directly relevant to the group's task, they will be particularly effective in overcoming status generalization effects (Cohen and Roper, 1972).

Since the Cohen and Roper study, several additional experiments have demonstrated the basic effectiveness of this technique (Freese and Cohen, 1973; Freese, 1974; Pugh and Wahrman, 1978). However, as a method of intervention, it has one disadvantage. It is not sufficient just to modify the performance expectations low external status members hold for themselves (Katz and M. Cohen, 1962; Cohen, 1972). Doing this will increase their assertiveness, but their efforts will be resisted by the high external status members, who don't want to relinquish their own advantage and are likely to interpret those efforts as a self-oriented, illegitimate status grab. The result is a status struggle. To truly overcome status generalization it is necessary to modify the expectations held by both high and low external status members. This may not always be practical in actual small groups, where the low external status members may not have the power to manipulate the expectations held by others. If, for instance, you are the only black member of the school board, how much power do you have to manipulate the expectations held by your conservative white opponents?

The second intervention technique we will consider overcomes this disadvantage. However, it is still in the testing stage and is not yet as clearly established by empirical evidence as is the first. In considering the development of status in mixed-sex groups, Meeker and Weitzel-O'Neill (1977) suggested that women might be able to defuse the status struggle they would otherwise face with men if, in their efforts to achieve influence, they appeared to be motivated by a desire to help the group rather than to aggrandize themselves. This desire to help the group is the socioemotional variable we have called group-oriented motivation. We contrasted it with the more purely self-interested motive of self-orientation.

We have argued that group-oriented motivation is a basic factor that affects status in small groups. Drawing on Meeker and Weitzel-O'Neill, Ridgeway (1978) argued that the member's perceived motivation in the group will have its greatest impact when the member enters the group with low external status characteristics. The reason for this is a legitimacy dynamic set in motion by external status characteristics (Meeker and Weitzel-O'Neill, 1977). The high and low performance expectations created by status characteristics specify the quantity and quality of task-related behaviors initially expected from a member. Following Meeker and Weitzel-O'Neill, Ridgeway (1978) suggested that as long as a member's task efforts fall within the range expected of someone with his or her status characteristics, those efforts are considered "legitimate."

To make this notion of legitimate task efforts a bit clearer, let's consider an example. Imagine some friends are helping you move an old refrigerator into your upstairs apartment. One of your friends has had summer jobs with a professional moving company. Another has never moved anything heavy before. In this situation, moving expertise is an external status characteristic that creates high performance expectations for your skilled friend, and low expectations for the inexperienced one. Given his expertise you expect your skilled friend to contribute more to the task. Therefore, when he dominates the "how are we going to do this" discussion and gives lots of advice, you consider his high task efforts appropriate and "legitimate." However, when your inexperienced friend tries to give you advice you are annoyed. Since you presume that he doesn't know what he is talking about, his high task efforts seem illegitimate. He must keep his contributions in proportion to the skill level implied by his status characteristics for them to be considered legitimate.

When efforts to deal with the task are legitimate, there is no need to question the member's motivation in making them. However, when members try to go beyond what is expected of them given their status characteristics, the rest of the group will want to know why. What are their motives? To help the group solve the task (group-oriented motives)? Or to aggrandize themselves (self-oriented motives)?

If the answer is self-aggrandizement, the member's extra illegitimate task efforts will be ignored. However, if the member appears to be group-oriented in intention, those added task efforts will be taken more seriously. If the efforts seem competent, they are likely to influence the group's decisions. As a result the group-oriented member's rate of participation and influence level will rise, increasing his or her status in the group.

When a person enters a group with high external status, a high level of task-related effort will be expected of him or her. Consequently, virtually all the task-related behaviors the member wishes to engage in will be considered legitimate by the rest of the group, and the member's motive for engaging in them will not be questioned. Therefore, Ridgeway (1978, 1982) argues that the generalization of *high* external status will not be affected by the member's apparent motivation.

However, the generalization of *low* external status *will* be affected by motivation. If a person comes to a group with low external status characteristics but does not want to end up on the bottom of the group's status hierarchy, he or she will have to engage in a more task-related behavior than is expected. This is the only way the person can increase his or her participation and influence rates to achieve higher status. Yet, at the same time, all those extra task efforts will be considered illegitimate by the rest of the group, and the person's motivation will be questioned by the other group members. If the person is found to be group oriented in motive, the added task efforts will be allowed, and the person's status in the group should improve. Consequently, offering the appearance of being group oriented might be a technique by which the generalization of low external status characteristics could be blocked.

The advantage of this approach is that it allows you to improve your status in the group by modifying your own behavior. It is not necessary to first modify the performance expectations others have for you. However, as yet there is only study to support the effectiveness of this technique. Ridgeway (1982) conducted an experiment in which the female member of an otherwise male group attempted to contribute substantially to the group's task efforts but accompanied her efforts with behaviors indicating that she was either self or group oriented. The self-oriented woman's efforts to influence the group were rejected, and she ended up at the bottom of the group's status hierarchy. However, when the woman appeared group oriented to the others, she was much more successful in attaining moderate to high influence and status in the group. When a male in a female group appeared self or group oriented, it did not substantially affect the status and influence he achieved. As predicted, then, motivation blocked the generalization of low external status but not high.

These results make it clear that motivation can overcome the generalization of low status that women face in mixed-sex groups, as Meeker and Weitzel-O'Neill (1977) suggested. However, we don't yet know whether motivation would have the same effect if the status characteristic were something other than sex—say race or age. Ridgeway (1982) argues that motivation should have the same effect no matter what the status characteristic is, but this must be confirmed by further research.

It appears, then, that the pervasive impact of status characteristics on group status structure can be reduced or overcome. Doing this requires that we manipulate one or the other of two basic sources of status in groups: either performance expectations, which really reflect perceived competence, or a socioemotional variable, the member's perceived motivation. These two factors, together with the status characteristics, objective competence, and dominance behaviors that go with them, determine the status hierarchies of virtually all small groups.

STATUS EQUILIBRATION AND STATUS INCONSISTENCY

Status Equilibration and the Maintenance of the Status Order

You may have noticed from our discussion of status evolution that the various sources of status often affect one another. Being high on one usually encourages the group to see you as being high on others. These variables tend to go together because of a preference on the part of group members for a single consistent status hierarchy. The process of lining up members' rankings on the various dimensions of status so that they are roughly consistent with one another is called *status equilibration* (Kimberly, 1966).

There are several reasons why most groups tend to evolve a single consistent status system. First of all, it gives the group a simpler, more clear-cut social structure that should make the process of coordinating the members' behavior easier. By aiding the structural integration of the group, it makes it easier for the group to successfully pursue its goals. Second, a single consistent status system is easier to maintain than a complex, overlapping, inconsistent one, and results in a more stable group structure. For instance, if members who were low in one status dimension were nevertheless high on another, they might feel encouraged to press for higher status in the group. This, in turn, would keep the group's status system in a constant state of flux and distract the group's attention from other activities. On the other hand, if members who are low on one status dimension are also low on most other dimensions, they have little basis on which to argue for a change in status, making the status system easier to maintain. This example suggests as well a third reason why groups tend to evolve a single consistent status system. The members who, in the process of status evolution, begin to emerge as high on some ranking have a vested interest in having themselves declared to be high on other dimensions as well, since this will solidify their power.

Finally, it has been argued that inconsistent status rankings are psychologically stressful for people because of the conflicting expectations placed on their behavior (Goffman, 1957; Sampson, 1963, 1969; McCranie and Kimberly, 1973). Others in turn supposedly find it difficult to deal with status-inconsistent people because they do not know whether to treat them as people of high or low status. This is a version of the argument we encountered earlier when we discussed how people combine information on inconsistent status characteristics.

This last argument is more psychological and interpersonal in emphasis, while the others focus more on problems of group structure and power. The last argument is also the one traditionally cited as the major reason why status equilibration occurs in groups. However, as we shall see, recent evidence suggests that this argument may not be as valid as was once thought (Crosbie, 1979).

Once the group has evolved a stable status hierarchy, the members tend to maintain it by insuring that they are ranked on subsequent activities in a way that is consistent with their current status rankings. Thus the status equilibration process becomes a process by which a group's status structure is maintained over time. Once again citing Whyte's classic 1943 study of the Nortons, the street-corner gang in Boston, we find a beautiful illustration of this. One activity the Nortons did together was to go bowling. Whyte noticed that, interestingly enough, the members' bowling scores lined up almost perfectly with their positions in the gang's status hierarchy. "Doc," the leader, almost always scored the highest.

Alec was a gang member who was at the bottom of the status hierarchy. When he bowled alone, he bowled quite well, often scoring higher than Doc's average. But when Alec bowled with the rest of the gang, he could never manage to bowl as well as he was able; somehow he always had an off night.

On one occasion, Doc had the idea of staging a competition among the bowlers in the gang, and he collected some prize money to be given to the top scorers. Alec was determined to prove his skill and announced his intentions to the rest of the gang. The other members clearly saw this as a challenge to the group's status system. When after the first few frames Alec was indeed ahead, the rest of the gang began to heckle and harass him. Under pressure Alec began to make mistakes. Ultimately he stopped even trying. Between turns he began going out and having drinks, with the results that he became "flushed and unsteady on his feet" (Whyte, 1955). In the end, his bowling score had fallen from first to last place. As one of the members said later, it wouldn't have been right if Alec had won.

Alec collapsed under pressure for two reasons. First, of course, was the direct pressure he felt from his groupmates' heckling. But second, Whyte (1955) implies that Alec had to deal with a certain amount of self-doubt as well. Although he knew he was a good bowler, he also knew he had low status in the group, and that fact eroded his confidence. In fact, when he was with the others, he shared their low performance expectation for himself. This combination of external and internal pressures is typical of the way groups encourage their members to behave in accord with their position in the status hierarchy. In this way, the status system of the group becomes self-maintaining.

The Behavior of Status-Inconsistent Members: Is It Unusual?

As we noted earlier, several writers have argued that status inconsistency is psychologically stressful and that it makes interaction with others more difficult. A number of these writers followed up on this idea, suggesting that, as a result, group members with inconsistent status ranks (that is, those who are high on some dimensions and low on others) will act differently than those with consistent status rankings (Benoit-Smullyan, 1944; Fenchel et al., 1951; Homans, 1961; Sampson, 1963, 1969; Kimberly, 1966; Galtung, 1966; Fleishman and Marwell, 1977; Zelditch and Anderson, 1966). An example of a person with inconsistent status ranks is a Ph.D. truck driver or a woman who has been appointed foreman of a crew of men.

These theories argue that the behavior of status-inconsistent group members will be different in several ways (Crosbie, 1979). First, because they are often treated in accord with their low status rankings, when they would like to be treated according to their high status rankings, they should show greater dissatisfaction with the group than other members. Second, they are likely to feel a certain amount of injustice in their situation, and therefore, should be more interested in changing the system than other group members. Finally, due to interaction difficulties, they should be more likely to withdraw from interaction with other group members.

Do people with inconsistent status rankings really show these distinctive behaviors in small groups? Until recently several writers thought the answer was yes (Sampson, 1969; Fleishman and Marwell, 1977; McCranie and Kimberly, 1973). But now there is new evidence that suggests status-inconsistent people behave no differently than other group members. Crosbie (1979) conducted an experiment designed to test the major theories of the effects of status inconsistency on behavior. At first glance, it appeared that most of the theories produced positive results. However, when Crosbie statistically controlled for the simple effects of the person's original high and low status rankings (rather than the inconsistency introduced by their combination), he found that the status inconsistency effects disappeared. Very few of the previous researchers had made these important corrections in their data. But those who had, had also found no significant effects for status inconsistency (Crosbie, 1979). These findings led Crosbie to conclude that status inconsistency is not a psychological or interactional problem for most people. Rather, the effects usually ascribed to status inconsistency were simply due to holding a low rank on one or more status dimensions.

So, it is having low status in the group, not status inconsistency, that encourages members to be dissatisfied with the group, to want to change it, or to withdraw from interaction. Crosbie argued that if earlier studies were analyzed this way, they too would show no independent effects of status inconsistency. At this point, then, it is probably best to conclude that people are capable of handling inconsistent status rankings without particular difficulty. Indeed, our earlier discussion of status characteristics theory suggests that people simply combine inconsistent status rankings and deal with one another on the basis of the average that results. Consequently, there is no reason to expect that status-inconsistent members will behave differently in the group than other members. This brings us back to our earlier point that status equilibration is more important for the maintenance of the group's status system than it is for the personal consistency needs of the individual members.

DISTRIBUTIVE NORMS AND EQUITY

At the beginning of this chapter we noted that status structures are not only a means for organizing the group, but are also a system for allocating rewards. Our discussion of reward allocation carried with it two implications that deserve renewed attention now. First, in general, rewards tend to be distributed in a way that is consistent with a person's status rank. In a sense, this is just an extension of the notion of status equilibration. Second, the perceived fairness, or justice, of the way the status system distributes rewards will have an important impact on the stability of that system. This is usually called the problem of distributive justice.

Let us look more carefully at these two points, beginning with the second. Behind the notion of perceived injustice is the idea of a shared norm defining what a just distribution of rewards is. To feel injustice, one must compare one's situation to this norm and find a discrepancy. A neighborhood kid, for instance, might be paid four dollars for mowing a lawn. Whether or not he thinks this is fair will depend on the norm his reference group has for what is a just price for lawn mowing. In this case, chances are his reference group is his other young friends who also mow lawns. If they say four dollars is fair, he will be satisfied with it. But if they say they get six dollars for a lawn, he will be outraged and feel he has been done an injustice. Studying how people make such comparisons and how they react once they define the situation as inequitable has been the special concern of a set of researchers called *equity* theorists.

Equity Theory

Most equity theorists work within the tradition of exchange theory (for example, Homans, 1961, 1974; Adams, 1963, 1965; Walster et al.,

1973; Walster, Walster, and Berscheid, 1978). They argue, much as we did earlier, that groups evolve equity or justice norms for distributing rewards as a way of maximizing the collective rewards available to the group. Without such norms, destructive competition among the members would diminish the rewards available to any member. To avoid this, groups evolve standards of fair distribution that can be used to manage conflicts of interest among the members. Since these norms are important to the stability of the group, members are taught to take them seriously. As a result, violations of distributive justice norms in a relationship are upsetting to people, resulting in guilt if the person receives more than he or she should, and anger or dissatisfaction if the person receives less. To relieve this distress, the person will make some attempt to restore equity in the relationship.

In our society, say the exchange theorists, the prevailing norms of justice are based on *equity*. A distribution of rewards is equitable when group members receive rewards in proportion to their inputs or investments in the group (Homans, 1961; Adams, 1965; Walster et al., 1978). This means that if one member contributes more than another to the group, he or she should receive more rewards in return. We can contrast an equity norm of justice with an *equality* norm, which holds that group members should each receive an equal share of rewards regardless of their contributions. There is some tradition for this as well in American society, although equity norms predominate.

Group members generally bring equity norms with them from the larger society where they have been learned. The equity or inequity of the group's allocation of rewards is then determined by comparing it to these norms. As Berger, Zelditch, Anderson, and Cohen (1972) point out, when people make such comparisons they usually take more into account than simply the strictly local comparison between the rewards they have received and those received by another member of their group. They are likely to consider an entire referential structure containing general social knowledge about the status value of various characteristics and behaviors, and the rewards that should go with these things. Thus you might decide that, in comparison to your groupmate, Mike, who put about as much into the group as you did, you were not treated unfairly. But if your referential structure suggests that people with attributes like yours and Mike's should be more highly rewarded than you were, you might decide that the group was unfair to both you and Mike. The concept of referential structure, then, illustrates how people make justice comparisons, not only with their groupmates, but also with an understanding of the larger social context in which the group operates.

People will act to restore equity, say equity theorists. Basically they can do this in one of two ways. First, they can change the ratio of the rewards they are getting to the inputs they are contributing in order to achieve *actual equity*. Interestingly, equity theorists argue that people feel unhappy when they are inequitably *overrewarded* as well as when they are underrewarded (Adams, 1965; Walster et al, 1978). If they receive more than they think they deserve, they feel guilty. If they receive less, they are angry. If they were overrewarded, for instance, to restore equity they could give back some of the reward. Or, what is more likely, they could increase their inputs so that they "deserve" the higher rewards they received. Adams (1963) showed that people did this when they were made to feel overpaid for their jobs: they compensated by working harder. Another way to restore actual equity would be to convince the rest of the group to change the system for distributing rewards to a more equitable one. In other words, you could try to convince the group to change things so that you get less if you are overrewarded or get more if you are underrewarded. However, human nature being what it is, it seems more likely that people will use this method of restoring equity when they are getting less than they deserve, rather than more.

A second technique for restoring equity is to distort your own perception of your inputs and rewards to achieve *psychological equity* (Walster et al., 1978). Rather than changing your actual behavior, you simply convince yourself that things are different than you first thought. For example, if you are overrewarded, you might decide that the value of your contributions is really higher than you thought. Therefore you deserve those rewards after all. "Sure I'm paid a lot," you may say, "but I'm worth it." Achieving psychological rather than actual equity is much more painful if you have been underrewarded. It means deciding that your contributions were not worth as much as you thought, and, therefore, that low rewards are all you deserve.

Equity theorists say people are most likely to resort to the mental tricks of achieving psychological equity under three conditions (Walster et al., 1978):

1. When you don't have the power to change either your own inputs or the group's reward system 'enough to create true equity.

2. If you are not personally responsible for the inequity: it is often easier to resort to a psychological justification rather than making the effort to change things (Walster et al., 1973).

3. The more costly it is for you (in personal sacrifice or effort) to restore actual equity, the less likely you are to do it, and the

more likely you are to rely on psychological equity (Walster et al., 1978).

Equity and the Status System

Now that we understand the basic principles of equity theory, let us apply them to the problems of reward distribution in groups. There are two ways in which we can do this. First, we can view power and prestige as rewards and examine the status system itself as an example of equitable or inequitable reward allocation. Second, we can look at the way the group distributes other collective rewards earned by the group as a whole. Considering these problems will bring us back to our earlier point that rewards tend to be allocated in a fashion consistent with the status system.

STATUS AS A JUST REWARD.   One way to view a status system is to consider a member's external status characteristics, dominance behaviors, competence, and likeability as contributions or inputs to the group deserving of proportionate rewards of power and prestige. As the group evolves its status structure some members may feel that power and prestige are not being distributed equitably. Generally such feelings develop out of disagreements over the weight or value of particular characteristics that are being treated as contributions to the group. For instance, women in a mixed-sex group might resent the fact that sex is treated as a relevant input for distributing power and prestige. In another group, some members might feel that socioemotional variables such as friendliness should count for more than they do in the distribution of status.

For a group to maintain a stable system it is vital that these disagreements be worked out, and that the majority of members come to see the status system as just. It is for this reason that perceived competence (as reflected in performance expectations) plays such a large role in the justification of status systems. When we examined the evolution of status, we found that the most powerful determinants—dominance behaviors and external status characteristics—gave rise to differential expectations of task competence, which in turn often shaped actual task performance. If you ask most groups to explain why certain members have more power and prestige than others, the answer that so-and-so is a white male or is very dominant is highly unlikely. Rather, it typically will be that so-and-so is better at the group activities than the other members (Lee and Ofshe, 1981). Differences in perceived competence, then, are vital for legitimating the power and prestige order—for asserting that it is, in fact, equitable.

It is only by such legitimating assumptions that low-status members can be induced to accept the status system as it is. That is why the Norton gang felt it just wouldn't be right if Alec out-bowled Doc. If Alec had won it would have challenged the legitimacy of the status system, suggesting that power and prestige was not distributed equitably on the basis of competence and merit. This in turn would have invited efforts to restore equity by changing the status order of the gang.

When a group member feels the status system is inequitable, he or she may, in fact, try to change it. But, as Alec found out, the other members who profit by the system are likely to resist. Most particularly they are likely to resist any redefinition of relevant inputs to the group that would make their current status seem inequitable. For instance, if older members have higher status due to seniority, they are likely to resist the efforts of younger members to declare seniority irrelevant to the group activities. In other words, people try to maintain the status quo when they benefit from it. They often do this, however, by convincing themselves and others that the status quo is, in fact, equitable.

If an aggrieved member cannot change the status system, the member may reduce his or her inputs to the group. Recall that Crosbie (1979), when he tested his status inconsistency theories, concluded that the effects he found—withdrawal from group interaction, dissatisfaction, and a desire to change the system—were, in fact, the result of low status. Presumably, low-status members are the most likely to feel that the status system is inequitable. It is not surprising, then, that they should be dissatisfied with the group since this is a reaction to feeling inequitably underrewarded. Neither is it surprising that they should want to change the system, or failing that, reduce their inputs to the group by withdrawing from interaction. Both these reactions are efforts to restore equity.

When several people in a group perceive the status system to be inequitable, they may form a coalition and use their combined power to force a redefinition of the status hierarchy. (We will have more to say about coalitions in the next chapter.) However, whenever a significant minority of members feel the status system is unjust, it is problematic for the group even when they do not come together in a coalition. Such a group will suffer from constant status struggles among the members. This in turn erodes cohesiveness and impairs the group's ability to effectively pursue its goals. Maintaining the perceived equity of the group's status system, then, is vital for the continued survival of the group.

REWARDS AND STATUS.   Groups often acquire, through their collective efforts, extra resources, benefits, privileges, or material rewards that must be distributed among the members. For instance, a group of students might earn money from some group project, like organizing a car wash, or an amateur baseball team might purchase a certain amount of equipment that could be shared among the players in some way. How will the distribution of rewards, other than power and prestige, be related to the status system?

If an equity norm is employed, the members should receive rewards in proportion to their status rank. This, of course, assumes that the members accept the status system as just and, therefore, feel that the higher-status people deserve their positions because of their greater contributions and perceived competence.

Under what conditions do group members use an equity norm to determine the fairness with which rewards are distributed? This is an important question, because it is only when an equity principle is invoked that group members should react to perceived injustice with efforts to restore equity to the system. As we shall see, two conditions are necessary for a group to divide up rewards by an equity rule.

Cook (1975) argues that for an equity assessment to be made at all, it is first necessary that the members have a clear sense of where they each stand on the relevant evaluative dimensions associated with the rewards. For our purposes this means that the group must have a clearly established status hierarchy that carries with it clear expectations for the way each member should perform in the activities relevant to the rewards. Only with this information can members determine who "deserves" a greater proportion of the rewards.

Without such clearly ranked performance expectations—either because the group is newly formed or because the status hierarchy is in flux—it is virtually impossible to distribute rewards according to an equity principle. Instead, the simple equality principle will be employed. But what if an outsider distributed rewards unequally among members of such a group? Imagine a group of students who are assigned a project to present together to the class. The professor inspects each student's contribution to the project and grades them differentially. What effect does this unequal distribution of grades have on the group's status system? Cook's (1975) data suggest that students will assume (rightly or wrongly) that the unequal distribution of grades is equitable and, therefore, that they reflect true differences in merit. As a result they will use differences in rewards to create differences in status, power, and prestige among themselves. The outside rewards will transform the status hierarchy. As Cook (1975) notes, paraphrasing Homans (1961), groups in this situation come to see what *is*, as what is *right*.

A well-established status hierarchy with clearly ranked performance expectations for the members is, then, a necessary condition for invoking an equity principle for the distribution of rewards. However, it is not the only such condition, as Parcel and Cook (1977) discovered. They found that it was only when members had information on one another's *actual performances* in the activities leading to the rewards that an equity principle was used to divide up those rewards. Without information on actual performances, members divided the rewards equally even when the group had a clear status hierarchy. These results are quite interesting, although we should maintain an element of caution in regard to them. The groups Parcel and Cook studied were quite small (two persons) and composed only of female college students. It is possible that larger, nonstudent, or mixed-sex groups might act differently.

However, if Parcel and Cook are right, then it appears that informal groups do rely on equity to distribute rewards where there are clear differences in actual performances, or goal-related efforts. Simple *expectations* of differential performance, however, are not enough. Ideally, then, a low-status member, if he or she outperformed higher-status members, should receive a greater proportion of the rewards. However, due to the self-fulfilling nature of the expectations associated with high and low status, such upsets occur rather rarely. Remember Alec's unsuccessful efforts to out-bowl Doc. Consequently, the employment of equity principles even in situations where the test is actual performance will usually result in the higher-status people receiving greater rewards. It was, after all, Doc and his two lieutenants who won the prize money in the Nortons' bowling contest.

Equally interesting, however, is Parcel and Cook's finding that, when information on actual performance is lacking or unclear, rewards are divided *equally*. Why does this happen? Why don't the high-status members take a greater share of the rewards in that situation as well? To do so plainly would appear arbitrary and unjust—and would invite revolt on the part of low-status members. But there are also certain advantages, on occasion, to dividing rewards equally. Lerner (1974) has pointed out that while equity principles emphasize the differences among members, equality principles emphasize what they have in common. As a result, an equal division of rewards may serve to unify the group and increase its cohesiveness. Informal groups, then, are likely to prefer equality in the division of rewards in situations where there are no clear differences in performance because it allows them to express and enhance the solidarity of the group.

We see, then, that the distribution of rewards, and the perceived fairness of that distribution, is intimately related to the status system of the group. The status system, through the medium of differential performance, often determines who gets the greater share of collective rewards. But it is also true that, when an outsider passes out unequal rewards to the group members, this in turn can reshape the status structure. The status hierarchy can only be maintained if the members feel that it itself represents an equitable distribution of power and prestige based on contributions to the group. Similarly, high-status members must justify receiving a greater share of collective rewards with evidence that they have actually outperformed lower-status members. Failing this, or when, for some other reason, a significant number of group members feel the status system or its reward allocations are unjust, the group's cohesiveness and ability to pursue its goals will be seriously impaired.

SUMMARY

Due to its central role in controlling the activities and goals of the group, the status hierarchy is the most important aspect of group structure. We can define a group's status structure as the pattern of power and deference relations among the members. The status structure of most groups are characterized by a series of ranks occupied by members who share different degrees of power and prestige. The observable signs of a member's power and prestige are his or her rate of participation in group discussion, the type of evaluation this participation receives from other group members, and the degree of influence he or she wields.

Groups evolve their status systems in response to two different forms of pressure: (1) the need to organize in pursuit of the group's goals, and (2) the need to avoid destructive competition over the rewards to be gained from group activities. This gives the status system a dual aspect, first as a mechanism for organizing and utilizing talents, and second as a mechanism for allocating rewards. These two aspects come together in the types of behaviors and attributes members use to achieve high status in groups. There are four behavior or attribute categories that function as sources of status in small groups: external status characteristics, dominance behaviors, objective competence, and the socioemotional factors of likeability and group-oriented motivation. Three—external status characteristics, dominance behaviors, and objective competence—affect status through the medium of performance expectations, which are assumptions members develop about each other's abilities at the group task. The four factors together illustrate the mix between the individual's assertion of power and the group's choice to grant deference and influence that underlies the status process of groups.

To understand how the various sources of status work together to determine the status members attain, we examined the process of status evolution under two conditions. First, we considered the case of groups whose members begin as initial equals in terms of their status in the larger society. Early accounts suggested that status differences develop in these groups as members, through interaction, begin to recognize objective differences in one another's abilities and performances. However, more recent evidence challenges this view, showing that status hierarchies often develop too quickly to be based on assessments of objective abilities. Instead there is evidence that status differences often begin with nonverbal dominance gestures, which lead to more sophisticated linguistic control over who participates in group deliberations. These factors in turn affect the development of performance expectations and perceived likeability that become the foundation for status. Group-oriented motivation seems to enhance status by giving the group some reassurance about the way power will be used by various members if it is granted to them.

Next we examined the process of status evolution in groups whose members are differentiated by external status characteristics. Status characteristics theory has shown that differences in external status generalize to differences in power and prestige within the group. This occurs through the medium of the differing performance expectations associated with high and low status characteristics. Performance expectations tend to affect actual performance in a self-fulfilling manner. We noted that dominance behaviors are also more likely from people who have high external status characteristics relative to the group.

Because status characteristics tend to generalize to status in the group, even when they are completely irrelevant to the group task, we examined two techniques for overcoming status generalization. The first alters performance expectations by adding on additional status characteristics that are inconsistent with the offending characteristic. The second uses the communication of group-oriented motivation to defuse the resentment a person with low external status faces when he or she makes a bid for high status.

With an understanding of the status evolution process we turned to the issues of status equilibration and status inconsistency. Most of the time, when a group member is ranked high on one dimension of status, the group tends to rank him or her high on the others as well; this is the process of status equilibration. It allows groups to achieve and maintain a single consistent and stable status hierarchy. It has been argued that one of the reasons why groups develop consistent status systems is that inconsistency causes psychological and interpersonal problems. However, we noted recent evidence contradicting this view.

For a status system to persist and serve the group effectively, it must be perceived by the members as being fair, or just, both in itself and in the way it distributes rewards acquired by the group. We turned to equity theory for an explanation of how and when members judge the fairness of the status system and how they react to apparent inequity. We noted that, in general, rewards are distributed in accord with the status system. However, this must be justified by maintaining differences in performance at the group task, or the status system may be challenged as inequitable.

7

Leadership

We all feel a basic conflict between our desire for independence and our need to belong. In light of that conflict, the notion of the group leader takes on special emotional significance, for he or she alone seems to unify the capacity for independent action with the solidarity of the group. A leader seems to be an individual who is completely himself or herself, and yet also who is completely at one with the group. When we think of such leaders, we tend to recall those charismatic students who, when we were in high school, used to do everything right, the "natural" leaders, like Doc from the Norton gang.

And yet, how accurate is this cultural stereotype of the group leader? How does it match up with the more pedestrian reality of a committee and the routine leadership of its chairperson? We often simply assume that every group has a—that is, one—definite leader. But is this true? For instance, in a group of three or four adult friends who work together, is there usually a clear leader? Generally not. As we shall see, leadership is a complex, highly variable phenomenon that develops out of the interaction of the specific group, its environmental situation, and the nature of its members. It has little to do with the romantic notion of "natural" leaders.

How then can we define leadership? Crosbie (1975) argues that its essential focus is the exercise of decision-making rights and obligations in the group. Stogdill (1974) discussed leadership in terms of the initiation and maintenance of structure in the interaction of the members and in the role expectations they form for one another. Many others would add that these decision-making and structure-initiating actions are carried out as part of the process of pursuing group goals (Cartwright and Zander, 1968; Gibb, 1969). Putting these together, we see that the core of leadership is three-fold:

1. The exercise of an executive function in the group
2. The assumption of responsibility for structuring behavior

3. The directing of decisions as part of the group's effort to pursue its goals

The distribution of these executive rights and responsibilities among the members constitutes the group's *leadership structure* (Crosbie, 1975). Employing the notion of a leadership structure, rather than a single leader, allows us to deal with the possibility that groups may have several leaders, or even no leaders. In a *differentiated* or *pluralistic* leadership structure, decision-making rights and responsibilities are distributed among several group members. In an *integrated* structure they are concentrated on a single member who may rule with the help of one or two informally delegated "lieutenants" or right-hand friends. We will examine these and other types of leadership structures and inquire as to how they arise.

It would seem obvious that the concept of leadership structure is intimately related to that of the status structure. Leaders, of course, are almost always the highest status members in the group. In fact, there is usually a close correspondence between each member's position in the status hierarchy and his or her location in the leadership structure. Because of this association, the members most likely to be selected as group leaders are those who have the characteristics that give them high status. That is, they tend to be group members who rank high in external status characteristics, dominance behaviors, perceived competence, and likeability. The key indicator of those in leadership positions is also an indicator of high status: leaders talk more than others in the group —they dominate the group's discussion (Riecken, 1958; Burke, 1974).

Why, then, do we distinguish between leadership structure and status hierarchy? The answer lies in the distinctive meaning of the leadership structure for the group. A leader (for convenience, let us take the case of a single group leader) may be the group's highest-status member, but he or she is much more than that as well. In addition to the rewards of status, he or she has been entrusted with a special obligation, the stewardship of the group. For whatever reason, the group members have developed a shared belief that this person is best suited to manage the group's affairs. This belief is expressed in group norms that define the right of the leader to make decisions and structure group activities, and the obligation of the group members to comply with the leader's directives (Crosbie, 1975). The leadership structure, then, rests on a distinctive set of norms that define a kind of contract between the leader(s) and the group.

According to this contract leaders are granted the privilege of executive authority, which carries with it a degree of autonomy in decision making that the followers have relinquished. In exchange, leaders are expected to exercise their authority in the interests of the group as a whole. This expectation places limits on the range of decisions leaders may make and still expect willing compliance from group members. It also creates the essential paradox at the heart of group leadership: leaders both control the group and are controlled by it. Although they are in charge and are expected to define the group's direction, they can only lead it where it is willing to go. Chowdry and Newcomb (1952) illustrated this nicely in a study of four actual groups, one religious, one political, and the last two a medical sorority and fraternity. They measured the members' opinions on a number of issues, particularly those relevant to their own group. They also asked all the members to predict the opinions of their fellow members on these same issues. Interestingly, the group leaders estimated their fellow members' opinions more accurately on matters of concern to the group than did other members. In other words, leaders had their fingers closer to the pulse of group opinion than anyone else. As the authors point out, this greater sensitivity to the group's opinions was vital to their leadership positions because only with it could they lead the group where it wanted to go.

An essential part of the normative contract between a group and its leaders is that the exchange of rights and authority for duties and obligations must be a just and equitable one. Leadership is like status in this way. It is very important that the leaders appear to the members to deserve their positions. They must be judged to have the skills and motivation to offer the group the services required. As long as this condition is met, the leaders will exercise their authority *legitimately* in the eyes of the members and will receive the willing compliance of the group.

As we shall see, the way leaders achieve their positions in the group often effects the perceived legitimacy of their authority. There are two primary ways that leadership positions in groups are obtained. If the group is located within a larger organization, the leader may be *appointed* by that organization. The Chief Justice of the Supreme Court, for instance, is appointed from the outside; so might be the foreman of a work group. As long as the right of the outside agency to appoint the leader is accepted by the members, and the person appointed is viewed as reasonably deserving of the position, externally appointed leaders will have legitimate authority in the group (Read, 1974).

More common to small groups, perhaps, is the situation where leaders *emerge* from the interaction of group members themselves. This can occur in a relatively formal fashion, as when a committee elects a chairperson or a club elects a president. Or it may happen more informally, as when one person gradually takes on a leadership position in a group of friends. Since emergent leaders are created by groups themselves, and base the legitimacy of their positions entirely on their relationship to them, these are the leaders who will be the focus of our attention in this chapter.

To maintain their legitimacy, leaders must uphold their normative contract with their followers in several ways. Besides seeming qualified for their positions and appearing to have achieved them fairly, leaders must confine the exercise of their rights and authority to accepted channels. Generally, the authority of leaders is limited to matters pertaining to the group. If the head of a work group, for instance, attempts to control the nature of the members' off-hours activities, he or she will be met with cold stares rather than normative compliance.

Legitimacy requires that the privileges of leadership not be abused in other ways as well. A leader who appears to use his or her authority too exclusively for personal ends at the expense of the group will risk rebellion, as we shall see. So will any leader who fails to meet the group's expectations for helping it manage its problems.

Clearly, the authority group members hand over to leaders comes with many strings attached. Followers are far from powerless. They have the critical resource of *support,* not only individually, but also collectively. When subsections of the group's membership band together to use the collective power of their support either for or against a leader, we say they have formed a *coalition.* The operation of coalitions is part of the intricate power exchange between leaders and members that is at the foundation of group leadership.

By now, several points should be clear. As we have seen, leadership is defined in terms of the rights to direct decision making and initiate structure in the group. In addition, a group's leadership structure is closely associated with its status structure. However, we distinguish between status and leadership because of the special nature of the transaction between leaders and followers upon which leadership is based. In exchange for executive authority and the right to expect compliance from group members, leaders are obligated to assume a special responsibility for the group's welfare. The tenets of this contract between leaders and followers are expressed by a set of norms that define the group's leadership structure and outline the range of privileges and duties appropriate to various members.

With this basic view of group leadership in mind, we are ready to go on to a more thorough examination of the leadership process. We will begin with a more detailed discussion of the nature and sources of group leadership. Then we will turn to the leadership structure itself, examining the factors that affect its emergence and the various forms it may take. Taking up the leader's impact on the group, we will look more closely at the issue of the power of leaders and the style with which they wield their power. Finally, we will consider the coalitions group members form either to support or to oppose the leadership structure.

THE NATURE OF SMALL-GROUP LEADERSHIP

The Trait Approach

The first attempts to understand group leadership focused on the traits of those in leadership positions. People who become leaders must be superior individuals, it was assumed. They must have some fundamental characteristics to offer their followers, ones which would allow them to emerge as leaders in almost any group. Given this hypothesis, the best way to understand leadership is to find those characteristics that distinguish leaders from their followers.

After more than fifty years of research, this approach has produced little more than a maze of inconsistent findings (Stogdill, 1948; 1974). What makes some people leaders in one group or situation, it turns out, is not necessarily what makes them leaders in the next. We should not be surprised by this result. If we turn to actual groups and ask what kinds of persons usually become the leaders, we come up with numerous and divergent answers, depending on the particular type of group we consider. The leader of a gang is usually the one who best represents the group's ideals, as well as the one who makes good decisions. The most influential member of the President of the United States' "brain trust" is usually the best "idea person." In a friendship clique, the most influential one might be the wittiest, or the most sociable one.

The search for natural leaders is clearly the wrong way to approach the phenomenon of group leadership. The type of traits that distinguish a group's leader will depend on the needs and demands of the particular group. Not surprisingly, then, people who have attempted to pull leadership-trait research together and extract from it some coherent conclusions generally come up with lists similar to the following (Stogdill, 1974). Leaders tend to be higher than the rest of the group in 1) those particular abilities that are necessary to help the group attain its goals, 2) social skills that help the group function smoothly, and 3) motivational factors related to their desire for recognition or prominence (Shaw, 1981; Carter, 1954). Such lists define few distinctly individual traits of leadership and rely instead on definitions of group need.

The specific traits that would fall into the first two categories would vary substantially from group to group depending on each one's circumstances and the nature of its goals. In one group political know-how might be critical, in another creativity or the ability to distinguish good ideas. Even the social skills that groups require vary considerably with the formality of the group, its particular social conventions, and the personalities of its members.

Only the third category, motivational factors, is truly a distinctive trait of an individual, rather than a need or requirement of the group. This motivational factor is akin to the confidence or dominance factors that we saw were so important in status attainment. Since leaders are generally the highest-status members, these same factors operate here. So it seems that the single distinguishing personality characteristic of leaders is that they want to be leaders and have the self-confidence to try to attain the position.

Even confidence does not guarantee that you will become a leader, however. Beckhouse et al. (1975) conducted an interesting study of an all-male group which was composed of one naive member and two confederates of the experimenter. The naive member was someone either high or low in his perception of himself as a leader. This subject was appointed by the experimenter as the group leader. However, in half the groups, the confederates were instructed to resist the subject's leadership efforts and take over the job themselves. In this situation even the "natural" leaders were unable to assume the leadership role and were forced to begin acting like followers. In the rest of the groups the confederates acted passively, forcing the subject to take the lead. When this happened, even those subjects who were nonleaders by personality acted in a leaderlike way. The only difference was that the subjects who saw themselves as leaders asserted themselves more dramatically in the leader role than those who did not. The work of Beckhouse et al. demonstrates that even confident, assertive people can only be leaders when the group wants them to be so.

Obviously, then, the "trait" approach is not the best way to study leadership. In its failure, however, it has pointed the way to a more productive avenue of inquiry. We need to analyze leadership in terms of the needs and demands of particular types of groups and their members, and of the functions that leaders perform for the group in regard to these needs.

Leadership Functions and Roles

In the three-part list of leadership traits, you may have recognized in the first two, abilities related to group goals and social skills, our old,

Table 7.1. Leadership Functions and Roles

	Social Structure (relationships among members)	Culture (relationships among ideas and values)
Instrumental (Task) Activity	SQUARE 1 Dimension of social activity: (a) the division of labor (b) the structure of authority —guidance functions LEADER ROLES: (a) task organizer (b) executive decision-making	SQUARE 2 Dimension of cultural symbols: Knowledge, information LEADER ROLES: (a) idea person, analyst (b) synthesizer
Expressive (Socioemotional) Activity	SQUARE 3 Dimension of social activity: (a) network of affective ties (b) solidarity LEADER ROLES: (a) best liked (b) harmonizer (joker, host roles)	SQUARE 4 Dimension of cultural symbols: Values LEADER ROLES: (a) style setter (b) symbolic figurehead, consensus creator

Source: Adapted from Michael S. Olmstead, *The Small Group,* Copyright © 1959 by Random House, Inc. Reprinted by permission of the publisher.

familiar dimensions of task and socioemotional activities. In Chapter 1, if you recall, we emphasized how the basic problems of pursuing group goals and managing relations among the members placed fundamental demands on all small groups, which each had to meet in some degree if it was to survive. We argued that group members evolve two basic tools to address these problems: a social structure, and a group culture. Since we have inquired into the nature of group structure over the last several chapters, it will be familiar to you as the pattern of relationships among the members, the group's organization. Culture we will deal with in more detail in the next chapter. But for now we can say that *culture* is the rules, values, ideas, information, and beliefs group members use to guide and interpret group activities. A member can help the group manage its task and socioemotional problems by contributing to the creation and operation of either its social structure or culture.

Olmstead (1959; Olmstead and Hare, 1978) used this insight to create a fourfold table of the types of roles a leader could play in a small group. Table 7.1 is adapted from his conception. Each of the four squares represents a potential area of concern in group life that can give rise to a particular type of leadership role.

Persons performing one of these leader roles exercise a leadership function in that area of group life. That is, they help the group create and direct its use of social structure and culture in pursuit of task and socioemotional accomplishments. Let's look at the types of roles created in each quadrant of the chart to make this a little clearer. Leadership in square 1 focuses on organizing and directing the activities of the group members in such a fashion that the group goals can be pursued. This means creating a division of labor, delegating authority for various aspects of the group task, and generally organizing and administrating task activities. It means saying, "You do this, and you over there do that, so we can get this job done." In square 2 leadership is also concerned with the task, but it has more to do with the generation and application of ideas and information that the group needs to pursue its goals. Coming up with a new idea on how to approach a problem or pulling together the ideas of others are examples of the leadership activities that might be involved.

Square 3 moves on to the socioemotional dimension of group life. Leadership here means taking the initiative in resolving interpersonal conflicts, providing relief when tension builds up in the group, and in general seeking ways to maintain smooth, positive relations among the members. A wisecracking friend or the host at a party exercises this type of leadership. In square 4 we find a type of socioemotional leadership that is rarely seen in short-lived laboratory groups but is often vital in natural small groups. Leadership here means representing and expressing the group's values, and helping it to define new ones. A teenager who sets the style for his or her friends is an example. These kinds of leaders star at what the members most admire or value. They provide a symbol around which the members can rally.

The types of behavior delineated in Table 7.1 are not of equal concern to all groups. An informal friendship group, for example, is likely to put most of its energies into issues relating to squares 3 and, perhaps, 4. An adult self-help group might concentrate on squares 2 and 3. A working committee will be most concerned about squares 1 and 2. A multifunctional group like the family, on the other hand, is likely to pay some attention to all four areas of concern, although the emphasis it gives to each will probably change with time and circumstances.

The more important the issues associated with one of these squares are to a group, the greater the potential for some member or members to perform a leadership function in regard to them. Consequently, it is the relative concern a group devotes to each of these areas of group life that determines the number of leadership roles that may potentially emerge within the group. Since task and socioemotional activities are vital to all groups, regardless of their relative emphasis, virtually all groups evolve more than one leadership role.

At this point, however, we need to make it very clear that we are discussing leadership *roles* here, not persons. Any single leadership role can be played by one person or shared among several group members, or perhaps even played alternately by different group members. In addition, the different leadership roles that most groups have may be performed by separate people, concentrated in a single leader, or divided up in some complex way among the members. Leadership roles, then, describe types of leadership functions that are available to be performed in the group. This is different from the leadership structure of the group, which describes the way responsibility for performing these functions is distributed among the group members. Our next task is to understand the types of leadership structures groups may evolve to perform the leadership functions created by their purposes and circumstances.

THE LEADERSHIP STRUCTURE

Leaderless Groups and Leadership Functions

We have argued that a group has a leadership structure when it has evolved a set of normative beliefs about the way responsibility for structuring behavior and directing group decisions should be distributed among the members. Considering this definition forces us to recognize, first of all, that not all groups will develop a normatively defined leadership structure that is clearly recognized by the members. As Crosbie (1975) has noted, there are a substantial number of small groups that are relatively leaderless in that they have no agreed-upon method of dividing up decision-making responsibilities. These are usually informal primary groups that have no particular task to work on. Their outside environment is relatively benign in that it poses few crises for which the members turn to the group for assistance. In general, the members themselves come from similar backgrounds, are external status equals, and have similar abilities. Their goals when they get together are simply fun and relaxation (Feldman, 1973; Crosbie, 1975). The kind of friendship cliques students form at college are a good example. These sort of informal peer groups often lack a normatively defined leadership structure.

What happens then to the leadership functions we have just discussed? Are these groups different in that they have no need for anyone to perform any leadership functions, or do they manage them in some other way? It seems likely that in these groups, like all others, decisions must occasionally be made, interpersonal relations must be looked after, behavior must be coordinated. There will be a need for members to take the initiative in these matters. So there are leadership functions to be fulfilled in these groups too. While there are leaderless groups, then, there are no groups that do not have to perform at least some leadership functions.

The answer must be that leaderless groups manage their leadership functions without evolving a definite, agreed-upon structure for doing so. Different members simply spontaneously assume responsibility for directing a particular decision or looking after a particular interpersonal issue in an informal, continually changing fashion. As a result, no one member consistently performs any particular leadership role and no normative expectations develop about who is in charge of what. But collectively the group members manage to perform, at least minimally, the necessary leadership functions. A group of friends trying to decide where to go on a Friday night is an example. After a lot of talk and general milling around, agreement is reached on Joe's pizza place. But no definite leadership structure is responsible for the choice. Rather, at various points in the discussion, individual members spontaneously step in, try to focus the group's options, and push it to a decision. After several rounds of this, agreement is finally reached.

This kind of anarchic system for managing leadership responsibilities is probably only possible in groups like this, where there is little concern about task accomplishment and few pressing problems posed by the outside environment. However, there is one major advantage to this system. In leaderless groups no member needs to surrender his or her decision-making rights to others on a permanent basis. While relinquishing personal decision-making rights relieves a member of some responsibilities, it also restricts his or her freedom of action. Most people react negatively to restrictions on their freedom unless they feel it is necessary to attain other desirable benefits (Brehm, 1966).

The Emergence of Normative Leadership Structures

The fact that leaderless groups exist induces us to ask why other groups evolve clear, normatively defined leadership structures. What makes group members willing to endure the restrictions of freedom necessary to evolve a well-defined leadership structure?

Jones and Gerard (1967) have delineated four factors likely to encourage the emergence of a defined leadership structure in groups. The first is the complexity of the tasks or activities the group engages in. With complex activities there are simply more decisions to be made and more steps to be taken. A desire for efficiency or some sense of order in approaching a difficult task makes most members willing to relinquish some of their decision-making freedom in return for a simplified, organized decision-making system. The complex problems of running a city, for instance, make most city councils more than willing to turn some of their decision-making rights over to a system of subcommittees and chairpersons who will attack the problems in a coherent way. Those members who do the most to initiate and structure this decision-making system emerge as the most powerful in the leadership structure that is created.

A second factor encouraging the emergence of leadership structure is the commitment of the members to attaining a group goal. The more involved the members are in the group's goal achievement, the more willing they are to make sacrifices to aid in that achievement. An athletic team, for instance, will be willing to follow the directives of a team captain if it helps win games. A group of teenagers might be willing to turn leadership functions over to a popular, socially successful member if they feel that will increase the group's social standing. We should note, however, that commitment to group goals will encourage leadership emergence only if the members feel such a structure is an aid to goal attainment (Crosbie, 1975). The members of a leaderless friendship group might feel committed to group activities, but still not feel that a defined leadership structure would be helpful in carrying them out.

Crises or stress from the outside environment represent a third variable that encourages the development of defined leadership structures. In an interesting experiment Hamblin (1958) caused a crisis in game-playing groups by continually changing the rules by which they won or lost. Faced with this situation, the groups gave a great deal of influence over group decisions to just a few members. This did not happen in similar groups which were not confronted by a crisis. The urgency of meeting a crisis or threat to the group induces members to relinquish some of their freedom of action in favor of a clear leadership structure. Think of the power of the president in times of war. This may also be why gangs have such clear-cut leadership systems. Gangs exist in conflict with other gangs and groups in their area. Sometimes they engage in illegal activities that cause trouble with the police. Consequently, they face continued threats and crises from the outside environment. In response to these crises they create strong, well-defined leadership systems.

It is possible for a group to face crises or threats from the inside also. For example, a group may evolve a clear-cut leadership structure to avoid constant bickering and disagreement among the members. This is an obvious possibility in a decision-making group like a committee, but it could occur in primary groups as well. A group of people living together, for instance, a family, college roommates, or children at camp, might evolve a defined leadership structure to manage potentially divisive personal conflicts among the members.

Group size is the fourth factor in stimulating emergence of leadership structures. The more people in the group, the more difficult it becomes to coordinate everybody's activities without a distinct leadership system. Again, in the interests of efficiency, members become more willing to cede leadership functions to a defined few as the group size grows (Hemphill, 1950; Bass and Norton, 1951; Reynolds, 1971). We would expect to find many more leaderless dyads and triads than we would groups of six or seven.

We can conclude that groups are more likely to establish a defined structure to manage their leadership functions when either internal or external forces make the organization of group activities more difficult, or require the group to have the capability for quick and efficient action. Increases in group size and task complexity increase the organizational difficulties the group faces. Group enthusiasm about achieving its goals as well as threats or crises increase the group's willingness to relinquish decision-making rights to a defined few in the interests of effective, disciplined action.

Integrated and Pluralistic Leadership Structures

Let us turn now to groups who manage their leadership functions by means of a normatively defined leadership structure. In these groups some people will be in leadership positions and others in follower positions. Members may be in a leader role in regard to some types of group activities, and not others. For instance, a member might play the leader in maintaining interpersonal relations and a follower in regard to other activities, representing group values, perhaps, or coordinating task activities. So even in a group with a defined leadership structure it is still possible to have either an integrated or a pluralistic leadership system.

In an integrated, or fused, leadership structure, the highest-status group member performs or directs the fulfillment of all the leadership functions in the group. The aid of one or two delegated lieutenants may be enlisted to do this. Bales and his colleagues called the person at the head of an integrated leadership structure a "great man" (or great woman) leader because he or she has the skill to be many things to the group at once (Borgatta, Couch, and Bales, 1954). This person might direct task activities, embody or express group values, arbitrate personal disputes, and provide ideas and information to the group, thus combining several leadership functions in one person. He or she fills task and socioemotional leader roles in both the social-structural and cultural spheres of group life. Doc was such a person in the Norton gang. He organized group activities, represented the group to outsiders, introduced new ideas and innovative activities to the group, dealt with members' personal problems, and generally was at the center of group life.

A pluralistic leadership structure is somewhat different. Leadership positions are held by a small subgroup of the members rather than by a single dominant person. Usually the members of the leadership clique specialize in performing different leadership functions, or roles, for the group. One member might play a leadership role with regard to task activities, another might take charge of socioemotional relations or the expression of group values.

Pluralistic leadership systems have some advantages, in that the group has a wider pool of talent from which it draws leadership services. The various members of the leadership circle are allowed to specialize in fulfilling those leadership roles for which they have the greatest enthusiasm or ability. However, there is also a major disadvantage to a pluralistic structure: it is only effective as long as the leaders successfully coordinate their actions. For instance, among the President of the United States's advisers, leadership in foreign policy is divided between two people, the national security adviser and the secretary of state. In recent years, rivalry between men in those positions has kept this leadership structure from operating smoothly, causing persistent problems in the foreign policy area. Integrated leadership structures do not face this additional organizational obstacle. Thus, there are advantages and disadvantages to both types of leadership structure. Neither is inherently superior to the other.

Why Do Groups Have One Type of Leadership Structure Rather than the Other?

MEMBER DIFFERENCES.   Why do some groups develop an integrated leadership structure while others rely on a system of specialists to fulfill the necessary leadership functions? Common sense tells us that the members of groups may vary in their talents and inclinations. We could suggest that in some groups there may be people capable of performing specialized tasks but no one person capable of being all things to the group.

How reasonable is this suggestion? Are not minimal skills for organizing task efforts, suggesting task ideas, dealing with interpersonal conflicts, and expressing group values pretty widely dispersed among us all? These are, after all, the basic activities of daily life, and most of us can perform them adequately. And there is, in fact, no guarantee that groups will evolve a talented leadership structure. Therefore, differences in the personalities of groupmates cannot adequately account for the development of integrated or pluralistic leadership structures. This is not surprising, given the general failure of personality traits to explain group leadership.

THE STRUCTURAL INCOMPATIBILITY OF SOME LEADER ROLES.   We must look to factors arising out of a group's circumstances, goals, and organization if we are to account for its leadership system. Bales and Slater (1955; Slater, 1955) were among the first to attempt to explain the development of pluralistic leadership structures in this way. They argued, you may recall, that the behaviors necessary to direct the group's task efforts were inherently incompatible with those required for socioemotional leadership. As a result, they felt that most groups would develop a differentiated structure in which one leader specialized in task issues and another managed the socioemotional arena. The following, drawn from several sources, summarizes their argument (Bales and Slater, 1955; Slater, 1955; Bales, 1956, 1958; Burke, 1967).

In order to coordinate the group's behavior and direct it toward a goal, some ideas must be preferred over others and some members will become more active in task activities, thereby denying opportunities to others. As a result, inequalities will develop among the members in terms of task activities. The development of this inequality causes a certain degree of resentment, frustration, and interpersonal tension among the members. Since the person who is most active with respect to the task is viewed as the source of these inequalities, he or she will be the target of some degree of hostility, as well as of appreciation for aiding the group's task efforts. This hostility reduces the task leader's effectiveness in resolving the tensions created by the inequalities of participation. If the tension is to be resolved, someone other than the task leader must take over the job. The result, then, is the differentiation of task and socioemotional leadership roles, and the emergence of two different types of leaders in the group.

Bales and Slater (1955; Slater, 1955) supported their argument with studies of laboratory discussion groups. They found that the most talkative person in the group was rated by the rest of the members as having the best ideas. This was clearly the task leader. However, this person was usually not the best-liked member. Instead, it tended to be a person who was average in task activity but high on socioemotional activity who was chosen as best liked. This was the socioemotional leader.

Bales and Slater's argument seems convincing on the surface, and their concept of two group leaders, one directing goal activities and the other managing interpersonal relations, is appealing. However, as always, further research has shown that reality is a bit more complicated. Separation between task and socioemotional leadership does occur, but it is not as structurally inevitable or widespread as Bales and Slater suggested.

LEADER LEGITIMACY AND THE INCOMPATIBILITY OF ROLES.   Several subsequent researchers have suggested that the differentiation between task and socioemotional leadership might be much less common in natural groups than in the laboratory groups Bales and Slater studied (Levinger, 1964; Leik, 1963; and Mann, 1961). Verba (1961) argued that the incompatibility between task and socioemotional leader roles is only likely to occur when the position of the leader has relatively low legitimacy in the group.

Following Verba, Burke (1967, 1968) suggested that the scenario proposed by Bales and Slater would only hold true when highly task-oriented behavior is not very acceptable, or legitimate, in the eyes of the group. He argued that when a group adopts a very task-oriented ethic (high task legitimacy) the dominance of task activities and inequalities introduced by the task leader are expected by the rest of the group. As a result they do not cause tension among the members and do not make the group dislike the task leader. In addition, the fact that the task leader does not have to fight to get task activities accepted by the rest of the group keeps the task leader from having to concentrate almost entirely on task activity just in order to prove him or herself. This frees the task leader to engage in socioemotional behavior as well, and, because he or she is not disliked, it allows the task leader to lead in socioemotional issues too.

Therefore, under conditions of high task legitimacy, an integrated leadership structure should emerge. However, when the group is not as highly committed to goal attainment, the directive, task-oriented behaviors of the task leader seem illegitimate and are resented. As a result the differentiation of leadership roles should occur as Bales and Slater suggested.

Burke (1967) tested these ideas on four- and five-person groups attempting to discuss and resolve a human relations problem. His results confirmed his argument. Under conditions of high task legitimacy, inequality in task participation did not cause hostility toward the task leader. The task leader was freed to engage in socioemotional behavior as well, and, as a result, an integrated leadership structure emerged. When the group did not adopt a task ethic, however, the behavior of the task leader was resented, and someone else became the socioemotional leader, creating a pluralistic leadership structure.

Burke (1971) went on in another study to show that the legitimacy of the leader's position in the group, as well as the legitimacy of task activity, affects the integrated or pluralistic nature of the leadership structure. When group members elect their leader, that leader usually has high legitimacy (Read, 1974). However, when leaders simply emerge from the group process, they must prove themselves to the group and generally have slightly less legitimacy. By chance, the groups Burke (1971) studied developed a third leadership pattern as well that had even lower legitimacy. In a few groups someone other than the duly elected leader took over the direction of task activities. Burke called these counterelected leaders.

Burke argued that the less legitimate the leader's position, the more his or her directive task behaviors would be resented, and the more likely the group would be to develop separate task and socioemotional leaders. This is just what he found. A pluralistic leadership structure with separate task and socioemotional specialists was most common when the task leader was counterelected, next most common when he (subjects were males) emerged on his own, and least likely when he was elected by the group.

Burke (1971) uncovered some additional results as well that are worth commenting on. Even when the task leader lacked legitimacy, Burke discovered it was not his high rate of task activity, *per se*, that aroused resentment. It was instead his preoccupation with task issues at the expense of socioemotional ones that caused tension. Of course, it is part of Burke's argument that when a task leader lacks legitimacy, that leader will become preoccupied with the task in order to prove him- or herself to the group. But the point is, if a task leader recognized this problem, and made an effort to maintain high levels of socioemotional activity as well as task behavior, an integrated leadership structure might result despite low legitimacy. We might note the similarity of this situation with one we discussed in the last chapter, in which a person with low status characteristics succeeded in engaging in an illegitimately high level of task activity if he or she gave evidence of being group oriented and cooperative.

One clear implication of Burke's research is that there is no *inherent* incompatibility between the role of task leader and that of socioemotional leader, as Bales and Slater had suggested. Indeed, more recent writers have suggested that even Bales and Slater's original data did not point to a true incompatibility between the roles (Lewis, 1972; Bonacich and Lewis, 1973; Riesdesel, 1974). It is clear that one person *can* play both roles. Whether this occurs or separate task and socioemotional leaders develop depends on the perceived legitimacy of the task leader's directive task activities. It is clear that a number of factors affect this perception of legitimacy, including the group's commitment to goal attainment, the legitimacy of the leader's position, and the extent to which the leader matches high task activity with high socioemotional behavior.

Recently, some additional factors have been suggested as well. Eskilson and Wiley (1976) were interested in the way the sex of the leader affects leadership performance in both sexually homogeneous and mixed-sex groups. Interestingly, they found that the apparent legitimacy of a leader's position affected the female leaders' task activity differently than it did the male leaders'. All the leaders in these three-person groups were appointed, but in some groups the experimenter used a lottery to decide which members to appoint to the leader position. In others the experimenter appointed a member supposedly on the basis of superior task-related test scores. Here, the leader appeared to "deserve" his or her position more, and therefore had higher legitimacy. For males the results were just as Burke (1971) would predict. Leaders with lower legitimacy (appointed by lottery) engaged in slightly more task activity, presumably in an effort to prove themselves. But for female leaders, the results were quite the opposite. Female leaders engaged in much more task activity when their position was highly legitimate (appointed by test scores). It was as though being appointed leader by an outside authority on a legitimate basis freed the female leaders to engage in task activity.

Fennell et al. (1978) suggested an interesting argument to explain these results. Drawing on Meeker and Weitzel-O'Neill (1977), they argued that in our society both males and females consider it more legitimate for males to take the lead in task matters, at least in public or organizational settings. In mixed-sex groups this occurs because sex is an external status characteristic in our society, with higher status assigned to males over females (see Chapter 6). But in same-sex groups the same thing happens for a slightly different reason. Because it is "empirically usual" for men rather than women to be in the task-oriented leader positions of most organizations in our society, men are considered to be more legitimate candidates for task leader roles than women. As a result, in all-male groups, every member feels he is potentially a legitimate candidate for task leader. But in all-female groups it is not entirely legitimate for any member to seize the task leader position (Fennell et al., 1978).

Remember Burke's argument that, when the task orientation of the leader is not quite legitimate to the group, a separation is likely to occur among leader roles? We should expect, then, to see more pluralistic leadership structures in female groups and more integrated structures in male groups. This is exactly what Fennell found. In a pilot study of 10 male and 10 female problem-solving groups, each with 4 members, they found that 60 percent of the male groups but only 30 percent of the female groups developed an integrated leadership structure with a single dominant leader. On the other hand, none of the male groups but fully half (5) of the female groups developed what the authors called a "specialist" type of leadership structure. In this pluralistic system some members became leaders, or specialists, in a particular aspect of the group proceedings, for instance, asking questions or synthesizing and summarizing the group's ideas. However, no one member was a leader overall. Because of the way Fennell and her colleagues recorded group behavior, we cannot be sure that one of these specialists was, in fact, a socioemotional leader. But we do see a differentiation of leader roles, rather than a fusing of them in one person, which is analogous to that discussed by Burke. And once again, this differentiation of leader roles was caused by the low legitimacy of task-oriented behavior for the group members.

Fennell and her fellow investigators only studied the effects of legitimacy on sex differences in leadership structures. But their findings suggest that the legitimacy assumptions created by the "empirically usual" dominance of some groups over others in our society might effect other categories of people as well. For instance, certain racial and ethnic groups are underrepresented in positions of task authority in our society. Perhaps, then, differentiated leadership structures would be more common in groups composed of these people as well. These are speculations, however, that must be verified by further research.

SCAPEGOATING AND LEADERSHIP STRUCTURE.   Scapegoating, a disturbing but interesting group phenomenon, occurs when one member is made the victim of all the group's accumulated tensions and hostility. One of the most succinct—and distasteful—expressions of how scapegoating works came from Adolf Hitler. When asked if it would be better if there were no Jews in the world, he said, "No . . . We should have then to invent him. It is essential to have a tangible enemy, not merely an abstract one" (Rauschning, 1940, quoted in Hoffer, 1951). By victimizing a low-status member in this way the group drains off its frustrations and hostilities without having to deal with their original source. Following an early suggestion by Bales (1953), Burke (1969) argued that scapegoating could provide groups with an alternate way of managing the tension and frustration caused by the illegitimately high task activity of a leader. As a result it would affect whether the group developed an integrated or pluralistic leadership structure.

To test this notion Burke (1969) looked particularly at discussion groups that were not very task oriented in their concerns. When a leader concentrated on the task under these conditions of low legitimacy, hostility directed toward the lowest-status member was more common. The more hostile the group was toward the low-status member, the less hostile it was to the illegitimately active leader him- or herself. It did in fact seem that the low-status scapegoat was absorbing the hostility that should have been directed toward the overly task-oriented leader. When someone was scapegoated, the leader was not disliked despite low legitimacy. As a result, it was possible for the task leader to become the group's socioemotional leader as well, resulting in an integrated leadership structure. Scapegoating, then, appears to be an alternative to the development of a pluralistic leadership structure under conditions of low task or leader legitimacy.

Although perhaps not common, scapegoating does occur in natural groups. Gang members, for instance, sometimes pick on a low-status member as a safe way of expressing the frustration and hostility they feel toward their domineering leader. Still, as a mechanism for dealing with the illegitimate task activity of a leader, it seems much less common than a differentiated leadership structure.

What makes a group resort to the scapegoating alternative? Burke felt the answer lay in the task leader's treatment of low-status members. If an illegitimately task-oriented leader personally picks on a low-status member, he or she opens a channel for the transference of the group's hostility from the leader to the scapegoated member. Indeed, Gallagher and Burke (1974) found that this kind of leader behavior under low legitimacy conditions did stimulate scapegoating, with the result that an integrated rather than differentiated leadership structure developed. So scapegoating is probably most common when the leader personally instigates it in an effort to increase his or her own power.

Fortunately, scapegoating is not the only technique available to a leader who wants to achieve an integrated leadership structure despite low legitimacy. Gallagher and Burke's (1974) data suggest a more posi-

tive alternative. When the leaders they studied not only did not scapegoat the low-status members, but actually showed positive support for
them, something unusual happened. Not only did scapegoating not
occur, but the legitimacy of the task leader was increased, possibly due
to the increase in his or her socioemotional activity. As a consequence,
a separate socioemotional leader did not develop, and an integrated
leadership pattern was the result. It seems, then, that a group may
evolve an integrated leadership structure even under conditions of low
task or leader legitimacy if the leader does something to redirect or
counter the group's hostility.

THE COMPLEXITY OR DIVERSITY OF GROUP GOALS.   It has been suggested that the nature of a group's goals is another factor that affects
its development of a pluralistic rather than integrated leadership system. Unlike Bales, Slater, and Burke, the proponents of this argument
have not been particularly concerned with the separation of task and
socioemotional leadership roles. Rather they have simply been interested in the distinction between groups that distribute leadership roles
among several members and those that concentrate on one person.

The basic argument is that, when groups are faced with complex
tasks requiring many types of skills, they are more likely to develop a
set of specialists to lead them than when their task is simple or unitary
in nature (Cartwright and Zander, 1968; Crosbie, 1975). Dunphy (1972),
for instance, suggests that many multifunctional primary groups develop pluralistic leadership structures. The obvious example is the "col-
league" type of family, where husband and wife have leadership rights
over different aspects of family life (Miller and Swanson, 1958). Feldman (1973) similarly suggests that all groups where the members actually live together face such a myriad of changing tasks and problems
that it is difficult for them to function well with an integrated leadership
system. As a result, pluralistic leadership systems are probably more
common in groups such as families (see Box 7.1), roommate groups,
college fraternities and sororities, kids at camp, and so on than they are
in groups that confront less diverse tasks. On the other hand, integrated
leadership structures are probably more common in more narrowly
focused task groups such as organizational task forces and specialized
committees.

It is clear that the factors affecting the development of pluralistic
and integrated leadership structures are very complex. We have seen
that the legitimacy of the leader's directive task activity is one of the
most important of these. The complex way the perception of legitimacy
is affected by the external circumstances of the group (for example,

whether the leader has been appointed from outside, or whether it is empirically usual for such a person to be leader) and by its internal processes (for example, its goal commitment) is a good illustration of the intricate manner in which the circumstances and purposes of a group combine to determine the nature of its leadership structure. In addition we have seen that diverse goals and the occurrence of scapegoating can affect the type of leadership structure that emerges. It seems more than likely that there are many as-yet-undiscovered factors that are important as well, and which await future research.

Now that we have some understanding of the processes by which leadership structures arise and of the factors that affect the shape of those structures, we are ready to take up the question of the leader's impact on the group. We will approach this question by focusing on the issue of a leader's power over the group. First we will consider factors affecting the amount of power a leader wields. Then we will look at the question of *leadership style,* by which we mean the manner in which a leader exercises his or her power in the group.

LEADERSHIP POWER AND STYLE

The Power of a Leader

There are two types of power that a leader might exercise in a group. The first, which we might call *legitimate power,* derives from the power invested in the leader's position by the norms defining the group's leadership structure. We take power to be the ability to effect a change in another's behavior. When a leader exercises legitimate authority, he or she can generally call on the power of group support to achieve willing or, if necessary, enforced compliance.

One factor that affects the amount of legitimate power a leader has is the nature of the group's leadership structure. The leader in an integrated leadership system performs several leader roles for the group at once (that is, the task organizer, the idea person, the social harmonizer, the representative of group values, etc.). Each of these roles provides a basis of legitimate power. As a result the leader in an integrated leadership structure is likely to wield more legitimate power than any one of the leaders in a pluralistic system.

The amount of power the group has invested in each of these roles will affect a leader's legitimate power as well. For instance, a group composed of relative equals in external status and abilities might invest much less power in its leader roles than would a group

Box 7.1   Leadership Structure in American Families

What kind of leadership structure does the American family have? Of the two answers to that question, one comes from our past and is quite straightforward. The roots of American culture are in the patriarchal traditions of Western Europe, and these prescribe an integrated leadership structure with the husband and father as the sole primary decision maker. In the classic form of this system, the husband was the final authority on all matters. Although he might delegate certain decision-making duties to his wife, he always retained the right to overrule her. There were few if any areas of family life on which the wife had sole authority in her own right.

That is the old tradition. But from the beginning, the economic conditions and egalitarian political ideals of the country have worked to undermine it. Even in colonial America, where the patriarchal leadership of the husband was legally established, the relative scarcity of women made wives valuable and probably increased their practical decision-making role (Carr and Walsh, 1978). However, the basic notion that husbands, not wives, have the authority in families was still alive and well in the nineteenth century. A popular Currier and Ives engraving used to decorate marriage certificates of the time lists the duties of husbands and wives by citing biblical quotations (Goodman and Marx, 1978). Among the items under the husband column is: "Husbands shall dwell with their wives according to knowledge, giving honor unto them, as unto the weaker vessel." The wife, on the other hand, receives the following commandments: "Wives submit yourselves unto your husband as unto the Lord," and, "A wife's desire shall be to her husband (i.e., she shall be subject to him)," and also, "The wife hath not power of her own body, but the husband."

There are still echoes of these notions of family leadership in the customs of our own time. The traditional Christian marriage vows still require the husband to love, honor, and cherish his wife while she promises to love, honor and obey him. Our language also contains references to the expected leadership of the husband in a family (Goodman and Marx, 1978). For instance, the person with the greater power is the one who "wears the pants" in the family, even if it is the wife. One would never say a family leader is the one who wears the skirt.

Things have changed rapidly in recent times, however. The notion that husbands have authority over their wives as a matter of right is no longer accepted by many Americans. Increasingly, young brides drop the word "obey" from their marriage vows. And words like "henpecked," to describe husbands who don't run their wives' lives, are not entirely fashionable any more. The American family is shifting

Box 7.1   *(continued)*

to a pluralistic leadership structure where husband and wife share decision-making responsibilities. Actually, the ideal of the egalitarian family has been with us for some time, but it has only gained widespread approval in recent times.

Studies of power and decision-making in the contemporary American family show that in most the wife does have her own distinct decision-making rights (Scanzoni and Szinovacz, 1980; Ericksen et al., 1979). She is therefore a coleader in the family with her husband. However, she usually still does not exercise as many leadership roles, or as important ones, as her husband. Her husband, in other words, still often has greater power than she does in the family. Thus, although most families have a pluralistic leadership structure, relatively few match the egalitarian ideal of equal power between husband and wife. Husbands generally bring higher status and income to the marriage, and, as we know, this leads to influence. When a wife works, or has high status characteristics such as education, her power also goes up (Ericksen et al., 1979).

The American family has changed from an integrated to a pluralistic leadership structure for complicated reasons. From the standpoint of factors that account for leadership structure in other small groups, it is the legitimacy issue that seems most responsible for changes in the family. The growing number of women who work and the growth in women's rights have eroded the patriarchal norms that gave a husband the legitimate right to rule his family. Husbands no longer have that right on an *a priori* basis. As two well-known family sociologists have said:

> Some husbands today are just as powerful as their grandfathers were—but they can no longer take for granted the authority held by older generations of men. No longer is the husband able to exercise power just because he is the "man of the house." Rather, he must prove his right to power, or win power by virtue of his own skills and accomplishments in competition with his wife. (Blood and Wolfe, 1960)

Once the husband's legitimate right to supreme authority is gone, the leadership roles in the family are up for grabs. As the adult members, the husband and wife compete for these roles on the basis of the status and influence they are able to achieve. Although the final outcome often favors the husband, that is not always true. And in either case, both spouses achieve some leader roles and are brought into a joint leadership structure.

whose members differ dramatically in status. A group facing a threat or crisis, on the other hand, might hand over sweeping power to its leader(s) (Jones and Gerard, 1967). Also the specialized nature of a group's purposes might induce it to give much more power to some leader roles than others. For instance, in a committee, task-oriented leader roles generally carry more power than socioemotional ones. If there is a separate socioemotional leader in such groups, he or she usually has less legitimate power than the task leader (Bales and Slater, 1955). The legitimate power of a leader, then, is affected both by the number of leader roles he or she plays in the group and by the degree of power invested in each of those roles.

Occasionally, a leader's legitimate power does not prove strong enough to gain compliance to his or her directives. This sometimes happens under conditions of controversy, when the support of the group fails the leader. For instance, when the president backs a controversial issue like abortion, or using troops to intervene abroad, or changing the social security system, his cabinet erupts in squabbling, and the members of his own party nervously say that they may not be able to support him in Congress. The power of his office alone is not sufficient to ensure support on such a tricky issue. The power of leaders can also fail when they go beyond their areas of authority, or when for some reason the leader's legitimacy is questioned by the group.

In order to get compliance when their legitimate power is insufficient, leaders must draw upon the second type of power—personal power resources—to supplement their authority (Crosbie, 1975). By *personal power resources,* we mean the rewards, punishments, and ability to persuade that the leader commands as an individual rather than by authority of the leader position. This type of power may be wielded by any member who has access to some rewards or punishments valued by the other members. The president, for instance, often uses personal power resources to rally support for controversial policies. He invites wavering supporters to the White House for lunch, or he calls them on the phone and tells them how much it would mean to him personally if they could help him out.

By virtue of being high-status members of the group, leaders generally command significant personal power resources, which they can exercise on these occasions. Virtually any trait, possession, or ability to take action can serve as a personal power resource as long as it is of significance to the other members and is controlled by the person in question (Emerson, 1962; Cartwright and Zander, 1968). Therefore, we cannot give a complete list of the leader's potential resources for exercising personal power over the members. However, we can mention a few categories of resources that are likely to be available to a leader.

In the last chapter we saw that status rests ultimately on the group's expectation of a member's performance at the task and their sense of him or her as cooperative and likeable. As the highest-status member of the group, a leader in good standing is usually considered both competent and generally well-liked. These twin foundations of status give the leader *expert* and *referent power* over the other members (French and Raven, 1959). Group members comply with a leader's directive because his or her assumed expertise (expert power) convinces them that the leader's judgment is probably right. When the president says, "Support me because my policy is based on secret intelligence reports," he is drawing on expert power. In the case of referent power, members comply because they personally like the leader and want his or her approval. When the president uses personal charm to marshal support, he is using referent power. Finally, as high-status members, leaders usually control a substantial share of the collective rewards generated by the group. Their ability to affect the distribution of these rewards *(reward power)* is an additional source of power that can be used to induce compliance (French and Raven, 1959; Crosbie, 1972). Leaders use reward power when they "buy" a member's support by offering the member extra rewards.

Leaders, then, wield a substantial amount of power in groups, both through the legitimate authority vested in their positions and through their personal resources as high-status group members. However, no matter how much power a leader has, he or she can still choose the style in which it will be exercised. A leader with a great deal of power can still wield that power in a group-oriented or democratic way. A relatively weak group leader may yet be highly directive and authoritarian within the limits of his or her resources. Our next task, then, is to look at the style with which leaders exercise their power and the impact this has on the group.

Leadership Style

Leaders exercise their power in different ways. They do this partly out of the nature of their personal skills, disposition, and ideology. But they also shape their style to some extent in reaction to their followers (Hollander, 1978). As a result, although there may be some general consistency due to personality factors, any individual's leadership style will vary somewhat from group to group.

Studies of leadership style have generally focused on two related clusters of stylistic behaviors. The first cluster distinguishes between a democratic or participatory style on the one hand, and a directive, authoritarian style on the other. The second cluster focuses on whether the leader is primarily task oriented in motivation and concern, or person oriented. Since task-oriented leaders are generally more directive and person-oriented leaders often encourage group participation, the two clusters are related. However, they are not quite the same thing. We will look at each of these and try to gain some insight into their effect on the group's behavior.

AUTHORITARIAN VERSUS DEMOCRATIC LEADERS.   From 1938 to 1940, Lewin, Lippitt, and White conducted what became a classic series of studies on the reaction of groups to authoritarian and democratic leaders (Lewin and Lippitt, 1938; Lewin, Lippitt, and White, 1939; Lippitt and White, 1952; White and Lippitt, 1960). The researchers formed clubs of 11-year-old boys and instructed their adult male leaders to behave in an authoritarian, democratic, or laissez-faire manner. Then they recorded the impact of the leader's style on the boys' behavior. We have already alluded briefly to these studies in an earlier chapter, but since they have had a powerful impact on the study of leadership in groups, we will look at them in some detail here.

The authoritarian leader in these groups dictated all the group activities and was generally controlling and directive. He kept fairly aloof from the boys, gave few explanations for his decisions, and was personalistic in his praise or criticism. In contrast, the democratic leaders encouraged the boys to take part in discussions of group policies and helped their groups come to decisions on them. Democratic leaders avoided making policy decisions themselves and tried to participate as regular group members.

Although primarily interested in the authoritarian-democratic distinction, a laissez-faire leader style was studied as well to provide an additional type of contrast. The laissez-faire ("hands off") leader was friendly but basically did not lead the group. He did not encourage or guide group decision making. He simply responded to questions and gave help when asked.

The differences among the leaders' styles are summarized in Table 7.2. To ensure that the observed differences in the boys' reactions were due to the leaders' behavior, the researchers matched the boys in the various clubs on several factors including personal characteristics and interest in the group. Also, over the course of the 21 group meetings, each club's leadership style was changed at least once.

As field theorists, Lewin and his colleagues were interested in the entire atmosphere, or "social climate," created by authoritarian and democratic leaders and wanted to see what effect these climates had on the members' behavior. As a consequence they observed and recorded all aspects of the boys' behavior during the course of the club meetings and followed up with detailed interviews in the boys' homes. To further compare group reactions they staged a number of experiments, such as having the leader arrive late or leave the group to work on its own.

The results of the studies were very interesting. They found, first of all, that groups reacted in two different ways to an authoritarian style of leadership. Most reacted by dependently leaning on the authoritarian leader for all directions, showing almost no capacity for taking the

Table 7.2. Definitions of Lewin's Three Leadership Styles

Authoritarian	*Democratic*	*Laissez-faire*
1. All determination of policy by the leader.	1. All policies a matter of group discussion and decision, encouraged and assisted by the leader.	1. Complete freedom for group or individual decision, with a minimum of leader participation.
2. Techniques and activity steps dictated by the authority, one at a time, so that future steps are always uncertain to a large degree.	2. Activity perspective gained during discussion period. General steps to group goal sketched, and where technical advice is needed the leader suggests two or more alternative procedures from which choice can be made.	2. Various materials supplied by the leader, who makes it clear that he will supply information when asked. He takes no other part in work discussion.
3. The leader usually dictates the particular work task and work companion of each member.	3. The members are free to work with whomever they choose, and the division of tasks is left up to the group.	3. Complete nonparticipation of the leader in determining tasks and companions.
4. The leader tends to be "personal" in his praise and criticism of the work of each member, but remains aloof from active group participation except when demonstrating.	4. The leader is "objective" or "fact-minded" in his praise and criticism, and tries to be a regular group member in spirit without doing too much of the work.	4. Infrequent spontaneous comments on member activities unless questioned, and no attempt to appraise or regulate the course of events.

initiative in their activities. The boys in these groups expressed little frustration, tension, or anything else (Hare, 1976).

In contrast to this apathetic response, another group reacted to the authoritarian leader with aggression, frustration, and rebellion. These two reaction patterns are opposite sides of the same coin. One is a capitulation in the face of the dominating leader, bringing with it a collapse of personal direction and autonomy on the part of the members. The other is a rebellion, an attempt to fight back against the dominating authoritarian leader.

Figure 7.1 summarizes the members' reactions in democratic, apathetic-authoritarian, aggressive–authoritarian, and laissez-faire groups. We will focus on the democratic–authoritarian contrast. The atmosphere created by a leader's power style seemed to affect four general aspects of a group's behavior. First of all, it clearly affected the individuality and capacity for autonomous action the boys showed. For instance, when the democratic leader left the room the boys kept right on working on their projects, but in authoritarian groups work stopped when the leader left. The generally higher dependence on the leader in authoritarian groups meant that the boys did little other than what they were told to do.

A second effect was on the emotional tone of the group. The atmosphere in democratic groups was generally friendlier and more open. On the other hand, hostility and aggression were more common in authoritarian groups, and, not surprisingly, more scapegoating occurred. Related to the emotional tone of the group was a third factor, the nature of the relationships the boys formed with one another. Possibly because more of their attention was focused on the dominating leader, boys in the authoritarian groups did not form as close ties with one another as they did in democratic clubs.

Finally, the researchers felt there were differences in task performance under democratic and authoritarian leaders. Authoritarian groups spent more time working on their projects and were slightly more productive. However, Lewin and his colleagues argued that the *quality* of work produced by democratic groups was higher, and that these groups were more genuinely interested in their work. As we shall see, this was their most controversial conclusion.

In summary, then, Lewin, Lippitt, and White argued that leadership climate affected leader-member relations, socioemotional relations among the members, and task effectiveness. In general, they rated democratic groups as superior in all three. Since these studies have appeared they have been criticized for their manifest ideological bent. They were conducted at the start of World War II by a refugee (Lewin) from Hitler's Germany, and their purpose was clearly to defend the virtues

Figure 7.1. Group Members' Reactions to Three Leadership Styles

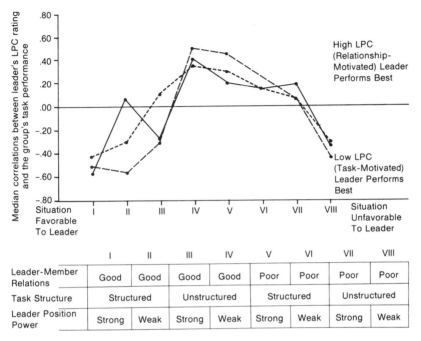

Graph shows median correlations between leadership style and group performance for Fiedler's (1964) original studies (---), Hardy's (1971, 1975, Hardy et al., 1973) validation studies (——), and the Chemers and Skrzypek (1972) study (— —). Source: Adapted from Fred Fiedler, "Recent developments in research on the contingency model," in Berkowitz (ed.), *Group Processes* (New York: Academic Press, 1978), p. 216. Reprinted by permission.

of democracy over authoritarianism. However, Lewin was also a careful and skilled researcher. As a result, a good many of the results of this pioneering study have stood the test of time.

Particularly well-supported have been the findings of greater member satisfaction and more positive socioemotional relations in democratically run groups (Shaw, 1955; Morse and Reimer, 1956; Rosenbaum and Rosenbaum, 1971). The major cause for these results is probably the fact that democratic leaders encourage greater participation in group discussion and decision making. Because members have a greater chance to express their own opinions and shape group decisions, they are likely to feel more closely identified with the group's activities and more satisfied with the results. Also, because members participate more, rather than simply listening to the leader's directions, they have a chance to talk more with each other (Gilstein, Wright, and Stone, 1977). The results are closer relations among the group members and, often, a more friendly atmosphere.

We should point out, however, that these results were obtained within the context of American society, where a high value is placed on democratic behavior. In another culture, where more traditional or authoritarian relations among people are emphasized, group members might be annoyed by the efforts of a democratic leader to include them in the decision making. In this situation, the failure of the leader to meet the members' expectations might lead to lower, rather than higher, member satisfaction. The effects of leadership style, then, are relative to the expectations of the members. However, in our own society members generally react more positively to, and are more satisfied with, a democratic leadership style that encourages member participation.

The Lewin team's conclusions about the task effectiveness of groups and their leadership styles have not fared as well. Further work has shown that there is simply no consistent, across-the-board relationship between a group's productivity or ability to attain its goals and the directive or participatory nature of its leadership (Stogdill, 1974; Shaw, 1981). As we shall see, task effectiveness depends on a number of factors besides leadership style, including the nature of the task and the group's circumstances.

The key difference between democratic and authoritarian leaders is the extent to which they encourage the rest of the members to participate in making the group's decisions. This distinction has some interesting consequences for leaders as well as for members. There is some evidence that it is more difficult to be a good democratic leader than an authoritarian one (Shaw, 1955, 1981). Many people can pass out orders effectively, but it takes a higher level of skill and a greater degree of group trust to draw out and utilize effectively the differing abilities of the group members. Especially given the particular importance of trust from the group to the successful exercise of democratic leadership, we should not be surprised to learn that there is a tendency for leaders to revert to a more authoritarian style when their legitimacy in the group is lower (Carter et al., 1951; Crockett, 1955) or when discussion or stress in the group threatens their control (Fodor, 1978). Think what happens when students in a classroom are unruly and hostile to the instructor. The instructor responds with harsher commands and stricter, more authoritarian controls. Again we see that group members affect the power style their leaders exhibit as well as being affected by it in turn.

TASK- VERSUS PERSON-ORIENTED LEADERS.   Because of the holistic orientation of field theory, Lewin, Lippitt, and White were interested in all aspects of a group's reaction to its leader's power style. The next set of research we will consider takes a narrower approach. It asks the question, how does leadership style affect a group's ability to accomplish its task effectively? The distinction between directive and participatory leadership offers no clear-cut answers to the question.

Fiedler (1964, 1967) argued that the impact of leader style on task effectiveness depends on its appropriateness to the group's situation and goals. It is, in fact, the interaction between group circumstances and leadership style that makes a group more or less effective at its task. It is not the leader alone. Consequently, Fiedler called his approach a *contingency model* of leader effectiveness.

The dimension of leadership style Fiedler focused on developed out of empirical experience observing groups. Group leaders were asked to rate their groupmates on a series of scales. Fiedler found that leaders who rated their "least preferred co-worker" (fellow group member) rather positively differed in their leadership style from those who rated their least-liked groupmate quite negatively. A leader who rates high on the least-preferred co-worker (LPC) scale, then, thinks rather positively about all group members and does not make a large distinction between most-liked and least-liked members. High-LPC leaders tend to be person oriented in style in that they make a priority out of their relationships with their groupmates. They want to be liked and supported. On the other hand, low-LPC leaders feel less obligated to like all their fellow members, making a dramatic distinction between those they prefer and those they don't. Their first concern tends to be with the task, not with their relationship to the group. Because task-oriented, low-LPC leaders tend to be more directive, there are, as we noted, some similarities between this distinction and the participatory-directive distinction (Fiedler, 1967). However, the two are not identical.

Fiedler (1978) has argued that the best way to understand the distinction between person-oriented and task-oriented leadership styles is to view it as a motivational hierarchy, or system of priorities. For the task-oriented leader, accomplishing the task is a goal that takes precedence over relationships with the members. For the person-oriented leader, the priorities are the reverse. When the group situation is difficult or problematic, leaders put all their energies into accomplishing their first priority goals, to the neglect of others. However, when they feel the situation is more firmly in control, they relax and pursue secondary goals as well (that is, personal relations for a task-oriented leader, task directives for a person-oriented leader).

To determine what kinds of group situations are most appropriate to person- versus task-oriented leadership styles, Fiedler (1964, 1967, 1978) has pointed out that we must first know how favorable the group situation is to control by a leader. This, in turn, depends on three contingencies (ranked in order of importance):

1. *The quality of the relationship between the leader and the members.* Is the leader personally liked and respected in the group or not?
2. *The nature of the task.* Is it a highly structured task in which what must be done is clear-cut and straightforward? Or is it unstructured in that it is ambiguous, can be approached from many points of view, and perhaps requires a complex or creative solution?
3. *The power of the leader's position.* It will obviously be easier for leaders to control the group situation when the position they hold carries a great deal of legitimate power.

Fiedler used these three situational factors to classify group situations from "very favorable" to "very unfavorable" to leader control (Figure 7.2). He then predicted that groups will perform more effectively with a task-oriented leader when the situation is either highly favorable or very unfavorable. In a favorable situation the group is ready to go. They like the leader, the task is clear-cut, and the leadership position carries substantial legitimate authority. Here, the task-oriented leader moves the willing group directly to its task. The person-oriented leader's emphasis on relationships is unnecessary in this situation and may even seem interfering (Fiedler, 1978).

When the situation is highly unfavorable, the leader has poor relations with the members, the task is ambiguous, and the leader position carries little authority. In this rather disastrous circumstance, a person-oriented leader focuses almost entirely on improving relations with the members, and the task goes by the wayside. However, the task-oriented leader is willing to ignore what the members think of him or her and pressures the group to address the task. As a result, only the task-oriented leader manages to get the group to accomplish anything.

In conditions of moderate favorableness, it is the person-oriented leader under whom the group can perform best. In these situations either the leader has good relations with the members but faces a complex, unstructured task, or the task is clear-cut, but relations with the members are bad. In the former, person-oriented leaders draw on their good relations with the members to encourage greater member participation and bring a wide range of ideas to bear on the task, the approach needed to accomplish a complex, poorly defined task. In the latter, the concern with relationships shown by person-oriented leaders helps them transcend the group's dislike of them and allows them to focus the group on the clear-cut task. In either of these situations a task-oriented leader neglects the key problem of relating to and dealing with the group members.

As Figure 7.2 shows, Fiedler's own studies (Fiedler, 1964) and two sets of more recent validating studies (Hardy, 1971, 1975; Hardy et al., 1973; and Chemers and Skrzypek, 1972) substantially support his arguments. Let's look at this graph a moment. The numbered sections (I through VIII) along the horizontal axis describe the group situation as it goes from "very favorable" to the leader to "very unfavorable" to the leader. The points graphed above each roman numeral show the correlation between the leader's LPC rating and the group's task performance in situations of that degree of favorableness to the leader. Low correlations (that is, −.60, −.40, and so on) mean that groups with *low*-LPC (task-motivated) leaders performed best. We can see from the graph that, both in Fiedler's original study and later studies, this happened when the group situation was either very favorable (sections I through III) or very unfavorable (section VIII) to the leader. In the middle sections of favorableness (IV through VII), we see that the correlations between the leader's LPC and group performance were fairly high (that is, +20, +40). This means that groups with *high*-LPC (relationship-motivated) leaders performed best under these conditions of moderate favorableness.

Fiedler's work has been criticized for overreliance on one measure of leader style, the perhaps too-simple LPC scale, and for reliance on rather weak correlations between leader style and group effectiveness. However, the bulk of subsequent research has supported Fiedler's basic argument (Shaw, 1981). We can conclude, then, that the relationships we have described between leader style, group situation, and task performance are generally valid.

It is clear, then, that the style with which leaders wield their power has a significant impact on group behavior. In our society, as we have seen, leadership that encourages member participation seems to create more positive socioemotional relations and greater satisfaction on the part of the members. The impact of leadership style on a group's effectiveness at achieving its goals is more complex, however, depending on the nature of the group's goals, the leader's relationship with the members, and his or her legitimate power. Further research will undoubtedly uncover additional factors as well. In general, however, it seems that groups perform more effectively under directive, task-oriented leaders when their situation is either highly favorable or very unconducive to task accomplishment. Under more moderate conditions they function best with a relationship-oriented leader.

Figure 7.2. Tests of the Contingency Model

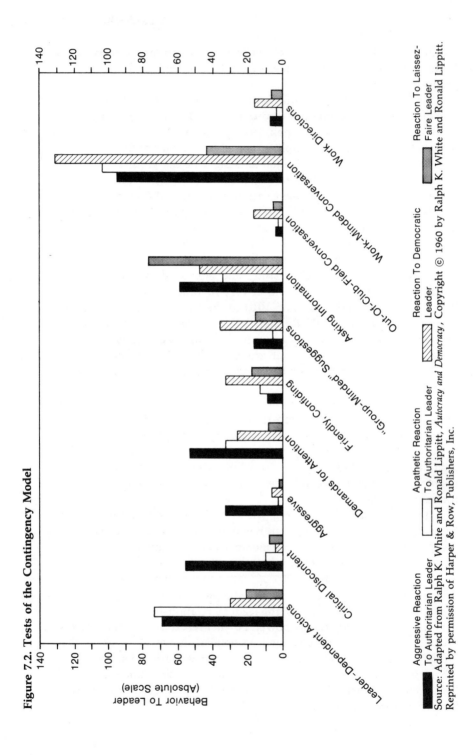

Source: Adapted from Ralph K. White and Ronald Lippitt, *Autocracy and Democracy*, Copyright © 1960 by Ralph K. White and Ronald Lippitt. Reprinted by permission of Harper & Row, Publishers, Inc.

Groups affect their leader's behavior as well as vice versa. If the group views a leader with suspicion or creates difficulties for him or her, for instance, many leaders will react by behaving in a controlling manner. Fiedler suggests that the area of group life to which the controlling behavior will be directed will depend on whether the leader is person oriented or task oriented in style. In general, leaders are more effective if they learn to wield their power in a fashion that the members consider appropriate to the situation (Hare, 1976). The effects of leadership style, then, flow out of the dynamic relationship between leaders and followers that develops as they confront the group's situation and goals. We are reminded again of what Hollander (1978) has called the *transactional* nature of the leadership process in groups.

LEADERSHIP MAINTENANCE AND COALITION FORMATION

Maintaining Leadership

Once a leadership structure emerges in a group, it tends to be fairly stable. Since it is thoroughly intertwined with the status system, it is maintained by much the same means. The norms defining the leadership structure are enforced by the group and are used to define new situations in such a way that they support the existing system. Leaders also take an active role in maintaining their positions. One of the best ways they can do this is by leading the group into activities at which they personally excel and avoiding ones at which they don't. Short and Strodtbeck (1963), for instance, found that gang leaders whose positions were threatened tried to lead their groups back into the violent street fights at which they excelled—and on which their reputations had originally been built.

Organizing the support of other group members is another way leaders maintain their positions in the face of difficulties. They may strike a deal with a number of group members to support them through the crisis in exchange for future rewards. Sometimes other members, usually of high status, will spontaneously organize themselves in support of a threatened leadership structure, most likely because they themselves benefit from the status quo. When members pool their power resources to influence the group like this, we say they have formed a *coalition*. In this case it is a conservative coalition organized to maintain the existing leadership structure.

Conditions that Undermine Leadership

Although group leaders usually manage to maintain their positions, they do not always do so. They are most vulnerable to a fall when they violate the basic terms of their normative contract with their followers. These terms generally require reasonably competent performance of leadership functions and equitable treatment of the members in the distribution of rewards and costs. Failure at either can make the leader appear undeserving of his or her authority.

Because of their ability to redirect group activities, and because of the attributes by which they gained high status in the first place (external status, dominance, perceived competence), leaders are usually able to maintain the appearance of competence under the group's normal conditions. But when external circumstances throw the group into a very different situation, this appearance of competence may be threatened. This can happen in many ways. For instance, rapid changes in the outside environment might create a crisis situation in which any leader is bound to fail. Hamblin (1958) found high leader turnover in these conditions. Or the leader may loose his or her ability to provide the group with vital resources. If, for instance, a husband who is the primary leader in his family loses his job, his position may be threatened (Wolfe, 1959). With the wife left as the family breadwinner, the leadership position may pass to her.

Finally, changing group circumstances may require new skills from the leader that he or she does not possess. For instance, Suedfeld and Rank (1976) noted that revolutionary leaders who successfully lead their groups to power in their societies, often find that very different skills are required to run them after the revolution. The ones who managed to maintain their leadership positions in the ruling group were those able to respond with flexibility and new skills.

Besides failing to perform well, a leader can fail to allocate group resources in an equitable fashion. We saw how the appearance of equity was necessary for the maintenance of the status system. It is not surprising, then, that leaders too must appear fair and equitable to keep their followers' support. If they behave inequitably, particularly by overrewarding themselves or underrewarding their followers, they risk being deposed.

REVOLUTIONARY COALITIONS.   The major means group members have for deposing a leader or changing the leadership structure is the formation of revolutionary coalitions. In this situation some set of group members combine their power resources for the explicit purpose of opposing a leader's directives, or even taking control of the group themselves.

When they do this, members generally try to form the "cheapest" coalition they can (Gamson, 1961). That is, they try to form a coalition that will have just enough power and resources to succeed, but not a great deal more. The reasoning proceeds this way: if you form a coalition with people who bring more power than you need, you will have to pay them off in proportion to their contribution; yet their extra contribution of power will have gained you nothing that you couldn't have gotten for less.

Leaders can probably provoke the formation of revolutionary coalitions in many ways. However, we have solid evidence that one such path is through the inequitable use of group resources. For example, Lawler (1975), in one study, compared groups in which a leader usurped an inequitably large share of the group winnings with groups in which the leader behaved equitably. As one might imagine, more frequent and more severe revolutionary coalitions were directed toward the inequitable leader. This occurred even in the face of possible retaliation from the leader and was not inhibited by status differences among followers.

However, for coalitions to be formed, Lawler found that it was important members felt their fellow groupmates would also be disenchanted with the leader—and likely to support an insurgent action. This finding is supported by an earlier study by Michener and Lyons (1972) in which members were much more willing to form coalitions against an inequitable leader when they felt that others in the group did not support the leader. Lawler suggests that the simple fact of inequity on the part of the leader is not enough for revolutionary coalitions to form. The members must also feel that such inequitable behavior or other circumstance has drained away the leader's legitimacy and support in the group. In that situation revolutionary action is likely.

The link between a leader's usurpation of group rewards and the formation of revolutionary coalitions has been documented by Webster and Smith (1978) as well. Even when the group was working on a cooperative task, they found that clearly inequitable behavior on the part of the leader produced revolutionary coalitions a majority of the time. However, Webster and Smith were particularly interested in what the revolutionary coalitions did with the group's resources once they had seized control. Would they seek revenge and keep everything for themselves? Or would they try to reestablish equity, allocating to the leader neither more nor less in resources than he or she deserved?

Reassuringly, the revolutionary coalitions studied by Webster and

Smith usually redistributed resources according to equity once they came to power, even when that meant an absolute loss to themselves. Two factors affected their tendency to do this. First, they were more likely to redistribute equitably if they justified their own rebellion in terms of the injustice and unfairness of the leader. In other words, when they established referential equity norms (see Chapter 6) as the basis of their revolution, they felt pressure to stick by those norms themselves once they seized control. Second, an important factor was their sense of some reasonable basis for deciding what each member actually deserved. When they felt there was such a basis, the revolutionary coalitions were more likely to behave equitably once in power. There was an exception, however. In a situation where the leader's inequity was truly extreme, the members showed a tendency to temper their concern for equity by a degree of retribution against the leader.

Clearly, leaders have many resources with which to maintain their power, but they must use these resources to maintain the basic tenets of their normative contract with their followers. Followers have power resources as well, most particularly the power of their support. And if no single member has power resources greater than the leader, they do have the ability to form coalitions, either in support or opposition to the leadership structure. Therefore, a leader who repeatedly or seriously fails to live up to the group's expectations for competence and fairness can expect to lose legitimacy and face the possibility of being deposed.

SUMMARY

Leadership consists of the exercise of an executive function in a group, the assumption of responsibility for making and directing decisions and structuring behavior as part of the group's efforts to maintain itself and pursue its goals. The distribution of these executive rights and responsibilities among the members constitutes the group's leadership structure. A member's position in the leadership structure generally corresponds closely with his or her position in the group's status hierarchy. The members chosen to occupy leadership positions in the group are those with the highest participation rates and the credentials necessary for high status. However, the leadership structure is distinguished from the status structure by its control of decision-making rights and by the special nature of the transaction between leaders and followers upon which it is based. In exchange for the right to expect compliance from members, leaders are held responsible for the group's welfare. The tenants of this contract between leaders and followers are expressed by a set of norms that define the leadership structure and outline the range of privileges and duties appropriate to each member.

Early attempts to understand group leadership searched for personality traits that would distinguish leaders from followers. The failure of this approach to produce any consistent findings suggested that the type of skills required of a leader depended on the goals, needs, and circumstances of the group. Consequently, it is necessary to analyze leadership in terms of the organizational problems created by the group's purposes and circumstances, and in terms of the leadership functions to be performed in regard to those problems. We presented a fourfold classification of leadership functions that may be performed in small groups. They were: the task organizer, the idea person, the social harmonizer, and the representative of group values. Which of these roles dominate in a group depends on the nature of its goals and situation.

A group's leadership structure determines how responsibility for performing the group's various leadership functions, or roles, is divided among the members. Small groups exist that are leaderless in that they lack a normatively defined leadership structure. However, leadership functions must be performed in these groups as well, usually by the group as a whole on a spontaneous basis.

Most groups develop a normative system for apportioning leadership roles among the members. The factors of group size, degree of commitment to the group's goals, task complexity, and external or internal crises all encourage the creation of a clear, normatively defined leadership structure. This can be an integrated structure in which all leader roles are invested in a single dominant member. On the other hand, it may be a pluralistic structure in which leader roles are divided among a subset of group members who jointly rule the group.

In seeking reasons why a group might develop a pluralistic rather than integrated system for managing its leadership functions, we considered several hypotheses. The idea that the cause might lie in differences among the members' personalities was rejected as generally inadequate. Bales and Slater's (1955) notion of the structural incompatibility of task and socioemotional leader roles was examined in some detail. Under conditions of low task or leader legitimacy, some opposition between task and socioemotional leadership can develop, leading to a pluralistic leadership structure. However, there appears to be no inherent incompatibility between the two types of leader roles. In addition, when leaders instigate scapegoating it can discourage the development of pluralistic leadership structure, while complex or diverse group goals encourage it.

The power a particular person wields in a group depends on two factors: degree of legitimate authority, and control of personal power resources. The number of leader roles a leader performs for the group, and the power invested in each of those roles, contribute to his or her legitimate authority. Additional rewards and costs controlled by the leader as an individual determine personal power. No matter how much power leaders have, they can still choose to exercise that power in different ways. Evidence suggests both that leadership style affects the behavior of the group and that the group situation affects the style with which a leader exercises his or her power. In our society a democratic leadership style that encourages member participation generally results in higher member satisfaction. However, there are no consistent differences in productivity between authoritarian and democratically run groups. To understand group productivity or effectiveness it is necessary to take into account the nature of a group task, leader-member relations, and leader power, in addition to leadership style. According to Fiedler's (1967) contingency model, groups work more effectively under a directive, task-oriented leader when their circumstances are either very favorable or very unfavorable to leader control. Under conditions of moderate favorability, group effectiveness is higher with a person-oriented leader.

Once leadership structures are established in a group they tend to be fairly stable. The leadership structure is maintained in much the same way as is the status structure: by defining group activities in a way that confirms it. Leaders, for instance, direct the group to activities at which they excel or can easily control, and generally they use their control of resources to maintain the support of group members. Group members may also form conservative coalitions to support the leadership structure if they feel they benefit from it. However, if leaders fail to meet the terms of their normative contract with their followers by failing to supply the expected competence and fairness, their positions may be undermined. Particularly if leaders use their positions to inequitably usurp group resources, they will lose legitimacy and may face organized resistance in the form of a revolutionary coalition. This process emphasizes for us the delicate interdependence between leaders and followers in a group. Leaders only have the power to lead the group where it is willing to go.

8

Small-Group Culture

WHAT IS GROUP CULTURE?

What do we mean when we say group *culture?* Of all the standard concepts of social science the notion of culture is the most elusive. As Fine (1979) has noted, quoting from Herskovits (1948), culture, in the final analysis, consists of the "things people have, the things they do, and what they think." Group members develop, enact, and maintain their group culture through interaction with one another, but, as Fine also points out, culture is not interaction itself, rather it is "the content, meanings, and topics of interaction" (Fine, 1979). For instance, in a group of friends, the recurring topics of conversation, the shared jokes and opinions about the world, the tradition of meeting for drinks together on Saturday night are all elements of the group's culture.

How can we make sense out of these amorphous patterns or habits that members share together, which constitute group culture? The first step is to realize that it is not just a random jumble of ideas and practices. Rather these ideas and practices are put together in loosely organized sets that are meaningful to the group members in that they encapsulate for them their understanding of what the group is like and how it relates to its environment. When a group creates a culture, then, it gathers together information and *orders* it in relation to the group's goals and the needs of the members (Roberts, 1951; McFeat, 1974). As a consequence a group's culture has an organizational structure that gives it a certain internal logic, a general consistency and coherence. It is the way information is organized in the culture that gives it significance to group members. It is also what gives the culture of a particular group its distinctive style, feeling, and meaning. The importance of this factor led Geertz (1957) to define culture as "an ordered system of meaning and symbols in terms of which social action takes place."

We must be careful to point out, however, that because group cultures have some internal order and coherence does not mean there are no loose ends, no bits of belief in one aspect of group life that contradict group beliefs in another area. It is probably best to view group cultures as loosely ordered collections of information, beliefs, symbols, values, and practices. Within this collection are various modules of beliefs and practices, usually associated with some important aspect of group life, that are more tightly and consistently organized. Because these more highly ordered modules describe the group's basic beliefs and its favorite traditions and rituals, there is close agreement on them among the members. Most teenage groups, for instance, have very elaborately worked out and well-organized conceptions of what is "cool behavior," because this aspect of identity achievement is very important to such groups. Cultural information dealing with less important aspects of the group is likely to be much more amorphous and less widely shared among the members.

Where Is Culture Located?

It is possible, then, to view group culture as the group's organized system of information about itself, its environment, and what it does. But where is this system of information located? In the minds of individual members? In some abstract collective reality of the group as a whole? Neither answer seems ideal. Yet we need some response to the question if we are to avoid treating group culture as a mysterious, ethereal quality of groups, rather than a concrete aspect of their daily lives.

Keesing (1974) has suggested a solution to this problem that we will draw upon here. He presents his argument in terms of the cultures of larger societies, but it can be applied to small groups as well. Keesing makes an analogy between a culture and a language, each of which he views as an informational code. Group members share their culture in the way native speakers share a language. That is, they share the broad design of the cultural code and its deeper organizing principles, but as individuals they may differ somewhat in their interpretation of its specifics.

According to Keesing (1974), group culture exists in the mind of the individual member as his or her *theory* of the code being followed by the other members, of the nature of the game they are playing together. Each member's theory of his or her group's culture may be largely unconscious. But it is what members use to interpret events in group interaction, and it is one of the factors that shapes their own decisions on how to behave in return. They use their groupmates' reactions to their own behavior to confirm or modify this theory of their group's culture.

Group culture, then, really comes alive in the interaction among the group members. The behavior of the members in relation to one another is the concrete place where the culture of the group as a whole actually lives (Geertz, 1973). When members meet, each with their own theory of the group culture, they enact together their shared symbols, meanings, ideas of themselves and their situation. Even though the members' conceptions of their culture are not identical, these shared meanings emerge from their mutual adjustments to one another and the substantial overlap among their views.

The organized system of information that is a group's culture exists, as a result, in two different places in two slightly different ways. The culture of the group as a whole exists in its truest sense in the interaction among the members. During any one interaction sequence, however, only a part of the total group culture is enacted. For the whole of the group culture to continue, rather than just the part being acted on now, it must be preserved in the knowledge of the individual members. But, as we have noted, what the individual carries with him or her is not a complete and accurate picture of the group culture, but is a personal theory of it. So a slightly different version of a group's culture exists in the minds of the individual members than the version that appears in interaction. Out of the interplay of these two versions, or faces, of culture, the group's own unique culture is enacted, modified, and maintained.

For a researcher to describe the culture of a particular small group, he or she must gather information on both these faces of the culture. The group members must be interviewed for their own understandings of the group and its practices. In addition, interaction among the group members must be observed and analyzed independently by the researcher. From the two sets of information a composite picture can be constructed. Necessarily, this composite will be an abstraction rather than a simple reflection of the culture as it exists. However, it is likely to prove highly useful in understanding the life of the small group.

Culture, Social Structure, and Norms

It is possible to define group culture in such a way that it incorporates all aspects of group life, including the group's social structure. Indeed, Herskovits's definition quoted at the beginning of this chapter can be read in this way. However, we would like to take a narrower view of culture, one that would allow us to distinguish between culture and social structure. This will enable us to discuss the relationship between a group's social structure and its culture. It will also make possible a view of culture as an independent tool that group members evolve to manage their basic problems of task, environment, and interpersonal relations. After we have considered this problem, we will take up the issue of the relationship between a group's culture and its norms.

How then do we distinguish between culture and social structure? The way has been pointed already by our emphasis on culture as an ideational system, as an ordered set of information or ideas. This ideational system contains much information that is directly relevant to the social structure. For instance, it usually includes a definition of the group's task, a sense of what skills are necessary to accomplish the task, and what is considered the best way to go about doing it. But these are ideas, understandings, and not the social structure itself.

As the preceding chapters have shown us, a group's social structure is its actual pattern of relationships among the members. It consists, in other words, of who has higher status than whom, who talks to whom, who likes whom. Clearly these relationships will reflect in many ways the system of ideas that makes up the group's culture. If the culture assumes that certain skills are most important for the group's goals, perceptions of the distribution of those skills among the members will be an important determinant of the group's status structure. A group member who seems to embody the group's values (an aspect of its culture) is likely to gain influence over the other members (an aspect of social structure). We can conclude, then, that a group's culture and its social structure are interdependent: a change in one affects the other. Furthermore, they are deeply intertwined in the actual ongoing flow of behavior in a real group. But they nevertheless remain analytically distinct aspects of the group's total way of life. Culture is the ordered system of ideas group members use to guide and interpret their interaction together. Social structure is the pattern of relationships among the members that emerges from that interaction.

Since culture is a system of ideas, it includes the group's norms, which are, after all, ideas about the way the members should act and what they should believe. In Chapter 5 we distinguished among three classes of norms: procedural, role, and cultural norms. Procedural and role norms contain the group's basic rules for behavior. Cultural norms are a little different. They define the beliefs, values, and symbols to which you must adhere to be a group member in good standing. A radical political group, for instance, will have some basic values that its members must accept, such as socialist ideals, certain beliefs—such as whether revolution is necessary to achieve socialism—and certain symbols, such as a group emblem with a raised fist on it. These are the group's cultural norms. Procedural, role, and cultural norms are all contained in the group culture. However, it is the cultural norms that outline the most distinctive elements of a group's cultural system, that is, the beliefs, values, and symbols by which a group expresses its own identity.

Although all the group norms are contained in the culture, most group cultures contain additional information and ideas that members share but which do not have the status of norms. For example, a group of friends who are not a political group might still share a set of political beliefs. These beliefs are not group norms for the friends in that adherence to them is not required of the members. And yet the group members draw upon these beliefs in a daily way, and they are in some sense part of the group culture. So, although the important beliefs, values, and symbols in a group culture will have the status of norms, the culture may contain some nonnormative beliefs and information as well.

Group culture, then, is best thought of as a group's store of shared information that it uses to guide and interpret its actions. It contains the group's norms but is distinct from its social structure. It is made up of four general types of information (Peterson, 1979):

1. Agreed-upon *rules for behavior*—what we have called procedural and role norms
2. *Values*—assumptions or statements that rank goals and behavior in terms of their importance to the group
3. *Beliefs*—statements about the world and the way the group operates in it that often serve to justify the group's values and behavioral rules
4. *Symbols*—ideas or objects the group uses to represent its beliefs, values, and basic identity, and which usually have an emotional meaning for the members

Each of these four information types can be seen clearly in a sample culture, of a college sorority, for instance. The sorority sisters' agreements about when they can have men in their rooms, if they must attend sorority meetings, how they should dress, and how friendly they should be are all examples of rules of behavior. Assumptions about the importance of dating and social success or of studying and getting good grades are examples of the sorority's values. Its beliefs can be seen in its assessment of itself as a popular group on campus, or its sense that the men of a particular fraternity are more fun to date than others. For symbols, the sorority has its Greek name, its sorority pin, its songs and rituals, information which it uses to represent its own distinctive identity. All of these are part of the sorority's group culture.

Now that we have a general notion of what we mean by *culture,* we can turn to a more specific analysis of the culture of small groups. Since small groups are situated within the larger organization of society, we need to distinguish more carefully between the culture of groups themselves and their larger cultural context. The problem of the creation of culture in small groups will be approached next. And we will then look at the factors to which group culture responds, the types of cultural products that are created, and the qualities that affect their adoption and maintenance by group members. Supplied with this better understanding of the operation of small-group culture, we will turn again to tl e relationship between the cultural products of small groups and the larger society.

GROUP CULTURE AND SOCIAL NETWORKS

The members of virtually any small group in our society are also members of other social entities ranging from the larger society to other small groups. As a result, small groups exist within an extensive network of interconnecting relationships, which link them to the beliefs and practices that define the culture of society as a whole, as well as to the cultures of surrounding large organizations and neighboring small groups. It is in relation to this larger social network that small groups develop their own distinctive cultures (Roberts, 1951; McFeat, 1974; Fine, 1979).

This background network of relationships has several important implications for small-group culture. First of all, it provides pathways along which cultural information flows from the outside society into the group. Just as importantly, the cultural creations of small groups are carried by their members back along these pathways to other small groups and to the larger society. This two-way flow of cultural information is called a *diffusion* process. It allows small groups and the larger society to influence one another's norms, beliefs, and values.

Most powerful, of course, is the influence of the larger society over the norms and beliefs of the small groups. Virtually all small groups shape their culture in relation to the general concerns and prescriptions of the larger culture. For some groups this consists of a simple transmission of these concerns into the group culture. A group of college friends might transmit the larger society's concern over achievement into their own group by adopting norms emphasizing studying, getting good grades, and preparing for an occupation. But other groups show the larger culture's influence by their reaction against its dominant values and norms. When a group of kids adopt punk-rock-style dress, they are reacting against the values and standards of established, well-to-do society. The strength of a group's cultural reaction can vary from a mild variation on mainstream values to full-fledged opposition, such as that shown in gangs and other deviant subgroups.

Blueprints and Idioculture

The larger culture influences small groups in a second way as well. Besides norms and values for the behavior of its citizens, the larger culture also contains some general notions of what specific types of small groups in its midst should be like. It does this by providing a set of normative *blueprints,* which outline the general type of behavior expected to characterize each of the most common kinds of small groups operating within it. For instance, most of us have a set of general normative expectations for what a committee—one of the more recurrent small-group forms in our society—should be like, expectations which outline the range of behaviors generally thought to be appropriate to, and characteristic of, a committee. Interestingly enough, a bunch of youths in a tough neighborhood also acquire from the larger society a normative blueprint for what a teenage gang should be like. It should have a strong leader, emphasize toughness, and fight for its turf.

Each of us, as socialized members of the larger culture, bring these normative blueprints with us when we form any common group, a committee, a family, a romantic relationship, a friendship group, a work group, a teenage gang, or the like. Because this blueprint originates in the larger culture and is consequently shared by the prospective members of a newly forming group, it provides some initial cultural norms for the group. If a member violates these norms by introducing inappropriate material—for instance, highly personal or emotional information in a committee—he or she will likely be checked even though the group is still in the formative stage without a distinctive culture of its own.

Occasionally, of course, people come together to form a new or unusual type of small group, one for which there is no blueprint provided by the larger culture. An example might be a group of senior citizens who decide to live together in a commune or a group of young people who join together in a group marriage. They will be on their own, forced to innovate the basic nature of their group's culture as well as its own distinctive concerns. However, chances are that in doing this, the members of such a group will borrow from the blueprints learned from other groups (for instance, the family or friendship group, or the roommate association), to piece together the foundation for their new type of group. This is a situation we will discuss later in the chapter.

However, for now, it is important to realize that most small groups use a basic blueprint, provided by the larger culture, to establish the foundation on top of which they erect their own unique culture. Fine (1979) calls the distinctive culture of a group its *idioculture.* Because groups create their idioculture in relation to the larger social networks of which their members are a part, and to a normative blueprint from the outside, they are in a position to evolve interesting variations on, and responses to, the larger cultural tradition within which they exist. Indeed much of what people seek from their small groups is a kind of reaction to, and help in coping with, the surrounding social context. College students turn to one another to deal with university life and the problems of youth, and they create through their efforts a distinctive student culture that both adopts the values of the larger society and satirizes them. This process illustrates for us how small groups play their roles as the linking mechanism between individuals and large-scale organizations, both maintaining the connection between the two and providing a buffer zone to absorb conflicts.

Because small groups are in the distinctive situation of creating idiocultures that are, in many ways, a commentary on the larger cultural tradition, some have argued that most innovations in the larger culture originate, in fact, in the idioculture of small groups (Fine, 1979; Fine and Kleiman, 1979). It is in the face-to-face encounters of small groups that people actually evolve new habits of speech, shared beliefs, and ways of doing things. The members of these groups then carry these idiocultural practices out to other groups, and occasionally they catch on quite widely throughout society (Fine, 1979). Virtually all social movements, for instance, the women's movement and the antinuclear movement, began as small groups, a collection of like-minded people meeting in somebody's living room. The same is true of religious cults like the "Moonies" or the Jonestown group. The beliefs and attitudes shaped or created by these groups have spread to varying, sometimes large, segments of the population.

The fact that the idiocultural creations of small groups occasionally diffuse outward into the surrounding society brings home the point that small-group culture influences the larger cultural tradition as well as vice versa. It also makes clear to us that group culture, while heavily influenced by outside factors, is never totally determined by them. In evolving an organized cultural response to these factors, the group develops some autonomy from them and, so, can imbue its culture with distinctive characteristics of its own.

THE CREATION OF IDIOCULTURE

How does a group create its culture? Why do certain bits of information become part of the group culture and not others? Fine (1979) tried to answer such questions by looking at the contents and topics of interaction that developed, over time, in Little League teams. He found that for a cultural item to be created and continue to be used by a group it had to meet five different criteria:

1. The cultural "item," or the basic information out of which it was created, had to be *known* to the group members.
2. It had to be *usable* in the group context, in the sense that it did not violate any norms of acceptable, proper behavior.
3. It tended to be *functional* for the group in that it supported the group's goals or the individual needs of the members.
4. The item itself, or the manner in which it was introduced to the group, had to be *appropriate* in that it supported the group's status heirarchy.
5. It needed to be *triggered*—that is, introduced into the group—by some event or occurrence in group interaction.

Fine views these five criteria as progressively smaller filters through which information must pass before it is adopted into the group's idioculture. At each level more and more information is strained out so that, in the end, only information that is rather well matched to the group's circumstances survives to become an ongoing part of the group culture. In this way, the members of a small group select from the vast amount of information available to them a small sample from which they create a distinctive group culture.

We need to look more closely at each of these selective criteria to understand better what they are and how they operate. Doing so will allow us to take up two other traditions of research that also touch upon the problem of culture creation. The first is a laboratory-experimental tradition from social psychology; the second is based on field work in anthropology. This broader consideration should give us added insight into the nature of small-group culture and its relationship to the ongoing life of the group.

Known Culture

The concept of known culture refers us back to our point that small groups are situated within larger networks of social relations. The members of a small group bring with them from their other groups, relationships, and the larger society itself a large repertoire of *known cultural information*. The store of information each member brings to the group forms its *latent* culture. Out of the reservoir of latent cultural content the group will derive the ideas and information that will become part of the group's outer manifest culture (Fine, 1979; Becker and Geer, 1960).

However, you might ask, how does a group create its own unique culture if it bases it entirely on known information from the outside? The answer lies in the nature of cultural creation. New cultural items, such as opinions, jokes, judgments about reality, are not generally created out of thin air (Fine, 1979). Rather they consist of novel combinations, interpretations, or usages of *familiar* information (Stein, 1968). The slang word "bad," for instance, was created by using a very familiar negative word in a new way that made it a compliment. In just this way, groups take information from their repertoire of known culture and restructure it to create their own distinctive idioculture.

Usable Culture

Less clear than the concept of known culture is Fine's notion of usable culture. He defines *usable* as meaning "mentionable in the context of group interaction" (Fine, 1979), and he seems to refer to the process by which certain elements of known culture are excluded from the arena of group interaction because they violate certain of the group's basic norms of appropriateness. However, Fine does not say much about the basic nature of the norms that groups use to define usable information, except to suggest that they are situationally specific and emerge out of the distinctive personalities, ideologies, and moralities of the individual members. He gives the example of norms defining taboo or sacred topics. In some of the Little League teams he observed, he noted that cursing, for instance, was standard behavior. But on one team, which adopted a more self-consciously religious attitude, such behavior was unacceptable—that is, unusable.

For our purposes here we will expand the notion of usability to cover two sets of norms that members use to edit out certain elements of their known cultural repertoire. The first is that which we described as providing the basic blueprint for a particular type of group. Adult women, for instance, have certain basic expectations about the types of information and topics of conversation that are appropriate to a peer group of women friends. (It's all right to talk about problems with men, for example.) These same women have a different set of expectations for the information it is appropriate to introduce into a romantic relationship with a man. (Man problems would not be an appropriate topic there.) So these cultural blueprints not only provide certain how-to information for building different types of small groups, they also establish an initial set of normative filters by which some of the members' known information is brought into the group and the rest is held back.

The normative expectations that make up these blueprints are, of course, themselves an element of the members' latent, known culture. When members join a group of a particular type, they retrieve from their known repertoire the appropriate set of blueprint norms, which they then use as first criteria by which to decide what information is or is not admissible to the group. Because group members bring these blueprint norms from the larger culture, they provide criteria of usability that operate from the first moments of the group's formation, affecting from the beginning the idioculture it develops.

As criteria of usability, blueprint norms continue to operate throughout the life of the group. However, once the group has been in existence for a while and begins to develop a distinctive culture of its own, a second set of norms emerge that also define certain information as more usable than other kinds. These are the distinctive idiocultural norms to which Fine referred when discussing his notion of usability. One group of friends, for instance, may evolve idiocultural norms that make the introduction of information on one's sexual life quite legitimate, while, in another friendship group, personal sexual information may be taboo. The source of such norms will often be in the personal dispositions and beliefs of the members. But they must be adopted by the group as a whole before they become effective filters for what is usable in the further construction of the group's idioculture.

As Fine points out, these norms are rarely simple, across-the-board prohibitions of certain topics. Rather they tend to be situationally founded norms that define particular types of information as appropriate under certain situations, but not under others. For instance, in some adult friendship groups it is considered appropriate to open up emotionally in a relaxed situation where alcohol is being consumed, but not otherwise.

The effect of both sets of usability norms (those from the cultural blueprint for the group and those from the group's own idioculture) is to point the development of group culture in a particular direction and keep it going that way. They provide a technique by which information from the outside that might challenge the group's idiocultural beliefs is edited out. Knowing the group's norms, most members will simply never introduce contrary information into the group. When they do, they are likely to be checked by the rest of the group. Furthermore, the offending information is likely to be rejected rather than taken up as part of the group culture. In this manner, usability norms become a mechanism by which groups preserve their distinctive idioculture (once it has developed) in the face of a constant influx of potential cultural information from the members' outside networks.

Functional Culture

The idea that information is selected for inclusion in the group culture on the basis of the way it supports group goals or satisfies members' needs is a very important one. It brings us to one of the basic explanations for the fact that groups develop and maintain organized cultural traditions in the first place. As we noted in Chapter 1, a group's culture, like its social structure, is a tool the members develop to deal, on the one hand, with their task goals and environment and, on the other, with the problems of individual relations and group maintenance. Consequently, information that appears useful to the members in meeting these problems—that is, which is functional in this way for the group—is more likely to be adopted into the group culture than information that is not so useful.

Is GROUP CULTURE FUNCTIONAL?   The idea that the cultural rules, beliefs, values, and symbols of groups undergo a kind of selective pressure to become better adapted to the group's circumstances has been somewhat controversial. We can all of us cite examples of apparently arbitrary cultural beliefs and practices that have persisted for some time. How is it more functional, for instance, for a football team to call itself the Tigers rather than the Panthers? Yet once the choice is made, it may make all the difference in the world to the team's fans. Expressing this view, turn-of-the century sociologist William Sumner (1906) headed a chapter of his book on culture with the phrase "The Mores Can Make Anything Right." But recently there is evidence that this statement is not as generally true as Sumner thought.

In developing and maintaining cultural beliefs and practices, people in groups do respond, at least to some degree and in some circumstances, to the reality of the group's circumstance (Jacobs and Campbell, 1961; Weick and Gilfillan, 1971; Sherif and Sherif, 1969; MacNeil and Sherif, 1976). As we noted when discussing deviance and social control (Chapter 5), the ongoing process of interaction in a face-to-face group encourages a fairly high rate of spontaneous innovation in ideas, usages, and practices (Jacobs and Campbell, 1961; Moscovici, 1976). Also, as we have seen, the location of groups in larger social networks means a constant influx of outside information, even though this information is edited down by norms of usability. Consequently, groups usually do have available to them alternative information from which a cultural belief or rule different from the one currently held could be constructed. Given the presence of this implicit choice, it seems likely that cultural items that are clearly poorly adapted to the group's circumstances will be gradually abandoned in favor of more functionally appropriate ones.

Let's consider an example to make this a little clearer. A group of adult friends get together on an irregular basis for dinner or a movie. Right now, the rule is that whoever wants the group to gather must contact all the other members and arrange for an event. Since that requires much effort and calling back and forth, the friends find they don't meet as often as they would like. Thus their rule for organizing a get-together is not very functional for their goal of seeing one another frequently. If the friends can find a simpler way of arranging meetings, chances are they will adopt it and abandon the old rule. There are many ways this might happen. First of all, the friends, just struggling with their cumbersome method, are likely to come up with spontaneous improvements. For instance, someone might suggest that at the end of each meeting they all agree when and where to meet next. Also, as members of other groups they might borrow methods they have seen used elsewhere. Given the better alternatives around them, it seems unlikely that their awkward old rule will last long.

Our point, then, is that, given the opportunity, most groups in most circumstances will replace less functionally appropriate cultural items with more functional ones. As we shall see there are several caveats that must be attached to this statement, however. For instance, what happens if the group has no standard by which to judge how functionally appropriate a cultural item is? Also, are there not circumstances when a simple desire for stability will cause a group to maintain a particular cultural norm? These are issues we will take up shortly.

However, for the moment let us turn to an experiment conducted to test the effect of the functional appropriateness of a cultural item on its persistence in a small group. This study focuses on only one type of cultural item, a group's belief about the circumstances confronting it. We would call such a belief a cultural norm. However, there is every reason to believe that the logic behind this experiment could be applied to other types of cultural items as well. This experiment is interesting because it gives us an idea of the circumstances in which group culture is selected to be functional and the circumstances in which it is not.

MacNeil and Sherif (1976) argued that the circumstances of group life to which particular cultural norms respond are often ambiguous. There is rarely one absolutely clear way in which these circumstances could be understood, even by people from similar cultural backgrounds (as most group members are). On the other hand, these circumstances are also rarely so totally ambiguous that there are not some limits on what appears to be a reasonable or realistic interpretation of them to the members. These limits of reasonableness are usually set by the standards of the larger culture within which the group operates and by the structure of human perception.

Perhaps an example would make this clearer. Imagine five friends talking together at a party. Suddenly tempers flare and there is a dramatic argument between two of them. When it is over, everybody wonders what happened. If you asked each member to describe what they saw and what it meant, would they all give you the same answer? No, the situation was too ambiguous. Each person will have his or her own interpretation. However, the situation was not so ambiguous that there isn't a certain limit in the range of interpretations that would seem reasonable to the members. For instance, if one of the arguers insisted, "I was not shouting, I never shouted," the others would probably turn in agreement and say, "I'm sorry, but you *were* shouting." The idea that nobody shouted is not a reasonable version of what they saw. This is what MacNeil and Sherif mean when they say that there are limits of reasonableness in the group's interpretation of its own behavior and the events around it.

Left to their own inventiveness and sense data, without the help or hindrance of outside influence or preestablished norms, MacNeil and Sherif argue that most groups will settle on a cultural norm that falls within this realistic or reasonable range in its interpretation of the group situation. Such norms, evolved by the members in direct response to the group's present circumstances, are considered by MacNeil and Sherif to be the least arbitrary, most "natural" (that is, functionally appropriate) norms available to the group, given its membership. In contrast, norms from the outside or from the group's own past, if they were formed under conditions that do not or no longer apply to the group, will be relatively arbitrary in relation to the group's present situation. MacNeil and Sherif argue that the more arbitrary a cultural norm is in this regard, the less successful the group will be in maintaining it over time. Highly arbitrary norms will gradually be replaced by less arbitrary ones.

To test these notions, MacNeil and Sherif used groups of people making judgments about the illusory movement of a stationary light in a darkened room. This is the same autokinetic situation described in Chapter 5 during the discussion of norm formation. Because it is an optical illusion, judging the distance the light moves is a highly ambiguous task. However, studies have shown that it is not totally ambiguous in that there is a range within which most people's answers fall if they are left to make judgments on their own (Sherif and Harvey, 1952; Hood and Sherif, 1962). When a group of people observe the autokinetic effect together, they generally agree upon a norm for the extent of the light's movement that falls within this range of reasonableness. Such norms are what MacNeil and Sherif considered to be "natural" norms for an autokinetic situation. The authors wanted to show that the further a norm was outside the "natural range," the more rapidly it would be replaced in the group culture.

To do this, comparisons were made among the norms groups adopted under three different conditions. In the "natural" condition, groups of naive subjects were allowed to form their own norm for how much the light moved. After 30 trials one member of each four-person group was replaced by a new person, and so on over several "generations" of members. This allowed the authors to measure the extent that the group's cultural norm was passed on to new members.

The other two conditions were slightly different in that the first generation of members consisted of three confederates and one naive subject. In the "moderately arbitrary" condition the confederates gave estimates of the light's movement that were outside the usual reasonable range, but not too much so. However, in the "most arbitrary" condition, confederates gave estimates well outside the reasonable range. As we would expect from conformity studies, the one naive subject went along with the confederates, allowing the group to adopt moderately or very arbitrary norms. As in the natural condition, after 30 trials one person, in this case a confederate, was removed and replaced by a naive member. After 30 more trials, another confederate was removed and replaced by a naive subject, and so on over several generations. Since the new members were taught the arbitrary norms, this allowed those norms to become established, or "encultured" in the group. After four generations all confederates had been removed.

The question is, did the more arbitrary norms persist as well as the "natural" norms after all the confederates were removed? Figure 8.1 tells the story. The natural norm wavered a bit over generations but remained within the same range. However, both the moderately and the most arbitrary norms gradually decayed towards the natural norm. The most arbitrary norm collapsed almost at once and was replaced by something rather close to the natural norm. These results led MacNeil and Sherif to conclude that the persistence of a cultural norm is inversely proportional to its perceived arbitrariness in relation to the group's circumstances (see Figure 8.1).

MacNeil and Sherif are aware that this kind of change toward more functionally appropriate cultural norms will not occur under all circumstances or in all aspects of group life. Rather they suggest three interrelated factors that will affect the extent to which this occurs. First is the ambiguity of the objective situation to which the cultural norm

Figure 8.1. The Persistence of Arbitrary and Nonarbitrary Norms over Eight Generations of Group Culture

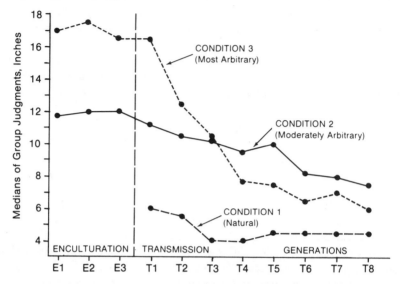

Source: Mark K. MacNeil and Muzafer Sherif, "Norm Change Over Subject Generations as a Function of Arbitrariness of Prescribed Norms," *Journal of Personality and Social Psychology*, 1976, 34:762–773, Copyright 1976 by the American Psychological Association. Reprinted by permission of the authors.

applies. A delinquent group's need to deal with the police is a fairly clear reality in relation to which the group can develop norms. However, the complex needs, motives, and insecurities of the members of a friendship group represent a much more ambiguous group reality. The more clear-cut the objective situation, the greater the pressure to adopt a functionally appropriate norm in relation to it.

The second factor is the perceived reasonableness of the norm in relation to the group's situation. Obviously, the greater the ambiguity of the situation, the greater the range of cultural norms that will seem reasonable. When the situation is extremely ambiguous, almost any kind of cultural norm will seem like a reasonable response. It will be "anything goes," and there will be no reason to consider one norm more functionally appropriate than others.

The final factor affecting the ability of an arbitrary norm to persist is the strength of the influence processes behind the norm. This is an important point because it refers to the way the structure of the group, and the role the cultural norm plays in regard to that structure, affects the norm's persistence. When a cultural norm supports the existing status hierarchy and social structure, conformity pressure will be brought to bear to maintain it, even if it is, or has become, arbitrary in relation to the group's current situation. We will have more to say about this when we discuss structurally appropriate culture.

We can see, however, that, while there are clear pressures on groups to prefer cultural usages and norms that are functionally appropriate to the group's circumstances and goals, there are also countervailing pressures that sometimes emerge from the desire to preserve the social structure of the group. It is the desire for structural stability that gives weight to traditional cultural norms in groups even when they become inappropriate to the group's goals. This should remind us that the test of functionality is only one of the tests applied to cultural items when they are considered for inclusion in the group culture. Most functional items are more *likely* to be adopted, and to persist longer once they have been adopted. But this does not mean that no functionally inappropriate item will ever be adopted or that items that have been adopted are all indispensible to the group's welfare, or even were always the most appropriate ones available (Merton, 1968).

Two other researchers, Weick and Gilfillan (1971) have also been interested in specifying the conditions under which a group's cultural norms will be changed to become more functionally appropriate. They distinguish cultural norms whose arbitrariness is "warranted" from those that are "unwarranted." Arbitrary norms are unwarranted if group members can find alternatives that are more reasonable or functionally appropriate. MacNeil and Sherif's arbitrary autokinetic norms were unwarrantedly arbitrary. Cumbersome procedures for organizing a group meeting are unwarrantedly arbitrary if simpler procedures are readily available. Weick and Gilfillan agree that unwarranted arbitrary norms should gradually be replaced by less arbitrary norms through spontaneous innovation and norm modification in the course of interaction.

Warrantedly arbitrary norms are another matter, however. These norms are arbitrary only in the sense that they have been adopted on a strictly preferential basis from among a set of equally reasonable and functionally appropriate alternatives. For instance, when the office softball league decides to play regularly in one local park rather than another, that is a warrantedly arbitrary norm because it represents a choice between two equally reasonable alternatives. This concept is important because it underscores the fact that there is no such thing as the single-most functionally appropriate set of cultural norms for a given group under given circumstances. Rather, there is generally a broad range of functionally acceptable alternatives amongst which groups choose in an idiosyncratic way. Weick and Gilfillan argue that groups will have no difficulty maintaining warrantedly arbitrary norms over time, because they are as functionally appropriate to the groups' circumstances as the available alternatives.

The data Weick and Gilfillan (1971) report generally support their argument. Their experiment is interesting because it used a group setting closer to everyday experience than did MacNeil and Sherif's autokinetic experiment. Using three-man groups of male college students, each group was given a cooperative game to play for which there were several successful strategies for winning. Some of these strategies were relatively obvious and easy to use, others were much more difficult. A group choice of one easy strategy over another constituted a warrantedly arbitrary cultural norm. However, employing a difficult strategy when easy ones were fairly obvious was unwarrantedly arbitrary. Their data showed that when confederates planted a difficult strategy in a group, over succeeding generations of members it was abandoned and an easier one developed. This result was obtained from a more realistic setting than that used by MacNeil and Sherif. Yet it clearly supports their conclusion that, all other things being equal, unwarrantedly arbitrary cultural norms are abandoned in favor of more functionally appropriate ones.

However, when Weick and Gilfillan's confederates planted an easy strategy in the groups (a warrantedly arbitrary norm) it was maintained fairly well. Weick and Gilfillan note, however, that even when a group's strategy (that is, cultural norm) was maintained, it did not go on utterly unchanged from one generation to the next. Rather, succeeding generations employed subtly different variations of the same strategy so that the norm was preserved in its principle but varied in its style. They argue that this kind of process is probably closer to the way cultural norms are maintained in most real small groups. That is, they are preserved in their main outline but are never unchanging.

AREAS OF FUNCTIONAL CONCERN.   So far we have discussed the functional appropriateness of cultural items simply in terms of their relationship to the group's goals and circumstances. Now we would like to be a bit more specific. If a group is to create a culture that helps it adjust to its circumstances and pursue its goals, what kinds of problems must this culture tackle? Are there certain problems of group life that a group's culture must address if it is to succeed in being functional for the group? These problems are what we call *areas of functional concern* for group culture. Considering these will help us see how cultural items such as symbols and values can be functional for a group as well as the norms we have discussed so far.

McFeat (1974), an anthropologist who has devoted a great deal of effort to the study of small-group culture, has argued that there are three areas of functional concern in relation to which groups create and structure cultural information. Two of these are familiar to us: the task area of adapting to the environment and pursuing goals, and the socioemotional area of group maintenance and the satisfaction of members' needs. The third area is an information-organizing one: cultural information must be ordered in such a way that it can be used effectively and preserved as long as it is needed.

Let us first take up the task area of functional concern. McFeat argues that, to survive, a group must develop and order cultural information into values, beliefs, and practices that allow it to stabilize its relationship with the outside environment in such a way that its goals can be pursued. To accomplish this, a group must first of all gather together information about its surroundings and structure that information into a cultural representation or interpretation of the group's environment and goals. This cultural representation will consist of the group's judgments or beliefs about the nature of the situation in which it exists, the reality that surrounds it, and its understanding of the goals it will pursue. McFeat calls this *the group's shared task definition*.

Second, groups must use their information about the task and their situation to create strategies for pursuing their goals. These strategies usually include beliefs about different social-structural arrangements that are felt to be best for accomplishing the group goal. A committee, for example, might adopt the idea of breaking into small subunits to solve difficult problems. Another group might believe a strong leader is essential to their plans. Strategy information will also include "how-to" lore in regard to skills relevant to the task. For instance, students in a graduate seminar might develop a cultural lore on how to locate and organize material for a classroom presentation. Children at school might develop a lore on how to pass notes in class without being caught.

The group's task definition and strategy information constitute the cultural complex by which the group addresses its task demands. McFeat calls this the "cultural core" of a group because of its basic concern with the group's adaptation to its environment. Clearly, the array of norms, beliefs, and values defining this cultural core will be under pressure to become more functionally appropriate. That is, there will be pressure to alter these items to make them represent the group's objective environment more effectively and to allow the group to effectively pursue its goals in that environment. Indeed, these are precisely the types of cultural norms studied by MacNeil and Sherif (1976) and Weick and Gilfillan (1971). MacNeil and Sherif demonstrated movement toward more functionally appropriate norms defining the nature of the group's environment. Weick and Gilfillen show similar pressures on norms dealing with strategy information.

The cultural core complex is important in any group whether it be task oriented in nature or a primary group. But there is always more to group culture than simply the cultural core (Keesing, 1974). McFeat argues that groups must also develop and order cultural information they can use to manage the group's socioemotional problems. Groups do this by creating cultural devices that help satisfy the needs of individual members, resolve conflicts among them, and weld them together under a distinctive group identity. The group's ordering of information to respond to these issues produces that aspect of small groups to which we most commonly refer when we say *culture*. Hess and Handel (1967), for instance, talk about the way families express their common definitions of themselves—that is, explain themselves to themselves—through the development of symbols, group rituals, repeated themes asserting core values and beliefs, and myths and narratives that illustrate and emotionally resolve recurrent family conflicts.

A persistent conflict in small groups, for instance, is that between the members' needs and desires as separate individuals and their collective concerns as a group. All forms of social organization must face this issue, but it is particularly critical for small groups. There, the ability of the group structure to develop a stable autonomy independent of the whims of individual members is much more limited. One person can actually destroy or severely disrupt a small group in a way that a lone individual cannot affect a larger organization. Consequently, developing cultural practices by which the members can simultaneously feel affirmed in their individuality and united in their collectiveness is an important aspect of group maintenance. A family, for instance, might use a tradition of holiday dinners for this purpose. A group of college friends might engage in an occasional all-night "bull session" for the same reason. The commitment-building techniques we discussed in Chapter 4 offer some additional examples of the ways groups do this.

McFeat (1974) notes that the more stable a group's adaptive relationship to its environment, the more energy it will be able to devote to elaborating its complex of cultural items addressed to socioemotional group-maintenance needs. The more elaborate the group's *expressive culture*, as it is called, the more distinctive an identity a group will have for its own members and outsiders alike. A teenage gang that acquires its own jackets and rituals and nicknames will have a more distinctive identity for itself and others than one without these cultural devices.

However, all groups must develop at least some group identity and expressive culture in order to manage their socioemotional problems effectively enough to survive. This means that the norms defining a group's complex of expressive culture will also be subject to some pressure to be functionally effective. Cultural symbols, practices, and beliefs that do not adequately address the group's socioemotional problems should be abandoned when more effective cultural innovations come along. For instance, a family might try to have formal sit-down dinners every Sunday as a way of increasing their sense of togetherness. But what if it doesn't work? What if the kids rebel against the formality by acting up and the parents get mad as a result? The dinners become a tense ordeal. They are no longer functionally effective for increasing family togetherness. As a result they are only likely to continue until someone comes up with a better substitute. Perhaps nice weather will encourage the family to take a picnic on Sunday instead. If everyone has fun, informal Sunday outings may gradually replace formal dinners, because they do a better job of giving the family a feeling of sharing and togetherness.

So the symbols, values, and practices of expressive culture are under some pressure to be functional as well. However, the goals they serve are the socioemotional needs of the group rather than its task problems. Socioemotional problems are generally much more complex and ambiguous than task demands. Consequently, the range of possible cultural devices that would be functionally appropriate for the group is much greater in expressive culture, and there is much greater opportunity for warrantedly arbitrary choices in that area.

McFeat's (1974) third area of functional concern does not involve a specific content area of group culture in the way that task and expressive culture do. Rather, it deals with the internal coherence with which task and expressive culture are structured. Following Roberts (1964), McFeat argues that cultural information must be organized in such a way that it can be stored, retrieved, used easily, and transmitted to new members. If this is not done the group will not be able to use and preserve what effective cultural information it has developed. As a result, its attempts to manage its task and socioemotional problems will be severely weakened.

What kinds of organizational properties make cultural information easy to store in the memory of group members, to call up through group processes, and to teach to new members? McFeat (1974) conducted a number of experiments to find out. His results suggest that the key aspects are relative simplicity (both in terms of the logical structure of the cultural complex or device and the amount of information organized within it), redundancy (in that important information recurs in many places), and explicitness (in that group members are aware enough of the cultural device to clearly articulate it).

How, you might ask, can a group organize all its important cultural information into a simple, redundant, explicit structure? The answer is that it cannot. Rather, task and expressive culture is usually broken down into little modules of related information that pertain to some specific aspect of the group's task or socioemotional circumstance. For instance, a family's tradition for Thanksgiving dinner is a single, internally organized module of information in its expressive culture. Its method for making important family decisions (perhaps a family conference) is a single module of information in its task culture.

The information in these modules is organized along lines of simplicity, redundancy, and explicitness. For example, the information describing the family's Thanksgiving tradition will be simplified to a basic outline of events that *must* occur (for example, everybody must dress up, there must be a formal dinner, and certain menu items must be served). Even though additional things happen as well (sometimes there are guests, sometimes it is just family), it is just the simplified basic outline that is remembered and passed on from year to year. The information in the outline is explicit, in that all the family members can articulate it, and it is redundant in that it is stored in the minds of several family members at once. So if Mom forgets to buy sweet potatoes, someone else in the family will say, "Where are the sweet potatoes? How can we have Thanksgiving without sweet potatoes?" In this way the tradition can be passed on unchanged from year to year and taught to the younger children as they grow up. Because these modules of information have a coherent internal organization, they describe well-formed contexts, or conveyances of meaning, that provide consistency in a group culture (McFeat, 1974). However, the organization among the various modules of information in the whole culture is usually somewhat looser.

Individual modules of information also vary in the tightness and coherence of their organization and, hence, in the ease with which they can be stored, retrieved, and transmitted. The modules most likely to be tightly ordered are those that develop in relation to some recurrent, pressing aspect of the group's task or socioemotional situation. Perhaps it will be financial struggles for a family or the "big game" for rival athletic teams. In these problematic areas it is most vital for the group's survival that cultural information be developed that is easy to use and preserve. Where the group faces its greatest challenge to its survival, then, you are likely to see the greatest preference for information that is not only effective in regard to the problem, but is functional from an organizational point of view, in that it is ordered in a coherent, easy-to-use fashion.

One of the ways groups create well-ordered cultural devices out of information relevant to task or socioemotional problems is through the development of cultural models (Roberts, Arth, and Bush, 1959; Roberts and Sutton-Smith, 1962; Roberts and Foreman, 1971; McFeat, 1974). Models consist of small-scale symbolic representations of some elements of the group's task or socioemotional reality that are perceived to be in persistently ambivalent or conflicting relation to one another. For instance, a group might use the stylized competition of a game to represent its own struggles with achievement and success in its social environment. In models the elements in this conflict are organized in such a way that they are brought together and reconciled on a symbolic level. By acting out a model, group members achieve a resolution of the conflict on an emotional or ideational level, aiding them in the management of the less easily resolved actual conflict. Examples of models are games, myths, rituals, and repeated stories.

Models help groups cope with threatening uncertainties and conflicts in group life, not only by bringing relevant cultural information to bear on the problem, but also by organizing that information in an evocative, memorable fashion. A gang, for example, might repeat the story of a heroic feat by one of its now almost-legendary past members. The story is a dramatic encapsulation, a model, of the primary struggles the group faces, and its valued ways for overcoming them. By repeating the story, the gang members gain some information about the group's goals and its strategies for achieving them. But just as important, they get a vicarious emotional experience of heroic success in living up to the group's values and overcoming the uncertainties of its problems. Buoyed by this experience, they feel more ready to encounter an actual conflict the group faces in the present. Models, then, can provide coherent, evocative summaries of the group's values as they are brought to bear on the recurrent problems in its life.

At this point, it might be helpful to stop and remind ourselves of the progress of our argument. We are interested in why groups adopt some beliefs and practices rather than others. Fine (1979) suggested that cultural items must be *known, usable, functional, structurally appropriate,* and *triggered* by events to be included in the group's culture. We have seen that the cultural items selected or created from the store of known and usable information, and ultimately preserved in the group culture, tend to be those that are more functionally appropriate, in that they address the group's task and socioemotional problems in a reasonable way and are organized in a usable manner. Although groups tend to preserve functionally appropriate information over unwarrantedly arbitrary information, there is still a large range of idiosyncratic choice among the many possible cultural items that are functionally acceptable. Finally, in addition to pressures to select more functionally appropriate cultural items, groups often also have countervailing pressures arising from the group structure, which may seek to preserve group traditions regardless of their present functionality. It is this problem of the effect of group structure on the creation of idioculture that we will take up next. After we have discussed the issue of structural appropriateness, we will go on to the effect of triggering events in the creation of group culture.

Structurally Appropriate Culture

Some cultural items that would be quite functional from a task or socioemotional point of view are never introduced into the group, or, if they are, don't persist because they do not support the power and prestige structure of the group (Fine, 1979). As we have periodically noted, cultural ideas often have significant implications for the social structure. The way group culture defines the task will have a great deal to do with who is perceived to have skills relevant to the task and, therefore, who legitimately should have power in the group. If, for example, the office softball team defines its task goals as recreation and fun, the most powerful people are likely to be the socially skilled ones. But if it decides that the goal is to play good softball, it is the best players whose status will be increased. There are many subtler ways in which cultural ideas can uphold or undermine the power and prestige of particular members in the group as well.

Because of the social-structural implications of differing cultural notions, members of a newly forming group will usually try to define the group culture in a fashion that makes the most of their own skills and preferences. As we have seen, however, some will be more successful than others, and a status hierarchy will generally take shape rather quickly. Out of this process, a newly forming group evolves not only a status structure, but also an idioculture that justifies and reinforces that structure.

Fine (1979) gives an illustration of this in his discussion of the nicknames his Little Leaguers developed for one another. Nicknames often have evaluative connotations. For high-status members the nicknames had a positive quality, like "Superstar" for a well-liked, good hitter. Nicknames for low-status members, on the other hand, often had a joking, teasing quality. In a play on his name, one low-status boy was called "Smell-Ton," for instance, and another was called "Maniac." In the next year, the boy called Maniac was older and played better, moving up to middle status in the group. His nickname was changed to "Main Eye" to match his new status (Fine, 1979).

After the status structure of a group emerges, those members who benefit from it have a vested interest in preserving cultural beliefs, or accepting new cultural practices, that legitimate their power. As a result they are likely to use their influence in the group to maintain cultural traditions that are important to their prestige and to scorn cultural innovations that threaten it.

This makes it difficult for new cultural ideas to catch on in the group unless they are introduced by high-status members themselves or, at least, approved of by them. Fine (1979) uses the example of an unusual haircut, which, after it was adopted by the number two boy on the team, was quickly emulated by several other members. The highest-status boy on the team then announced that he thought it was "stupid," although he carefully excepted Wiley, the number two boy, saying it looked good on him. After that, no one except one low-status boy adopted the new haircut, and he was teased about it. We should not be surprised by this effect, since it is really part of the deviance and social control process we discussed in Chapter 5. If you recall, deviance and innovation which was accepted from a high-status member was punished in a low-status member. The highest-status members were actually expected to take the lead in innovating new cultural practices for the group.

The result of the unofficial veto power of high-status members over new cultural items is that the group culture is continually screened for its appropriateness to the status structure, even as it is changed and adapted to new circumstances. It may have occurred to you, however, that the vested interests of high-status members may occasionally incline them to maintain cultural traditions after their functional appropriateness has played out. Changing conditions may make the favorite traditions of high-status members unwarrantedly arbitrary.

When this happens, the group finds itself saddled with a culture that is no longer effective in managing its task or socioemotional problems. There are several possible outcomes. First, the group members may do nothing about the problem, with the result that the group limps along unhappily, or perhaps even founders and is disbanded. Or the high-status members might recognize that, to preserve their standing, they must introduce some effective changes themselves. Whether or not this happens will depend on the type of changes demanded and on the leadership skills of the high-status members.

However, there is also a third possibility in this situation. A coalition of group members may simply override the wishes of the high-status members and change the group culture, even though it means transforming the status hierarchy. Sherif and his colleagues (1961) give an example of this from their field experiment on boys at camp (described in Chapter 4). When the two groups of campers began to engage in heavy competition with one another, one group was dissatisfied with its ability to successfully match its rivals. The members of this group insisted on redefining their culture so that it took a more aggressive, hostile view of their rivals, even though this meant changing their group leader. As you might imagine, this "mutiny" situation is not all that common in small groups. As we noted in the last chapter, it tends to occur when a group is failing to achieve a goal to which it is highly committed, or when it is experiencing a severe threat from the outside.

Triggering Events

For any group, the range of all possible cultural items that are known, usable, functional, and structurally appropriate is still very large. How does it happen that a group picks one set of these possibilities rather than another? The answer has to do with the way group culture is affected by the unique contingencies of ongoing interaction. Fine (1979) argues that the impetus to introduce some specific piece of cultural information comes from the "spark" of a triggering event in the group interaction. One member laughs in a sudden distinctive way that inspires another member to dub him with a specific nickname. According to Fine, any event that produces a response from the group may serve as a trigger, but repeated events are particularly likely to lead to cultural formation. For instance, if one member is presistently late to group gatherings, jokes, wisecracks, and stories are almost bound to develop around the fact. Novel or unusual events are also powerful triggers to cultural formation. The day their losing team finally won will be celebrated by the team members in tale after tale.

The notion of triggering events points out for us the way the actual content of a particular group's idioculture flows out of the details of group interaction in a spontaneous, not wholly predictable way. One things leads to another. The criteria of usable, functional, and appropriate culture only narrows the pool of known cultural items that it might occur to a member to introduce into the group. It is the triggering events of ongoing interaction that cause a member to select one rather than another of those items out of the pool, or to recombine several known items in a new way. The ever-changing contingencies of interaction are the sparks behind the continual process of cultural innovation.

However, simply because a triggering event causes a member to introduce a new cultural item into the group arena does not mean that that item will be adopted into the group culture on a more permanent basis. That will depend on,the other members' judgment of the item's usability, its task, expressive, or informational functionality, and its structural appropriateness. So these screening criteria operate twice: first in the mind of the individual member who will decide whether to introduce the item in the first place, and second in the shared judgment of the rest of the group, who either reject or adopt the item. Spontaneous triggering events mediate between these two levels of cultural screening.

For any distinctive idiocultural item to enter the group arena, it must be sparked by a triggering event. However, there are usually areas of group life where the stage is so set for cultural formation that almost any event will serve to trigger the process. Most obvious is the fundamental need faced by all groups to develop at least a minimal definition of their task and self-identity. But beyond this, a group may also have some recurrent, nagging problem or conflict in its daily life, perhaps the area of interpersonal relations or the group's self-definition. There might be a problem of sibling rivalry in a family, for instance, or competition for dates among college friends. A problem like this hangs around in the background during group interaction, often just below the members' conscious awareness, but it is ever-present nevertheless. In this situation, any little event can trigger something in the mind of a member, causing them to introduce some cultural idea that might be used to manage the problem (see Box 8.1). It is easier, then, for cultural information to be triggered into the group if it is relevant to the group's conflicts and problems. As a result, groups tend to develop more elaborate culture in those areas of group life that are most important to the group or most troublesome.

We can see, then, that the process by which groups create their idioculture is quite complicated. The members bring with them from their other social contacts a pool of known cultural items. However, based on the blueprint norms for the group and its own evolving internal norms, certain of these cultural items become usable in the group context. Of these usable items, those which are more functional, in that they help the group accomplish its goals, tend to be preferred over less functional items. However, the importance of functionality in adoption and persistence of a cultural item varies considerably with a number of factors. Also there is usually a wide range of functionally acceptable cultural items amongst which the group chooses in an idiosyncratic way. Functional or not, cultural items usually must be structurally ap-

Box 8.1   The Sweetest-Smelling Baby in New Orleans

Families develop rich, distinctive group cultures. Any child knows this who has spent the night at a neighbor's and found everything different: the taste of the spaghetti, how people acted at supper, the TV programs the family watched, what they talked about, when the kids had to bathe or go to bed, if they were allowed to eat sweets. Since families develop such elaborate group cultures, they are a good place to watch the process of cultural creation. In *Pentimento,* playwright Lillian Hellman recounts an amusing scene from her own family which illustrates how cultural items can be introduced into a group, struggled over, and finally adopted or rejected. The situation is two days before the opening of Hellman's first play:

. . . I had gone to have dinner with my mother and father, who had not read the play, had not seen the rehearsals, had asked no questions, but, obviously, had talked to each other when they were alone. Both of them were proud of me, but in my family you didn't show such things, and both of them, I think, were frightened for me in a world they didn't know.

In any case, my mother, who frequently made sentences that had nothing to do with what went before, said, in space, "Well, all I know is that you were considered the sweetest-smelling baby in New Orleans."

She had, through my life, told me this several times before, describing how two strange ladies had paused in front of our house to stare at me in the baby carriage and then to lean down and sniff me. One of them had said, "That's the sweetest-smelling baby in town." The other had said, "In all New Orleans," and when my mother told our neighbor about her pleasure in this exchange, the neighbor had said of course it was true, famously true, I always smelled fresh as a flower. I didn't know that my mother had never until that night told my father or, if she had, he was less nervous than he was two nights before the opening. Now, when she repeated it, he said, *"Who* was the sweetest-smelling baby in New Orleans?"

"Lillian," said my mother.

"Lillian? Lillian?" said my father. "I was the sweetest-smelling baby in New Orleans and you got that information from my mother and sisters and have stolen it."

"Stolen it?" said my shocked mother. "I never stole anything in my life and you know it. Lillian was the sweetest-smelling baby in New Orleans and I can prove it."

"It's disgraceful," said my father, "what you are doing. You have

Box 8.1   *(continued)*

taken what people said about *me, always said about me,* and given it to your own child."

"Your child, too," said my mother.

"That's no reason for lying and stealing," said my father. "I must ask you now to take it back and not to repeat it again."

My mother was a gentle woman and would do almost anything to avoid a fight, but now she was aroused as I had never before seen her.

"I will take nothing back. You are depriving your own child of her rightful honor and I think it disgraceful."

My father rose from the table. "I will telephone Jenny and prove it to you," he said.

He was giving the phone operator the number of his sisters' house in New Orleans when my mother yelled, "Jenny and Hannah will say anything you tell them to. I won't have it. Lillian was the sweetest-smelling baby in New Orleans and that's that." She began to cry.

I said, "I think maybe you're both crazy." I went to the sideboard and poured myself a large straight whiskey. My father, holding the phone, said to me, "Sweet-smelling, are you? You've been drinking too much for years."

"Don't pay him any mind, baby," said my mother, "any man who would deny his own child." (Hellman, 1973)

From the standpoint of family culture, what happened? The parents wanted both to express their pride in their daughter and to connect her unfamiliar adult accomplishments to the family lore. The triggering event was the dinner. There they were, face to face before the big opening. Something needed to be said. Since the family culture prohibited outright expressions of pride, Hellman's mother dredged through her known, usable information and came up with an item from Lillian's past, the sweetest-smelling-baby story. It was functional in two ways: it was an indirect expression of pride in Lillian, and it associated her current achievement with the familiar past. However, as we know, a cultural item can't just be functional, it must also be structurally appropriate to be adopted into the culture of the group as a whole. Hellman's father was the highest-status member of the family. He objected that *he* was the sweetest-smelling baby. Passing that title on to Lillian was structurally inappropriate, and he wasn't going to let it happen. It didn't. Lillian as the sweetest-smelling baby did not make it into the whole family culture.

propriate, in that they support the existing status hierarchy, if they are to catch on for long. Finally, to be introduced into the group in the first place, cultural items must be triggered by some event in the group's life.

IDIOCULTURE AND THE LARGER CULTURAL CONTEXT

Now that we have a better idea of what idioculture is and how it is created, we can return with greater understanding to the relationship between small-group culture and the culture of society as a whole. To gain a deeper insight into the complex interdependence between these two levels of culture we will look at two examples of their mutual influence. We will first discuss how groups can innovate new patterns of relationships among people that can be disseminated into the larger culture. We will then examine the way cultural models that exist in the larger culture become the foundation for certain types of small groups.

Novel Groups and New Blueprints

At the beginning of this chapter we emphasized the fact that the larger culture contains normative blueprints for the most common groups operating in its midst. Where do these blueprints come from in the first place, and how are new ones created? The answer, of course, is from the idiocultural innovations of small groups. We have often noted that people form groups to meet personal needs and accomplish goals that they cannot achieve on their own. Many of these goals and needs arise from the demands of living in the larger society. One of the things small groups do, then, is to develop, through their idioculture and social structure, patterns of relationship and concerns that help people manage the demands of society.

The existing group blueprints are the results of these efforts in the past. Particular types of group arrangements, innovated by groups themselves, worked well within the surrounding organizational context. Because they were useful, they diffused outward to other groups and gradually became institutionalized in the culture of society as a whole. The increasing use of the decision-making committee is a recent example of such diffusion.

However, these blueprints, once established, do not become rigid. They are constantly subject to innovation and modification by the groups formed in accord with them. Most of these modifications are just personal variations that do not diffuse outward to other groups. But when a group's innovations respond to changing social conditions affecting a major sector of society, they are much more likely to spread widely, and ultimately to modify the basic blueprint of the group type. For example, the fact that most women as well as men work these days is forcing families to innovate new relationships among their members that will probably modify our basic normative expectations for the family itself.

Occasionally, changing social situations will lead people to improvise a new type of small group, one for which there is no blueprint in the larger culture. If the changing circumstances are ones that seriously affect a large segment of the population, rather than just a few people, then improvisations of this type may lead to the formation of a new social blueprint for a novel group type. Our general cultural blueprint for the type of groups we call T-groups developed in just this way. Experiments with T-group-like arrangements have been going on for some time. However, the changing social and cultural circumstances of the 1960s encouraged these experiments on a wide scale, and, gradually, a new group type entered our cultural repertoire. Perhaps, with the aging of the population that will occur as the baby boom generation reaches retirement, we will see a similar spread of innovative senior citizen groups. We can conclude, then, that it is the innovations of group idiocultures that create the normative blueprints for new types of groups in our society. That brings us full circle then. The larger society shapes the culture of most groups by providing a normative outline of the basic range of behaviors expected to characterize a group of that type. But small groups, by developing their idioculture out of and in reaction to this blueprint, in turn, may modify the blueprint itself and ultimately create new ones.

Groups Founded on Cultural Models

The cultural devices we call "models" were introduced as the creations of group culture. Most such models do originate in face-to-face interaction, but there are some models that have been progressively formalized and institutionalized as part of the larger culture. In general, this has occurred because the models deal with conflicts, problems, and ambivalences whose source is in the demands of the larger society on the individual. A classic example of such cultural models are games. What is interesting to us here is that there are a whole category of small groups formed for the primary purpose of acting out such models provided by the larger society. Let us look more closely at the example of groups founded on the cultural models we call games.

Games are internally consistent, well-ordered cultural complexes that deal with strategies for exercising mastery and overcoming opposition (Roberts, Arth, and Bush, 1959; Roberts, Sutton-Smith, and Kendon, 1963; Roberts and Chick, 1979; Roberts, Chick, Stephenson, and Lee, 1981). They are models of achievement and the exercise of control under differing circumstances, and their outcomes are usually determined primarily by strategy, physical skill, or chance (Roberts, Sutton-Smith, and Kendon, 1963). Roberts and his colleagues have noted that in our own society, where the emphasis is on the control of events through effort and calculation, games of physical skill and strategy predominate.

Roberts further argues that, by participating in games, people have an opportunity to express and symbolically work through conflicts and stress they feel about real achievement situations. In an achievement-oriented society like our own, many people have these kinds of conflicts. Participating in sports and games allows them to work through tensions that are not only stressful to them but may even interfere with their successful management of the real achievement situations posed for them by the larger society. They may also learn a few helpful points that will aid them in dealing with competition of all sorts (Roberts and Sutton-Smith, 1962; Sutton-Smith, Roberts, and Kozelka, 1963).

The point for us here is that to play most games it takes a group. A great many small groups in our society form for the express purpose of acting out a game of one sort or another, from canasta and bridge to baseball and racquetball. The cultural models for competition and achievement that such games represent become the foundation of these group's idiocultures. By allowing people to act through these models, game groups help their members deal with tension and difficulties acquired from the society at large. In doing so, they help their members go back into that society and function effectively. Game groups operate as buffer zones absorbing some of the conflicts and problems created for individuals by the larger culture, which in turn allows individuals to continue to support that culture. They illustrate for us once again the complex interdependence between the culture of small groups and that of the society in which they operate.

SUMMARY

In this chapter several basic points have been made about small-group culture. Group culture was defined as the members' store of shared information about the group, its surroundings, and its behavior.

This store of information is acted out in the content, meanings, and topics of interaction among the members. Group culture is not just a random jumble of information, however. Rather, it is information that the group has organized into distinctive patterns of rules, beliefs, values, and symbols, which are used to give meaning to group life. These patterns of culture are what gives each group its own distinctive quality and style. Culture, then, is a system of ideas. It includes the group's norms, but it is not limited to them. It is analytically distinct from the social structure, which is a pattern of relationships among the members. However, the two are interdependent since both are tools by which the group grapples with its task and socioemotional problems.

To understand the particular culture small groups develop, it is necessary above all to recognize that groups are located in larger social networks that connect them to the cultures of neighboring small groups, surrounding large organizations, and the society as a whole. Since small groups evolve their distinctive culture in relation to this larger social network, they are heavily influenced by it. However, they are in the unique position of creating cultural ideas and practices that are in many ways a commentary on the culture of society as a whole. As a result, groups often create new cultural ideas that sometimes spread to and influence society in turn.

We viewed the process of creating group culture as one by which people select, from the information they have acquired from their social networks (*known* culture), certain items to be introduced into the group and recombined into new cultural forms. Following Fine (1979), we argued that four criteria guide this selection process. The information must be *usable* in the group context, in that it does not violate norms of proper behavior in the group. For most small groups we bring with us, from the larger culture, a set of general expectations for the types of behavior expected to characterize that group. These form a normative blueprint by which the usability of culture information is first judged. After the group has developed its own distinctive idiocultural norms, these too are used to judge the acceptability of particular information.

In addition to being usable, cultural information is more likely to become a stable part of the group culture if it is *functional* for the group —if it addresses pressing task and socioemotional problems and is organized in a way that makes it easy to remember, apply, and transmit to new members (McFeat, 1974). We reviewed experimental evidence showing that groups tend to preserve functionally appropriate information in their cultures much better than information that is *unwarrantedly arbitrary* in regard to the group's circumstances. However, groups still have a large range of idiosyncratic *(warrantedly arbitrary)* choice among the many possible cultural items that are functionally acceptable (Weick and Gilfillan, 1971).

The third criterion is that, for inclusion in the group culture, information must be *structurally appropriate* in that it supports the status hierarchy of the group. This means that information is unlikely to enter the group culture unless it is approved of by the high-status members. It also means that occasionally high-status members will maintain existing group traditions that justify their power even after these norms have become functionally inappropriate. Finally, to enter group culture, an item must be *triggered* by some event in the interaction of the members. Triggering events explain how the actual details of group culture develop from the ongoing process of interaction in a spontaneous, not wholly predictable way.

With a better understanding of the operation of group idioculture, we returned to the relationship between small-group culture and the culture of society as a whole. To gain a deeper insight into the complex interdependence between these two levels of culture, we explored two examples of their mutual influence. We looked at the way small groups in fact create for the larger society the blueprints for new types of groups. We then discussed groups formed on the basis of cultural models, such as games, provided by the larger society.

III

Small Groups
in Society

9

Task Groups and Productivity

Now that we know something of the fundamental processes that apply to small groups in general, we are going to shift gears a bit. In this chapter and the next we intend to delve into processes and problems that are specific to two different types of groups in our society: task groups and primary groups. Understanding the particular problems and issues of these groups will involve an application of analytical tools we have already learned, as well as the acquisition of new information. Our goal is to gain some new insight into the actual operation of the two major types of small groups that structure our lives.

Task groups will be the focus of this chapter. Task groups, of course, are groups created to accomplish some specific goal. The goal can consist of making a decision, solving a problem, creating a group product, or carrying out an activity. Whenever a group is constituted to perform a task, the distinctive question raised is, "How successful will it be?" The major focus of our exploration will be to understand what makes some task groups productive while others bog down in frustration or simply become content to go nowhere.

As we shall see, this is an extremely complex problem. Like so many other group characteristics, productivity (task success) is something that *emerges* from the interaction of skills and personalities of the members, the nature of the task, the group's structure and norms, and the influence of the outside environment. As an end result of a complex system of interdependencies, it provides a good illustration of the almost seamless web of interacting parts that constitutes the essence of group life. However, it does not yield simple answers. We shall have to rely on conditional answers that specify the impact of various factors on a group's productivity, given particular circumstances.

After exploring the basic factors affecting productivity, we will turn our attention to some particular problems that may afflict that most ubiquitous of task groups, the committee. Although committees are used to make a great many major decisions in our society, they have a rather poor reputation. Everyone has heard the saying, "It couldn't have been done any worse if it were done by a committee." Why do committees have a reputation for producing low-grade, poorly organized decisions and products? Most of the time, the reputation is undeserved. However, as we shall see, committees can be vulnerable to some particular decision-making difficulties that *can* occasionally lead to very bad decisions. We will examine these difficulties in terms of the problems of creativity in groups, and a process called "groupthink."

THE USE OF TASK GROUPS IN SOCIETY

Before delving into the determinants of a group's productivity, we need to establish a framework for understanding the use of task groups in our society. We will do this by briefly discussing two issues: first, why and when problems are assigned to task groups rather than to individuals, and second, whether groups are, in general, a good way to accomplish things. How well do groups manage a task, compared to the way an individual might? Exploring this second issue will help us understand whether the widespread use of task groups in our society is in fact justified.

Why Have Task Groups Proliferated?

We have often noted that large organizations, when faced with some task to accomplish, are likely to put a group in charge of it. Private corporations, government agencies, politicians, educational institutions, are all equally likely to appoint a committee, task force, or study group when faced with a difficult problem. The use of task groups has become habitual for individuals as well. When faced with a complicated task like moving, or a troublesome community issue like a debate over schools, taxes, zoning, or neighborhood safety, most Americans organize a task group to deal with it. Why has the use of task groups become so widespread?

There are two reasons. One arises from the types of problems large organizations increasingly confront; the other, from the history of our knowledge about groups and their impact on people's productive efforts. Let's deal with the types of problems typically assigned to groups first. Groups are attractive tools for task accomplishment when the task is rather complex, of large-scale, or politically or emotionally sensitive. Groups seem more appropriate to large-scale or complex tasks because they combine the skills and energies of several people. When a task involves very serious consequences, conflicts of important values or interests, or matters on which people have strong feelings, groups are attractive because they diffuse responsibility for the decision over several people. No one person is on the spot.

The growing size and complexity of American society is increasing the number of complex and/or sensitive tasks that major organizations face. The larger scale and growing interdependence of business, government, and service institutions requires more complex planning and decision making and arouses more conflicts of interests and values. As a result, people within these institutions increasingly appoint committees. The major impetus for the proliferation of task groups, then, comes from their increasing use by large organizations to manage their affairs. From working within these organizations, individuals also learn the task group habit and apply it to the accomplishment of tasks in their own lives.

A second reason for the increasing use of task groups by large organizations is more historical. We have referred on several occasions to pioneering group-process studies of workers in the Hawthorne Electric plant in the 1930s (Roethlisberger and Dickson, 1939). These studies were originally undertaken by scientists attempting to understand how external environmental factors like lighting, pay structure, and job organization affected workers' productivity. The researchers made the unexpected discovery that, while external factors were quite important, the informal relations among the workers were also critical in determining productivity. The revelation of the importance of groups to workers' productivity created a new school of thought in business management called the human resources approach. People working within this school have sought techniques for harnessing the power of groups to the goals of the large organization. As a result of the growth of the human resources approach, the use of groups to accomplish tasks has become an increasingly popular management technique. There is every reason to expect that the movement to install small task groups within large organizations will continue in the future (Hackman and Morris, 1978).

Are Groups a Good Way to Accomplish Tasks?

Do groups really perform better than individuals? The answer depends both on the nature of the task at hand and on the skills of the individual we are comparing to groups. Groups can usually produce a higher quality or more accurate product than an average member could alone if the task involves solving a problem or learning new material (Shaw, 1981; Hare, 1976; Davis, 1969; Rotter and Portugal, 1969). On the other hand, if the task involves making a judgmental decision, the evidence is more equivocal. Groups do not necessarily make better judgments than individuals. Walker (1974), for instance, found that judicial decisions made by three-judge panels were reversed by higher courts about as frequently as those made by individual judges. There is, however, no indication that groups do worse than individuals on judgmental decisions (Hare, 1976; Shaw, 1981). Finally, a task could simply require a lot of effort, like moving furniture. Groups will obviously be faster than individuals on a task like that.

In general, then, groups *are* superior to most individuals at many, although not all, tasks. Groups have three advantages over a single person, since they possess:

1. A greater variety of judgments and skills to rely on
2. A better opportunity to discover and correct errors as they go (Shaw, 1981)
3. More energy and effort to bring to bear on the task

However, it usually takes a group longer to complete a task than it does an individual, especially if you consider all the hours put in by all the members together (Taylor and Faust, 1952; Kelley and Thibaut, 1969).

Groups usually outperform their average members, but can they ever outperform their best, most-skilled members? Would an organization be better off locating the most-skilled member and giving the task to him or her alone? If the task is clear-cut and simple with one best solution, groups are more likely to recognize the competence of the best member, follow his or her suggestion, and end up performing as well as that person could alone (Kelley and Thibaut, 1969). Many physical tasks—moving an awkward piece of furniture into a house or freeing a car stuck in the mud—are relatively simple (if exhausting) because the goal is clear-cut and solutions that work are easy to recognize from those that do not. Adding up group finances or figuring out how much water the city used last year are also simple tasks because they require routine calculations rather than new ideas or careful thinking. Groups can manage tasks like these as well as their best members.

However, some tasks are very complex with many steps to be thought through and put together. Consider what is involved in devising a balanced budget for a city or deciding on a foreign policy for the United States. In the process of discussing all the various aspects of complex tasks, group members may interfere with one another's thinking and, in the confusion, either disturb or not recognize the skills of the group's best members (Faucheux and Moscovici, 1968; Davis and Restle, 1963; Lorge and Solomon, 1960; Schoner, Rose, and Hoyt, 1974). As a result the group may not do the job as well as the best member might have alone (but it is still likely to outperform the average member.) In fact, if the task is so extraordinarily difficult that none of the members can do it alone, working together in groups probably will not help (Shaw, 1981).

However, there is a middle ground between a very simple task, where the group performs as well as its best members, and a very complex task, where the group performs worse than its best members. When the task is of intermediate difficulty, challenging but not impossible to solve, group members may stimulate and learn from one another, as well as just adding together their skills. This is a true interaction effect in which the mutually stimulating impact of the members makes the group's productive capacity more than merely the sum of the individuals involved. As a result, the group as a whole actually outperforms even its most-skilled member (Goldman, 1965; Laughlin and Johnson, 1966; Shaw and Ashton, 1976). This might happen, for example, when TV scriptwriters get together to discuss the plot for a soap opera, or a team of scientists bounce around ideas for a new experiment. Students sometimes experience this when they discuss ideas for a class project with their colleagues.

On average, then, our society probably *is* justified in its increasing reliance on task groups to address important problems. Occasionally these problems might be better handled by a single very skilled person. However, in the complexities of large organizations, that most-talented person may not be easy to locate, and a group will handle the problem better than the average person will. Some problems may be more complex than either individuals or groups can handle (for instance, solving the world's energy problems), but groups will not do worse on these than most individuals. In most situations groups will produce higher-quality decisions and solutions than will most individuals, and, occasionally, groups will even outperform highly skilled individuals. Groups, then, are not a bad tool for accomplishing many kinds of tasks.

WHAT MAKES GROUPS PRODUCTIVE?

Some groups are very effective at accomplishing their tasks, while others fail. Why? Hackman and Morris (1975) have offered three general "summary variables" that control a group's task effectiveness:

1. The *effort* the members bring to bear on the task
2. The *knowledge* and *skills* the members effectively apply to the task
3. The *task performance strategies* they use to carry out the task

We will repeatedly see the effects of these variables on group performance. Our explanations for the way various factors affect productivity will most frequently turn on the way these factors alter the group's effort, knowledge and skills, or task strategy.

However, a moment's consideration will make it clear that behind each of these apparently simple variables are very complex group processes. The effort expended on the task, for instance, might reflect group norms, or the cohesiveness of the group, or the external rewards available to the group, or a wide variety of other factors. To understand productivity, then, we must consider the entire situation of the group, its structure and norms, its environment, and the needs and skills of its members.

In discussing how various aspects of the group affect its task performance, we must keep in mind the socioemotional dimension of group life as well. A group can only focus its energies and skills on its task when it is not being distracted or disturbed by the members' concerns over their relationships with one another. In Chapter 1 we mentioned that most task groups adopt an emotionally cool, work-oriented attitude that deemphasizes the members' personal reactions to one another. In other words, people are not required to like one another, just to be able to work together.

This work-oriented atmosphere does not mean that socioemotional problems disappear, however. Members must still manage their relationships with one another and deal with personal needs. To be very productive, then, task groups must strike an appropriate balance between attention to the demands of the task and attention to their relations with one another. A group can fail to achieve this balance by either over- or underemphasizing socioemotional problems. Neglect of members' needs and reactions to one another can lead to bickering, hostility, frustration, and inefficiency. Overemphasis on feelings and relationships may lead to a happy, intimate group, but it can distract time and energy from the task, too. The more successful a group is at striking an appropriate balance between task emphasis and attention to socioemotional issues, the greater its productive potential.

With these general considerations in mind, let us turn now to a consideration of the many factors that influence a group's task performance. We will begin by presenting an overall paradigm for understanding group performance. We will use this paradigm to organize our discussion of the way specific factors like group structure or members' abilities affect a group's task performance.

A Paradigm for Understanding Group Performance

Steiner (1972) has pointed out that any task group begins with a certain *potential* for productivity. That is, it has a potential amount of effort it could bring to bear on the task it faces, a given store of knowledge and skills to address those demands, and a number of possible strategies available to it. However, as we all know, there is often a big difference between a group's potential and what it actually achieves. Steiner attributes that difference to what happens in the actual *process* of group interaction, the steps the members take to deal with the task and how, in the process, they react to and influence one another. Putting these points together, Steiner suggests that a group's actual productivity will equal its potential productivity minus losses due to faulty group processes.

Steiner's approach is helpful because it separates factors that contribute to a group's potential to manage its task from the process of interaction that determines the effect of these variables on actual productivity. Figure 9.1 provides a more detailed diagram of this view of group performance. This paradigm, from Figure 9.1, will be used to organize our discussion of the impact of various factors on group productivity.

A group's potential productivity is determined by three general classes of factors:

1. *Individual-level factors*—the skills, knowledge, and personal characteristics that the members bring to the group
2. *Group-level factors*—the group's structure, norms, cohesiveness, and so on
3. *Environmental-level factors*—factors that come from outside the group, including, most importantly, the task with which the group is confronted, and also, the rewards offered by the organization or social situation in which the group operates and the degree of stress put on the group by its environment

The impact of each of these variables is mediated by the way the actual process of interaction develops in the group. This is a complex business. The potential input factors shape the nature of the interaction that occurs in the first place. We have seen, for instance, how aspects of group structure such as status hierarchy pattern members' behavior

Figure 9.1. Group Productivity: From Potential to Performance Outcome

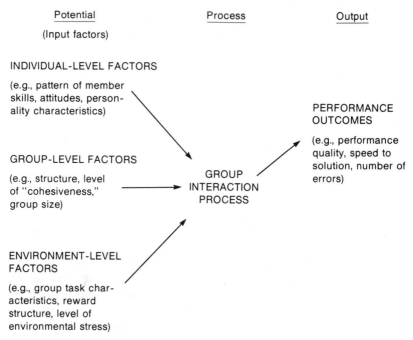

Potential   Process   Output
(Input factors)

INDIVIDUAL-LEVEL FACTORS

(e.g., pattern of member
skills, attitudes, personality characteristics)

GROUP-LEVEL FACTORS

(e.g., structure, level
of "cohesiveness,"
group size)

GROUP
INTERACTION
PROCESS

PERFORMANCE
OUTCOMES

(e.g., performance
quality, speed to
solution, number of
errors)

ENVIRONMENT-LEVEL
FACTORS

(e.g., group task char-
acteristics, reward
structure, level of
environmental stress)

Source: Adapted from J. Richard Hackman and Charles C. Morris, "Group Tasks, Group Interaction Process, and Group Performance Effectiveness: A Review and Proposed Integration," in L. Berkowitz, ed., *Advances in Experimental Social Psychology*, vol. 8 (New York: Academic Press, 1975), p. 50. Reprinted by permission.

toward one another. However, these potential input factors do not entirely determine what actually goes on as the group process takes shape. Events occur together in a spontaneous, unpredictable way that alter the impact of a potential variable such as members' skills. Out of this process the group's actual task performance emerges. As a result our separation between factors affecting a group's potential and its interaction processes cannot be an absolute, categorical one.

Our next step is to examine individually the various input factors that determine a group's productive potential. We will begin by looking at the impact of the group task and other environmental factors, and then turn to group-level factors, and, finally, to individual factors. After that, we will discuss some general models for understanding actual group process and look at some types of process effects that can occur.

The Impact of the Task and Other Environmental Factors

TASK DEMANDS.   No single factor has as great an impact on the operation and success of a task group as the nature of the task itself. People organize themselves in different ways when confronted with a task like shoveling snow than they do when, say, playing football or choosing a weapons system for the U.S. government. Consequently, much of what we can say about the impact of group and individual factors on productivity must take into account the kind of task at hand. Actually, we have already had a sample of this in our discussion of whether groups are better task accomplishers than individuals. If you recall, our answer depended on the type of task the group faced.

What we need, then, is some method for classifying tasks in terms of the type of demands they make on a group. It is these task demands that condition the impact on productivity of other variables like group structure or members' skills. There are many ways group tasks could be classified. We have already distinguished between tasks that involve problem solving, the carrying out of an activity, the creation of a product, or decision making. Steiner (1972) has devised a fairly elaborate typology of tasks in terms of the nature of their solutions and the strategies necessary to perform them. Shaw (1973) has analyzed people's reactions to group tasks in terms of basic dimensions, such as whether the tasks have one or many solutions or involve mental or manual work. However, researchers as yet have neither carried through on these more elaborate task classifications nor connected them clearly to the other factors that we want to discuss. Consequently, we will rely instead on a much simpler classification system that nevertheless makes clear the major types of demands a task may place on a group.

Herold (1978) proposed a distinction between the technical demands made by a task and its social demands. *Technical demands* refer to the skills and knowledge necessary to accomplish the task. *Social demands* refer to the types of interactions among the members the task requires. Both social and technical demands vary from "easy to satisfy" to "complex" or "difficult to satisfy," resulting in the 4-box table shown in Table 9.1.

Technical demands are simple when the procedures necessary are obvious to members and easily available to them, like passing buckets of water in a fire brigade. They are difficult when ready solutions are neither available nor obvious and a search must be performed to find an appropriate way of meeting them. Creating new special effects for a movie is an example of a technically difficult task. Social demands are

Table 9.1. A Classification of Group Tasks by Technical and Social Complexity

| | | Complexity of Technical Demands | |
		LOW	HIGH
Complexity of Social Demands	LOW	Both technical and social demands are simple and routine. *Examples:* pushing a stalled car; carrying out a routine, highly structured task which arouses no strong feelings	Social relations are routine but technical demands are high. *Examples:* the tasks faced by a swim team or a relay team in some sport like track or cycling
	HIGH	Task is technically simple but interpersonally problematic. *Examples:* Deciding how to distribute funds among various programs, or distribute rewards among group members	Both technical and social demands are complex. *Examples:* Producing a creative product; a jury deciding an important case; a committee making an important policy decision; problems of human relations

Source: Adapted from David M. Herold, "Improving Performance Effectiveness of Groups Through a Task-Contingent Selection of Intervention Strategies," *Academy of Management Review*, 3, p. 317. Reprinted by permission.

simple when each member can work on a different part of the task and little interaction is required as, for example, when digging a ditch. Social demands are also simple when the required interaction, even if considerable, is mundane and not likely to cause interpersonal difficulties. For instance, three people surveying a construction site must be in constant communication with one another, but the nature of their interaction is not complex. However, if the task demands extensive and potentially problematic interaction among the members, it is high in social difficulty. An example might be a school board trying to decide on a desegregation plan. When a task is emotionally charged or has very serious consequences, it is particularly likely to be high in social difficulty (Herold, 1978).

Table 9.1 gives examples of the types of tasks that would fall into each of Herold's four categories. As a further elaboration, we might point out that most of the tasks that fall into the low-social, high-technical demand category are what some writers call "coacting" tasks rather than "interacting" tasks (Fiedler, 1967; Steiner, 1972; Nixon, 1979). In coacting tasks, group success depends on adding up the individual contributions of all the members, the way the overall score of a ski team is the sum of the individual athletes' performances. More common in task groups are interacting tasks where members must coordinate their efforts, often each performing a different aspect of the task. Playing football, for instance, is an interacting task. The social demands in interacting tasks are obviously more difficult than in coacting tasks.

To perform well at its task, a group must distribute its efforts, skills, and strategies in a way that matches the complexity of the social and technical demands of the task (Hackman and Morris, 1978; Herold, 1978). If a group's task is socially simple, and the members or, say, the group leader focuses a great deal of time on relationship problems, effort will be wasted that might better be spent on the task. The members of a relay team of swimmers, for instance, would do better concentrating on the technical problems of swimming than on becoming better friends with their teammates (assuming they do not allow the team relationship to deteriorate entirely). If the task is technically well defined but socially difficult, it is relationship problems that should be addressed if the group is to perform well. How many city councils or school boards, for instance, bog down on budget issues when the facts under discussion are not really the problem; rather, a conflict of interests or personal ideology is at stake. Groups face their most difficult challenges when the task is both socially and technically difficult. Interestingly, as we argued earlier, these complex, often controversial problems are precisely the ones government and business organizations are most likely to refer to groups to solve.

EXTERNAL REWARDS AND ENVIRONMENTAL STRESS.   In addition to its task, there are two other environmental factors that affect a group's potential for productivity. If a task group operates within a larger organization, that organization may offer rewards to the group for its task performance. The nature of these rewards can affect the group's productivity. The most important distinction here is between *cooperative* situations, where the group as a whole is rewarded for its performance, and *competitive* situations, where rewards go to individual members based on their personal performance.

In a classic study, Deutsch (1949) found that rewards which encouraged cooperation led to high member motivation, a greater division of labor and coordination of activities, and more positive interpersonal relations. This, in turn, led to high productivity both in terms of quality of products produced and the amount of time required. The nature of the rewards, in other words, shaped the structure and processes of the group, which in turn affected productivity.

Blau (1954) confirmed these results in his study of interviewers in a public employment agency whose job was to place as many applicants as quickly as possible. In one group a cooperative atmosphere encouraged interviewers to share information on job openings and to help one another place applications. As a result, productivity was high. In another group the interviewers competed with one another. In an effort to outperform each other, interviewers hoarded information on job openings and, as a consequence, everybody's placement rate declined.

The superiority of a cooperative reward structure, however, is limited to tasks where the members are dependent on one another for overall success (Okun and DiVesta, 1975; Goldman, Stockbauer, and McAuliffe, 1977). When the group members can work independently of one another on what we called a coacting, or *additive*, task, a competitive reward structure may be just as effective or even superior to a cooperative one. This makes sense, since the effect of cooperative rewards is to improve coordination and specialization among the members' task activities. If the task doesn't require this, cooperative rewards will not improve productivity (Shaw, 1981).

Somewhat related to the factor of reward structure is the factor of environmental stress. When groups must accomplish their task under conditions of great stress—as, say, soldiers in combat, or the president's security advisors during a dangerous international confrontation, must—this naturally affects their performance. Outside stress makes it harder for members to trust one another and coordinate their behavior together (Kelley et al., 1965). In other words, it greatly increases the social difficulty of a group's task. As a result only more cohesive groups whose members have good interpersonal relationships will manage to perform well under high-stress conditions (Shils and Janowitz, 1948). (However, as we shall see later, very high cohesiveness under stress conditions can sometimes cause discussion groups to make poorly considered decisions [Janis, 1972].)

Groups that regularly face a certain degree of stress or violence in the conduct of their tasks may try to deal with the added socioemotional problems by developing a group culture that encourages emotionality among the members and emphasizes getting "psyched up" for the task. Nixon (1977), for instance, reports that teams engaged in relatively violent contact sports like football do better when such emotionality is emphasized. (In lower-stress sports, however, such emotionality interferes with group performance, draining energy away from the task.) Similarly, a fanatic paramilitary group like the Ku Klux Klan might use a high degree of emotionality to whip up its members for a violent endeavor.

We can conclude, then, that the nature of a group's task is the most important environment-level factor affecting its productivity. It is useful to classify group tasks in terms of complexity of the technical and social demands they pose for a group. A group will do best when it uses its skills, efforts, and strategies in a way that matches the demands of its task. When a group operates within a larger organization, the cooperative or competitive nature of the rewards it receives from the organization also affects its productivity. Unless the task is a socially simple, coacting one, groups usually perform better with a cooperative reward structure. Stress is another environmental factor that affects productivity by increasing the social difficulty of any task. Groups perform better under stress if they have good socioemotional relations among the members.

Group Characteristics Affecting Productivity

The structure and characteristics of a task group naturally are a major determinant of its productive capability. In discussing the effect of group-level factors, we will review briefly the impact of many aspects of group structure and culture that we have dealt with in earlier chapters. We will see the impact of group culture in the way norms affect productivity. The effects of group structure can be seen in the impact of status, leadership, communication, and group size. Finally, we will see how cohesiveness, too, has a significant impact on productivity.

GROUP NORMS.   A task group will never perform well if it does not embody a value for high productivity in its norms. If it does do this, the group can use its reward structure, conformity pressures, and social control processes to increase each member's involvement in the task. But not all task groups do value high productivity. Recall that the factory work groups in the Hawthorne studies developed and enforced on the members norms for moderate, not high, production. Members who produced too much ("rate busters") were pressured to slow down, just as the slow ones were pressured to speed up.

Low or moderate productivity norms may reflect the members' lack of interest in the task or, perhaps, their greater interest in social relations among the members. Students assigned to work together on a class project, for example, may in fact have little interest in their task and spend most of their "work" time socializing. Similarly, a suburban bridge club may enforce rather relaxed playing standards to allow opportunity for general conversation. However, lower productivity norms may also reflect a task group's ambivalent or negative relationship with the larger social context within which the group functions. The men in the Hawthorne groups feared their employers would exploit them if they were too productive. A committee might feel their report will never be read or taken seriously by the larger organization; as a result, they put little effort into its preparation.

Cultural norms specifying the type of behavior appropriate to various task groups also affect productivity. They do this by affecting the strategy or approach to a problem a group adopts (Argyris, 1969; Hackman, 1975; Hackman and Morris, 1975). Argyris has suggested that the emotionally cool, work-oriented assumptions most of us share as part of our cultural blueprint for task groups lead us to behave in an emotionally "conservative" fashion in such groups. Feelings are expressed circumspectly, personal risks are avoided, deviant ideas are generally suppressed. For socially simple tasks, these norms are perfectly appropriate for high productivity. But when the tasks are socially difficult—and many of those turned over to groups are—these norms can impair the group performance. This makes it hard for the group to face its complex interpersonal issues directly and it discourages the suggestion of deviant but possibly creative ideas that might help the group solve a troublesome social or technical issue.

Finally, Hackman and Morris (1975) argue that many of the kinds of tasks groups face are basically familiar to us. For example, we are all acquainted with tasks requiring the group to discuss a series of options and choose among them on the basis of some specified criterion. This is what a group of friends do when they decide what movie to go to. It is what the finance committee of a corporation does when it chooses an investment strategy. Because we are familiar with tasks like these, we share common assumptions about the types of strategies and procedures that are appropriate to them, and we bring these assumptions with us when we take part in a task group. The trouble is, our common patterns of decision making may not, in a specific case, be the best way to solve the task. An individual working alone might break through these habits of thinking. But in a group, habits become norms, and they inhibit the group member's ability to see through them to a more innovative approach. Group norms, then, shape the effort members put into a task and the way they apply their individual skills and knowledge to the problems at hand.

STATUS RELATIONS AND COMMUNICATION.   To make use of the efforts, skills, and personality differences of its members, a task group must develop an organizational structure that can coordinate its different people efficiently in relation to the task. A key aspect will be the extent to which the group's status structure corresponds to task-related abilities of the members. Since status confers influence, and because high-status members talk more, the group tends to spend more time discussing the ideas of high-status members than searching for other alternatives (Maier and Hoffman, 1960). As a result, task groups produce higher-quality decisions, solutions, or products in a shorter time if the most-skilled members occupy the high-status positions.

Riecken (1958) illustrated this in a classic experiment. He gave hints about the best solution to the group task to (1) the most talkative member in some groups (talkativeness usually indicates high status) and (2) to the least talkative member in others. When the most talkative member had the crucial information, the best solution was adopted by most groups. But when it was in the hands of the least talkative member, most groups rejected the best solution. It is important, then, to have the most-skilled members in the high-status positions.

This can sometimes be problematic for a group. Objective skill at the task is an important determinant of a member's status, but, as we saw in Chapter 6, it is not the only determinant. Status is also affected by factors such as external status characteristics, dominance, and likeability, that may or may not be associated with objective competence.

The type of status structure best able to utilize the members' abilities often depends on the task the group faces. We know from Chapter 4 that the flow of communication is usually governed by the status structure. Communication, of course, is essential to the process of accomplishing a task. We saw in our discussion of communication networks that open, decentralized communication is best if the group task is ambiguous, technically complex, or requires innovation. It seems likely that socially complex tasks as well would require free-flowing discussion. To achieve open communication, the size of the status differences among the members would have to be relatively small. Groups faced with a technically or socially complex task, then, would do better if they organized themselves democratically with a relatively flat status hierarchy.

Actually it is interesting that many groups faced with innovative tasks, such as "think tank" groups or advertising writers, do exactly this. As we have noted elsewhere, they function in rather open democratic work groups despite the hierarchical structure of the large organizations within which they operate. In some industries, such as home-computer companies, technology is changing so fast that new, freshly trained people must have as much voice in decisions as more experienced people if the company is to keep up. These industries, too, try to avoid large status differences among their members in order to facilitate open communication and innovation.

We know, then, that open communications tend to be good for complex tasks. But what if the group's task is not complex? Will the reverse be true? Yes. When the group task is technically or socially simple and highly structured, clear lines of authority and centralized communications lead to more efficient task performance. For instance, if the group's job is to clear trash off the beach after a holiday, or to address envelopes for a political group, open communication is unnecessary and time-consuming. It would be more efficient simply to have one or two members take charge of the group and direct it from the middle of a centralized communication network. This will be easier to achieve with a focused, hierarchical status structure.

Whatever status system the group evolves, it is most important that it be accepted as fair by the group members. If members feel that status differences are unfairly large (or small), or that the wrong people are in positions of influence, they will direct their energies toward arguing about those problems, increasing socioemotional activity in the group at the expense of task effort. Alternatively, they may become alienated and withdraw from the group effort, reducing the cohesiveness and motivational unity of the group. Either way, the group's task effectiveness will be reduced.

As an aside, we might note that maintaining member satisfaction with the status structure might sometimes conflict with creating a status structure that is more appropriate to the task. Consider a group with a complex task that requires a democratic status system—for example, weighing the evidence against an accused murderer or resolving a serious family conflict. The group may, however, have some members who, because they are more skilled or perhaps have personal needs for dominance, will be unhappy with only slight status differences. Similarly, group members who are all of similar background and external status might resent the establishment of a strictly hierarchical status system even if it is efficient for the task. Tension caused by conflicts like these often leads task groups to compromise between the organizational structure needed to be efficient and that needed to satisfy members' needs.

LEADERSHIP.   Let's turn now to the way a group's leadership structure affects its potential productivity. Since we reviewed some of this material in Chapter 7, we will be brief here. First of all, there is evidence that task groups perform more effectively when they develop a clear, normatively defined leadership structure rather than maintain an informal, leaderless system (Goldman and Fraas, 1965; Walker, 1976). Hare (1976) argues that if several members exercise specialized leader roles in a pluralistic system, the group will be more productive than if it has a single leader. His basic point is that with pluralistic leadership, more members are actively brought into the group's decision-making process, increasing everybody's shared sense of responsibility for the group's efforts.

Certainly this is true. However, we should remember that pluralistic leadership structures also have the added problem of coordinating the behaviors of the leaders. If the task is technically and socially simple (see Table 9.1) this added problem might just be an unnecessary inefficiency. If the task is extremely difficult socially—making a controversial decision, for instance—the added problem of coordinating the leaders might prove too much to handle, with the result that the group might collapse into bickering or go nowhere. So perhaps a pluralistic leadership structure is only superior for certain types of tasks: those which are simple to moderate in social difficulty but technically more complex. Usually these fall into the category of planning or decision-making tasks that require the group to consider a wide variety of information and make complicated decisions, but which are not of great emotional or personal consequence to the members. A corporate committee working out the production schedule for a new product or a group of students organizing a routine class presentation are examples. However, when the task is simple technically and socially, or of moderate technical difficulty but very troublesome socially, an integrated leadership system will probably be more effective.

Probably more important than leadership structure, however, is the behavior of those in leadership positions. In general, a group will perform more effectively if its leaders direct and structure its activities (Stogdill, 1974). However, as we saw when we discussed Fiedler's (1967) theory of leader effectiveness (Chapter 7), the extent and nature of the directive activities that are needed depend on the task. A group will perform better under a directive, task-oriented leader if its task is either socially and technically simple or very complex. If we look at Table 9.1, this means tasks that fall in either the upper-left-hand quadrant, such as pushing a stalled car, or in the lower-right-hand quadrant, such as making a controversial policy decision. The lower-left-hand and upper-right-hand quadrants of Table 9.1 describe tasks of moderate or mixed levels of social and technical difficulty. With this sort of task, a more relationship-oriented leader who encourages member participation will be better at making the group perform effectively.

One of the major ways a leader can help or inhibit a group's problem-solving or decision-making capabilities is by affecting the number of ideas and alternatives that are brought up for discussion. If the group's task is fairly complex technically, there will be no obvious ways to solve it. Therefore, the more distinctly different task ideas the group generates, the better the ultimate solution the group is likely to achieve (Hoffman, 1961). Whether the group views the generation of different, even conflicting, ideas as productive or sees it instead as an example of deviance to be controlled, depends a lot on how the leader acts. Leaders can encourage their members to question existing group ideas and offer alternative opinions by lending their personal support to members who wish to do so and making clear their approval of dissent. In this way a leader can help a group avoid excessive conformity pressures that might limit its ability to develop high-quality, complex decisions and solutions. On the other hand, as we shall see when we examine "groupthink," leaders can do just the opposite by disapproving of conflict and emphasizing their own views too strongly.

GROUP SIZE.   An additional aspect of a group's structure that affects productive potential is size. By now, you will not be surprised to hear that the precise effects of group size depend, like so much else, on the kind of task the group faces. If we consider the advantages and disadvantages of increasing group size, the results we are about to present will be a bit clearer.

When a group gets bigger, its pool of talent grows, as does the diversity of personalities and viewpoints. As a result its decision-making and problem-solving resources grow, but so do the potential organizational problems. Also, as group size increases, a distinct leadership structure is more likely to emerge, which, as we have seen, is a plus for productivity. On the other hand, as this happens, participation rates for the members become more unequal, and as a result it gets harder and harder for some members to get their opinions heard. Because of these countervailing effects, Steiner (1972) concludes that, for most tasks, group productivity increases with group size up to a certain point, after which it levels off and then actually declines.

Moderate size groups, then, tend to be most effective. How do we define "moderate"? Variables such as the group's circumstances, its task, and its members' abilities make no clear-cut answer possible. But recall from Chapter 1 that Slater (1958) found that groups with five people were most satisfactory to their members. Somewhere between four and ten members is probably best for most tasks.

How then does the optimum group size vary with the type of task? Steiner (1972) and Shaw (1981) point out that if the group's task is an additive or coacting one (shoveling snow), group performance is just the sum of individual efforts, and so larger size is an advantage. The more people you have to help you work, the faster it will go. If the task is such that it can be solved if any one group member can figure it out (for example, why a car doesn't work), again, large groups will be better because of their greater talent pool. However, if, for the group to complete the task, each and every group member must be able to solve it, then a smaller group would clearly be best (Steiner, 1972). Finally, it is probably moderate-sized groups whose members are most likely to stimulate one another into performing even better than their most-talented members might alone, which would be most helpful on interacting tasks of some technical difficulty.

COHESIVENESS.   The last group-level factor to examine in relation to productivity is cohesiveness. We know from Chapter 4 that cohesiveness increases both members' commitment to group goals and the power the group has to influence their behavior. If the group norms define productivity as a goal, then the members of a cohesive group are likely to put increased effort into accomplishing the task. And if some member lags behind, the group is likely to use its power of influence and control to bring that member in line. As a result, cohesive groups that value productivity are in general more effective at their task (Hare, 1976).

There are some exceptions, however. If the group task is mainly a coacting one (running on a high school track team or selling Girl Scout cookies), a certain element of competition among the members, as long as it does not destroy the unity of the group, will improve the group performance even though it will reduce cohesiveness (Nixon, 1977). A second exception is more problematic. Sometimes the increased conformity pressures in high-cohesive groups can inhibit the diversity of thought the members engage in, which in turn limits the group's ability to perform well at technically complex tasks. We will look at this in more detail when we examine Janis's (1972) notion of "groupthink."

It should be clear by now that no factor other than the task itself affects a group's potential to perform effectively more than its organizational structure and characteristics. A group's norms, status system, leadership structure, cohesiveness, and size all have a major impact on what it can accomplish. We have approached these group-level factors as determinants of a group's performance potential. However, we have often had to refer to their impact on the actual process of group interaction in order to understand their effects. This serves to illustrate once again that the structure and process of task groups, like all groups, are interdependent, and a group's task performance is something that emerges out of the interaction of the two.

Members' Characteristics and Productivity

Individual-level factors—the skills, attitudes, and personalities of the members themselves—represent the final link in our triangle of input factors affecting group productivity. Obviously, a group can accomplish more if some or all of its members are highly skilled at the task. However, the specific mix of abilities among the members is important, too. You might assume that a group would perform best if everyone had a similar level of ability, but actually this does not seem to be the case. In general, groups composed of members with diverse abilities outperform more homogeneous groups with the same overall skill level (Goldman, 1965; Laughlin, Branch, and Johnson, 1969).

We see similar effects when we turn to the attitudes and personalities of the members. In general, heterogeneous groups produce a better product than homogeneous ones. This is particularly the case if the members differ with respect to their overall personality profile (that is, their whole pattern of personality attributes). Hoffman (1959) found that groups whose members differed in overall personality produced better and more innovative solutions to management problems. Even when the task was socially difficult, involving conflicts of values and interests, rather than just technically problematic, the heterogeneous groups still outperformed homogeneous ones (Hoffman and Maier, 1961).

The key to understanding these results is to view diversity as a problem-solving *resource* for the group. People with different abilities, backgrounds, and personalities approach problems in various ways . A person whose viewpoint diverges from yours might suggest an idea you might never have thought of, even if you have the greater ability. In a sense, then, you can look at task group members as tools in a tool box. For most tasks, particularly more complex ones, it is better to have five or six different tools in the box than to have five or six copies of the same tool. With a wider variety of skills and personalities, the group has the potential to generate more alternative solutions to its task, and, as a result, it is more likely to end up with a good final product.

To take advantage of diversity, however, it is vital that the members have a cooperative, committed orientation to the task. Without this commitment, diversity can become a source of dissension and personal conflict rather than stimulation. It is also necessary that the members not be so different from one another that they don't "speak the same language." Finally, it is helpful if, despite their divergent personalities, the members are reasonably compatible in terms of their personal needs (Hare, 1976; Shaw, 1981). However, as long as these conditions are met, a mixture of abilities and personalities is a source of creative contrast that can help the group do its job efficiently and well. This is an interesting point, since we often implicitly assume that the more similar people are, the more efficient they will be in group action.

We are now ready to move from a consideration of factors that affect a group's potential for productivity to that of the interaction processes by which this potential is translated into actual task performance. We have seen how environmental-, individual-, and group-level factors all shape the interaction that takes place among the members as they grapple with their task. However, these factors do not wholly determine what actually occurs as the members deal with one another and the task. While it would be impossible to specify the whole range of processes that might occur in different types of groups dealing with varying kinds of tasks, we can give some sense of the basic dynamics involved and some of the process effects that can occur.

Group Process and Task Performance

We begin our examination of group interaction and task output by considering a model of the group problem-solving and decision-making process. Not all group tasks have problem solving or decision making as their primary focus. However, even when the task consists of carrying out an activity, such as playing a game, or creating a product, such as writing a report, the group must still discuss problems of strategy and make decisions as to procedure. Therefore, understanding group interaction in regard to problem solving seems critical to task performance in most situations. After we have discussed a model of the problem-solving process, we will go on to consider a major effect that emerges out of group discussion, the polarization of group opinion.

A MODEL OF GROUP PROBLEM-SOLVING PROCESSES.   Hoffman (1961, 1965, 1978, 1979) has outlined a theory of the group problem-solving process that has been quite influential in the study of group performance. His conception uses the general approach of field theory. Hoffman views problem solving as a process in which the group changes over the course of discussion to become more attracted to some potential solutions and less attracted to others. The attractiveness of a particular solution is conceived of as its positive or negative *valence* to the group members. (Recall from Chapter 2 that the concept of valence comes straight from Lewin's field theory.) Valance is measured by the number of positive or negative comments made about a particular alternative as it is discussed.

The group's valence toward a given solution or decision is the sum of the individual members' reactions to it. Those who have some prior acquaintance with the group task may have some valence toward particular solutions before group discussion begins. However, the assumption is that the group as a whole goes through a complex process of warming up to various solutions, considering alternatives, and perhaps later backing off from some ideas and reapproaching others. These changes, in the alternatives favored by the group occur as a result of the process of mutual stimulation and influence that goes on as the members talk with one another.

Hoffman makes a number of assumptions to describe how this process moves (or fails to move) toward a conclusion in which the group adopts a particular solution to its problem. First of all, he argues that a solution must achieve a certain minimum valence (or favorableness) before it is a candidate for adoption as the group's final decision. Often, in the course of discussion, more than one of the suggested alternatives will pass this minimum adoption threshold. Once beyond it, the amount of positive valence a solution accumulates in the eyes of the group increases the likelihood of its adoption. In the end the group will adopt the solution with the highest valence. The more strongly each member has personally favored the adopted solution, the more satisfied he or she will be with the group's decision. Hoffman (1978, 1979) has accumulated substantial research evidence confirming this description of the problem-solving process in groups with varying tasks and structures.

Using this model to observe groups grappling with problems, Hoffman has been able to offer some interesting insights into the subtlety of the processes of mutual influence by which groups gradually come to a decision. He notes that, often well in advance of the members' explicit remarks to that effect, particular solutions acquire a favorable valence and move toward acceptance, or a negative one and become *de facto* rejects. In other words, the influence processes by which various solutions move forward or backward in the group's opinion are often implicit and not overtly acknowledged by the members. Thus by the time some members announce, "Well, I guess we're down to two choices," the group has often already implicitedly decided to favor one of these choices and rejected the other (Hoffman, 1978). The explicit discussion that follows will serve to rationalize and justify that decision rather than to truly choose between the two.

We can use Hoffman's model to conceptualize the way environmental-, group-, and individual-level factors impinge on the process by which groups come to favor some solutions and reject or fail to consider others. This, along with the spontaneous development of group interaction, determines the extent to which a group lives up to its productive potential. The nature of the task and outside environmental pressures structure the demands placed on the group and the sort of solutions likely to be discussed in the first place. The pattern of abilities and personalities similarly will affect the variety of task ideas considered and, to some extent, the way members react to one another's suggestions. The status system is likely to have a substantial impact on the solution adopted, as high-status members use their prestige and persuasiveness to increase the valence of some ideas and decrease that of others. Recall the Maier and Hoffman (1960) finding that groups spend more time debating the ideas offered by high-status members than searching for alternatives. The behavior of group leaders will also greatly affect which solutions are favored and the variety of options entertained. Group norms will shape the members' initial preferences, the diligence of their search for solutions, and their reactions to novel solutions. This in turn may mean certain solutions that occur to individual members are never introduced into the group discussion or, if they are, are swiftly rejected.

Many more examples of the possible impact of group, environmental, and individual factors on the process of group decision making could be given. However, this brief overview should suffice to suggest the general way these factors shape discussions as groups move toward making task decisions. In addition to the impact of these potential factors, there are, as we have said, spontaneous processes that develop from the group discussion itself. These, too, affect the final group decision. One of the most important of these processes, the group polarization effect, will be examined next.

GROUP POLARIZATION OF ATTITUDES AND BEHAVIOR.   Some years ago a group of researchers interested in individual risk-taking behavior discovered something unusual. After a group discussion of risk-taking situations, the members seemed willing to endorse riskier decisions than they had previously (Wallach, Kogan, and Bem, 1962, 1964). This was called the "risky shift" phenomenon, and it aroused considerable interest since it seemed to imply that groups made people more extreme and less responsible than they might be on their own. A barrage of research soon established that the term "risky shift" was a misnomer, because what was really happening was that group discussion was enhancing the prevailing initial leanings of the group members. If the group members were leaning toward risk, discussion made them, on average, riskier; but if they initially favored caution, discussion would make them more cautious. As a result the phenomenon has been renamed *group polarization* (Moscovici and Zavalloni, 1969). It has since been shown that group polarization effects are not just limited to issues involving risk and caution. Group discussion can make people favor more strongly or dislike more adamantly all sorts of attitudes and behaviors toward which the group has an initial positive or negative inclination (Meyers and Lamm, 1976).

Group polarization is of interest because it is an effect that emerges entirely out of the actual process of group interaction, and because it influences the decisions task groups make. While it does not always or inevitably affect all discussion groups, it regularly and reliably affects most of them (Lamm and Meyers, 1978). What could possibly cause group polarization?

Several theories have been proposed, and, from the fact that no one can supply all the answers, it is clear that several processes are involved. However, if we put them all together, the general picture that emerges is something like this. There is evidence that, although people generally like to agree with others on matters that reflect upon themselves, most people would like to appear, not just average, but a bit better than average (Festinger, 1954; Brown, 1974; Jellison and Arkin, 1977; Lamm and Meyers, 1978). When they enter into a group discussion they are exposed to the attitudes and opinions of the other group members. If these opinions reveal that the group is learning toward a particular stance, group members may get the feeling that opinions in that direction are more socially valued than other attitudes. This is particularly likely if the group's initial leanings coincide with a dominant value or norm in the outside society. In various groups, for instance, members may get the impression that it is socially valued to appear willing to take risks, or to be hard-nosed, or to be cautiously concerned with the facts, or to be sympathetic and lenient.

When members sense (or think they sense) a social value for a certain direction of opinion in the group, some may react by trying to more closely live up to that value. To do this they may pick a position that is a bit further in the valued direction than the average opinion in the group, and argue for it. Their goal is to gain approval in the eyes of themselves and others. However, in making their argument they are likely to persuade some members to agree with them and, by example, encourage others to take the argument even further. In a gradual process of "one upping" one another in their efforts to appear desirably distinctive, the group members gradually talk each other into adopting a more extreme position than they originally advocated (Lamm and Meyers, 1978).

Group polarization, then, is a result of several processes. Ironically, one is the social comparison process, and the conformity pressures it creates (see Chapter 5). Another is people's desire to appear just a bit distinctive from others in a socially valued way. And finally, there are the effects of persuasion and informational influence. Group polarization has been shown to affect the decisions made by a variety of actual task groups, including juries (Davis, Bray, and Holt, 1978), judges (Lamm and Meyers, 1978), and many other groups dealing with social, business, and legal decisions.

Does the group polarization effect mean that people in groups will make worse decisions than they would alone? Not by any means. Whether a polarized decision turns out to be a better or worse one is entirely dependent on the context and nature of the problem the group is deciding on. And we already have seen that groups usually make better decisions than individuals. However, for our purposes it is important to understand that group polarization is one process is one effect that mediates the nature of the decisions task groups make and the sort of solutions they adopt.

CREATIVITY AND GROUPTHINK: THE PROBLEM OF THE COMMITTEE

We have outlined the fundamental processes that affect a group's task performance. Now let us turn to some specific problems faced by discussion groups like the committee. Like most task groups, committees have the capacity to perform quite well, and usually they do a more than adequate job. On the other hand, they can sometimes produce stunningly bad decisions. Why? As task groups, committees are prone to all the problems of structure and process we have discussed so far, and these partially account for their failures. However, there are two other types of problems that afflict discussion groups which we have yet to discuss: (1) creative thinking in groups, and (2) the phenomenon called "groupthink." We will discuss these issues with a special focus on what they tell us about the types of failures committees are prone to.

Already we have seen signs of potential trouble in the group decision-making processes. We have seen the way cohesiveness raises pressures for conformity and social control, for instance. We have also noted the kind of "bandwagon" process by which certain ideas develop high valence in the group, and by which group polarization occurs. As a particular viewpoint begins to surface as the most popular one, the social processes of discussion groups sometimes sweep the members along to a decision that, from the outside, seems ill considered. When this happens, the members can make two types of decision-making errors. First, they can too quickly close in on one choice without seriously considering all the available alternatives. Second, once they begin to favor an idea, they may no longer critically evaluate it, with the result that they overlook serious flaws that cause problems later. During the Watergate incident, which forced President Nixon to resign, Nixon and his advisors decided early on to pursue a cover-up plan when they might have just come clean on a slightly embarrassing scandal. Why didn't they see the potential risks involved in an illegal cover-up scheme? The military experts who planned the attempted rescue of the American hostages in Iran failed to anticipate the problems that caused the disastrous failure of that mission. Again, why? The two decision-making errors outlined above may account in part for the kind of faulty planning involved in both these incidents.

Creative Thinking in Groups

Now let's consider how these potential trouble spots might affect a discussion group's ability to produce a truly creative decision. Most researchers agree that creativity involves 1) the generation of a wide range of ideas, particularly novel or unusual ones, and 2) critical evaluation to produce a novel combination of those ideas uniquely suited to the problem at hand (Stein, 1968). If a group closes in too quickly on a particular alternative and suspends critical evaluation of it, both these key steps in creative thinking will be disrupted. While groups are capable of creative decision making, then, the problems they are prone to reduce the likelihood that they will live up to their creative potential. As a result, it probably is true that most committees do not produce highly creative decisions.

The way group processes limit genuine creativity can be seen in the results of a phenomenon called "brainstorming." We have often noted that the thoughts of others can stimulate you to come up with different ideas. There is also evidence that the presence of other people stimulates you physically, too, increasing your energy level (Zajonc, 1965). You may recall from Chapter 2 that this is called "social facilitation." Aware of effects like these, an advertising executive named Osborn (1957) suggested that putting people in groups would be a better way to generate new ideas than having them work alone. In these brainstorming groups, all critical evaluation would be suspended so that everybody in the group could throw out whatever ideas came to mind, good or bad. The results, Osborn thought, would not only be more ideas, but more creative ideas.

Brainstorming caught on and became something of a fad in the 1950s. However, the results were not what Osborn predicted. In the end, research showed that brainstorming actually produced *fewer* ideas per person than did individuals working alone (Lamm and Trommsdorff, 1973). Furthermore, the ideas brainstorming groups produced were of no higher quality or originality than those of individuals. In fact, what seems to happen in brainstorming groups is that the members fall prey to "one-track thinking" (Taylor, Berry, and Block, 1958). Group members do stimulate each other to new ideas, but they are all ideas of the same type. Totally different ideas are neglected (Kleinhans and Taylor, 1976). The result is a limiting, rather than broadening, of creative thinking. It seems clear, then, that groups do not usually inspire great creativity, even if they can generally perform a task or solve a problem better than an individual. In fact, group members can usually be more truly innovative on their own.

Groupthink

The same type of one-track thinking that limits creativity in groups can also cause problems for groups facing complex, important decisions under crisis conditions. In our society important policy decisions are often made by high-level, prestigious committees. Examples might be the governing board of a corporation, the joint chiefs of staff, the president's advisors, a "blue ribbon" committee, or a variety of other such groups. With the prestige they receive, and their sense of doing important work, groups like this can become extremely cohesive, creating a sense of high morale and superconfidence among the members. As we know, cohesiveness usually increases productivity since it increases the effort the members put into the task. But, unfortunately, *very high* cohesiveness can also have negative side effects for decision making. It can make the group vulnerable to something Janis (1972) called "groupthink."

Groupthink is a very serious version of one-track thinking, or, as Janis calls it, of the *tendency for concurrence seeking* in highly cohesive groups. What happens is that a sense of self-confidence and loyalty to the group, its norms, and its past behavior, replaces critical evaluation of the task. Janis (1972) carefully analyzed the deliberation of government leaders and their advisers in situations where groupthink led to disastrous decisions, for instance, the Vietnam War and the United States' failed "Bay of Pigs" invasion of Cuba. He found that the groups responsible for these decisions shared illusions of invulnerability. They had a sense that their side just could not lose, which made them rationalize away warnings of disaster. Because they felt their group to be inherently moral, they never questioned the morality of their own decisions. This same tendency made them stereotype people who opposed them as incompetent or weak and treat their opposition too lightly.

The pressures to agree created by extreme cohesiveness can be seen in a number of other symptoms Janis discovered in these groups. Loyalty to the group became so important that members censored their own doubts or questions. As a result, nagging worries were rarely expressed, creating the illusion of unanimity even when members had substantial private doubts about the group's actions. If some member actually did voice concern or criticism of the group's thinking, he or she was usually directly pressured to get back in line, making it clear that dissent was considered almost disloyal. Because of this atmosphere, self-appointed "mind guards" emerged who took it upon themselves to protect the group from adverse information that outsiders might try to bring to the group's attention. Table 9.2 shows these symptoms of groupthink, the conditions which lead to it, and the problems it causes for decision making.

As you might imagine, groupthink keeps a group from considering all the alternatives it should and makes it much too sanguine about the risks involved in its preferred choice. Given the complexity and importance of major policy decisions, the result can be disaster. Raven (1974) has suggested that it was exactly this kind of groupthink phenomenon that lead President Nixon and his advisers to become involved in the Watergate cover-up, which ultimately brought down his presidency. Janis (1972) has shown that it was groupthink that caused the United States to enter the Korean War and to be unprepared for the attack on Pearl Harbor that started World War II. A similar type of thinking might cause a car company to market an automobile that shows serious signs of design failure—and might lead to millions of dollars in recalls.

Let's look a little more carefully at the antecedent conditions that cause groupthink. This will help us to understand when groups will be most vulnerable to groupthink and, also, what might be done to avoid it. Janis (1972) emphasizes high cohesiveness as groupthink's most important cause, particularly when it is combined with a directive leader who makes known early on the alternative he or she favors. Laboratory studies affirm that these two factors are indeed important contributors to groupthink but show that their mere presence may not always be sufficient to cause a full-blown case of the problem (Flowers, 1977; Cartwright, 1978). It may be necessary for the group to face some of the other groupthink preconditions as well. For instance, the group should be under stress, facing a crisis situation, and should be without established procedures for considering a wide variety of viewpoints (Janis, 1972; Janis and Mann, 1977). When all those factors come together in

Table 9.2. Analysis of Groupthink by Policy-Making Groups

Antecedent Conditions	Symptoms of Groupthink	Symptoms of Defective Decision Making
1. High cohesiveness	1. Illusion of invulnerability	1. Incomplete survey of alternatives
2. Insulation of the group	2. Collective rationalization	2. Incomplete survey of objectives
3. Lack of methodical procedures for search and appraisal	3. Belief in inherent morality of the group	3. Failure to examine risks of preferred choice
4. Directive leadership	4. Stereotypes of out-groups	4. Poor information search
5. High stress with a low degree of hope for finding a better solution than the one favored by the leader or other influential persons	5. Direct pressure on dissenters	5. Selective bias in processing information at hand
	6. Self-censorship	6. Failure to reappraise alternatives
	7. Illusion of unanimity	7. Failure to work out contingency plans
	8. Self-appointed mind guards	

CONCURRENCE-SEEKING TENDENCY →

Analysis based on comparisons of high- and low-quality decisions made by policy groups.

Source: Irving L. Janis and Leon Mann, *Decision-Making: A Psychological Analysis of Conflict, Choice, and Commitment*, Copyright © 1977 by The Free Press, a Division of Macmillan Publishing Co., Inc. Reprinted by permission of Macmillan Publishing Co., Inc.

any committee, whether it be an important policy-making group or a mundane subcommittee, groupthink is the likely, although not inevitable, result (see Box 9.1).

It is obviously frightening to think that groups making vital decisions affecting all of our lives might become victims of groupthink. What can be done to prevent it? Janis (1972) suggests several prescriptions for avoiding groupthink and improving the quality of decision-making in committees. They are all aimed at reducing the tendency to one-track, poorly evaluated thinking, which is the heart of groupthink. First of all, the leader can assign the role of critical evaluators to each member and make clear that it is critical thinking, not agreement, which is valued. Besides encouraging members to air their doubts, the leader should avoid stating his or her personal preferences among the alternatives being considered. This discourages members from agreeing with that view in order to please the leader. To encourage diversity of opinions, the group should periodically break down into subgroups that work separately on the same problem and then come together to hammer out their differences. In addition, outside experts, including those who disagree with the group, should be brought in and be heard. Once a consensus has begun to emerge, the group should make a "second chance" reevaluation of all the rejected alternatives. With these procedures, Janis (1972) argues, cohesive groups can avoid the dangers of groupthink, even under the pressure of crisis situations.

Obviously, then, there are real reasons why committees have the reputation for producing ill-considered decisions. It is important to realize, though, that these are the exceptions to the usual good, if not extraordinary, work committees do throughout our society. The fact is task groups have the ability both to greatly improve on the performance capacity of most people, or to fall very short of it. Which it will be depends on the success with which the group's organization and norms take advantage of the members' skills, and apply them appropriately to the task. The more we understand about the fundamental group processes involved, the better we become at designing groups that live up to their high productive potential. Given the growing importance of task groups in our society, this is an endeavor that has important implications for us all.

SUMMARY

The use of task groups to make decisions, solve problems, create products, and carry out activities has become increasingly common in

Box 9.1   Groupthink and the Attempted Rescue of American Hostages in Iran

By April 1980, the personnel of the American embassy in Iran had been held hostage for five months. Subjected to constant taunts from the Iranians, and with negotiations breaking down, the American government attempted a military rescue of the hostages. It was a dismal failure. Only a few hours into the attempt, dust storms and mechanical problems forced down three of the eight helicopters, leaving too few to complete the mission. In the effort to return to base, accidents and confusion led to the death of eight American soldiers.

The American people reacted with dismay, demanding to know how the mission could have failed so badly and why it had not been better planned. The decision to attempt a rescue had been made by the president and his national security advisers. Plans for the mission had been developed by the military joint chiefs of staff. Were these task groups subject to groupthink in deciding upon the rescue plan? Certainly the baseline conditions were there. Both groups were highly prestigious and likely to have high morale and cohesiveness. Both faced a crisis and felt a decision had to be made soon. But were the other conditions also present? Did groupthink occur?

A complete answer requires detailed information on the decision that is not yet available. However, we can make some guesses based on then–national security adviser Zbigniew Brzezinski's (1982) account of deliberations among the president's advisers, and on accounts of military considerations at the Pentagon (Middleton, 1981).

First, let us consider the presidential advisory group, which consisted primarily of the president, the vice-president, Brzezinski, the secretaries of state and defense, the director of the CIA, and the chairman of the joint chiefs of staff. Although this group did not develop the rescue plan, it decided a rescue *should* be attempted, and gave the go-ahead on the military's plan. Besides cohesiveness and a crisis situation, the group, by Brzezinski's account, had two additional antecedent conditions of groupthink. They were relatively insulated in that outsiders, particularly ones with dissenting views, were not brought into the deliberations. Instead, concerns with secrecy led to private discussions in isolated circumstances, often without the knowledge of the men's own staffs. Secondly, the breakdown of negotiations made many in the group feel there was little alternative to the military options, favored from the beginning by some influential members. Both factors would have increased the tendency for concurrency seeking in the group.

Box 9.1   *(continued)*

According to Brzezinski, the group did consider options other than the rescue plan: it considered a number of large-scale punitive military actions against Iran; the president rejected, only two days before the rescue attempt, a plan to cloak the rescue in a larger assault on Iran; and, on the other side, the secretary of state argued against any military action whatsoever.

It is here that we see a few symptoms of groupthink. The final decision was taken at a meeting when the dissenting secretary of state was out of town. When his representative spoke up for further diplomatic efforts, direct pressure was applied by the secretary of defense, who dismissed the ideas as "not impressive" (Brzezinski, 1982). The group, and by now, the president, clearly favored a military option and did not wish to hear about other alternatives. Although the group reviewed the details of the military rescue plan, they appeared to accept uncritically the military's assessment of its feasibility and concurred with its judgment that eight helicopters would be enough. Here the group's extreme concern with secrecy played a part, since they were worried that more helicopters would increase the chance of detection.

All in all, it seems that the presidential group did display some symptoms of groupthink in their uncritical acceptance of the military's plan and in the quick dismissal of diplomatic options. However, in other ways, they performed well. They considered a number of options, they were aware of the risks involved, and had developed contingency plans to abort the mission if it failed.

If the presidential group showed only moderate problems of groupthink, it is possible that the military planning groups who devised the plan may have suffered much greater problems. Here we are on shaky ground in terms of evidence, since accounts of the military deliberations behind the rescue plan are not available. However, interviews with knowledgeable military people suggest that decision-making errors were made (Middleton, 1981). Information on past helicopter operations suggested that more helicopters would be needed. While more helicopters increased tactical and security problems, there were alternatives available for overcoming these problems. Evidently these points were not considered fully. Also, the total mission procedure was not fully rehearsed. Because all branches of the military were involved, the command structure at the lower levels was unclear. Finally, obsessive concern with secrecy meant that many participants did not know the full plan until shortly before its execution. Were these problems a result of groupthink? We do not know for sure. However, these are the types of errors that groupthink can produce. It is likely that the hostage rescue plan failed for a number of reasons, of which groupthink was a primary one.

our society. Large organizations are primarily responsible for this trend, although individuals, too, have acquired the habit of creating groups to deal with difficult tasks. The increasing use of small task groups in government, business, and service organizations has its roots in the growing social and technical complexity of the tasks confronting these organizations and in the development of the human resources approach to organizational management. In most situations groups produce higher-quality decisions and solutions than the average member would working alone, although only occasionally do they do better than a high-skilled individual might. Groups are often somewhat slower than individuals in general, however.

Understanding what makes some groups very productive while others bog down in frustration or just happily go nowhere is a very complex process. The group's entire situation must be taken into account, including the nature of the task, its structure and norms, the needs and skills of its members, and the pressures from the outside environment. To approach the problem we used Steiner's (1972) notion that a group begins with a certain potential for productivity, based on the task it faces and the human resources it has to address the task. The actual process of group interaction determines the extent to which the group lives up to (or falls short of) this potential. We organized our discussion of productivity in terms of environmental-, group-, and individual-level factors (input factors), which contribute to a group's productive potential, and in terms of the effects of group interaction by which this is translated into actual task performance (Hackmann and Morris, 1975). This distinction between these two categories is not a neat one, however. Input factors shape interaction among the members, but do not wholly determine it. Interaction in turn affects the impact of the input factors.

The demands made by the group task, the nature of the rewards offered by the organization in which the group operates, and the stress placed on the group are all environmental factors that affect productivity. Of these, the most important is the task itself, since its demands determine what is required for the group to be effective. We classified tasks according to complexity, both of the technical and the social demands made on the group. A task is technically difficult if it requires elaborate skills and if its solution is not obvious. It is socially difficult if its solution requires potentially problematic interaction among the members. Environmental stress increases the social complexity of tasks. Rewards from the outside environment can encourage cooperation or competition among the group members, which also affects productivity.

Among the group-level factors affecting task performance are the group's norms, status relations and communication patterns, leadership structure, size, and cohesiveness. A group will never be productive if its norms do not encourage the members to give their full effort to the task. This may happen if the group is alienated from its organizational context, feels it may be exploited, or is, in fact, more interested in social activity. In order to make use of the efforts and skills of its members, a task group must develop a status structure that coordinates its different people efficiently in relation to the task and yet is acceptable to the members. For technically complex tasks a relatively flat status hierarchy that encourages open communication is probably best. But when the task is technically and socially simple or socially very difficult, clear lines of authority and a more hierarchical status system may be needed. The leadership structure and behavior of those in leadership positions is also important. One of the major ways a leader can help or inhibit a group's problem-solving or decision-making capability is by affecting the number of ideas and alternatives that are brought up for discussion.

The optimum size of a group depends on the nature of the task it faces. However, since size increases both a group's resources and its organizational problems, increasing size usually improves task performance up to a certain point, after which further increases cause a leveling-off and decline in performance. Cohesiveness increases the members' commitment to group goals. If the members value productivity, it will usually improve task performance. However, the increased conformity pressures that come with cohesiveness can sometimes interfere with critical thinking in decision-making groups. The pattern of abilities and personalities are individual-level factors that affect a group's productive potential. In general, heterogeneous groups perform better than homogeneous ones.

The impact of these input factors is mediated by the actual process of face-to-face interaction among the members. We described this process in terms of the way particular notions under discussion grow or decline in favorableness in the group's eyes (Hoffman, 1965, 1979). We also discussed the way various input factors might influence this process. Next, we turned to the way group members, through a kind of "one-upping" process, sometimes induce one another to adopt a group decision that is more extreme (although in the same direction) than that which they initially favored. Group polarization, as this is called, arises from the process of interaction itself and can affect the nature of a group's performance.

With this basic understanding of group productivity in hand, we turned to some special problems of discussion groups such as committees. We attempted to explain the sporadic but sometimes dramatic failures of committees in terms of the way conformity pressures and the influence of members on each other can sometimes produce one-track thinking in groups. This tendency inhibits creative thinking and can be seen in the disappointing results of group brainstorming as a technique for producing novel ideas. In highly cohesive groups facing a crisis situation, one-track thinking and a sense of overconfidence can lead to the much more serious problem of groupthink. Janis (1972) argues that groupthink among high-level policy groups, like the joint chiefs and the president's advisers, has been responsible for some disastrously bad decisions in situations like the Vietnam War. However, groupthink can be prevented by adopting a number of leadership and organizational procedures that encourage a diversity of opinions, active dissent, and a critical evaluation of all alternatives. These techniques are part of a growing movement to apply our knowledge of group performance to the practical problem of designing groups that will live up to their full productive potential.

10

Primary Groups

Probably nothing has more emotional significance in our lives than primary groups—that is, our families, friends, lovers, neighbors, and coworkers. Upon these groups we anchor our self-identities, and from them we receive the basic emotional support that gives meaning and pleasure to life. Through them we link ourselves to larger, more impersonal organizations and causes, and with their help we manage our lives in a complex bureaucratic society. Like all small groups, primary groups evolve status heirarchies, communication networks, a leadership structure, and a group culture—the basic structural and cultural processes vital to all groups. These processes operate in primary groups according to the same principles as in other groups. Therefore, we will not repeat our earlier discussion of them here. Rather, we will focus on those processes that distinguish primary groups from more task-oriented groups.

In Chapter 1, if you recall, we noted three defining characteristics of primary groups:

1. Significant emotional attachments among the members and a relatively personal quality to interaction
2. Relative permanence (compared to task groups)
3. A diffuse, nonspecific purpose

Indeed, the business of primary groups seems to be the selves of the members—and the effect of members' relationships on those selves. These characteristics give the primary group its powerful impact on the self-concept, -beliefs, and -attitudes of the individual. They also account for its critical role in the maintenance and change of the larger social structure. It is largely through primary groups that people are socialized to accept the norms and values of larger social institutions and pressured to adhere to them. For instance, it has been shown that most recruits to the religious cult called the "Moonies" are attracted first by the warm, accepting primary group offered by the members, and only through that do they come to accept the norms and beliefs of the religion (Lofland and Stark, 1965; Lofland, 1966, 1977). A similar process seems to operate for more conventional religions as well (Stark and Bainbridge, 1980). Thus what lies at the heart of primary-group existence, and distinguishes it from other groups, is the particularly intense and complex interplay among pressures from the outside society, the emotional dynamics of the group, and the needs and identities of the members. This interplay will be at the center of our consideration of primary groups.

To understand the distinctive processes of primary groups, then, we need to look not only within these groups but outside them. Consequently, we will begin with an analysis of the nature of contemporary primary groups and their relationship to the larger society. This will give us a glimpse of the concerns that dominate different primary groups and will suggest in turn the role these groups might play in the life of the individual. After this overview we will turn our attention to a more detailed analysis of two types of primary groups: the family, and resocialization groups such as self-help groups and T-groups. Since the family is the core primary group both for our social structure and in the lives of most people, we need a more thorough understanding of what it does, and how it is changing. Resocialization groups are less central to our society than the family, but they offer an interesting example of the new types of primary groups that have been created in recent years. They also provide a good illustration of a basic quality of all primary groups: the interdependence between the selves of the members and the emotional life of the group.

THE DIFFERENTIATION OF PRIMARY GROUPS IN CONTEMPORARY SOCIETY

The forces of social change we call modernization, that is, industrialization, urbanization, and bureaucratization, all increase the extent to which our daily contacts with others are conducted according to impersonal, task-oriented standards. These forces increase the size and impersonality of the institutions we deal with from the businesses we work for and buy from to the government agencies we rely on. They also increase people's geographic mobility as they move from one house and job to another. Finally, modernization has greatly increased the diversity of life-styles available to people, bringing with it greater personal choice, but also greater uncertainty and change. Each of these changes makes the formation of enduring primary-group relations more difficult.

Turn-of-the century observers predicted that the forces of modern-ization would destroy the primary group entirely (Toennies, 1887; Wirth, 1934). Clearly this has not happened. Instead people have reacted to modernization by transforming the nature and type of pri-mary groups they rely on to meet their needs for emotional support and self-definition. In response to people's increasingly mobile and diverse life-styles, primary groups have become both more specialized in func-tion and more differentiated from one another (Litwak and Szelenyi, 1969; Dunphy, 1972). It is this new system of specialized primary groups that we need to understand.

Most people's lives in a preindustrial society are organized around a small number of overlapping and multifunctional primary groups: a kinship group, the community, and perhaps a religious group. In mod-ern industrialized societies these traditional primary groups survive, but they have become narrower and more specialized. Some of their func-tions have been taken over by the new types of primary groups people have created to deal with the urban environment. For instance, in an industrialized society where there is a greater choice of occupations and life-styles, children do not necessarily follow in their parents' occupa-tional footsteps. Consequently, as children reach adolescence they may find they want or need to know things that their parents can't teach them and want experiences that can't be found in the family. They turn to their peers, to teenage friendship groups for the socialization they need. In this way the function of adolescent socialization has moved out of the family and into more-specialized peer groups (Dunphy, 1972).

To grasp the relationship between present day primary groups and contemporary society, then, we need to examine the types of specializa-tion that have occurred in the traditional primary groups of family, kin, and neighbors and in the varieties of new primary groups that have sprung up to supplement them. Understanding this will give us an idea of the dominant issues and emotional concerns of different types of contemporary primary groups, how these issues are related to the larger social structure, and, as a result, the nature of the effects these groups are likely to have on their members.

Specialization in Traditional Primary Groups

Let's look first at the specialization that has occurred in the tradi-tional primary groups of kin, family, and community. When we refer to family we mean the nuclear family of parents (one or two adults) and their live-at-home children. Kin, on the other hand, are a person's close relatives outside the nuclear family household, people such as grown brothers and sisters, grandparents, aunts and uncles, and cousins. Community groups are essentially neighbors, those people who live near you. We will consider changes in kin and family first, then turn to neighbors.

In a classic article Litwak and Szelenyi (1969) pointed out that modernization has forced both kin and neighbor groups to change in important ways from the traditional definition of a primary group. Recall that primary groups have been defined as affective in nature, relatively permanent, face-to-face, and diffused in purpose. Modernization has made some of these characteristics almost impossible for kin and neighborhood groups to maintain. By looking at the way these groups adapted to the loss of some primary characteristics, Litwak and Szelenyi were able to suggest the ways in which kin and neighbor groups have become differentiated from one another and more specialized in the functions they perform for their members. These changes have in turn affected the types of tasks that remain the special province of the nuclear family.

In our society, most people treat the bonds of kinship as permanent. That hasn't changed. However, to continue as a true primary group, kin must also maintain bonds of emotional concern and commitment. Urban industrialization has threatened this by increasing the extent to which people move around. No longer do people live their entire lives in close proximity to their relatives. As a result many kin groups have lost the dimension of regular face-to-face interaction.

Kin groups have survived in the face of this loss by means of the improved communication links and techniques of long-distance travel that modernization has also provided (Adams, 1968). However, the fact that most people's kin groups are scattered over a larger geographic area has narrowed the functions these groups can perform. Litwak and Szelenyi suggest that contemporary kin specialize in providing the kind of services and emotional support that require long-term ties but not immediate on-the-spot assistance. For instance, families in a Detroit sampling reported it was relatives they would turn to, not friends or neighbors, if they needed help with serious needs, such as a long-term illness or extended child care (Litwak and Szelenyi, 1969). Likewise, in situations of major financial need or major life disruption, such as a divorce, people are most likely to rely on relatives. However, problems of everyday emotional support or short-term emergency aid are left to other groups which they can deal with on a regular face-to-face basis.

The geographic dispersal of kin groups has had an effect on the nuclear family as well. When relatives live far away, the nuclear family is relatively isolated and on its own. Even though it retains all the traditional features of a primary group—permanence, face-to-face interaction, affectivity, and diffused purpose—its human resources are limited to the knowledge and skills of its one or two adult members and the children. Often these resources are not adequate to provide the full range of socialization and self-development that its members need to successfully establish lives in an urban industrial society. We have already noted that families are no longer much help in securing occupations for their children or teaching them job skills. However, they can still provide basic acceptance and everyday emotional support, as well as the kind of general socialization that shapes our basic personalities, attitudes, and opinions. The nuclear family, then, has specialized in providing the close daily emotional contact that allows for the socialization of young children, the anchoring of personal identity, and the satisfaction of individual needs (Parsons and Bales, 1955; Weigert and Hastings, 1977; Laslett, 1978). We will discuss this more thoroughly when we examine the specific case of the contemporary family.

The mobility associated with urban industrialism has affected neighborhood groups as well. If you live in a neighborhood very long these days, virtually all your neighbors will change. Between 1975 and 1980, 45 percent of all Americans moved at least once (U.S. Bureau of the Census, 1981a). And yet, people still do develop friendly, supportive relations with their near neighbors in many, if not all, places. Neighbor groups have survived, say Litwak and Szelenyi (1969), by developing informal norms and techniques that ensure newcomers can get to know their neighbors quickly. It is the norm in some neighborhoods, for instance, to walk up to a family when they are moving in and introduce yourself, and perhaps offer to help. Similarly, newcomers who have come from such neighborhoods may make a point of calling on their new neighbors and introducing themselves. In the suburban neighborhoods of highly mobile professionals, there are often even organizations such as the "welcome wagon" or "newcomers club" that make a point of bringing new arrivals into the neighborhood group. In this way neighbors in many areas maintain some degree of primary relations, although the emotional depth of these relations are circumscribed by the loss of permanence.

What friendly neighbors do have, however, is close proximity to one another. This allows them to give one another quick, on-the-spot help in short-term emergencies (Litwak and Szelenyi, 1969; Gordon, 1977). When your sofa is being delivered on the day you have to attend an important meeting, what do you do? You take a key to the next-door neighbor and ask them to let the delivery people in while you are at your meeting. Neighbors also provide one another with everyday information on matters such as how to fix the fence or keep your kids from playing in the street. While people rely on relatives for serious, long-range problems, they go to neighbors for small, immediate needs. Indeed, Gordon (1977) points out that, at least for his Irish sample, people prefer to ask neighbors for small favors even when they have kin in the immediate neighborhood. This underscores the fact that people in an industrialized society think of their kin and neighbor groups as specialized in different sorts of aid and support.

Each of the three primary groups discussed so far has survived modernization by narrowing its focus and developing techniques for dealing with problems posed by people's greater mobility. However, specialization has not been the only consequence of that change. In Chapter 1 we pointed out that the distinction between primary groups and task groups represents, not a dichotomy, but rather the polar extremes of a continuum along which real groups can be arranged. The changes forced on kin and neighbor groups have moved them a little further from the ideal type of primary group on that continuum. Although both are still clearly more primary- than task-oriented in concern, each has shifted a bit closer to the middle. The loss of face-to-face relations among kin has lowered (but not eliminated) the intensity of the emotional bond. The loss of permanence among neighbors has similarly reduced the strength of the affective tie. Only the family has remained at the far extreme of the primary continuum.

The reduction in primary qualities of neighbors and kin groups has not usually meant an absolute loss in primary attachments for the individual, however. Rather people have created new primary groups to fill in the gaps left by the narrower, contemporary versions of family, kin, and neighbors. As a result people now meet their needs by assembling a "package" of several differently specialized primary groups, rather than by belonging to one or two all-purpose groups. Each of the three groups discussed so far specializes in meeting a different aspect of its members' needs for emotional support, socialization, identity development, and mutual assistance. The nuclear family (or equivalent living group) provides daily emotional contact and primary socialization and is usually the focus of most adults' emotional lives. Kin supplement this with aid and advice for major problems that are more than the family alone can handle. Neighbors in turn provide short-term supplemental assistance and information. This, of course, leaves several roles open for additional groups to provide help with one's occupational identity, with extrafamilial personal concerns, or with self-change.

Before we go on to other groups, however, we should comment on some individual variations from this general picture of the way people use primary groups to organize their lives. Although most people build their lives around a family group, the number who do not is increasing. "Nonfamily households," as the census calls them, grew from 18.8 percent of all households in 1970 to 26.1 percent in 1980 (U.S. Bureau of the Census, 1981c). About 14 percent of these nonfamily households are made up of unrelated people living together. Some are same-sex roommates, but most are mixed-sex groups of unmarried people. These people have formed living groups that are alternatives to the nuclear family. Such groups function in their lives about as a family would, but they have a different structure that is usually more voluntary and less permanent. Although the percentage of people living in these groups is still quite small, their increase in recent years suggests that even the more-specialized form of the family is not always flexible enough to meet some people's needs in a mobile society.

The bulk of nonfamily households, however, are made up of people who live alone. Some do this involuntarily and only temporarily, for instance, after a divorce or widowhood. Others, however, choose to live alone. Single people do not organize their primary attachments around a core family or living group of any kind. Rather they turn to other groups with whom they have more intermittent contact—romantic partners and friends, for example—for the kind of emotional sustenance most people draw from their families. As we continue our discussion of various primary-group roles, we should keep in mind that we are describing the dominant pattern in our society. We must remember that not everyone lives according to this pattern.

Specialization in Other Primary Groups

To supplement the traditional primary groups, people in our society have created or put new emphasis on four additional primary groups: friendship groups, co-worker groups, interest groups, and resocialization groups. Of these, only resocialization groups are truly a new creation. The others have existed since preindustrial times but were quite different in membership and importance from their contemporary versions. People have always had friends, for instance. They have usually developed primary bonds with their co-workers as well. However, in a preindustrial setting, most people worked at home in farming, home manufacture, or a family-run business. As a result most of their co-workers, and indeed their personal friends, were either relatives or neighbors. This kind of overlapping membership in primary groups is called *multiplexity*, because the members play multiple roles *vis-à-vis* one another (Verbrugge, 1979; Gluckman, 1962). It was because of high multiplexity that traditional primary groups were able to serve so many functions for their members. However, in that situation co-worker and friendship groups were not often distinct types of groups on their own.

Urban industrialization has changed that. The friendly, informal relations that most of us have with our work associates are usually quite separate from the relations we have with kin and neighbors. We go to our co-workers for the specialized information and support we need to manage the demands of our job. It's the people we eat lunch with at work or those we chat with in the office, who we rely on for support and advice in dealing with a difficult boss, or encouragement to apply for a new position, or for a needed bit of human relief from an impersonal environment.

People also turn to co-workers to help manage their occupational identities. We spend a third of our lives working, and our relationship to work becomes an important part of our self-concept. This relationship is in turn mediated by the primary attachments we form with co-workers. For instance, most people judge their skill or success at work more by the opinions of their co-workers than by outside objective standards. If the people you work with think you do a good job, it really doesn't matter so much what others think. Your relations with your co-workers particularly affect your own sense of satisfaction with your job. Even when it is objectively unpleasant, like picking up garbage, or dangerous, like fighting a war, or even demeaning, close relations with co-workers can make a job bearable and help you maintain a sense of security and self-worth.

Modern friendships are less differentiated from other primary groups than are co-worker groups. People still do choose many of their friends from among their neighbors, relatives, and co-workers. These are, after all, the people they are most likely to encounter in their daily lives. If you recall from Chapter 4, proximity is an important factor in interpersonal attraction.

The emotional significance of friendships in most people's lives is usually not as great as that of family. And yet, there is a distinctive quality to the friendship bond because it is a purely voluntary affective tie. Unlike kin, neighbor, or co-worker groups, friendships are not supported by institutional structures, blood ties, or social arrangements. They survive only through the special efforts their members make to keep up the friendship. This makes friendships more vulnerable and less stable than other primary groups, but it also gives them a special quality that most people value. When a friend helps you out in a difficult time, you are especially touched. You know he or she didn't have to do it. Your friend *chose* to help you.

This quality of choice is the defining characteristic of friendship, determining the specialized functions it performs. Because friendships are not part of larger institutional arrangements, people can search more broadly for friends than they can the members of most other primary groups. This gives them a greater opportunity to match themselves up with others who are very similar to them in background, attitudes, and beliefs. As we saw in Chapter 4, similarity is the key to interpersonal attraction and friendship (Byrne, 1961; Newcomb, 1961). The fact that friends are usually so similar to one another allows them to get quickly past superficial concerns and speak directly to the most immediate, distinctive concerns of their personal lives. This is what gives good friends that sense that the other knows just what they feel when there is trouble with a lover or anxiety about a career. Because friends focus on one another's unique characteristics and concerns, they help each other define and affirm their own individuality. This, then, is the specialized function of friendship groups in our society (Litwak and Szelenyi, 1969). They help their members work out, and feel secure in, the distinctive details of their own personalities.

As people's lives change over time, the aspects of themselves they wish to emphasize change as well. In fact there is evidence that people tend to specialize in the type of people they seek for friends. Some people repeatedly look for friends among those they work with, others choose friends from neighbors, still others prefer people with whom they have no other primary-group contact (Verbrugge, 1977, 1979). These tastes in friendships very likely reflect the aspects of the self that are most important to the person at the time. Co-worker friends, for instance, have their professional selves in common. They can help each other with the problems of self-definition that arise in relation to their occupations. They deal with events like career crises, or questions such as, "Am I ambitious?" or "Is this the right kind of job for me?" On the other hand, people who choose friends who are unrelated to their family, neighborhood, or work may be seeking others who can affirm a distinctive self that exists outside the confines of society's traditional work and home categories. For instance, a schoolteacher who likes to dance might choose other disco devotees for friends to affirm an identity as an outgoing, adventurous, and fun-loving person. The issues of selfhood most important to you at a given time, then, determine those, among the pool of available "similar others," you choose for personal friends. As these issues change, so, for the most part, will your friends.

The fact that friendship groups specialize in the unique aspects of their members' personalities gives them some distinctive characteristics. They tend to develop highly specialized group cultures full of inside jokes, rituals, and special concerns relevant only to the specific people who are members. Because the group culture is so specialized, it can't easily be transferred to different people (Ridgeway, 1981b). If a new person is brought into the friendship the whole group culture has to be restructured to include the concerns and feelings of the new member. This, of course, causes a serious disruption of the group. As a result, membership turnover in friendship groups is not as common as in some other groups. Rather than recruiting new members when old members are lost, most friendship groups simply shrink or disband. This adds to the fragility of the friendship bond in a society like ours. From a human point of view that is perhaps unfortunate, since friends provide a type of affection and information about ourselves that is an important complement to that supplied by family and kin.

When people are confronted with a substantial change in their social circumstances, or when they desire to change those circumstances themselves, they increasingly turn to a new type of primary group, the resocialization group (Dunphy, 1972). Examples are self-improvement groups, encounter groups, therapy groups, consciousness-raising groups, assertiveness-training groups, marriage-counseling groups, and so on. What these groups have in common is their shared aim in helping their members change old self-concepts and habits of living.

Why have so many of these groups sprung up in recent years? Living in a complex, rapidly changing society is not easy. It requires people to play a diverse set of roles every day, and to change those roles frequently. Sometimes the change is voluntary. Perhaps you decide to change careers, or become more assertive on the job, or break off a romantic relationship. But just as often the change is thrust upon you. You are fired and forced to move to find work, or your marriage collapses when your spouse leaves you. Each of these transitions means giving up old roles and the sense of self you invested in them, and re-establishing yourself in new roles. This necessitates a great deal of relearning and, particularly, emotional readjustment. The continual intensifying of modernization has meant that people go through more and more of these difficult transitions over the course of their lives. Other more traditional primary groups are not always adequate to meet people's needs in these situations. To fill in the gaps people have created groups that specialize in readjustment. We will have more to say about these groups later in the chapter.

The final primary-group type to be considered is the interest group. This is really a grab-bag category of primary-type groups whose members are brought together by a specific shared interest. In a sense, they are clubs. An example might be a small, close-knit political group that plays an important part in the lives of its members. In our society such groups usually have political beliefs that are out of the mainstream, often to the far left or right. Some of these groups might be rather deviant in their behavior, for instance a fanatical paramilitary group that plots violent action. Close-knit religious groups are also primary-oriented interest groups. Interest groups make people feel united in the expression of a particular view of life. They allow people to create and express an identity as a particular type of person (for example, a religious person, or a political radical) which goes beyond that which they can express in their occupational and family groups.

There are a wide variety of interest groups in our society: grass-roots political action groups, bridge clubs, book clubs, and so on. However, not all function as primary groups for their members. Some are more task oriented in emphasis. To decide whether a specific interest group operates as a primary group, it is necessary to look at the members' dominant concerns. If the focus is on issues of self-definition and on the relationships among the members as much as the accomplishment of external tasks, the group probably functions as a primary group in the lives of its members.

We see, then, that there are several varieties of primary groups in our society. Each fills a slightly different niche in people's lives, focusing on different aspects of their identity and emotional needs. We can summarize the specialized concerns of each of the groups we have discussed as follows. We have also indicated the extent to which their specialization has altered their characteristics from that of the ideal-typical primary group:

1. The nuclear family specializes in basic emotional support and retains a high degree of all primary group qualities.
2. Kin specialize in assistance for major problems. Kin groups are high in permanence and moderate in affectivity and diffused purpose, but low in face-to-face contact.
3. Neighbors specialize in assistance for minor problems and short-term emergencies. They are low in permanence, moderate in affectivity and diffused purpose, and high in face-to-face contact.
4. Friends specialize in defining and affirming unique personal characteristics. Friends are moderate in permanence and diffused purpose, high in affectivity, and low in face-to-face contact.
5. Co-workers specialize in managing work identities and demands. They are high in face-to-face contact, low in permanence, and moderate in affectivity significance and diffused purpose.

6. Interest groups specialize in the expression of identities outside usual work and family categories. They are low on permanence and diffused purpose, moderate in affectivity, and high in face-to-face contact.

7. Resocialization groups specialize in emotional resocialization. They are low in permanence and high in affectivity, diffused purpose, and face-to-face contact.

Modern primary groups have become specialized in this way because of the pressures and demands of an urbanized, industrialized society. Making a living in such a society requires most people to move across a wide variety of social situations, each of which demands a slightly different type of identity. And, over the course of our lives, these situations change, we change jobs, we move from one place to another. Consequently, the type of primary groups we need to develop the aspects of our identity necessary to manage our lives change. The result is a greater need on the part of most people for more primary groups which are specialized in function. Furthermore, more and more of these primary groups must be of the sort that can be entered and left at will as the members' needs change. The last point is important. It has meant that the "growth sector" in primary groups in recent years has been in groups in which membership is entirely voluntary, like interest groups, resocialization groups, and friendships.

Of course most people organize their changing package of more voluntary primary groups around the core of less voluntary, more enduring groups like family and kin. The fact that one cannot dip in and out of family and kin groups in the way that one can friendships or interest groups allows for the development of deeper emotional attachments. It also provides for some continuity over time in self-identity, which is important for a sense of security and control over one's life.

More enduring groups like the family are also important for society's ability to maintain social control over its members. Enduring primary groups can apply consistent pressure on their members to abide by the norms and values of the larger society. Because they occupy a larger portion of people's lives, they influence their identities more strongly. As a result, these groups encourage their members to make society's values and norms part of their own personalities and beliefs in a way that constantly changing groups cannot.

However, even such enduring groups are more voluntary in nature and more likely to change over one's lifetime than has been true in the past. You have no choice who your kin are. But when you no longer live next door to your relatives, you can choose whether you will maintain primary group relations with them. Although the family continues to have substantial institutional support in society, the rising divorce rate shows that the family is also more voluntary than in the past. Since most divorced people remarry, it is clear that people still want to have a family as their core primary group. However, more people are changing families as they do other primary groups.

For the individual person, this system of specialized primary groups with changing membership has mixed consequences. The wider choice of groups offers the individual the potential of finding the "perfect package" of primary groups, one which almost precisely matches his or her needs. It also offers a flexibility in identity that people do need to adapt to the complex and changing demands of the larger social structure. Finally, the possibilities for personal self-expression are certainly much greater under this system. People have many more opportunities to become the kind of person they want to be.

However, the system exacts some emotional costs as well. When people change primary groups frequently, it is harder to maintain a sense of security and rootedness in life. These things come, after all, from our emotional relationships with others. When those change often, we are bound to experience substantial ups and downs in our sense of connectedness with others and, perhaps, be more prey to feelings of loneliness and isolation. Some writers have described this as a loss of *community* under our present system of primary groups (Back, 1978; Slater, 1976; Zablocki, 1980). By *community* they mean a sense of being united with others in a committed trusting way that allows your individual self to blend in with the group as a whole. It is difficult to achieve this feeling in a primary group that may break up at any moment, or in a society that emphasizes individuality, competition, and change. There are some who for a variety of reasons experience this loss of community particularly acutely. Zablocki (1978) suggests that these are the people most likely to join communes and cults that offer the commitment and community they seek. These people are, in a way, refugees from (or rebels against) our industrialized society and the primary-group system it has created.

Our system of primary groups carries other emotional risks as well. When people belong to several primary groups, they may be subject to painful crosspressures when the norms or cultures of those groups conflict. For instance, your parents may not understand or approve of your friends, or your spouse may think your professional colleagues are boring and snobbish. Also, although people can "shop" for that perfect package of primary groups to meet their needs, how many actually succeed in finding it? It is just as likely that people will be unable to locate the right sort of groups to give them the support they need. It is equally likely that when people belong to several changing groups, rather than a few enduring ones, some people will fall through the cracks in society, will get cut off from primary groups and, as a result, from the rest of society. This might temporarily be the case for someone who simultaneously lost both job and marriage. A middle-aged housewife whose husband runs off with another woman might find herself suddenly penniless and cut off from the couple-oriented suburban life where she had built her identity. Most people in these situations find their way back into new primary groups, but there is no guarantee that that will happen. Our primary group system is based on people finding their own relationships with others. There is no automatic mechanism to ensure that everyone has a place.

If you recall from Chapter 1, being cut off from primary groups leads to feelings of alienation, meaninglessness, and disconnectedness in life. We think of alienation and meaninglessness as a modern malaise because urban industrialization, and the primary group system we have created in response to it, make it likely that more people will fall through the cracks this way and, at least temporarily, be cut off from the primary groups they need. For the individual, then, our current system of primary groups represents a bigger gamble than that of the past. It trades greater personal freedom and the possibility of ideal, tailored-to-fit primary group attachments for an increased chance of finding yourself isolated and cut off from others. A very different type of primary group system than that of the past, it links people to a very different sort of socioeconomic structure.

With this overview of contemporary primary groups and the roles they play both in society and in the lives of their members, we are ready to take a more detailed look at some specific groups. We will examine the nuclear family first, the single-most important primary group in our society. After attending to some definitional matters, we will discuss the major tasks the family performs for society and its members, how those are changing at the present, and some of the strains that have been the result. We will turn next to that new and interesting primary group, the resocialization group. As one of the fastest-growing categories, these groups are worthy of attention in themselves. However, they are also interesting for how they illustrate the link between the emotional dynamics of a primary group and the identity development of its members. As we shall see from our analysis of the family, this is a vital process in all primary groups.

THE NUCLEAR FAMILY

Our society's cultural blueprint for the nuclear family dictates that it be composed of a married couple and children. However, reality is a bit more complicated. The family really begins as two people whose relationship has a sexual as well as affectional basis. As their relationship moves from one of intermittent dating to a more permanent living arrangement, it changes in form and importance from essentially a sexual friendship to a group more truly like a family. In the usual way of things, the couple will marry and have children, completing the transformation of their group into the full structural form of the nuclear family.

There are, however, a growing number of exceptions to this pattern. If the couple marry (or simply live together on a permanent basis) but do not have children, the group they form together will operate as a family even without certain traditional family functions, such as childhood socialization. On the other hand, the couple may have children but not stay together, leaving a family group composed of children and only one parent. This is an increasingly common family type in the United States. To perform the entire range of tasks traditionally assigned to the family requires the full structural form of two parents and children. However, its most vital emotional-support functions can be provided by a wide variety of other family configurations.

The most indispensable element of the family blueprint is the requirement that a group of people live together and maintain a deep and reasonably permanent commitment to one another. Most groups that meet these specifications function as families in the lives of their members. That fact, however, leads to a final distinction we must make. Over the course of their lives most people are members of two different nuclear families. The first is the one they are born into, the *family of orientation*. But the time comes when most people leave this family, transforming the relations they have with its members from those of a nuclear family to those of a kin group. Most will go on to create a new nuclear family in their lives through marriage, the *family of procreation*. Which of these families operates as the nuclear family in your life depends on which you live in at the present.

The nuclear family, more than any other primary group we have discussed, is an established institution in the larger social structure. Families are recognized as a basic unit in our society in the same way that government and economic institutions are. Our patterns of housing, economic support, consumption, community social organization, and child care are all organized around the family unit. As a result, the very organization of the larger society supports the existence of the family in a way that it does not a kin, friendship, or any other primary group. Of course, the nature of these supports has changed and even weakened in strength, with the result that the family has become more specialized and voluntary in basis than in the past (Aldous, 1977; Ryder, 1974; Glick, 1975). However, it remains a core unit of society.

For the family, the major consequence of being an institution in society is that it is charged with fulfilling a number of functions important, not only for its members, but for the maintenance of the social structure. This has kept the nuclear family a multifunctional primary group, even if it is more specialized now than in the past. As a result, the family still remains closer to the ideal primary group type than any other group. Four functions are delegated to families in our society: 1) Emotional support, 2) procreation, 3) socialization, and 4) the economic maintenance of individuals. To understand the nature of the contemporary family, we need to understand how it fulfills each of these functions. We will look at each in turn, starting with *economic maintenance*, since this is a major source of change in the family today, then turning to *socialization* and *emotional support*. Since *procreation* simply reflects the fact that families are society's method for organizing the production of the next generation, we will not deal with it separately from the others.

Economic Maintenance

One of the fastest-changing aspects of the family at present is the way it meets its economic goals. Our traditional image of the family presents the husband going out to earn the family's income while the wife stays home, managing the household and seeing to everyday needs like groceries and clothing. This was a reasonably accurate description of most American families during the first half of our century. However, since World War II married women have been moving into the labor force at an accelerating rate, causing a profound change in that picture. As of 1980, both the wife and husband bring home a paycheck in 54 percent of all U.S. families where at least one spouse is in the labor force (U.S. Bureau of the Census, 1981*b*). In other words, the average American family now has *two* incomes.

Most interesting for us is how these economic changes have altered the internal organization of the family. In one of the earliest and most influential attempts to apply what we know about small groups to an analysis of the family, Parsons and Bales (1955) suggested that the

American family has a differentiated leadership structure. Following Bales's theory of complementary group leaders, they suggested that the husband acts as the family's instrumental leader while the wife takes care of the group's expressive needs. They further suggested that a family with this division of labor would work more smoothly and happily than one without it.

However, remember (from Chapter 7) Burke's (1967, 1968, 1971) discovery that differentiation between task and socioemotional leaders occurs only when either the leader or the group task is not well accepted by the members. These conditions are not very applicable to reasonably happy families where the leadership of the parents and the family's activities are usually well-accepted by the members (Waxler and Mishler, 1970). Not surprisingly, then, attempts to seriously inquire into Parsons and Bales's view soon showed that reality was not so neat and simple. Wives, it seemed, engage in a substantial amount of instrumental behavior in their own families, even if they avoid such behavior in public places (Leik, 1963). Furthermore, when husbands take over more of the family's expressive activities, the family tends to be more, not less, happy (Levinger, 1964).

The problems of organizing a family as a small group, then, do not require an instrumental-expressive split between the roles of husband and wife. Why then did Parsons and Bales's theory seem so intuitively right to so many people? Possibly because our vision of the economic roles played by husbands and wives, and the sex-role expectations associated with them, led us to expect such a division of labor in the family. If the husband is the only one to go out and earn money for the family then it seems likely that he will have a greater impact on what the family does with that money. That in turn gives him greater influence over a wide variety of family decisions and casts him in a more powerful, task-oriented role. Without this economic power, the wife limits her controlling, instrumental behavior to everyday family decisions and to matters of the house and children. In accord with the expectations associated with the female role, this traditional wife is also likely to take responsibility for the emotional life of the family, although her husband participates in these concerns as well. The traditional division of labor between husband and wife, then, is not an organizational requirement of the family as a small group, but a product of the economic and gender roles each plays in the larger society.

As you might expect, the fact that many wives are working today is causing substantial changes in this picture. When wives work, they usually gain more influence over financial decisions, and their husbands tend to take on more child-care activities and, to a lesser extent, cooking and daily shopping tasks (Bahr, 1974; Aldous, 1977). However, in most cases the traditional division of labor is only altered, not completely abandoned. Working wives still usually have primary responsibility for the children and tasks like cleaning and laundry. Their husbands are still responsible for traditional masculine chores like home repairs and car upkeep (Aldous, 1977).

The employment of women alters the power structure of the family more dramatically. In our society's traditional patriarchal blueprint for the family, the husband was normatively prescribed to be the provider and head of the family, the one in charge when all was said and done. But when the family becomes as dependent on the wife's as on the husband's income, this cultural pattern is difficult to sustain. The wife's power and influence in the family is necessarily increased. If one or the other spouse is strongly committed to the traditional view of the family, these changes may be confusing and upsetting, and a source of serious conflict. However, for others less attached to the traditional norms, the greater equalization of power the wife's employment brings is a welcome relief that reduces rather than increases family conflict (Scanzoni, 1978).

The impact of women's changing economic role has been increased by the fact that it has coincided with a cultural questioning of traditional sex roles. As a result of both factors, the norms for how a family should operate and the roles husbands and wives should play are in a state of flux. In a sense the cultural blueprint for the family is up for grabs in our society. When society's norms for the family are in transition, a wide variety of family forms develop. At one extreme are people still adhering faithfully to the traditional norms. At the other are couples trying to work out for themselves new norms that allow them to run their family in a way better suited to their changing expectations and dual career life-style (Rapoport and Rapoport, 1971). In between are all sorts of altered family forms. The single-parent family has grown from 13 to 18 percent of all households in the last decade (U.S. Bureau of the Census, 1980). The "reconstructed family" is created when two single parents who have children marry and merge their families. The number of married couples who remain childless, and of couples who live together as a family without marrying, is also increasing. There may also be an increase in the number of people participating in experimental alternatives to the nuclear family, such as communes or groups of unrelated parents who live together and pool child-care. Changes in the way families manage their economic functions have not been the sole cause for this diversification, but they have been a major contributor to it.

Socialization

If the family's economic roles have changed, so have its socialization duties, which in fact have narrowed. Perhaps this is best illustrated by asking yourself, who is it that you go to for information about the social world? If you are past adolescence, chances are it will not be your family. Unlike former times, most of us now rely on other groups for occupational socialization, formal education, and much of our sexual and political knowledge. The family no longer offers specific socialization for most adult roles. What, then, is left of the family's socialization function? The answer, of course, is the basic raising of children.

Families have the enormous responsibility of producing newborn infants and teaching them how to be social, how to behave like reasonable members of society. Families inculcate in children the norms and procedures of society and help shape their children's personalities and identities in ways that enable them to operate in that society. From society's point of view, families vary in how well they succeed at this task. But from the children's, it is still *their* family, however it acted, that laid the foundation for their personality and taught them to be the person they are. People, of course, continue to develop throughout their lifetimes. However, since the later personality develops out of the earlier one, the experience of childhood socialization continues to affect the behavior and self-identity of the adult.

One of the most important ways it does this is by shaping the way people relate to groups. Childhood socialization creates a basic interdependence between one's sense of self and one's primary group memberships. As we pointed out in Chapter 2, a child learns his or her self through interaction with emotionally significant others like parents and siblings. Our first, most basic sense of who we are is learned from our families' responses to us while growing up. Because the self is learned in this way, it is a social thing. It is anchored in a set of relationships with others and can be altered by a change in those relationships. This creates a life-long interdependence between our self-identity and our primary group attachments. Given this interdependence, people enter some primary groups, leave others, and try to shape the emotional dynamics of yet others in an effort to express or change a basic aspect of themselves. The consequence is that, as a result of early learning in the family, the emotional lives of all primary groups, not just families, become intertwined with the selves of the members.

Childhood socialization affects the way adults relate to groups in more specific ways as well. A child comes out of his or her particular family experience fitted with basic tools for dealing with fundamental dimensions of group life such as power and affection. For instance, some families teach strict power differences between husband and wife, parents and children; others are very egalitarian. In some families there is a taboo against showing anger or hostility; in others, feelings, both good and bad, are expressed easily. These ways of managing power and affection learned in the family affect the type of primary-group relations the child creates with others as an adult. Also, children learn from their families basic habits of using groups in their lives. In one family the norm may be independence and a refusal to seek help from others except in serious situations. In another, kin and friends may be consulted freely and often on small as well as large matters. These norms of family culture will affect the ease with which the child, now grown, turns to others in his or her own life. The fact that the family no longer teaches the child much specific information about adult life has not removed its impact, then. Through its control over childhood socialization, it still remains the single greatest outside influence on adult personalities and on the emotional dynamics of the primary groups adults create.

Emotional Support

Modernization's most striking effect on the family has been to increase the significance of its emotional support function. As other aspects of society become increasingly impersonal in nature, the larger social structure has become more exclusively dependent on the family to meet the basic emotional needs of its members (Parsons and Bales, 1955). The effect has been to transform the family into an increasingly separate realm of "private life," distinct from the public world of jobs and money. In this private haven of the family people concentrate almost all their hopes for emotional satisfaction and self-realization (Berger and Kellner, 1975; Laslett, 1973, 1977, 1978).

Laslett (1978) suggests that this emotional intensification of the family came about through a series of specific changes in American family life over the last century. She argues that the nineteenth-century American family was much more likely to have boarders, servants, apprentices and other sorts of nonkin living within it. When people interacted with nonkin in their own households, it was difficult for them to see their family as something intensely different from the rest of the social world. Furthermore, Laslett argues, higher mortality in the nineteenth century meant that people had fewer surviving older relatives to draw upon for advice and help. As a result, they turned to people outside the family, making it still harder to accentuate differences between family and other primary attachments. Both factors made it less likely that one would look only to family members for basic emotional support (Shorter, 1975).

However, continuing economic development removed nonfamily from the household and increased the available pool of relatives. These changes were accompanied by a shift in the ideology of family living in the United States. Rather than seeing the family as the enforcer of society's norms, the family increasingly came to be seen as a refuge from that society, as a private place where emotions and solidarity could be emphasized in contrast to the impersonal competition of the outside world (Lasch, 1977; Laslett, 1978).

The combined effects of changing household composition, the greater availability of relatives, and changing beliefs about family life transformed the family into the exclusive emotional unit that it is now. This occurred through the alteration of family culture and childhood socialization. Each of the changes we have described encouraged twentieth-century families to develop their own distinctive group culture that distinguished more sharply between kin and nonkin and between the impersonal public world and the emotional private world of the family. As a result, children began to grow up in a family world that increasingly emphasized its own unique way of feeling, its own view of reality, and contrasted this with that of other groups. Furthermore, with only kin living in the household, the processes of early socialization, role modeling, and personality development occurred almost entirely through interaction with family members rather than outsiders.

The result has been to produce people who identify more strongly with their own distinctive family. They feel a more exclusive emotional bond with its members. The greater strength of this tie has probably increased the turbulence of adolescence, when children must differentiate themselves from the family group to make the transition to adulthood (Laslett, 1978). However, the adult who emerges is left with a sense of families as unique entities of great emotional significance. When such people establish their own families of procreation, they look to recreate that intense, emotional quality. In this way, then, structural changes in society, through the media of family culture and childhood socialization, have transformed the family into a group more intensely concerned with the emotional support of its members and more highly differentiated from other social institutions.

PROBLEMS FOR THE FAMILY.   It may have occurred to you that all this reliance on the family for emotional satisfaction raises some very high expectations for family life. How often can any real family live up to such expectations? Simply because the family has been assigned such a task by the society and its members in no way guarantees that, in practice, it can fulfill it. The socioemotional specialization of the family, by promising so much, has created the potential for serious frustrations. And many of the characteristic problems of contemporary families are a product of such frustration. For instance, there is evidence that the accelerating divorce rate in this country does not reflect a rejection of marriage *per se,* but rather a rejection of specific partners who haven't lived up to people's hopes (Bane, 1976; Carter and Glick, 1976). Laslett (1978) even speculates that concern about family violence and the growth in family counseling reflect the frustration of families that cannot live up to the enormous demands placed on them.

The problem is not only one of unrealistic expectations on the part of family members. It is also a problem of real need, for as the emotional support function is increasingly delegated to the family, people have few other places to turn to for real emotional gratification. This problem is compounded by the fact that nuclear families have limited human resources. All one's deepest needs must be satisfied by a rather small number of people. It simply doesn't always work (Sennett, 1970). When the family fails in its emotional support function, the result is tension, conflict, and even the potential dissolution of the group.

The difficulty of meeting its members' needs is not the only problem posed by the emotionally specialized family. The fact that people's deepest emotional identities are rooted in families makes them a powerful source of pain and conflict as well as emotional sustenance (Weigert and Hastings, 1977). Changes or serious discord in a family can threaten its members' deepest sense of security and well-being. It can even lead to what Weigert and Hastings call "identity loss." A person suffers from identity loss when some particularly meaningful type of bond with another, central to their self-identity, is destroyed or denied (Weigert and Hastings, 1977). If your spouse dies in an accident, you lose not only the person but also that whole part of yourself that existed in the relationship. When conflict turns the relationship between parent and child into one of hostility and rejection, each loses, not only the other, but that part of themselves that has been the beloved child or the good, caring parent. This loss can be painful indeed. If personal identity is rooted in emotional relations with family members, then the family has the power to disrupt that identity.

As Weigert and Hastings point out, the painful sorts of identity loss that take place in the family are not its members' fault. They come from the aging of a family over the life-cycle. Children grow up and leave home, disrupting the parental identity of the mother and father and forcing young adults to give up their childhood selves. Parents and spouses age and die, taking with them a unique aspect of ourselves.

However, families can also cause identity loss more directly. When their emotional needs conflict, family members may lock one another into confining roles, forcing each other to give up, or fail to develop, valued aspects of themselves. A wife who values security and financial success may force her husband to stay with his lucrative but (to him) boring job, when he really yearns to try something more adventurous but less secure. A husband who is threatened by his wife's success might keep her from achieving the professional standing she wants. The isolation and specialization of the nuclear family, then, can turn it into an emotional hothouse that can breed serious pain and discord, as well as security and self-realization.

The family is a distinctive and powerful institution in our society. Society as a whole relies on the family to produce and socialize children, to organize the economic maintenance of individuals, and to provide basic emotional support for its members. Individuals rely on the family to offer them a private refuge from the complex, impersonal nature of life in an urban, industrialized society—a place where they can anchor their personal selves and find emotional satisfaction. Together these demands make the family a multifunctional group that is nevertheless increasingly specialized in the emotional maintenance of its members. While the specialization makes the family more attentive to its members, it also puts a great deal of pressure on the family that is more than some marriages and parent-child relationships can bear. The way the family meets its economic goals is also changing with the result that our society's traditional patriarchal blueprint for the family has been undermined. With society's norms about the family in flux, the variety of family living arrangements we see around us has increased. Clearly, the family is in transition and subject to a certain degree of conflict and frustration. However, it is just as clear that the family is here to stay. Families are too important to our emotional well-being and too tightly intertwined with our identities to disappear, no matter how dramatically they are transformed by our efforts to live in a changing society (see Box 10.1).

RESOCIALIZATION GROUPS

Thinking about the family has underscored for us the closeness of the relationship between the self-identities of primary group members and the emotional dynamics of the group. In resocialization groups, people make explicit use of this relationship in an effort to change aspects of themselves. We are interested in looking more closely at resocialization groups for two reasons. First, as we noted earlier, they are an interesting and increasingly common example of the new primary groups people have created to manage the demands of life in a society characterized by change and complexity. They are on the frontier of change in our primary-group system. Second, resocialization groups provide a useful illustration of how a primary group's development is affected by the specific interpersonal orientations of the members and in turn can change those orientations. After we have gained some basic information on various types of resocialization groups, it is this second point that will be the focus of our concern. By understanding the interdependence between personality and group development in resocialization groups, we will gain insight into the nature of this interdependence in all primary groups. Finally, we will look briefly at the evidence on how well resocialization groups work.

Types of Resocialization Groups

There are at least three common types of resocialization groups in our society: *learning, therapeutic,* and *expressive* (Lakin, 1972). *Learning* groups attempt to teach specific skills in human relations. Such groups are often run by larger organizations to train management personnel, to increase worker sensitivity to problems of race relations or sex discrimination, or to promote smoother relations among the staff (Back, 1971). Individuals also pay fees to join some learning groups designed to teach specific interpersonal skills such as assertiveness. People form their own learning groups as well, such as consciousness-raising groups and self-help groups of many kinds. Learning groups may also be run as part of a course designed to teach people to understand basic group dynamics. Sometimes the emphasis is on learning at a theoretical or analytical level, but more often it is learning through feelings and experience that is emphasized, although this may be combined with analysis.

Therapeutic groups are those established as part of a program of

Box 10.1   Family Dynamics and Self-Esteem

The family is one of the best places to see how people's self-identities are intertwined with the dynamics of their primary groups. Abraham Tesser (1980) has an interesting idea of the way one part of ourselves, our self-esteem, affects family dynamics. People, Tesser maintains, try to keep their self-esteem as high as they can. However, self-esteem is strongly influenced by relationships to family members. So family members are constantly realigning their relationships with one another in an effort to preserve or improve their self-esteem. This does not always work, of course. Sometimes people are caught in a painful choice between preserving a close family bond and escaping low self-esteem.

Relationships with family members affect self-esteem in two ways (Tesser, 1980). If a member of the family is better than you at some skill, your self-esteem is threatened if that activity is important to your own self-identity. As an example, if you think you are the scholarly one in the family, but your sister wins the big scholarship, you feel threatened. The closer you are to your sister, the more threatened you feel. On the other hand, if a family member does better than you at a skill not all that relevant to your identity, you do not mind. On the contrary, you are proud. Your self-esteem is raised by being associated with such a successful person.

There are three variables here that determine how the other family member affects your self-esteem. First, there is the relevance of the other person's activities for your own self-esteem. If the two of you are very similar, this is high. Second, there is the question of who does best at the activities in question, you or the other person. Finally, there is the matter of how close the two of you are. The more you care about each other, the bigger the impact, positive or negative, of the other person on your self-esteem.

When a family member threatens your self-esteem, you will try to change one of these variables to correct the situation (Tesser, 1980); thus self-esteem affects family dynamics. For instance, if you think you are a good money earner, but your spouse gets a job and starts making more than you, what do you do? You could change your self-image, deciding that earning large amounts of money is not that important after all. You could also try to change who earns more, either by getting a better-paying job yourself or by giving your spouse a hard time. You might try to get your spouse to quit or only work part-time. Last, you could protect your self-esteem by becoming more emotionally distant from your spouse. As you can see, each alternative has its costs, and sometimes an alternative will

Box 10.1   *(continued)*

be blocked. Perhaps you cannot get a better-paying job, for example. Within the options they have, people usually try to choose the least painful choice.

Sometimes that choice is difficult. The other person has his or her needs as well, and they may conflict with your efforts to readjust the situation. Let us look at an example. The following is a conversation between a highly successful man and his 17-year-old daughter (Wilkes, 1977). The interviewer studying the family has noticed that the daughter, despite being a good student and respected member of the high school drill team, has surprisingly low self-esteem. She feels in the shadow of her father, who never fails. Father and daughter try to talk about the problem.

FATHER: Nancy, do you really think you're a loser?

DAUGHTER: Yes.

FATHER: Aw, no way, no way. I'm sure you can handle even the problems that you've had and that's going to make you better because you've had 'em. I never had those problems.

DAUGHTER: I know.

FATHER: But I'd be a better person if I'd had 'em. . . . But I guess I wonder why you say "I'm a loser."

DAUGHTER: Comparing me to you?

FATHER: Yes. What do you think? Take your track record. Look at the Yearbook. Look at the sweaters in the closet.

DAUGHTER: Do I compare me to you? No, I don't compare me. I try to beat you.

FATHER: Good.

DAUGHTER: I haven't yet, though. But I will. You wait.

FATHER: There's no point in banging your head against a steel wall if you don't have to.

INTERVIEWER: Are you a steel wall?

DAUGHTER: Well, he's your Superman. . . . The basic loser type of person I was referring to was one in social standing, not in academics. I don't worry about academics but I don't brag about it either. I mean (I'm) fifteenth (in my class). I guess it's good but it's not top ten. It's not number one. It's too far away for me. It makes me mad. . . . Dad said I couldn't be in the family if I gave up.

INTERVIEWER: You can't give up and be in this family?

DAUGHTER: Yes, if I give up, I get kicked out. What name would I have then? Nancy. Hi, my name's Nancy. Nancy what? Nancy.

FATHER: I don't remember saying that.

> **Box 10.1**   *(continued)*
> DAUGHTER: You did say that. I don't make those things up. It would be easier to give up than to keep going, you know.
> FATHER: Oh really? No, it wouldn't.
> DAUGHTER: You wouldn't because you always keep going.
> FATHER: That's right. It would be terrible to give up because then you have no hope. Then you always got to carry around that failure to try. That's worse than failing to succeed.
>
> (Wilkes, 1977)
>
> The father feels his daughter is younger and different enough that her achievements cannot threaten him. On the contrary, he feels it reflects badly on him if she does not try to do well. She, on the other hand, identifies closely with him and wants to achieve at things he values. But she is afraid she can never outperform him, and so feels caught between low self-esteem and losing her close relationship with her father. Their struggles between their affection for one another and their needs for self-esteem will affect the emotional dynamics of their family for some time to come.

psychological counseling. The members attend them in an effort to gain insight into their own emotional difficulties through the reactions of others. Such groups are usually led by a therapist of some sort. They can vary from an intense psychiatric group for severely disturbed people to a simple self-improvement group. In addition to classic group therapy they include things like marriage counseling and rap groups for Vietnam veterans.

Expressive groups focus on increasing the emotional openness and expressivity of members as a way of increasing personal well-being. The classic example is the Esalen encounter group, in which the emphasis is on nonverbal exercises oriented around physical contact among the members and on the freest and strongest expression of all feelings. The goal is to break through the barriers of everyday life to encounter the other members at an intimate emotional level (Back, 1971). People are attracted to expressive groups for the contrast they provide to the impersonal transactions that dominate life in a society like ours (Zablocki, 1978).

These three categories of groups are neither neat nor exclusive. For instance, learning to improve your understanding of human relations shades into the therapeutic goal of improving your own ability to deal with other people and manage your emotional problems. Furthermore, a certain degree of expressiveness is emphasized in all three group types, since it is only through open communication that the members can benefit from one another's reactions. All three types also rely on the basic technique of self-analysis in which groups proceed by self-consciously examining their own behavior. As a result, most actual resocialization groups draw techniques and goals from all three approaches.

How do Resocialization Groups Work?

What happens in resocialization groups that gives them the potential to change people? For an answer we will go to Bennis and Shepard's (1956) theory of the life-cycle of a self-analytic group. Their approach reflects something of the holistic, dynamic orientation of field theory. This is not surprising since they were both associated with the National Training Laboratory (NTL), an institution founded by Kurt Lewin, among others. NTL pioneered in the use of self-analytic groups to increase people's understanding of and ability to manage group situations. The phrase, T-group, comes from NTL, the "T" standing for training in group dynamics.

From observing a series of self-analytic groups, Bennis and Shepard developed a theory on how the interpersonal orientations of members give rise to certain group processes, which in turn allow the individual the opportunity to struggle with and resolve problems in their own interpersonal dispositions. We should emphasize that these processes only allow the possibility for individual change, they do not guarantee it. (Later we will look at some studies of how much change actually occurs in most real self-analytic groups.) In choosing to focus on Bennis and Shepard's approach we should not leave the impression that theirs is the only such theory. Several others are available that might have been used (for example, Bion, 1961; Schutz, 1958; Winter, 1976), and all agree on the basic processes involved. For our purposes, Bennis and Shepard's is one of the most useful, since it explicitly emphasizes the relationship between the personal orientations of the members and the changing emotional dynamics of the group. We will highlight this relationship to gain insight into the emotional dynamics of other primary groups as well.

Bennis and Shepard (1956) begin by pointing out that the same skill needed for people to improve their ability to relate to others and change themselves is also necessary for a group to work efficiently—that is, open, honest communication. They put it this way:

> The group can resolve its internal conflicts, mobilize its resources, and take intelligent action only if it has the means for consensually validating its

experience. The person can resolve his internal conflicts, mobilize his resources, and take intelligent action only if anxiety does not interfere with
his ability to profit from his experience, to analyse, discriminate, and
foresee. (Bennis and Shepard, 1956)

A self-analytic group progresses by overcoming obstacles to good communication among the members. This in turn means overcoming the
personal anxieties and conflicts of the members that limit their ability
to deal with each other in an open and honest way, so that they may
achieve the goals they want.

INTERPERSONAL ORIENTATIONS.   According to Bennis and Shepard,
most problems in dealing with others focus around two fundamental
dimensions of interpersonal relations: authority and affection. The self-
change people seek in resocialization groups usually entails an improve-
ment of their ability to manage one or both of these issues. Drawing on
Freud ([1922] 1949) and Schutz (1955), Bennis and Shepard argue that
a person who can manage these issues is a person who can act autono-
mously in relation to them. A person who is unconflicted about authority and power relations can deal with them rationally, allowing others
to have power over him or her when it seems reasonable, resisting when
it does not. Similarly, a person unconflicted about affection can respond
to each new person in terms of the actual affection offered, rather than
always approaching or avoiding others in a compulsive way.

    On the other hand, people who are anxious about authority or
affection usually show that conflict in a more rigid, less flexible way of
responding to others. Difficulty with authority can reveal itself in either
of two ways. *Overdependent* people manage anxieties about power by
habitually giving up power themselves and relying on others to take
charge and control things for them. They want others to take responsibility for the situation. *Counterdependent* people have the same anxieties
about power and authority, but deal with it in the opposite way. They
manage their fears by refusing to ever depend on others or let others
have power over them. They will always resist authority.

    Problems with affection are usually rooted in the fear of being
emotionally rejected by others. Efforts to manage this fear can also show
itself in two different ways. *Overpersonal* people try to avoid rejection by
always being nice, no matter what. They put all their efforts into making
everybody like them. *Counterpersonals* react in the opposite way. To avoid
rejection they avoid intimacy with others. In effect, they say, "You can't
reject me, I reject you first."

    These are the interpersonal orientations of the members, the aspects of their selves, which show themselves most clearly in the emotional dynamics of the resocialization group as it comes together and attempts to accomplish personal growth. Certainly, similar orientations affect the emotional life of other primary groups as well. By following Bennis and Shepard through the life course of an ideal T-group, we can see how the intertwining of personal orientations and group behavior can offer the possibility for self-change.

THE LIFE-CYCLE OF A T-GROUP.   When a collection of strangers come together in a self-analytic group, they are immediately faced with the problem of somehow organizing themselves into a group that can grapple with their problems. As we know from Chapter 2, the first problem will be that of power and authority. In effect, they will turn to the group leader or organizer and say, "You're in charge here, how do we start, what do we do?" This is what Bennis and Shepard call the dependence phase, in which the group as a whole acts the way overdependent members usually do: the group wants the leader to take responsibility for the situation. Generally, however, the T-group leader causes consternation by refusing to direct the group: "It's your group, what do you want it to do?" he or she may reply. The effect is to create a power vacuum in the group that brings to the fore the anxieties of both over- and counterdependent members.

After further efforts to win the approval of the leader make it clear that he or she will not take the lead, the group begins to get angry and frustrated. Now is the time when the counterdependents come to the fore. In this *counterdependent* phase the group may break into warring factions, each unwilling to accede to the others' proposals for structuring the group, but all unable to win power themselves. In the course of the conflict both over- and counterdependents find themselves acting out their anxieties.

It is up to those members who are relatively unconflicted about power to bring the group out of its destructive internal haggling and into the third phase of *resolution and catharsis*. By this time group members have begun to develop closer bonds, at least with those in their faction. Feeling more secure, they are more open to a direct confrontation. Now it may be perceived openly that the problem of the leader is holding up the group. It might even be suggested that the leader leave the room. The emotional effect of this confrontation is to open up the members, to allow them for the first time to discuss frankly their feelings about the leader as an authority figure. In the process, overdependents and counterdependents have the opportunity to work through some of their anxieties. Before long, unconflicted members usually suggest that the authority problem can be resolved by the members taking responsibility for their own actions rather than leaning on or fighting against the leader, and the leader is reaccepted by the group as just another member. In suggesting this resolution, unconflicted members not only help the group move on, they also demonstrate for the over- and counterdependents how power relations might be managed in a more flexible, less anxious way.

Of course, not all groups proceed this far. Some simply collapse in the bickering over control and structure. Members stop attending and the group dies. However, if the group does arrive at this stage of resolution and catharsis, say Bennis and Shepard, its attention turns to the second major problem: the affective relations among the members. Relieved by the resolution of the power struggle, the members feel a flush of unity and togetherness. In this *enchantment-flight* phase, the mood is one of harmony and acceptance, and any underlying tension or conflict that might challenge the appearance of unity is studiously avoided. Here, the group is treating the problems of affection much as overpersonals usually do.

Of course, this ideal harmony cannot last, especially if there are counterpersonals in the group. Eventually somebody broaches the fact that such harmony is just an illusion, an attempt to deny the reality of underlying interpersonal problems. Tension begins to surface, and the group moves into the *disenchantment-flight* phase. As Bennis and Shepard point out, counterpersonals dominate this phase much as overpersonals did the previous one. Counterpersonals band together to resist what they feel is the suffocating involvement of the previous stage. Overpersonals are upset and demand a more accepting atmosphere.

Again it is up to the members who are relatively unconflicted on matters of affection (not necessarily those who were unconflicted about power) to bring the group out of this bickering stage. They often attempt this under the goad of the coming end of the group sessions or some other outside demand. What is necessary is that the members begin to treat one another in a franker way, exchanging their real evaluations of one another. However, this must occur in a constructive atmosphere of mutual acceptance rather than counterpersonal rejection. Often the relatively unconflicted members help by acting this way themselves and serving as a model for others. The group's ability to move to this final *consensual validation* stage depends on the strength of the bonds that have developed among the members and on the level of trust they engender. If the group does manage to reach the penultimate stage where open, honest communication is possible for the first time, over- and counterpersonals will experience another, more flexible way of managing affection. This, of course, will allow them the opportunity for personal change.

As Bennis and Shepard admit, the picture they give is an idealized one. Not every T-group, or other resocialization group, goes through all the phases exactly as described, and most groups never make it to the final goal of consensual validation. However, other more recent observations and descriptions report a similar progression of concerns in self-analytic groups, generally confirming Bennis and Shepard's insights (Mabry, 1975; Winter, 1976).

For us, their theory provides a good illustration of the way resocialization groups work, even those that are not classic T-groups. By turning the members' attention back on themselves, resocialization groups bring to the fore that basic but often hidden agenda in all primary groups, the selves of the members. As the members self-consciously grapple with the basic emotional dimensions of group life, they bring out their personal skills, anxieties, and conflicts in relation to those dimensions. This transforms efforts to resolve group problems into a simultaneous struggle with personal difficulties. Because the members have different problems, they can help each other by challenging one another's conflicted interpersonal behaviors in a basically supportive atmosphere. This in turn offers the individual a real opportunity for change. This is the basic technique used by resocialization groups of all kinds, from Alcoholics Anonymous to assertiveness-training groups.

We have said that understanding resocialization groups will help us understand the emotional dynamics of other primary groups as well. Now we need to be more specific. What do resocialization groups teach us about groups like families and friends? We've seen that people bring to groups complex personal agendas in regard to themselves and others. These agendas have their roots in people's self-identity and in their habitual ways of managing interpersonal dimensions like power and affection. The encounter among these personal orientations creates the emotional dynamics of a group. This happens to some extent in all groups. But in the warm, nonspecific atmosphere of primary groups, these emotional dynamics dominate much of the life of the group—just as in resocialization groups. Consequently, as the members of primary groups grapple with the necessities of group life—establishing patterns of status, friendship, communication, and leadership—they bring to the fore their own identities, anxieties, and needs. As in resocialization groups, the struggle with group problems becomes a simultaneous encounter with the self. Because other primary groups are not self-analytic, this encounter among the members' selves is often not acknowledged explicitly, but it nevertheless dominates the life of the

group. And out of this encounter comes self-change, in desired or un-
desired ways. We do not form primary attachments with others without
being influenced by them. So this, too, is similar to resocialization
groups.

As already mentioned, the major difference between resocialization
and other primary groups is, of course, that the latter are not self-
analytic. Most friends do not self-consciously focus on the dynamics of
their group. As a result other primary groups are not likely to go through
the precise sequence of stages described by Bennis and Shepard, stages
which are driven by the process of self-analysis. Equally important,
other primary groups do not attempt to affect the nature or direction of
self-change that goes on within them. Outside these differences, however, there is an essential similarity in the relationship between the
members' selves and the concerns and dynamics of the group.

Are Resocialization Groups Effective?

Whether resocialization groups have desired effects on their members depends on a number of contingencies. First, the seriousness of the
problems brought to the group and the degree of change being sought
are important factors. It also depends on the group's mix of personalities
and the degree to which they manage to both support and challenge one
another. The skills of the leader are important here too, since he or she
can encourage or divert conflict among the members, and do much to
create a supportive atmosphere. Finally, most resocialization groups
meet for a limited number of sessions, and the available time may or
may not be sufficient to accomplish the desired change. Given all these
contingencies, perhaps we should not expect an overwhelming success
rate from resocialization groups.

A number of studies have attempted to assess the effectiveness of
resocialization groups more precisely. It is very difficult to measure the
types of change that are sought or might be achieved in resocialization
groups, particularly since they will vary from individual to individual.
As a result, studies attempting to assess such change have been fraught
with methodological difficulties. This must be kept in mind when considering their results.

However, the data existing suggest that resocialization groups do
change people's perception of themselves and to a lesser extent their
behavior as it is judged by others (Burke and Bennis, 1961; Friedlander,
1967; Lieberman, Yalom, and Miles, 1973; Shaw, 1981). Resocialization
groups do not seem to be very effective at altering their members' basic
underlying personalities (Baumgartel and Goldstein, 1967; McLeish and

Park, 1972; White, 1974; Ware and Barr, 1977). Participants, however, generally rate their experience in such groups as helpful. Lieberman, Yalom, and Miles (1973), for instance, found that 78 percent of the participants they studied in a wide variety of resocialization groups reported positive change, and 64 percent still believed that to be true six months later. However, friends and associates of the participants did not agree that they had changed so much, nor did they always feel the change had been in a positive direction (Lieberman et al., 1973). Some researchers have suggested that what resocialization groups actually do is reduce the gap between people's ideal self and their actual self-concept (Shaw, 1981). Thus it is not so much one's basic self that changes as one's self-awareness and self-acceptance. Presumably these in turn improve your ability to interact with others in a way that provides the satisfactions you want.

For some people, however, an experience with a therapy or experiential group may have more negative than positive effects. Such groups deliberately arouse one's personal anxieties. Some groups may do this without also providing the support necessary to deal with those anxieties, possibly making your problems worse rather than better. Lieberman et al. (1971, 1973) report that between 9 and 10 percent of participants suffer observable psychological harm. Much more rarely, there may even be a serious breakdown (Back, 1973).

We can conclude, then, that resocialization groups are moderately effective at improving self-awareness and self-acceptance. They do not seem to be effective at accomplishing deeper psychological changes. While most people find them a positive, constructive experience, there is some risk involved, and a few participants do end up worse off than before.

Regardless of their effectiveness, resocialization groups do address a set of needs that people in an industrialized society increasingly feel. People must learn to change themselves in response to changing demands placed on them by our society. Given their limited resources and specialized natures, the usual family and friendship groups are not always sufficient to the task. As a result, there is a real place for resocialization groups in our society, and, very effective or not, they are unlikely to disappear.

Resocialization groups do, however, appear to be changing in emphasis. A decade ago they were primarily oriented toward general personal change—encounter and sensitivity training groups, for instance. Now such groups appear to be on the wane, replaced by more focused and specialized change groups. The new groups deal with specific needs, for example, counseling battered wives, or learning to "think thin," or becoming more assertive. Partly, the shift reflects a movement away from the ideological views of the 1960s. But it also reflects the more general trend toward specialization of primary groups that has been the focus of this chapter. Because of this trend we should see continuing growth in these more specialized self-change groups.

As we have seen, resocialization groups provide a good illustration of a distinctive primary-group process. By self-consciously focusing on their own emotional dynamics, resocialization groups bring to the surface the intense, interdependent relationship between members' self-concepts, their habits of dealing with others, and the emotional relationships that develop among members. This interdependence lies at the heart of all primary-group life. It is what makes sense out of a group's cultural themes, rituals, and concerns. It is what allows primary groups to provide basic emotional support for members and influence their deepest beliefs. Yet in most primary groups this central interdependence is not explicitly articulated but rather operates just below the surface, recognized by all, but somehow hard to pin down. By bringing these processes into the open, resocialization groups provide a laboratory where much can be learned about primary groups, even if they, themselves, do not often achieve sufficient emotional depth to accomplish profound change in their members.

PRIMARY GROUPS AND A CHANGING SOCIETY

It is the close relationship between the life of the group and the selves of the members that distinguishes primary from task groups. It has been one of this chapter's themes that the nature of this relationship is in turn affected by the larger social structure within which the group operates. Since primary groups are the major means by which people manage their personal needs in relation to the larger society, when that society changes the demands people make of their primary groups change. Furthermore, primary groups, like task groups, are themselves units of social organization within that larger social structure. Therefore, when it is transformed, the institutional supports and cultural blueprints for various primary groups are also altered. The result is two sources of change, one from without and one from within, which come together to transform the structure and dominant emotional concerns of differing primary groups. These changes in turn alter the nature of the relationship between the selves of the members and the emotional life of the group.

It is this process from which derive today's primary groups which are more specialized, differentiated, and voluntary in basis than their predecessors. As we have seen, these new primary groups attempt to manage the needs of people increasingly accustomed to change and mobility in their lives. They offer their members greater opportunity to develop and express their unique feelings and personal characteristics, but they also create a greater possibility for personal frustration and feelings of alienation and dislocation. These tensions and opportunities are felt most acutely in the family, still the central, most traditional primary group in the lives of most people. The fact that the family has undergone rapid change in the last few years argues for continuing transformations in our primary group system. As the social structure changes, so will our primary groups.

SUMMARY

Few experiences in our lives have the emotional significance of our primary groups. We anchor our self-identities in them, rely on them for emotional support, and use them to create a sense of connection between ourselves and larger, more impersonal organizations and causes. The defining characteristics of primary groups—emotional attachments among the members, relative permanence, and diffuse purpose—account for their impact on individuals and their importance for the maintenance or change of the larger social structure. The development of communication networks, status hierarchies, leadership structures, and group cultures are as vital to primary groups as to any other group type. However, since such processes were discussed in previous chapters, the focus in this chapter was on those that define the distinctive role played by primary groups. It is the particularly intense and complex interplay among pressures from the outside society, the emotional dynamics of the group, and the selves of the members that lie at the heart of primary group existence.

Our current system of primary groups developed in response to the demands of an urban, industrialized, and increasingly bureaucratized society. These forces increased the degree of differentiation and specialization among traditional primary groups and fostered the growth of some new types of groups. They also made primary groups more voluntary in basis and more subject to change over the individual's life span. To understand how our contemporary system of primary groups works, we examined the specialized functions of each of the major primary group types. Increasing mobility and geographic dispersal have changed but not destroyed the usefulness of the modern primary group: kin groups have narrowed their focus to helping members with major needs but not offering on-the-spot reaction to every minor problem; the nuclear family manages basic emotional support; neighbors provide every-day assistance and short-term emergency help. Primary groups among co-workers help people manage the demands of their jobs and their occupational identities; personal friendships focus on the unique aspects of their members' personalities; and interest groups allow people to create a specific type of identity outside the confines of work and family. Resocialization groups fill in the gaps, helping people change themselves to adjust to their changing circumstances. The result of this differentiated system is that most people manage their needs by assembling a "package" of specialized primary groups rather than relying on a few multifunctional groups. For the individual this offers greater possibilities for self-realization but a larger risk of social dislocation, alienation, and emotional isolation as well.

This overview of contemporary American primary groups was followed by a more specific analysis of two groups: the family and resocialization groups. The family is a core unit in the lives of most people and in the organization of the larger society. Resocialization groups affect fewer people, but they offer a worthy illustration of the interdependence, between the selves of the members and the emotional dynamics of the group, that characterizes all primary groups.

The family is a basic, institutionalized unit of society. As such it continues as a multifunctional group, even though more specialized than previously. Nuclear families are expected to manage procreation, early childhood socialization, the economic maintenance of individuals, and provide primary emotional support. The way the family fulfills its economic role is being transformed by the increasing employment of women, which is changing the power structure, division of labor, and the cultural blueprint of the family. Although the family's socialization duties have been narrowed to those of early childhood, this still allows it a formative influence on the personalities and future group behavior of its members. Urban industrialism has increased the importance of the family's emotional support function, raising members' expectations for the intensity and quality of their family relations. Sometimes these demands are more than a particular marriage or parent-child relationship can sustain, and they can lead to the frustration and discord that is a problematic aspect of contemporary family life.

Thinking about the family underscores the importance of the relationship between the emotional life of primary groups and the selves of the members. To look more closely at this relationship we turned to resocialization groups, where this link is self-consciously manipulated in an effort to produce self-change. After discussing learning, therapeutic, and expressive varieties of resocialization groups, we turned to a consideration of how such groups work. We relied on Bennis and Shepard's (1956) description of the life-cycle of a T-group to clarify the way such groups bring to the fore underlying conflicts of power and affection. By self-consciously focusing on emotional dynamics, members' efforts to manage group problems simultaneously become opportunities to alter aspects of their selves. However, for many reasons, resocialization groups are not always very successful in changing their members in the way they wish. As the larger social structure continues to change, so will the variety and type of primary groups, and the nature of their relationship with their members.

Epilogue

GROUPS, INDIVIDUALS, AND SOCIETY: A FINAL COMMENT

We began this book by noting that small groups are *the* essential form of human social organization. We have seen them as social microcosms unto themselves. Within them people achieve personal status and esteem in the eyes of their fellows. Hierarchies of influence develop, and personal leadership is exercised. They are the home for human intimacy, for affection, warmth, and trust, as well as for anger and jealousy. They are the social factories in which people invent ideas, beliefs, and expressions of feeling about the social world and, indeed, whole ways of living.

We have also discovered that small groups are vital agents in the survival of both individuals and larger society. They are an essential tool that both rely on to accomplish difficult or complex tasks. They are the supporting structures in which individuals root their self-identities and on which they rely for satisfaction of their needs and for feedback about the social world. Larger social institutions, such as government, corporations, or universities, count on small groups to link them directly to the individuals within their domain and to harness the energy and beliefs of those individuals to the goals of the institution. Without them, the successful persistence of both individuals and large institutions would be in doubt. Although the specific types of small groups that predominate in our society will continue to change, it is safe to say that as a form of social organization, small groups are here to stay.

However, simply because small groups will not disappear in the future does not mean that they will necessarily develop to the benefit of all individuals or institutions in our society. There is always a degree of tension between the larger society, the mechanism of the small group, and the personal needs of the individual. The structure of the larger society is always changing. The economy goes up and down, new technology replaces old, and the social and physical environments we live in are reshaped by ongoing modernization. Consequently, the three-way tension among society, small groups, and individuals must be continually renegotiated in order for society to continue to function as an integrated social system.

Individuals are apparently seeking to balance the tension between the obligations of small groups and their own needs in an increasingly urban environment by dispersing their commitments over a wider variety of more voluntary and transitory groups. There is every reason to expect this trend to continue. When your commitments are divided among several, short-lived groups, your behavior is less controlled by any of them. This allows you greater freedom to change your life, opinions—and even self-image if necessary—to survive and succeed in a rapidly changing society. Right now, for example, industry and jobs are moving from the Northeast to Southern and Southwestern states. As a result thousands of people must sever their group ties in places like Detroit and Buffalo and move to Houston, Atlanta, or Phoenix in search of a good job and a chance for personal success. This is harder to do if your life has been rooted in a few all-encompassing and overlapping groups such as kin, neighborhood, and local job.

Economic necessity is not the only reason why Americans are moving toward more diversified, voluntary, and less-obligating small groups. American society values individualism and the freedom for people to become whatever they want. In pursuit of these values many want the freedom to break off group relations when they interfere with self-development or personal achievement. This too encourages a life lived through many and more transitory small groups. More and more, people hold several jobs, marry more than once, change friends, and live in many neighborhoods over the course of their lives. Given the union between the demands of the economy and the value we place on individualism, this trend should continue.

The consequences of this trend are not entirely positive, however. We have seen the importance of primary groups for the individual's sense of security, belonging, and identity, as well as for the larger society's ability to maintain social order. The growing diversity and voluntary nature of our small groups does not make deep primary attachments impossible, but it does make them harder to achieve. In all our lives, there is a growing probability that we will encounter periods when we cannot find the primary groups we need, when we will experience loneliness, alienation, and self-doubt as a consequence. This system also means that, at any given time, there will be a noticeable segment of the population detached from primary groups, and hence, from effective social control. The result is an undercurrent of unrest and even crime.

The difficulty of creating a system of small groups that allows people the freedom and flexibility they require and the security and connectedness they need, is a persistent problem of modern society. It has not been solved and is not likely to be in the near future. This problem reflects one aspect of that three-way tension we spoke of earlier, the strain between the requirements of the larger society and the needs of the individual.

In their efforts to moderate this strain people create specialized new primary and task groups designed to deal with specific problems of living in an increasingly urbanized, bureaucratic society. Recent years have seen the development of old age communes, computer conference groups, citizens' action groups, barter groups, open marriages, cohabitating couples, and a variety of other inventive forms. Because the problems to which they respond are likely to persist, the invention of new specialized small groups will continue. The future coherence of American society will be determined in part by our ability to link these proliferating new groups with both the needs of individuals and the demands of larger institutional structures.

This will not be easy. As the major institutions of our society have grown larger and more bureaucratic, some have lost touch with the small groups that link them to their clients. The difficulties educational institutions have maintaining effective links with teenage peer groups is a case in point. The inability of large governmental structures to maintain normative control over the small, powerful decision-making groups that operate within the government is another that has gained attention in the past decade. Much of the debate over the regulation of the intelligence community or the power of presidential advisers centers around the issue of maintaining effective links with small groups that have grown up within the official hierarchy.

What we see here is not just the tension between individuals and large organizations, but the tension between unofficial small groups and large institutions as well. This is the third leg of the three-way tension we mentioned earlier. The problem of institutions is not simply to build new small groups where they are now missing, but to establish contacts with those that already exist within the institutional structure.

There are many factors that make this process difficult. Some institutions—government and educational establishments, for instance—have relied heavily on the support of primary groups such as the traditional family and community. As the power of these groups, and the number of people affiliated with them, has declined, these institutions have not always been quick to recognize and contact the new groups that have taken their place. Also, as people have dispersed their commitments over many groups, the reduced power of any one has meant that broad-based institutions such as government and education must deal with a larger number and variety of small groups in order to forge effective links with their clients. This, too, makes the task more difficult.

Other types of institutions, such as businesses, have sometimes failed to understand the importance of small groups in the first place. Small groups don't usually appear in the corporate organizational chart, and yet they are vital to assuring the loyalty and effort of the people who make up a business. American automobile manufacturers, for instance, have found quality control difficult to achieve without small groups to link management with the production line. The increasing interest of American businesses in Japanese management techniques, with their emphasis on group relations, reflects a growing awareness of this problem.

A final factor that obstructs the forming of effective links between large organizations and their constituent small groups is the potential conflict of interests between the two. Sometimes large institutions want things from their people that the people do not want to give. For instance, government agencies may want more contact with families in order to increase social control, but the families may resist this as an invasion of privacy and a threat to personal freedom. Similarly, business may try to foster more company-based social groups in order to increase worker loyalty and productivity. Workers, however, may see this as an exploitative demand on their personal lives.

There is no simple solution to these conflicts. To gain their loyalty, large institutions may have to devolve real power and authority onto small groups whose operations are important to the institution's success. To gain some sense of control over the institutions that govern their lives, individuals will have to participate in these groups and work with larger organizational structures. The future effectiveness of our major business, government, and educational institutions, as they grow larger and more bureaucratic, will be strongly affected by their ability to balance growth against more significant links with their constituent small groups, and, through them, with their individual participants. The future coherence of our society, the growth of the crime rate, the level of disaffection among its citizens, and the status of many other social ills—and benefits—depend heavily on our ability to invent small groups that respond to people's needs in changing economic and social conditions.

References

ACOCK, ALAN C., JAMES J. DOWD, and WILLIAM L. ROBERTS.
1974   *The primary group: Its rediscovery in contemporary society.* Morristown, N.J.: General Learning Press.
ADAMS, BERT N.
1968   *Kinship in an urban setting.* Chicago: Markham.
ADAMS, J. STACEY.
1963   Towards an understanding of inequity. *Journal of Abnormal and Social Psychology* 67: 422–436.
1965   Inequity in social exchange. In L. Berkowitz (ed.), *Advances in experimental social psychology,* vol. 2, pp. 267–299. New York: Academic Press.
ALDOUS, JOAN.
1977   Family interaction patterns. *Annual Review of Sociology* 3:105–135.
ARGYRIS, CHRIS.
1969   The incompleteness of social psychological theory: Examples from small group, cognitive consistency, and attribution research. *American Psychologist* 24:893–908.
ARONSON, ELLIOT, and JUDSON MILLS.
1959   Effect of severity of initiation on liking for a group. *Journal of Abnormal and Social Psychology* 59: 177–181.
ASCH, SOLOMON.
1951   Effects of group pressure upon the modification and distortion of judgments. In H. Guetzkow (ed.), *Groups, Leadership and Men,* pp. 177–190. Pittsburgh: Carnegie Press.
1955   Opinions and social pressure. *Scientific American* 193:31–35.
BACK, KURT W.
1951   Influence through social communication. *Journal of Abnormal and Social Psychology* 46:9–23.
1971   Varieties of sensitivity training. *Sociological Inquiry* 41:133–137.
1973   *Beyond words: The story of the sensitivity training and encounter movement.* Baltimore: Penguin Books.

1978   *In search for community: Encounter groups and social change.* Boulder, Colo.: Westview Press.

BAHR, STEPHEN J.
1974   Effects on power and division of labor in the family. In L. W. Hoffman and F. I. Nye, *Working mothers,* pp. 167–185. San Francisco: Jossey-Bass.

BAKER, PAUL B.
1981   The division of labor: Interdependence, isolation, and cohesion in small groups. *Small Group Behavior* 12:93–106.

BALES, ROBERT F.
1950   *Interaction process analysis: A method for the study of small groups.* Cambridge, Mass.: Addison-Wesley.
1953   The equilibrium problem in small groups. In T. Parsons, R. F. Bales, and E. A. Shils, *Working papers in the theory of action,* pp. 111–161. Glencoe, Ill.: Free Press.
1954   In conference. *Harvard Business Review* 32:44–50.
1956   Task status and likeability as a function of talking and listening in decision-making groups. In L. D. White (ed.), *The state of the social sciences,* pp. 148–161. Chicago: The University of Chicago Press.
1958   Task roles and social roles in problem-solving groups. In E. E. Moccoby, T. M. Newcomb, and E. L. Hartley (eds.), *Readings in social psychology,* 3rd ed., pp. 437–447. New York: Holt, Rinehart & Winston.

BALES, ROBERT F., and PHILLIP E. SLATER.
1955   Role differentiation in small decision-making groups. In T. Parsons, R. F. Bales, and P. E. Slater, *The family, socialization and interaction process,* pp. 259–306. Glencoe, Ill.: Free Press.

BALES, ROBERT F., FRED L. STRODTBECK, THEODORE MILLS, and MARY E. ROSEBOROUGH.
1951   Channels of communication in small groups. *American Sociological Review* 16:461–468.

BANE, MARY JO.
1976   *Here to stay: American families in the twentieth century.* New York: Basic Books.

BASS, B. M., and F.-T. NORTON
1951   Group size and leaderless discussions. *Journal of Applied Psychology* 35:397–400.

BATES, ALAN P., and NICHOLAS BABCHUCK.
1961   The primary group: A reappraisal. *Sociological Quarterly* 2:181–191.

BAUMGARTEL, H., and J. W. GOLDSTEIN.
  1967   Need and value shifts in college training groups. *Journal of Applied Behavioral Science* 3:87–101.
BAUR, E. JACKSON.
  1960   Public opinion and the primary group. *American Sociological Review* 25:209–219.
BAVELAS, ALEX.
  1950   Communication patterns in task-oriented groups. *Journal of the Acoustical Society of America* 22:725–730.
BECKER, HOWARD S., and BLANCHE GEER.
  1960   Latent culture: A note on the theory of latent social roles. *Administrative Science Quarterly* 5:304–13.
BECKHOUSE, LAURENCE, JUDITH TANUR, JOHN WEILER, and EUGENE WEINSTEIN.
  1975   And some men have leadership thrust upon them. *Journal of Personality and Social Psychology* 31:557–566.
BEM, DARYL J.
  1967   Self-perception: An alternative interpretation of cognitive dissonance phenomena. *Psychological Review* 74:183–200.
  1972   Self-perception theory. In L. Berkowitz (ed.), *Advances in experimental social psychology,* vol. 6, pp. 2–62. New York: Academic Press.
BENNIS, WARREN G., and HERBERT A. SHEPARD.
  1956   A theory of group development. *Human Relations* 9:415–437.
BENOIT-SMULLYAN, E.
  1944   Status, status-types, and status interrelations. *American Sociological Review* 9:151–161.
BERGER, JOSEPH, BERNARD COHEN, and MORRIS ZELDITCH, JR.
  1966   Status characteristics and expectation states: A process model. In J. Berger, M. Zelditch, Jr., and B. Anderson (eds.), *Sociological theories in progress,* vol. 1, pp. 47–73. Boston: Houghton-Mifflin.
  1972   Status characteristics and social interaction. *American Sociological Review* 37:241–255.
BERGER, JOSEPH, THOMAS CONNER, and M. HAMIT FISEK.
  1974   *Expectation states theory: A theoretical research program.* Cambridge, Mass.: Winthrop.
BERGER, JOSEPH, THOMAS CONNER, and WILLIAM L. McKEOWN.
  1969   Evaluations and the formation and maintenance of performance expectations. *Human Relations* 22:481–502.
BERGER, JOSEPH, M. HAMIT FISEK, ROBERT Z. NORMAN, and MORRIS ZELDITCH, JR.
  1977   *Status characteristics and social interaction: An expectation states approach.* New York: Elsevier.

BERGER, JOSEPH, SUSAN J. ROSENHOLTZ, and MORRIS ZELDITCH, JR.
1980 Status organizing processes. *Annual Review of Sociology* 6:479–508.
BERGER, JOSEPH, MORRIS ZELDITCH, JR., and BO ANDERSON.
1966 *Sociological theories in progress,* vol. 1. Boston: Houghton-Mifflin.
BERGER, JOSEPH, MORRIS ZELDITCH, JR., BO ANDERSON, and BERNARD P. COHEN.
1972 Structural aspects of distributive justice: A status value formulation. In J. Berger, M. Zelditch, Jr., and B. Anderson (eds.), *Sociological theories in progress,* vol. 2, pp. 119–146. Boston: Houghton-Mifflin.
BERGER, PETER, and HANSFRIED KELLNER.
1975 Marriage and the construction of reality. In D. Brisset and C. Edgley (eds.), *Life or theatre: A dramaturgical sourcebook,* pp. 219–233. Chicago: Aldine.
BERKOWITZ, LEONARD.
1954 Group standards, cohesiveness and productivity. *Human Relations* 7:509–519.
1957 Effects of perceived dependency relationships upon conformity to group expectations. *Journal of Abnormal and Social Psychology* 55:350–354.
BION, W. R.
1961 *Experiences in groups and other papers.* New York: Basic Books.
BLAU, PETER M.
1954 Cooperation and competition in a bureaucracy. *American Journal of Sociology* 59:530–535.
1964 *Exchange and power in social life.* New York: Wiley.
1960 Patterns of deviation in work groups. *Sociometry* 23:245–261.
BLOOD, ROBERT O., JR., and DONALD M. WOLFE.
1960 *Husbands and wives: The dynamics of married living.* New York: Free Press.
BONACICH, PHILIP.
1972 Norms and cohesion as adaptive responses to potential conflict: An experimental study. *Sociometry* 36:31–41.
BONACICH, PHILIP, and GORDON H. LEWIS.
1973 Function specialization and sociometric judgment. *Sociometry* 36:31–41.
BORGATTA, EDGAR, ARTHUR S. COUCH, and ROBERT F. BALES.
1954 Some findings relevant to the great man theory of leadership. *American Sociological Review* 19:755–759.
BREHM, J. W.
1966 *A theory of psychological reactance.* New York: Academic Press.

BROWN, ROGER.
1974 Further comment on the risky shift. *American Psychologist* 29: 468–470.
BRZEZINSKI, ZBIGNIEW.
1982 The failed mission: The inside account of the attempt to free the hostages in Iran. *New York Times Magazine,* April 18:28–31, 61–78.
BUCKLEY, WALTER.
1967 *Sociology and modern systems theory.* Englewood Cliffs, N.J.: Prentice-Hall, Inc.
BURKE, PETER J.
1967 The development of task and social-emotional role differentiation. *Sociometry* 30:379–392.
1968 Role differentiation and the legitimation of task activity. *Sociometry* 31:404–411.
1969 Scapegoating: An alternative to role differentiation. *Sociometry* 32:159–168.
1971 Task and social-emotional leadership role performance. *Sociometry* 34:22–40.
1974 Participation and leadership in small groups. *American Sociological Review* 39:832–843.
BURKE, R. L., and W. G. BENNIS.
1961 Changes in perception of self and others during human relations training. *Human Relations* 14:165–182.
BYRNE, DON.
1961 Interpersonal attraction and attitude similarity. *Journal of Abnormal and Social Psychology* 62:713–715.
BYRNE, DON, J. L. CLORE, JR., and P. WORCHEL.
1966 Effect of economic similarity-dissimilarity in interpersonal attraction. *Journal of Personality and Social Psychology* 4:220–224.
CAMILLERI, S. F., and J. BERGER.
1967 Decision making and social influence: A model as an experimental test. *Sociometry* 30:365–378.
CAPLE, R. B.
1978 The sequential stages of group development. *Small Group Behavior* 9:470–476.
CARR, LOIS G., and LORENA S. WALSH.
1978 The planter's wife: The experience of white women in seventeenth-century Maryland. In Michael Gordon (ed.), *The American family in social-historical perspective,* pp. 263–288. New York: St. Martin's.

CARTER, HUGH, and PAUL C. GLICK.
1976   *Marriage and divorce: A social and economic study,* rev. ed. Cambridge, Mass: Harvard University Press.
CARTER, L. F.
1954   Recording and evaluating the performance of individuals as members of small groups. *Personnel Psychology* 7:477–484.
CARTER, L. F., W. W. HAYTHORN, B. SHRIVER, and J. LANZETTA.
1951   The behavior of leaders and other group members. *Journal of Abnormal and Social Psychology* 46:589–595.
CARTWRIGHT, DORWIN, and ALVIN ZANDER.
1968   *Group dynamics: Research and theory,* 3rd ed. New York: Harper & Row.
CARTWRIGHT, JOHN A.
1978   A laboratory investigation of groupthink. *Communications Monographs* 45:229–246.
CHASE, IVAN D.
1980   Social process and hierarchy formation in small groups. *American Sociological Review* 45:905–924.
CHEMERS, M. M., and G. J. SKRZYPEK.
1972   An experimental test of the contingency model of leadership effectiveness. *Journal of Personality and Social Psychology* 24:172–177.
CHOWDRY, K., and THEODORE M. NEWCOMB.
1952   The relative abilities of leaders and nonleaders to estimate opinions of their own groups. *Journal of Abnormal and Social Psychology* 47:51–57.
COHEN, ELIZABETH G.
1972   Interracial interaction disability. *Human Relations* 25:9–24.
COHEN, ELIZABETH G., and SUSAN ROPER.
1972   Modification of interracial interaction disability: An application of status characteristic theory. *American Sociological Review* 37:643–657.
COLEMAN, JAMES S.
1960   The adolescent subculture and academic achievement. *The American Journal of Sociology* 65:337–347.
COOK, KAREN S.
1975   Expectations, evaluations and equity. *American Sociological Review* 40:372–388.
COOLEY, CHARLES H.
1902   *Human nature and the social order.* New York: Schocken, 1964.
1909   *Social organization: A study of the larger mind.* New York: Scribner's.

COUCH, L., and J.R.P. FRENCH, JR.
1948   Overcoming resistance to change. *Human Relations* 1:512–532.

CROCKETT, W. H.
1955   Emergent leadership in small decision-making groups. *Journal of Abnormal and Social Psychology* 51:378–383.

CROSBIE, PAUL V.
1972   Social exchange and power compliance: A test of Homen's propositions. *Sociometry* 35:203–222.
1975   *Interaction in small groups.* New York: Macmillan.
1979   Effects of status inconsistency: Negative evidence from small groups. *Social Psychology Quarterly* 42:110–125.

CROSBIE, P. V., F. A., PETRONI, and B. G. STITT.
1972   The Dynamics of Collective Groups. *Journal of Health and Social Behavior* 13:294–302.

CROSBIE, P. V., B. G. STITT, and F. A. PETRONI.
1973   Relevance in the small groups laboratory. Mimeo. University of Arizona.

DAVIS, JAMES H.
1969   Individual-group problem solving, subject preference, and problem type. *Journal of Personality and Social Psychology* 13:362–374.

DAVIS, JAMES H., and FRANK RESTLE.
1963   The analysis of problems and prediction of group problem solving. *Journal of Abnormal and Social Psychology* 66:103–116.

DAVIS, J. H., R. M. BRAY, and R. W. HOLT.
1978   The empirical study of social decision processes in juries. In J. Tapp and F. Levine (eds.), *Law, justice and the individual in society: Psychological and legal issues,* pp. 326–361. New York: Holt, Rinehart & Winston.

DEUTSCH, MORTON.
1949   An experimental study of the effects of cooperation and competition upon group processes. *Human Relations* 2:199–231.

DEUTSCH, MORTON, and HAROLD B. GERARD.
1955   A study of normative and informational social influences upon individual judgment. *Journal of Abnormal and Social Psychology* 51: 629–636.

DEUTSCH, MORTON, and ROBERT M. KRAUSS.
1965   *Theories in social psychology.* New York: Basic Books.

DITTES, J. E., and H. H. KELLEY.
1956   Effect of different conditions of acceptance upon conformity to group norms. *Journal of Abnormal and Social Psychology* 53: 100–107.

DUNCAN, STARKEY, JR.
1972   Some signals and rules for taking speaking turns in con-
       versations. *Journal of Personality and Social Psychology* 23:283–
       292.
DUNPHY, DEXTER C.
1972   *The primary group: A handbook for analysis and field research.* New
       York: Appleton-Century-Crofts.
DURKHEIM, EMILE.
1893   *The division of labor in society.* New York: MacMillan, 1933.
1894   *Suicide.* Glencoe, Ill: Free Press, 1951.
EMERSON, RICHARD M.
1954   Deviation and rejection: An experimental replication. *American
       Sociological Review* 19:668–693.
1962   Power-dependence relations. *American Sociological Review* 27:31–
       41.
1964   Power-dependence relations: Two experiments. *Sociometry* 27:
       282–298.
ERICKSEN, JULIA, WILLIAM L. YANCEY, and EUGENE ERICKSEN.
1979   The division of family roles. *Journal of Marriage and the Family*
       41:301–313.
ESKILSON, ARLENE, and MARY GLENN WILEY.
1976   Sex composition and leadership in small groups. *Sociometry* 39:
       183–194.
EXLINE, R. V.
1957   Group climate as a factor in the relevance and accuracy of
       social perception. *Journal of Abnormal and Social Psychology* 55:
       382–388.
FAUCHEUX, CLAUDE, and SERGE MOSCOVICI.
1968   Studies on group creativity: III. Noise and complexity in the
       inferential processes. *Human Relations* 21:29–40.
FELDMAN, RONALD A.
1968   Interrelationships among three bases of group integration. *Soci-
       ometry* 31:30–46.
1973   Power distribution, integration, and conformity in small
       groups. *American Journal of Sociology* 79:639–665.
FENCHEL, G. H., J. H. MONDERER, and E. L. HARTLEY.
1951   Subjective status and the equilibration hypothesis. *Journal of
       Abnormal and Social Psychology* 46:476–479.
FENNELL, MARY L., PATRICIA BARCHAS, ELIZABETH COHEN, ANNE MCMAHON,
and POLLY HILDEBRAND.
1978   An alternative perspective on sex differences in organizational
       settings: The process of legitimation." *Sex Roles* 4:589–604.

FESTINGER, LEON.
1950   Informal social communication. *Psychological Review* 57:271–282.
1954   A theory of social comparison. *Human Relations* 7:114–140.
1957   *A theory of cognitive dissonance.* Stanford, Calif: Stanford University Press.
FESTINGER, LEON, HENRY W. RIECKEN, and STANLEY SCHACTER.
1956   *When prophecy fails.* Minneapolis: University of Minnesota Press.
FESTINGER, LEON, STANLEY SCHACTER, and KURT BACK.
1950   *Social pressures in informal groups: A study of human factors in housing.* New York: Harper & Row.
FESTINGER, LEON, and JOHN W. THIBAUT.
1951   Interpersonal communication in small groups. *Journal of Abnormal and Social Psychology* 46:92–99.
FIEDLER, FRED E.
1964   A contingency model of leadership effectiveness. In L. Berkowitz (ed.), *Advances in experimental social psychology,* vol. 1, pp. 149–190. New York: Academic Press.
1967   *A theory of leadership effectiveness.* New York: McGraw-Hill.
1978   Recent developments in research on the contingency model. In L. Berkowitz (ed.), *Group processes,* pp. 209–225. New York: Academic Press.
FINE, GARY A.
1979   Small groups and culture creation: the idioculture of Little League baseball teams. *American Sociological Review* 44:733–745.
FINE, GARY A. and SHERRYL KLEINMAN.
1979   Rethinking subculture: and interactionist analysis. *American Journal of Sociology* 85:1–20
FISEK, M. HAMIT, and RICHARD OFSHE.
1970   The process of status evolution. *Sociometry* 33:327–346.
FISHMAN, PAMELA.
1978   Interaction: The work women do. *Social Problems* 25:397–406.
FLEISHMAN, JOHN, and GERALD MARWELL.
1977   Status congruence and associativeness: A test of Galtung's theory. *Sociometry* 40:1–11.
FLOWERS, M. L.
1977   A laboratory test of some implications of Janis' group think hypothesis. *Journal of Personality and Social Psychology* 35:888–896.
FODOR, E. M.
1978   Simulated work climate as an influence on choice of leadership style. *Personality and Social Psychology Bulletin* 4:111–114.

FORD, GERALD R., and JOHN R. STILES.
1965   *Portrait   of   the   assassin.*   New   York: Simon   and
        Schuster.
FREESE, LEE.
1974   Conditions for status equality. *Sociometry* 36: 177–193.
1976   The generalization of specific performance expectations. *Soci-
        ometry* 39:194–200.
FREESE, LEE, and BERNARD COHEN.
1973   Eliminating status generalization. *Sociometry* 36:177–193.
FRENCH, JOHN, JR., and BERTRAM RAVEN.
1959   The basis of social power. In D. Cartwright (ed.), *Studies in social
        power,* pp. 150–167. Ann Arbor, Mich.: Institute for Social Re-
        search.
FREUD, SIGMUND.
1922   *Group psychology and the analysis of the ego.* J Strachey (trans.),
        London International Psycho-Analytical Press, 1922. New
        York: Liveright, 1949.
FRIEDLANDER, F.
1967   The impact of organizational training upon the effectiveness
        and interaction of ongoing work groups. *Personnel Psychology*
        20:289–309.
GALTUNG, JOHAN.
1966   Rank and social integration: A multidimensional approach. In
        J. Berger, M. Zelditch, Jr., and B. Anderson (eds.), *Sociological
        theories in progress,* vol. 1, pp. 145–198. Boston: Houghton-
        Mifflin.
GALLAGHER, JAMES, and PETER J. BURKE.
1974   Scapegoating and leader behavior. *Social Forces* 52:481–488.
GAMSON, WILLIAM A.
1961   A theory of coalition formation. *American Sociological Review* 26:
        373–382.
GEERTZ, CLIFFORD.
1957   Ritual and social change: A Japanese example. *American An-
        thropologist* 59: 32–54.
1973   *The interpretation of cultures.* New York: Basic Books.
GERARD, HAROLD B.
1953   The effect of different dimensions of disagreement on the
        communication process in small groups. *Human Relations* 6:
        249–271.
1964   Conformity and commitment to the group. *Journal of Abnormal
        and Social Psychology* 68:209–211.

GERARD, HAROLD B., R. A. WILHELMY, and E. S. CONOLLEY.
  1968 Conformity and group size. *Journal of Personality and Social Psychology* 8:79–82.
GIBB, C. A.
  1969 Leadership. In G. Lindzey and E. Aronson (eds.), *Handbook of social psychology*, vol. 4, pp. 205–282. Reading, Mass.: Addison-Wesley.
GILSTEIN, K. W., E. W. WRIGHT, and D. R. STONE.
  1977 The effects of leadership style on group interactions in differing sociopolitical subcultures. *Small Group Behavior* 8:313–331.
GLICK, P. C.
  1975 A demographer looks at American families. *Journal of Marriage and the Family* 37:15–26.
GLUCKMAN, M.
  1962 *Essays on the ritual of social relations.* Manchester, U.K.: Manchester University Press.
GOFFMAN, IRWIN W.
  1957 Status consistency and preference for change in power distribution. *American Sociological Review* 22:275–281.
GOLDBERG, S. G.
  1955 Influence and leadership as a function of group structure. *Journal of Abnormal and Social Psychology* 51:119–122.
GOLDMAN, EMMA.
  1931 *Living my life.* New York: Knopf.
GOLDMAN, M.
  1965 A comparison of individual and group performance for varying combinations of initial ability. *Journal of Personality and Social Psychology* 1:210–216.
GOLDMAN, M., and L. A. FRAAS.
  1965 The effects of leader selection on group performance. *Sociometry* 28:82–88.
GOLDMAN, M., J. W. STOCKBAUER, and T. G. MCAULIFFE.
  1977 Intergroup and intragroup competition and cooperation. *Journal of Experimental Social Psychology* 13:81–88.
GOLEMBIEWSKI, ROBERT T.
  1962 *The small group: An analysis of research concepts and operations.* Chicago: The University of Chicago Press.
GOODACRE, D. M.
  1951 The use of a sociometric test as a predictor of combat unit effectiveness. *Sociometry* 14:148–152.
GOODE, W. J.
  1960 A theory of role strain. *American Sociological Review* 25:483–496.

GOODMAN, NORMAN and GARY T. MARX
1978   *Society today.* New York: Random House.
GORDON, MICHAEL.
1977   Primary-group differentiation in urban Ireland. *Social Forces* 53: 743–752.
GRIFFITT, W.
1966   Interpersonal attractions as a function of self-concept and personality similarity-dissimilarity. *Journal of Personality and Social Psychology* 4:581–584.
GROSS E.
1954   Primary functions of the small group. *American Journal of Sociology* 60:24–30.
HACKMAN, J. RICHARD.
1975   Group influences in individuals. In M. D. Dunnette (ed.), *Handbook of industrial and organizational psychology,* pp. 1455–1525. Chicago: Rand-McNally.
HACKMAN, J. RICHARD, and CHARLES C. MORRIS.
1975   Group tasks, group interaction process, and group performance effectiveness: A review and proposed integration. In L. Berkowitz (ed.), *Advances in experimental social psychology,* vol. 8, pp. 45–99. New York: Academic Press.
1978   Group process and group effectiveness: A reappraisal. In L. Berkowitz (ed.), *Group Processes,* pp. 57–66. New York: Academic Press.
HACKMAN, J. RICHARD, and NEIL VIDMAR.
1970   Effects of size and task type on group performance and member reactions. *Sociometry* 33:37–54.
HAMBLIN, ROBERT L.
1958   Leadership and crises. *Sociometry* 21:322–335.
HARDY, R. C.
1971   Effect of leadership style on the performance of small classroom groups: A test of the contingency model. *Journal of Personality and Psychology* 19:367–374.
1975   A test of poor leader-member relations cells of the contingency model on elementary school children. *Child Development* 45:958–964.
HARDY, R. C., S. SACK, and F. HARPINE.
1973   An experimental test of the contingency model on small classroom groups. *Journal of Psychology* 85:3–16.
HARE, A. PAUL.
1952   A study of interaction and consensus in different-sized groups. *American Sociological Review* 17:261–267.

1976   *Handbook of small group research,* 2nd Ed. New York: Free Press.

HARVEY, O. J., and CONRAD CONSALVI.

1960   Status and conformity to pressures in informal groups. *Journal of Abnormal and Social Psychology* 60:182–187.

HEINECKE, C., and R. BALES.

1953   Developmental trends in the structure of small groups. *Sociometry* 16:7–38.

HELLMAN, LILLIAN

1973   *Pentimento.* Boston: Little, Brown.

HEMPHILL, J. K.

1950   Relations between the size of the group and the behavior of "superior" leaders. *Journal of Social Psychology* 32:11–22.

HEROLD, DAVID M.

1978   Improving performance effectiveness of groups through a task-contingent selection of intervention strategies. *Academy of Management Review* 3:315–325.

HERSKOVITS, MELVILLE.

1948   *Man and his works.* New York: Random House.

HESS, ROBERT D., and GERALD HANDEL.

1967   The family as a psychosocial organization. In G. Handel (ed.), *The psychosocial interior of the family: A sourcebook for the study of whole families,* pp. 10–29. Chicago: Aldine.

HOFFER, ERIC.

1951   *The true believer: Thoughts on the nature of mass movements.* New York: Harper & Row.

HOFFMAN, L. RICHARD.

1959   Homogeneity of member personality and its effect on group problemsolving. *Journal of Abnormal and Social Psychology.* 58:27–32.

1961   Conditions for creative problem solving. *Journal of Psychology* 52:429–444.

1965   Group problem solving. In L. Berkowitz (ed.), *Advances in experimental social psychology,* vol. 2, pp. 99–132. New York: Academic Press.

1978   The group problem-solving process. In L. Berkowitz (ed.), *Group Processes,* pp. 101–113. New York: Academic Press.

1979.   *The group problem-solving process: Studies of a valence model.* New York: Praeger.

HOFFMAN, L. RICHARD, and NORMAN R. F. MAIER.

1961   Quality and acceptance of problem-solving solutions by members of homogeneous and heterogeneous groups. *Journal of Abnormal and Social Psychology* 62:401–407.

HOLLANDER, EDWIN P.

1958   Conformity, status, and idiosyncracy credit. *Psychological Review* 65:117–127.

1960   Competence and conformity in the acceptance of influence. *Journal of Abnormal and Social Psychology* 61:365–369.

1964   *Leaders, groups, and influence.* New York: Oxford.

1978   *Leadership dynamics: A practical guide to effective relationships.* New York: Free Press.

HOMANS, GEORGE C.

1950   *The human group.* New York: Harcourt Brace Jovanovich.

1961   *Social behavior: Its elementary forms.* New York: Harcourt Brace Jovanovich.

1974   *Social behavior: Its elementary forms,* rev. ed. New York: Harcourt Brace Jovanovich.

HOOD, W. R., and MUZAFER SHERIF.

1962   Verbal report and judgment of an unstructured stimulus. *Journal of Psychology* 54:121–130.

HUSTON, TED L., and GEORGE LEVINGER.

1978   Interpersonal attraction and relationships. *Annual Review of Psychology* 29:115–156.

IWAO, SUMIKO.

1963   Internal versus external criticism of group standards. *Sociometry* 26:410–421.

JACOBS, R. C., and D. T. CAMPBELL.

1961   The perpetuation of an arbitrary tradition through several generations of a laboratory microculture. *Journal of Abnormal and Social Psychology* 62:649–658.

JANIS, IRVING L.

1963   Group identification under conditions of external danger. *British Journal of Medical Psychology* 36:227–238.

1972   *Victims of groupthink: A psychological study of foreign-policy decisions and fiascos.* Boston: Houghton-Mifflin.

JANIS, IRVING L., and LEON MANN.

1977   *Decision making: A psychological analysis of conflict, choice, and commitment.* New York: Free Press.

JELLISON, J. M., and R. M. ARKIN.

1977   Social comparison of abilities: A self-presentational approach to decision making in groups. In J. M. Suls and R. L. Miller (eds.), *Social comparison processes,* pp. 235–257. New York: Halsted.

JOHNS, A. WESLEY.
1970   *The man who shot McKinley.* Cranbury, N.J.: A. S. Barnes and Co.

JONES, EDWARD E., and KEITH E. DAVIS.
1965   From acts to dispositions: The attribution process in person perception. In L. Berkowitz (ed.), *Advances in experimental social psychology.* vol. 2, pp. 219–266. New York: Academic Press.

JONES, EDWARD E., KEITH E. DAVIS, and KENNETH J. GERGEN.
1961   Role playing variations and their informational value for person perception. *Journal of Abnormal and Social Psychology* 63:302–310.

JONES, EDWARD E., and HAROLD B. GERARD.
1967   *Foundations of social psychology.* New York: Wiley.

KANTER, ROSABETH M.
1968   Commitment and social organization: A study of commitment mechanisms in utopian communities. *American Sociological Review* 33:499–517.

1972a   *Commitment and community: Communes and utopias in sociological perspective.* Cambridge, Mass: Harvard University Press.

1972b   Commitment and the internal organization of milennial movements. *American Behavioral Scientist* 16:219–243.

KATZ, I., and L. BENJAMIN.
1960   Effects of white authoritarianism on biracial work groups. *Journal of Abnormal and Social Psychology* 61:448–456.

KATZ, I., and M. COHEN.
1962   The effects of training Negroes upon cooperative problem solving in biracial teams. *Journal of Abnormal and Social Psychology* 64:319–325.

KATZ, I., J. GOLDSTON, and L. BENJAMIN.
1958   Behavior and productivity in biracial work groups. *Human Relations* 11:123–141.

KEATING, CAROLINE F., ALLEN MAZUR, and MARSHALL H. SEGALL.
1977   Facial gestures which influence the perception of status. *Sociometry* 40:374–378.

KEESING, ROGER M.
1974   Theories of culture. In B. Siegal, A. Beals, and S. Tyler (eds.), *Annual review of anthropology,* vol. 3, pp. 73–97. Palo Alto, Cal.: Annual Reviews, Inc.

KELLEY, HAROLD H.
1951   Communication in experimentally created hierarchies. *Human Relations* 4:39–56.

1973   The process of causal attribution. *American Psychologist* 28:107–128.

KELLEY, HAROLD H., JOHN C. CONDRY, JR., ARNOLD E. DALKE, and ARTHUR H. HILL.

1965   Collective behavior in a simulated panic situation. *Journal of Experimental Social Psychology* 1:20–54.

KELLEY, HAROLD H., and JOHN L. MICHELA.

1980   Attribution theory and research. *Annual Review of Psychology* 31: 457–501.

KELLEY, HAROLD H., and M. M. SHAPIRO.

1954   An experiment on conformity to group norms where conformity is detrimental to group achievement. *American Sociological Review* 49:667–678.

KELLEY, HAROLD H., and JOHN W. THIBAUT.

1969   Group problem solving. In G. Lindzey and E. Aronson (eds.), *The handbook of social psychology* (2nd ed.) vol. 4, pp. 1–101. Reading, Mass: Addison-Wesley.

KELMAN, HERBERT C.

1958   Compliance, identification, and internalization: Three processes of attitude change. *Journal of Conflict Resolution* 2:51–60.

KIMBERLY, JAMES C.

1966   A theory of status equilibration. In Beyer, Zelditch, and Anderson (eds.), *Sociological theories in progress,* vol. 1, pp. 213–226. Boston: Houghton-Mifflen.

1967   States inconsistency: A reformulation of a theoretical problem. *Human Relations* 20:171–179.

1972   Relations among status, power, and economic rewards in simple and complex systems. In J. Berger, M. Zelditch, Jr., and B. Anderson (eds.), *Sociological theories in progress,* vol. 2, pp. 291–307. Boston: Houghton-Mifflin.

KIMBERLY, JAMES C., and LYNNE ZUCKER.

1973   Relations between status and power structures: Toward a general theory. *Sociological Inquiry* 43:151–157.

KLEINHANS, BRUCE, and DALMAS A. TAYLOR.

1976   Group processes, productivity, and leadership. In B. Seidenberg and A. Snadowsky (eds.), *Social Psychology,* pp. 407–433. New York: Free Press.

KOFFKA, KURT.

1935   *Principles of gestalt psychology.* New York: Harcourt Brace Jovanovich.

LAKIN, M.

1972   *Experimental groups: The uses of interpersonal encounter, psychotherapy groups and sensitivity training.* Morristown, N.J.: General Learning Press.

LAMM, HELMUT, and DAVID G. MEYERS.
1978   Group-induced polarization of attitudes and behavior. In L. Berkowitz (ed.), *Advances in experimental social psychology*, vol. 11, pp. 145–195. New York: Academic Press.

LAMM, HELMUT, and G. TROMMSDORF.
1973   Group versus individual performance on tasks requiring relational proficiency (brainstorming): A review. *European Journal of Social Psychology* 3:361–388.

LARSEN, OTTO N., and RICHARD J. HILL.
1958   Social structure and interpersonal communication. *American Journal of Sociology* 63:497–505.

LASCH, CHRISTOPHER.
1977   *Haven in a heartless world.* New York: Basic Books.

LASLETT, BARBARA.
1973   The family as public and private institution: An historical perspective. *Journal of Marriage and the Family* 35:480–492.
1977   Social change and the family: Los Angeles, California, 1850–1870. *American Sociological Review* 42:269–291.
1978   Family membership, past and present. *Social Problems* 28:476–490.

LAUGHLIN P. R., L. G. BRANCH, and H. H. JOHNSON.
1969   Individual versus triadic performance on a unidimensional complementary task as a function of initial ability level. *Journal of Personality and Social Psychology* 12:144–150.

LAUGHLIN, P. R., and H. H. JOHNSON.
1966   Group and individual performance on a complementary task as a function of initial ability level. *Journal of Experimental Social Psychology* 2:407–414.

LAWLER, EDWARD J.
1975   An experimental study of factors affecting the mobilization of revolutionary coalitions. *Sociometry* 38:163–179.

LEARY, TIMOTHY.
1957   *Interpersonal diagnosis of personality.* New York: Ronald.

LEAVITT, HAROLD J.
1951   Some effects of certain communication patterns on group performance. *Journal of Abnormal and Social Psychology* 46:38–50.

LEE, MARGARET T., and RICHARD OFSHE.
1981   The impact of behavioral style and status characteristics on social influence: A test of two competing theories. *Social Psychology Quarterly* 44:73–82.

LEIK, ROBERT K.
1963   Instrumentality and emotionality in family interaction. *Sociometry* 26:134–145.

LENSKI, GERHARD.
1954   Status crystallization: A non-vertical dimension of social status. *American Sociological Review* 19:405–13.

LERNER, M. J.
1974   The justice motive: "equity" and "parity" among children. *Journal of Personality and Social Psychology* 29:539–550.

LEVINE, JOHN M.
1980   Reaction to opinion deviance in small groups. In P. B. Paulus (ed.), *Psychology of group influence,* pp. 375–429. Hillsdale, N.J.: Laurence Erlbaum Associates.

LEVINGER, GEORGE.
1964   Task and social behavior in marriage. *Sociometry* 27:433–448.

LEWIN, KURT.
1939   Field theory and experiment in social psychology: Concepts and methods. *American Journal of Sociology* 44:868–896.
1947a   Frontiers in group dynamics: I. *Human Relations* 1:5–41.
1947b   Frontiers in group dynamics: II. *Human Relations* 1:143–153.
1948   *Resolving social conflicts.* New York: Harper & Row.
1951   *Field theory in social science.* New York: Harper & Row.

LEWIN, KURT, and RONALD LIPPITT.
1938   An experimental approach to the study of autocracy and democracy: A preliminary note. *Sociometry* 1:292–300.

LEWIN, KURT, RONALD LIPPITT, and RALPH K. WHITE.
1939   Patterns of aggressive behavior in experimentally created "social climates." *Journal of Social Psychology* 10:271–299.

LEWIS, GORDON H.
1972   Role differentiation. *American Sociological Review* 37:424–434.

LIEBERMAN, M., I. YALOM, and M. MILES.
1971   The group experience project: A comparison of ten encounter technologies. In L. Blank, G. Gottsegen, and M. Gottsegen (eds.), *Confrontation: Encounters in self and interpersonal awareness,* pp. 469–498. New York: Macmillan.
1973   *Encounter groups: First facts.* New York: Basic Books.

LIPPITT, RONALD, and RALPH K. WHITE.
1952   An experimental study of leadership and group life. In G. E. Swanson, T. M. Newcomb, and E. L. Hartley (eds.), *Readings in social psychology,* rev. ed., pp. 340–355. New York: Holt, Rinehart & Winston.

LITWAK, EUGENE, and IVAN SZELENYI.
1969   Primary group structures and their functions: Kin, neighbors, and friends. *American Sociological Review* 34:465–481.

LOFLAND, JOHN.
1966   *Doomsday cult.* Englewood Cliffs, N.J.: Prentice-Hall, Inc.

1977   Becoming a world-saver, revisited. *American Behavioral Scientist* 20:805–818.

LOFLAND, JOHN, and RODNEY STARK.

1965   Becoming a world-saver: A theory of conversion to a deviant perspective. *American Sociological Review* 30:862–875.

LORGE, IRVING, and HERBERT SOLOMON.

1960   Group and individual performance in problem solving related to previous exposure to problem, level of aspiration, and group size. *Behavioral Science* 5:28–38.

LOTT, ALBERT J., and BERNICE E. LOTT.

1961   Group cohesiveness, communication level, and conformity. *Journal of Abnormal and Social Psychology* 62:408–412.

1965   Group cohesiveness as interpersonal attraction: A review of relationships with antecedent and consequent variables. *Psychological Bulletin* 64:259–309.

MABRY, E. A.

1975   Sequential structure of interaction in encounter groups. *Human Communication Research* 1:302–307.

MACNEIL, MARK K., and MUZAFER SHERIF.

1976   Norm change over subject generations as a function of arbitrariness of prescribed norms. *Journal of Personality and Social Psychology* 34:762–773.

MAIER, NORMAN R. F., and L. RICHARD HOFFMAN.

1960   Quality of first and second solutions in group problem solving. *Journal of Applied Psychology* 44:278–283.

MAIER, NORMAN R. F., and A. R. SOLEM.

1952   The contribution of a discussion leader to the quality of group thinking: The effective use of minority opinions. *Human Relations* 5:277–288.

MANN, RICHARD D.

1961   Dimensions of individual performance in small groups under task and social-emotional conditions. *Journal of Abnormal and Social Psychology* 62:674–682.

MARQUIS, D. G., H. GUETZKOW, R. W. HEYNS.

1951   A social-psychological study of the decision-making conference. In H. Guetzkow (ed.), *Groups, leadership and men*, pp. 55–67. Pittsburgh: Carnegie Press.

MAZUR, ALLAN.

1973   A cross-species comparison of status in established groups. *American Sociological Review* 38:513–30.

MAZUR, ALLAN, EUGENE ROSA, MARK FAUPEL, JOSEPH HELLER, RUSSELL LEEN, and BLAKE THURMAN.

1980 Physiological aspects of communication via mutual gaze. *American Journal of Sociology* 86:50–74.

McCRANIE, EDWARD D., and JAMES C. KIMBERLY.
1973 Rank inconsistency, conflicting expectations and injustices. *Sociometry* 36:152–176.

McFEAT, TOM.
1974 *Small-group cultures.* New York: Pergammon Press.

McGRATH, J. E.
1964 *Social psychology: A brief introduction.* New York: Holt.

McLEISH, J., and J. PARK.
1972 Outcomes associated with direct and vicarious experience in training groups: I. Personality changes. *British Journal of Social and Clinical Psychology* 11:333–341.

MEAD, GEORGE H.
1934 *Mind, self and society.* Charles C. Morris (ed.). Chicago: University of Chicago Press.

MEEKER, B. F., and P. A. WEITZEL-O'NEILL.
1977 Sex roles and interpersonal behavior in task-oriented groups. *American Sociological Review* 42:92–105.

MERTON, ROBERT.
1968 Manifest and latent functions. In R. Merton, *Social Structure and Social Theory,* enlarged ed., pp. 73–138. New York: Free Press.

MEYERS, DAVID G., and HELMUT LAMM.
1976 The group polarization phenomenon. *Psychological Bulletin* 83: 602–627.

MICHENER, H. ANDREW, and MORGAN LYONS.
1972 Perceived support and upward mobility as determinants of revolutionary coalition behavior. *Journal of Experimental Social Psychology* 8:180–195.

MIDDLETON, DREW.
1981 Going the military route. *New York Times Magazine,* May 17: 103–12.

MILGRAM, STANLEY.
1965 Liberating effects of group pressure. *Journal of Personality and Social Psychology* 1:127–134.

MILLER, JAMES C.
1955 Toward a general theory for the behavioral sciences. *American Psychologist* 10:513–531.

MILLER, P. R., and G. SWANSON.
1958 *The changing American parent.* New York: Wiley.

MILLS, THEODORE.

1967   *The sociology of small groups.* Englewood Cliffs, N.J.: Prentice-Hall, Inc.

MOORE, JAMES C.

1968   Status and influence in small group interactions. *Sociometry* 31: 47–63.

MORENO, JACOB L.

1960   *The sociometry reader.* Edited with H. H. Jennings. New York: Free Press.

MORGAN, WILLIAM R.

1974   Bales' role theory: An attribution theory interpretation. *Sociometry* 38:429–444.

MORSE, N. C., and E. REIMER.

1956   The experimental change of a major organizational variable. *Journal of Abnormal and Social Psychology* 52:120–129.

MOSCOVICI, SERGE.

1976   *Social influence and social change.* Translated by C. Sherrard and G. Heinz. London: Academic Press.

MOSCOVICI, SERGE, and CLAUDE FAUCHEUX.

1972   Social influence, conformity bias, and the study of active minorities. In L. Berkowitz (ed.), *Advances in experimental social psychology,* vol. 6, pp. 149–202. New York: Academic Press.

MOSCOVICI, SERGE, and CHARLAN NEMETH.

1974   Social influence: II. Minority influence. In C. Nemeth (ed.), *Social psychology: Classic and contemporary integrations,* pp. 217–249. Chicago: Rand-McNally.

MOSCOVICI, SERGE, and M. ZAVALLONI.

1969   The group as a polarizer of attitudes. *Journal of Personality and Social Psychology* 12:125–135.

MUDD, S. A.

1968   Group sanction severity as a function of degree of behavior deviation and relevance of norm. *Journal of Personality and Social Psychology* 8:258–260.

NEMETH, CHARLAN, and JOEL WACHTLER.

1974   Creating the perceptions of consistency and confidence: A necessary condition for minority influence. *Sociometry* 37:529–540.

NEMETH, CHARLAN, JOEL WACHTLER, and JEFFREY ENDICOTT.

1977   Increasing the size of the minority: Some gains and some losses. *European Journal of Social Psychology* 7:15–27.

NEWCOMB, THEODORE.

1961   *The acquaintance process.* New York: Holt, Rinehart & Winston.

NIXON, HOWARD L., II.

1977   Cohesiveness and team success: A theoretical reformulation. *Review of Sport and Leisure* 2:36–57.
1979   *The small group.* Englewood Cliffs, N.J.: Prentice-Hall, Inc.

OKUN, M. A., and F. J. DIVESTA.
1975   Cooperation and competition in co-acting groups. *Journal of Personality and Social Psychology* 31:615–620.

OLMSTEAD, MICHAEL S.
1959   *The small group.* New York: Random House.

OLMSTEAD, MICHAEL S., and A. PAUL HARE.
1978   *The small group,* 2nd ed. New York: Random House.

OLSEN, MARVIN E.
1968   *The process of social organization.* New York: Holt, Rinehart & Winston.

OSBORN, A. F.
1957   *Applied imagination.* New York: Scribner's.

OUCHI, WILLIAM G.
1981   *Theory Z: How American business can meet the Japanese challenge.* Reading, Mass.: Addison-Wesley.

PARCEL, TOBY L., and KAREN S. COOK.
1977   Status characteristics, reward allocation and equity. *Sociometry* 40:311–324.

PARLEE, MARY B.
1979   Conversational politics. *Psychology Today* 12 (May): 48–56.

PARSONS, TALCOTT, and ROBERT F. BALES.
1955   *Family, socialization and interaction process.* Glencoe, Ill: Free Press.

PARSONS, TALCOTT, ROBERT BALES, and EDWARD SHILS.
1953   *Working papers in the theory of action.* Glencoe, Ill: Free Press.

PASCALE, RICHARD T., and ANTHONY G. ATHOS.
1981   *The art of Japanese management: Applications for American executives.* New York: Simon and Schuster.

PETERSON, RICHARD A.
1979   Revitalizing the culture concept. *Annual Review of Sociology* 5: 137–166.

PRESS, ARIC, MARTIN KASINDORF, PEGGY CLAUSEN, SYLVESTER MONROE, DANIEL SHAPIRO, JOHN TAYLOR, and DIANE CAMPER.
1982   The insanity plea on trial. *Newsweek* May 24: 56–61.

PUGH, MEREDITH, and RALPH WAHRMAN.
1978   Neutralizing sexism in mixed-sex groups: Do women have to be better then men? Paper presented at the American Sociological Association Meetings, San Francisco, Cal.

RAPAPORT, RHOANA, and ROBERT N. RAPAPORT.
1971   *Dual-career families.* Baltimore: Penguin Books.

RAUSCHNING, HERMANN.
1940   *Hitler speaks.* New York: G. P. Putnam Sons.
RAVEN, BERTRAM.
1974   The Nixon group. *Journal of Social Issues* 30:297–320.
READ, PETER B.
1974   Source of authority and the legitimation of leadership in small groups. *Sociometry* 37:189–204.
REYNOLDS, P. D.
1971   Comment on "The distribution of participation in group discussion" as related to group size. *American Sociological Review* 36:704–706.
RIDGEWAY, CECILIA L.
1978   Conformity, group-oriented motivation, and status attainment in small groups. *Social Psychology Quarterly* 41:175–188.
1981a   Nonconformity, competence, and influence: A test of two theories. *American Sociological Review* 46:333–347.
1981b   Small group culture and its transmission in urban society. Paper presented at "The Content of Culture: Constants and Variants," a conference in honor of John M. Roberts, Pomona College, November, 1981.
1982   Status in groups: The importance of motivation. *American Sociological Review* 47:76–88.
RIDGEWAY, CECILIA, and CARDELL JACOBSON.
1977   Sources of status and influence in all-female and mixed-sex groups. *Sociological Quarterly* 18:413–425.
RIECKEN, HENRY W.
1958   The effect of talkativeness on ability to influence group solutions of problems. *Sociometry* 21:309–321.
RIESDESEL, PAUL L.
1974   Bales reconsidered: A critical analysis of popularity and leadership differentiation. *Sociometry* 37:557–564.
RILEY, MATILDA W., R. COHN, J. TOBY, and J. W. RILEY, JR.
1954   Interpersonal orientations in small groups: A consideration of the questionnaire approach. *American Sociological Review* 19:715–724.
ROBERTS, JOHN M.
1951   Three Navaho households: A comparative study in small group culture. *Papers of the Peabody Museum of American Archeology and Ethnology,* Harvard University, vol. XL, no. 3.
1964   The self-management of culture. In Ward Goodenough (ed.), *Explorations in cultural anthropology: Essays in honor of George Peter Murdock,* pp. 433–454. New York: McGraw-Hill.
ROBERTS, JOHN M., MALCOLM J. ARTH, and ROBERT R. BUSH.

1959   Games in Culture. *American Anthropologist* 61:597–605.

ROBERTS, JOHN M., and GARRY E. CHICK.
1979   Butler county eight-ball: A behavioral space analysis. In Jeffrey Goldstein (ed.), *Sports, games, and play,* pp. 59–99. Hillsdale, N.J.: Lawrence Erlbaum Associates.

ROBERTS, JOHN M., GARRY E. CHICK, MARIAN STEPHENSON, and LAUREL LEE.
1981   Inferred categories for tennis play: A limited semantic analysis. In Alice T. Chiska (ed.), *Play as context,* pp. 181–195. West Point, N.Y.: Leisure Press.

ROBERTS, JOHN M., and MICHAEL FOREMAN.
1971   Riddles: Expressive models of interrogation. *Ethnology* 10:509–533.

ROBERTS, JOHN M., and BRIAN SUTTON-SMITH.
1962   Child training and game involvement. *Ethnology* 1:166–185.

ROBERTS, JOHN M., BRIAN SUTTON-SMITH, and ADAM KENDON.
1963   Strategy in games and folk-tales. *Journal of Social Psychology* 61: 185–199.

ROETHLISBERGER, FRITZ, and WILLIAM J. DICKSON.
1939   *Management and the worker.* Cambridge, Mass.: Harvard University Press.

ROSA, EUGENE, and ALLAN MAZUR.
1979   Incipient status in small groups. *Social Forces* 58:18–37.

ROSENBAUM, L. L., and W. B. ROSENBAUM.
1971   Morale and productivity consequences of group leadership style, stress, and type of task. *Journal of Applied Psychology* 55: 343–348.

ROSENBERG, CHARLES E.
1968   *The trial of assassin Guiteau.* Chicago: University of Chicago Press.

ROSENTHAL, R., and L. JACOBSON.
1968   *Pygmalion in the classroom.* New York: Holt, Rinehart & Winston.

ROTTER, GEORGE, and STEPHEN PORTUGAL.
1969   Group and individual effects in problem solving. *Journal of Applied Psychology* 53:338–341.

RYDER, N. B.
1974   The family in developed countries. *Scientific American* 231:123–32.

SAMPSON, EDWARD E.
1963   Status congruence and cognitive consistency. *Sociometry* 26: 146–162.
1969   Studies in status congruence. In L. Berkowitz (ed.), *Advances in experimental social psychology,* vol. 4, pp. 225–270. New York: Academic Press.

SCANZONI, JOHN H.

1978   *Sex roles, women's work, and marital conflict.* Lexington, Mass: Lexington Books.

SCANZONI, JOHN, and MAXIMILIANE SZINOVACZ.

1980   *Family decision-making.* Beverly Hills, Cal.: Sage.

SCHACTER, STANLEY.

1951   Deviation, rejection, and communication. *Journal of Abnormal and Social Psychology* 46:190–207.

SCHACTER, STANLEY, NORRIS ELLERSTON, DOROTHY McBRIDE, and DORIS GREGORY.

1951   An experimental study of cohesiveness and productivity. *Human Relations* 4:229–238.

SCHONER, BERTRAM, GERALD ROSE, and G. C. HOYT.

1974   Quality of decisions: Individual versus real and synthetic groups. *Journal of Applied Psychology* 59:424–432.

SCHUTZ, W. C.

1955   What makes groups productive? *Human Realtions* 8:429–469.

1958   *FIRO: A three dimensional theory of interpersonal behavior.* New York: Rinehart.

SEASHORE, S. E.

1954   *Group cohesiveness in the industrial work group.* Ann Arbor: University of Michigan Press.

SENNETT, RICHARD.

1970   The brutality of modern families. *Transaction* 7:29–37.

SHAW, MARVIN E.

1954   Some effects of unequal distribution of information upon group performance in various communication nets. *Journal of Abnormal and Social Psychology* 49:547–553.

1955   A comparison of two types of leadership in various communication nets. *Journal of Abnormal and Social Psychology* 50:127–134.

1964   Communication networks. In L. Berkowitz (ed.), *Advances in experimental social psychology,* vol. 1, pp. 111–147. New York: Academic Press.

1973   Scaling group tasks: A method for dimensional analysis. *JSAS Catalog of Selected Documents in Psychology* 3:8 (MS No. 294).

1978   Communications networks fourteen years later. In L. Berkowitz (ed.), *Group processes,* pp. 351–361. New York: Academic Press.

1981   *Group dynamics: The psychology of small group behavior,* 3rd ed. New York: McGraw-Hill.

SHAW, MARVIN E., and N. ASHTON.

1976   Do assembly bonus effects occur on disjunctive tasks? A test of Steiner's theory. *Bulletin of the Psychonomic Society* 8:469–471.

SHAW, MARVIN S., and P. R. COSTANZO.
1970 *Theories of social psychology.* New York: McGraw-Hill.
SHAW, MARVIN E., and G. H. ROTHSCHILD.
1956 Some effects of prolonged experience in communication nets. *Journal of Applied Psychology* 40:281–286.
SHAW, M. E., G. H. ROTHSCHILD, and J. F. STRICKLAND.
1957 Decision processes in communication nets. *Journal of Abnormal and Social Psychology* 54:323–330.
SHAW, MARVIN E., and L. M. SHAW.
1962 Some effects of sociometric grouping upon learning in a second grade classroom. *Journal of Social Psychology* 57:453–458.
SHEPARD, CLOVIS.
1964 *Small groups: Some sociological perspectives.* San Francisco: Chandler.
SHERIF, MUZAFER.
1936 *The psychology of social norms.* New York: Harper & Row.
1956 *An outline of social psychology.* New York: Harper & Row.
SHERIF, MUZAFER, and O. J. Harvey.
1952 A study in ego functioning: Elimination of stable anchorages in individual and group situations. *Sociometry* 15:272–305.
SHERIF, MUZAFER, O. J. HARVEY, B. J. WHITE, W. R. HOOD, and C. W. SHERIF.
1961 *Intergroup conflict and cooperation: The Robber's Cave experiment.* Norman, Okla: University Book Exchange.
SHERIF, MUZAFER, and CAROLYN W. SHERIF.
1953 *Group in harmony and tension: An introduction to studies in intergroup relations.* New York: Harper & Row.
1969 *Social psychology,* rev. ed. New York: Harper & Row.
SHILS, EDWARD A., and MORRIS JANOWITZ.
1948 Cohesion and disintegration of the Wehrmacht in World War II. *Public Opinion Quarterly* 12:280–313.
SHORT, JAMES F., JR., and FRED L. STRODTBECK.
1963 The response of gang leaders to status threats: An observation on group processes and delinquent behavior. *American Journal of Sociology* 68:571–579.
SHORTER, EDWARD.
1975 *The making of the modern family.* New York: Basic Books.
SIMMEL, GEORG.
1950 *The sociology of Georg Simmel.* Translated by Kurt H. Wolff. Glencoe, Ill: Free Press.
SLATER, PHILIP E.
1955 Role differentiation in small groups. *American Sociological Review* 20:300–310.

384   References

1958   Contrasting correlates of group size. *Sociometry* 21:129–139.
1976   *The pursuit of loneliness: American culture at the breaking point*, rev. ed. Boston: Beacon.

STARK, RODNEY, and WILLIAM S. BAINBRIDGE.
1980   Networks of faith: Interpersonal bonds and recruitment to cults. *American Journal of Sociology* 85:1376–1395.

STEIN, MORRIS I.
1968   Creativity. In E. Borgatta and W. W. Lambert, *Handbook of personality theory and research*, pp. 900–942. Chicago: Rand-McNally.

STEINER, IVAN D.
1972   *Group processes and productivity.* New York: Academic Press.

STOGDILL, RALPH M.
1948   Personal factors associated with leadership: A survey of the literature. *Journal of Psychology* 25:37–71.
1974   *Handbook of leadership: A survey of theory and research.* New York: Free Press.

STOUFFER, SAMUEL A., et al.
1949   *The American soldier.* Princeton, N.J.: Princeton University Press.

STRODTBECK, FRED, RITA JAMES, and CHARLES HAWKINS.
1957   Social status in jury deliberations. *American Sociological Review* 22:713–719.

SUEDFELD P., and A. D. RANK.
1976   Revolutionary leaders: Long-term success as a function of changes in conceptual complexity. *Journal of Personality and Social Psychology* 34:169–178.

SUMNER, WILLIAM G.
1906   *Folkways.* Boston: Ginn.

SUTTON-SMITH, BRIAN, JOHN M. ROBERTS, and ROBERT KOZELKA.
1963   Game involvement in adults. *Journal of Social Psychology* 60:15–30.

TAYLOR, D. W., P. C. BERRY, and C. BLOCK.
1958   Does group participation when using brainstorming facilitate creative thinking? *Administrative Science Quarterly* 3:23–47.

TAYLOR, D. W. and W. L. FAUST.
1952   Twenty questions: Efficiency of problem solving as a function of size of the group. *Journal of Experimental Social Psychology* 44:360–363.

TESSER, ABRAHAM.
1980   Self-esteem in family dynamics. *Journal of Personality and Social Psychology* 39:77–91.

THIBAUT, JOHN W., and HAROLD H. KELLEY.
1959   *The social psychology of groups.* New York: Wiley.

THOMAS, E. J.
1957 Effects of facilitative role interdependence in group functioning. *Human Relations* 10:347–366.

TOENNIES, FERDINAND.
1887 Gemeinschaft and Gesellschaft. In T. Parsons, E. Shils, K. Naegale, J. Pitts (eds.), *Theories of Society*, pp. 191–210. New York: Free Press, 1961.

TORRANCE, E. P.
1954 Some consequences of power differences on decision making in permanent and temporary three-man groups. *Research Studies, State College of Washington*, 22:130–140.

TUCKMAN, BRUCE W.
1965 Developmental sequence in small groups. *Psychological Bulletin* 63:384–399.

TURNER, JONATHAN H.
1974 *The structure of sociological theory.* Homewood, Ill: Dorsey.

U.S. BUREAU OF THE CENSUS.
1980 *Statistical abstract of the United States.* Washington, D.C.: U. S. Government Printing Office.

1981a *Geographic mobility March 1975 to March 1980.* Current Population Reports, Series P-20, No. 368. Washington., D.C.: U.S. Government Printing Office.

1981b *Household and family characteristics.* Current Population Reports, Series P-20, No. 366. Washington, D.C.: U.S. Government Printing Office.

1981c *Marital status and living arrangements: March 1980.* Current Population Reports, Series P-20, No. 365. Washington, D.C.: U.S. Government Printing Office.

VAN ZELST, R. H.
1952 Sociometrically selected work teams increase production. *Personnel Psychology* 5:175–186.

VERBA, SIDNEY.
1961 *Small groups and political behavior: A Study of Leadership.* Princeton, N.J.: Princeton University Press.

VERBRUGGE, LOIS M.
1977 The structure of adult friendship choices. *Social Forces* 56:576–597.

1979 Multiplexity in adult friendships. *Social Forces* 57:1287–1309.

WAHRMAN, RALPH, and MERIDITH D. PUGH.
1972 Competence and conformity: Another look at Hollander's study. *Sociometry* 35:376–386.

1974   Sex, nonconformity, and influence. *Sociometry* 37:137–147.

WALKER, THOMAS G.

1974   The decision-making superiority of groups: A research note. *Small Group Behavior* 5:121–128.

1976   Leader selection and behavior in small political groups. *Small Group Behavior* 7:363–368.

WALLACH, MICHAEL A., NATHAN KOGAN, and DARYL J. BEM.

1962   Group influence on individual risk-taking. *Journal of Abnormal and Social Psychology* 65:75–86.

1964   Diffusion of responsibility and level of risk taking in groups. *Journal of Abnormal and Social Psychology* 68:263–274.

WALSTER, ELAINE, ELLEN BERSCHEID, and G. WILLIAM WALSTER.

1973   New directions in equity research. *Journal of Personality and Social Psychology* 25:151–176.

WALSTER, ELAINE, G. WILLIAM WALSTER, and ELLEN BERSCHEID.

1978   *Equity: Theory and research.* Boston: Allyn and Bacon.

WARE, J. R. and J. E. BARR.

1977   Effects of a nine-week structured and unstructured group experience on measures of self-concept and self-actualization. *Small Group Behavior* 8:93–100.

WATSON, D., and B. BROMBERG.

1965   Power, communication, and position satisfaction in task-oriented groups. *Journal of Personality and Social Psychology* 2:859–864.

WAXLER, NANCY E., and ELLIOT G. MISHLER.

1970   Experimental studies of families. In L. Berkowitz (ed.), *Advances in experimental social psychology,* vol. 5, pp. 249–304. New York: Academic Press.

WEBSTER, MURRAY, JR.

1977   Equating characteristics and social interaction: Two experiments. *Sociometry* 40:41–50.

WEBSTER, MURRAY, JR., and JAMES E. DRISKELL.

1978   Status generalization: A review and some new data. *American Sociological Review* 43:220–236.

WEBSTER, MURRAY, JR., and LeROY SMITH.

1978   Justice and revolutionary coalitions: A test of two theories. *American Journal of Sociology* 84:267–292.

WEICK, KARL E., and DAVID P. GILFILLAN.

1971   Fate of arbitrary traditions in a laboratory microculture. *Journal of Personality and Social Psychology* 17:179–191.

WEIGERT, ANDREW, and ROSS HASTINGS.

1977   Identity loss, family, and social change. *American Journal of Sociology* 82:1171–1185.

WEST, CANDACE, and DON H. ZIMMERMAN.
1977   Women's place in everyday talk: Reflections on parent-child interaction. *Social Problems* 24: 521–529.

WHITE, K. R.
1974   T-groups revisited: Self-concept change and the "fishbowling" technique. *Small Group Behavior* 5:473–485.

WHITE, RALPH K., and RONALD LIPPITT.
1960   *Autocracy and democracy.* New York: Harper & Row.

WHYTE, WILLIAM F.
1943   *Street corner society.* Chicago: The University of Chicago Press.
1955   *Street corner society,* 2nd ed. Chicago: The University of Chicago Press.

WILKES, PAUL.
1977   *Six American families.* New York: Seabury Press for United Church of Christ and United Methodist Communications.

WILLARD, D., and F. STRODTBECK.
1972   Latency of verbal responses and participation in small groups. *Sociometry* 35:161–175.

WILSON, STEPHEN.
1978   *Informal groups.* Englewood Cliffs, N.J.: Prentice-Hall, Inc.

WINFREY, CAREY.
1979   Why 900 died in Guyana. *The New York Times Magazine,* February 25: 39–50.

WINTER, S. K.
1976   Developmental stages in the roles and concerns of group co-leaders. *Small Group Behavior* 7:349–362.

WIRTH, LOUIS.
1934   Urbanism as a way of life. *American Journal of Sociology* 44:3–24.

WOLFE, DONALD M.
1959   Power and authority in the family. In D. Cartwright (ed.), *Studies in social power,* pp. 99–107. Ann Arbor, Mich.: Institute for Social Research.

ZABLOCKI, BENJAMIN.
1978   Communes, encounter groups, and the search for community. In K. Back (ed.), *The search for community: Encounter groups and social change,* pp. 97–142. Boulder, Colo: Westview Press.
1980   *Alienation and charisma.* New York: Free Press.

ZAJONC, ROBERT B.
1965   Social facilitation. *Science* 149:269–274.

ZELDITCH, MORRIS, JR., and BO ANDERSON.
1966   On the balance of a set of ranks. In J. Berger, M. Zelditch, B.

Anderson (eds.), *Sociological theories in progress,* vol. 1, pp. 244–268. Boston: Houghton-Mifflin.

ZELDITCH, MORRIS, JR., PATRICK LAUDERDALE, and STEPHEN STUBLAREC.
1980   How are inconsistencies between status and ability resolved? *Social Forces* 58:1025–1043.

ZIMBARDO, PHILLIP G., W. CURTIS BANKS, CRAIG HANEY, and DAVID JAFFE.
1973   A Pirandellian prison. *New York Times Magazine,* April 8: 38–60.

Index

402   Index

dependent and independent,
63–65
extraneous, 64–65
Verbal latency, 172, 173
Verba, Sidney, 219
Verbugge, Lois M., 322, 324
Vidmar, Neil, 11

Wachter, Joe, 147, 167, 169
Wahrman, Ralph, 141, 188
Walker, Thomas G., 284, 296
Wallach, Michael, 303
Walsh, Lorena S., 226
Walster, Elaine, 41, 195–98
Walster, G. William, 41, 196
Ware, J. R., 349
Waxler, Nancy E., 332
Webster, Murray, Jr., 178, 183–85,
188, 241–42
Weick, Carl E., 156, 261–64
Weigert, Andrew, 320, 337, 338
Weitzel-O'Neill, P. A., 177, 189,
191, 221
West, Candace, 181
Westgate and Westgate West,
91–95, 104–5
White, Ralph K., 38, 69, 115,
230–34, 349

Whyte, William F., 160, 193
Wiley, Mary Glenn, 221
Wilhelmy, R. A., 154
Wilkes, Paul, 341–42
Willard, D., 167, 172
Wilson, Stephen, 100, 117, 161
Winter, S. K., 343, 347
Wirth, Louis, 318
Wolfe, Donald M., 227,
240
Worchel, P., 113
Work groups, 16
productivity in Japan and, 22–23
Wright, E. W., 233

Yalom, I., 348, 349

Zablocki, Benjamin, 328, 342
Zajonc, Robert B., 306
Zander, Alvin, 99, 100, 104, 115,
118, 205, 224, 228
Zavalloni, M., 304
Zelditch, Morris, 179, 183–86, 194,
196
Zimbardo, Phillip G., 67–68
Zimmerman, Don H., 181
Zucker, Lynne, 177–78